T0375146

Scuttlebutt

Tales and Experiences of a Life at Sea

Robert B. Kieding

iUniverse, Inc.
Bloomington

Scuttlebutt
Tales and Experiences of a Life at Sea

Copyright © 2011 by Robert B. Kieding

All rights reserved. No part of this book may be used or reproduced by any means, graphic, electronic, or mechanical, including photocopying, recording, taping or by any information storage retrieval system without the written permission of the publisher except in the case of brief quotations embodied in critical articles and reviews.

The views expressed in this work are solely those of the author and do not necessarily reflect the views of the publisher, and the publisher hereby disclaims any responsibility for them.

iUniverse books may be ordered through booksellers or by contacting:

iUniverse
1663 Liberty Drive
Bloomington, IN 47403
www.iuniverse.com
1-800-Authors (1-800-288-4677)

Because of the dynamic nature of the Internet, any web addresses or links contained in this book may have changed since publication and may no longer be valid.

Any people depicted in stock imagery provided by Thinkstock are models, and such images are being used for illustrative purposes only.

Certain stock imagery © Thinkstock.

ISBN: 978-1-4620-0431-7 (sc)
ISBN: 978-1-4620-0432-4 (ebk)

Library of Congress Control Number: 2011904436

Printed in the United States of America

iUniverse rev. date: 4/5/2011

Contents

SCUTTLEBUTT

"Scuttlebutt" is an old nautical term meaning shipboard rumors or gossip. The scuttlebutt was a cask with an opening called a "scuttle," and it was used for drinking water or other potables, around which crewmembers could be expected to gather and chat when weather or the captain's law allowed. Hence, the common phrase, "What's the scuttlebutt?" meaning "What's new?" The following pages are a collection of "scuttlebutt" dealing history, information, issues, perspective, and other topics of interest.

Santa Barbara is uniquely defined by its mountains, history, and climate, but very so much by its shoreline and waterfront. The waterfront is Santa Barbara's front porch, and it is inseparable from the heart of the community. It has been an essential part of local history and development from the arrival of the first ancient settlers until the present day. Santa Barbara has the only east-west shoreline on the west coast of North America, and the resultant mild climate and weather are further enhanced by its guardian Channel Islands that lie twenty-two miles off its shore. In addition, its waterfront teems with activities and social interaction. To many, that's where the action is in Santa Barbara.

There are many sub-communities at the waterfront: commercial fishermen who daily risk their lives at sea to make a living and sport fishermen who can pick their time and weather to fish for the sake of fun; relaxed day sailors and intense, athletic sailboat racers; professional skippers and crewmembers who make their living moving commercial vessels or yachts across the sea; mechanics and maintenance personnel who maintain, repair, wash, paint, and varnish boats and yachts; agencies who are concerned with the protection of property, safety, and rescues at sea; merchants who serve tourists and those who carry mysterious nautical wares whose purposes baffle the landlubber; people who make their homes on their boats, and those whose boats are their escape from the challenges of uptown daily life; activists who press for rights, change or the status quo, and those who wish to leave such passions behind; employees who work for restaurants, businesses, government to earn their daily pay; tourists who have but a few hours or days to sample what we locals too often take for granted; surfers, swimmers, hikers, idlers, and many more who are part of the melting pot that makes up Santa Barbara's waterfront community.

ADVENTURES AT SEA

We have all read and heard tales of tragic adventures at sea – severe storms, shipwrecks, lost at sea, injuries, and more. But have you ever considered that the real "hair raising" experiences seem to happen to the least qualified and least prepared boaters? When you pick up a book about real life adventures at sea, more often than not you find that the author or main characters knew very little about boating and the sea, and they found themselves in situations that could have been avoided if they had been more knowledgeable. They didn't take proper measures to prepare their boats, to learn to navigate, to check immediate and long term weather, to learn sound seamanship, or to prepare contingency plans. If they had followed these sound measures, there probably wouldn't be as many adventure at sea books as there are today.

It's great fun to read about such adventures, but it's usually better to read about them than experience them yourself. The sea has too many surprises in store without volunteering for more by being unprepared. Whether on a long voyage, a short race, or just a day sail, the same principles and procedures apply. You, your crew, your vessel, and your plans must be checked out before starting. Problems can be just as serious a half mile from Santa Barbara Harbor as off the stormy shores of Tierra Del Fuego.

The proper preparations for going to sea are similar to those of a pilot flying a plane. A good pilot continually plans for the unexpected. He has alternate landing locations in the event of emergency, and he has thought out and practiced remedial measures in the event of mechanical or electrical failure. His close attention to weather is well known by all.

A qualified sailor acts no differently. His contingency plans are no less important, although disaster usually strikes a boat at a slower pace. Since formal training leading toward a license is not required for recreational boating (perhaps it should be), it is up to each boater to take steps to develop knowledge and experience to avoid unplanned adventures at sea. Classes are offered by the Santa Barbara Sail and Power Squadron (www.sbpss.org), the Coast Guard Auxiliary (www.cgaux.org), private institutions, and boat charter and rental operations. There are many good books and videos available.

But there is simply no substitute for experience. It is amazing how many major voyages are begun before the skipper and crew have worked together, checked out their boat, and developed contingency procedures. "Shaking down" is a historic tradition in boating. Before tackling an island trip, a good deal of coastal sailing should be done, including practice in anchoring, reefing to reduce sail area in high winds, navigation, boat's systems operation, and safety drills. Before cruising to distant ports, several island trips should be made in a variety of conditions to secure as much practical experience as possible and to learn the peculiarities of your specific boat. Most successful blue water sailors had years of experience before they sailed beyond the horizon.

An understanding of all of your ship's systems is essential. I am constantly surprised at how many boaters have sailed or powered for years without even a basic understanding as to how the various systems on board actually work. As a result, they are incapable of repairing them, frequently have not maintained them, and wouldn't know where to begin to deal with emergency procedures associated with them. The first step is to collect manuals for all equipment on board, then file them in a plastic file box or a three ring binder for accessibility. Next, read them. If there are essential areas you don't understand, ask professionals for assistance. Select key spare parts to keep on board and familiarize yourself with how to install them.

Consider which systems could create major problems if failure occurs, and take steps to have the means to deal with them. Major systems to be concerned with are propulsion, plumbing, electrical, anchor, floatation, pumping, fire protection, and safety.

Navigation warrants special mention. You must know where you are and how to get to a safe destination under adverse conditions. Successful navigation depends on knowledge, common sense, and experience accumulated over many voyages. Electronics and other devices help a great deal, but your experience and native instincts may be what keep you off the rocks in extreme weather or limited visibility.

Maintain your boat and its systems. If you do it yourself, you will learn a great deal about your boat. If you have someone else do it, take the time to learn about your boat and discuss it with your maintenance person. Finally, develop contingency plans, just like the pilot. Think about what could happen before it actually does, and plan what you would do to counter the situation. If you're moving into a narrow, shallow channel with current, plan what you would do if you lost power. Is an anchor handy for fast deployment? If you hit unanticipated severe weather (in spite of your usual practice of carefully checking in advance), do you have alternate anchorages in mind? And so on. Your mind should be trained to plan ahead for contingencies on a continuous basis. And don't keep them a secret. Let your crew know. One plan should cover the absence or incapacity of the skipper. Another should cover informing all on board of the location and use of lifejackets and other life saving gear.

As you learn, practice, plan, and implement preventative measures before they are needed. The result will be smooth sailing, but, sadly, you may also eliminate the possibility of getting rich by writing a book on your "adventures at sea."

Sea Term -
- Three sheets to the wind –This term goes back to the 18th century and indicates a sailor's intoxicated condition. Its derivation indicates a condition of crew's carelessness as when sheets (lines) are poorly trimmed.

OUR CHANNEL CATCH

Santa Barbarans know that we live on a unique stretch of the Pacific Ocean and that there is a commercial fishing fleet that brings in its catch to be sold in stores and restaurants. But how many know what types of sea life are actually harvested from our waters? The variety and quantities may surprise you. Here's a partial list provided by Santa Barbara Fish Market at the Harbor:

Fish – swordfish, opah, albacore tuna, blue fin tuna, mako shark, thresher shark, angel shark, leopard shark, soupfin shark, yellowtail, ocean white fish, rock cod, rock fish, red snapper, halibut, white seabass, black seabass, sardines, mackerel, bonita, barracuda, king salmon, perch, sole, sand dab, pompano

Shellfish and other Products – spiny lobster, yellow rock crab, red rock crab, brown rock crab, spider crab, California king crab, box crab, oysters (farmed), black mussels (farmed), spot prawns, ridge back shrimp, pink shrimp, abalone (farmed), sea urchins, scallops (farmed), kelp (farmed), welk (snail)

Some are caught only during natural seasons. Others are caught year-round. Many are protected by laws that specify when and how many may be harvested and what fishing procedures may be used. Some have been prohibited due to reduced quantities. Some have graduated from the prohibited list because of increased populations due to their temporary protection.

Catch methods include nets, hook sand lines, long lines, harpoons, pry bars, crab traps, and oyster traps. The types of boats used are purse seiners, long liners, dive boats, draggers, and more. Much of the catch is made by local fishermen, but some are caught by vessels from as far away as Japan.

Sea Term

- Golliwobbler - The name given to a very large main staysail used by a schooner in light winds. It probably comes from *golliwog,* a slang word for something grotesque.

TRAVAILS of TRAVELER

The famous 2,225 mile Transpac Yacht Race from Los Angeles to Honolulu had recently finished. Roy Disney's giant sloop *Pyewacket* was the first boat to cross the finish line off Diamond Head after seven days and captured the coveted Barn Door Trophy. Seventy-two other boats followed as the days passed until the smallest boat crossed the line, still in hopes of winning its division on handicap.

We at The Chandlery, Santa Barbara's primary marine supply store, had provided electronics, equipment, rigging and other essentials for several of the entries, so we followed their daily progress reports over the Internet with interest. One yacht that we were rooting for was the 47-foot North Wind Sloop *Traveler* that turned out to be on an 18-day litany of challenges and trouble. Just an hour after their start, they had to return to the mainland to seek medical help for a crewmember who had sliced his finger with a rigging knife. They re-started nearly six hours later.

But their troubles weren't over. Skipper Michael Lawler, the skipper, wrote in his log:

Day Two - On the west side of San Clemente Island - *Traveler* accidentally headed into the middle of a major naval training exercise including live ammo, and we were forced by an escorting Navy helicopter to divert our course by 10 miles away from the direction to Hawaii.

Day Six at 2:00 A.M. - Barbara Burdick, *Traveler's* helmsman at the time, shouted out to her crewmates, 'I've lost the steering!' Next to 'we're sinking' or 'man overboard,' those are probably the most dreaded words you want to hear when you are over 400 miles out at sea. Within a few seconds, the entire crew of six men and two women jumped into action, identified the problem, got the boat under control and then fixed the steering. Somehow, the threaded steering arm had become disconnected from the rudderpost."

Day Seven - Again with Barbara at the wheel at about two in the morning, she called for help from the off-watch crew. The spinnaker pole had separated from the mast . . . and the spinnaker with the pole still attached was dangerously flying around the foredeck, out of control." After just a couple of minutes and with no serious damage, the pole was secured on the deck and the spinnaker was lowered and bagged safely.

Day Eight - The steering failed yet again, but it was an entirely different problem. The nut holding the sprocket to the chain somehow came loose so the steering wheel was not turning the rudder.

Day Eleven - The head of the spinnaker tore apart from the shackle at night. The spinnaker fell into the sea and was being dragged along the side of the boat. After several minutes, it was pulled back on to the foredeck and bagged. That sail is a lot heavier when it is soaking wet. *Traveler* had a spare spinnaker, but we were unable to launch it until we could see what the problem was at the top of the mast. Kurt Roll volunteered to be hoisted up to the top of the mast at dawn to repair the problem."

Because of the light wind, the race took longer than expected and, among other things, the toilet paper started running low. A sign was posted in the head, "Running low on TP, use sparingly." Two days later another sign was posted below it, "We are now really low on TP. Use both sides."

Traveler finished without further woes, but wait...

The spinnaker blew out in a strong gust just when we were about to take it down after crossing the finish line. Then we tried to start the engine and it wouldn't start. Fortunately, there were a couple of power boaters on board and they got it going.

In spite of their difficulties and giving their competitors a six hour head start, *Traveler* clawed her way back to the fleet and actually won second place in its class, Aloha B.

After their finish and festivities, the rest of the crew flew home. Undiscouraged by their experiences, Michael and Barbara soon headed on to Tahiti, planning to continue westerly around the world. After all, their sail number is 7315. "That's the number I picked for my boat so I could be reminded of the day I met the love of my life," Michael said. "I was walking down this very same dock at the Ala Wai Yacht Harbor two years ago (on July 31, 2005) when I saw Barbara on another boat. I asked if she wanted to join me for breakfast at the Hawaii Yacht Club, and she said yes. By our third date, we started planning to do this race together. Transpac is just the first leg of a three-year world cruise for us."

FRESH FISH

We were staying at a beachside motel in the Cambria area and craved a fine fish dinner. A nearby restaurant advertised fresh fish, and drove there with great anticipation of tasting fish caught off the central California coast just hours before. I was armed with knowledge acquired some years before after reading an article about how to determine if fish is fresh. It declared that fresh fish should "not be frozen, cooked, or preserved by any method other than cooling." And further, "the fish should not be taken below 32 degrees Fahrenheit, and that cooling had to be solely by ice. The article further discussed the number of "ice days" that were appropriate to be able to represent fish as "fresh". It was not a tight definition, but offered good guidelines. After thinking things over, I decided that the best test would be to select fish that had been caught recently. So I decided that the question to ask a waiter was, "Do you have any <u>local</u> fish on the menu today?"

I asked "Tad," our suntanned waiter in his form fitting short pants, "What do you have today that is local?" As so often has been the case when I ask that question, Tad gave me a blank stare and replied, "Let me check with the kitchen." With the restaurant's advertised specialty of serving only seafood, and with two major fishing ports within a few miles, I was sure that I would receive an affirmative answer. But I didn't. Tad returned to report that none of the restaurant's fish were local. We ordered anyway, but I found it hard to believe that the restaurant was buying fish from afar and not from the nearby fishing ports.

Considering all the restaurants and supermarkets that advertise "fresh fish" raises serious doubts as to whether many meet the definition.

For example, "Fresh Ahi" is caught off Hawaii, usually by Japanese fishing boats that deliver their catch to a processing ship that must then steam 3850 miles to Japan where the fish are then shipped to a Los Angeles, wholesale market, then to a restaurant where waiter "Tad" informs his customers that they are serving "fresh Ahi tonight". That is a pretty old Ahi, but actually safe to eat.

Or, consider "fresh Chilean sea bass". According to a Joint U.S. Department of Commerce report, it may not be what you think. Chilean sea bass is a deep-water species also known as *toothfish* that lives in southern ocean waters near Antarctica. The Chileans were the first to commercially market toothfish in the United States, hence the name *Chilean sea bass,* even though it is not really a bass and is not always caught in Chilean waters. Because of its white meat appeal, Chilean sea bass usually fetches premium prices in specialty markets and high-end restaurants. It is a huge vdeep-water fish that can live up to 50 years and grow to weigh over 200 pounds.

Some Chilean sea bass are caught by hooks attached to long-lines strung behind large commercial fishing boats off the coast of Chile, and then iced and shipped to the United States – fresh and not frozen. But the majority of Chilean sea bass are harvested in the far distant waters of Antarctica, frozen on-board factory vessels, and shipped from a few weeks to several months later. Both fresh and frozen Chilean sea bass are available for consumption in the United States. The U.S. imports about twenty million pounds of fresh and frozen Chilean sea bass, or somewhere between 15 to 20 percent of the worldwide Chilean sea bass catch.

Do you need to be concerned that you are getting safe to eat fish? No. All fish that is served in the United States in conformance with government regulations are perfectly safe. But, they may not meet your vision of "fresh fish". To buy fish that is just off the boats, go to a store or restaurant that carries fish that have been caught and sold by Santa Barbara's local commercial fishermen. For the very freshest, visit the Navy Pier at the Harbor on Saturday mornings and buy fish right off the fishing boats. Or, go to the Santa Barbara Fish Market at 117 Harbor Way at the Harbor and select fish and seafood that are caught on the local boats

Bon apatite!

WHY I DON'T DRINK COFFEE

It's a dark night and the seas are running high. The bitter cold cuts through to the bone and the sailor's hands are raw and bleeding. He stumbles off watch to the warmth of the galley to recharge his weary body with a scalding cup of coffee before falling into his bunk and a dreamless sleep until the mate sends him aloft once again to face the bitter storm.

All sailors drink coffee, right? Just watch television and movies, or read novels of the sea. Wrong. I don't, and it's actually *because* of the sea. In my early teens, I worked for Bill Irvine doing varnishing and maintenance, and periodically we delivered wooden sailboats and powerboats up and down the coast. On one trip, we were taking a six knot (6.75 MPH) powerboat to San Francisco. It was a rough and long trip, with Point Conception dishing out its harshest. But the trip was made even worse because we discovered that Bill had left our provisions on the dock. All we had to eat for three days were bananas and coffee. By the end of the trip I was having coffee and banana nightmares.

I still eat bananas, possibly because we had them both cold and baked for variety, but I have had coffee only once since that trip. I was doing business in Japan many years later. They made a "ceremony" of drinking coffee... I choked it down but I haven't had any since.

OUR CHANNEL ISLANDS

On a clear and sunny afternoon, standing on the isolated western point of Pelican Bay on Santa Cruz Island, I could feel a light westerly wind as it began sculpting scattered whitecaps over the channel. Surging swells rushing against the rocks and into the sea caves below me generated the only sounds that invaded complete silence. Santa Barbara's high mountains stood out as purple shadows twenty-two miles away.

Sighting across the familiar channel, I visualized the strident and endless activity that was taking place at the base of those hazy mountains – speeding cars, phones ringing, hurrying pedestrians, fingers flying over computer keyboards, deals in the making, crowded stores, the ceaseless roar of a thousand tires spinning down 101, and on and on.

I wondered again why I didn't return to these islands more frequently because most of the year, I too, am part of that distant roar across the channel. And once again, I was amazed at how few Santa Barbarans have ever visited this island sanctuary so close to their doorsteps; just twenty-two miles to reach one of the world's most scenic and natural wonders. Just twenty-two miles to leave behind their stresses for a day or more of absolute contrast to their daily lives.

The islands offer much more than isolated serenity. Inlets and coves provide private hideaways from the outside world. Most of the beaches are covered with pebbles, but higher up you can spread a blanket to lounge and picnic seemingly hundreds of miles from civilization. Hiking is wonderful, and topping an ascent, you become suddenly overwhelmed with a vast panorama of the deep blue, white-capped sea. I like to hike in early mornings, and used to enjoy mutually uncomfortable confrontations with the now, sadly, exterminated wild pigs of the islands. But wild birds and many small animals still abound to provide perspective and variety to a hiker. Of course, diving off the ocean rocks or your vessel opens the vast world of the deep where you can enjoy the view or seek a seafood lunch or dinner with a well-aimed spear. But most of all, the combination of the sea, the winds, the wildlife, and the island terrain become a total experience that can be found very few places on Earth.

Unlike today, it was not easy to get to the islands when I first visited Santa Cruz in 1950 as a young, paid deckhand on the schooner *Samarang*. There were no regular commercial passenger vessels, so the only practical way to get there was on a privately owned boat or as a crewmember on a commercial fishing vessel.

The inexperienced should not attempt a channel passage unassisted. The Santa Barbara Channel is the only location on the North American continent where the coastline runs west-east rather than north-south. This creates the unique climates of both the mainland and the islands. But it also results in the phenomenon named "Windy Gulch," where strong winds from the north bend around Point Conception and accelerate easterly down the outer one-fourth of the channel, creating steep seas and high winds that run its length and finally crash onto the beaches at Ventura. So be forewarned - a channel crossing is not for the inexperienced or unprepared. Happily, today there are many ways to get to the islands easily and safely.

There are a number of the commercial means to visit Santa Barbara's Channel Islands. They provide access ranging from day trips, overnight trips, camping, hiking, diving, private charters, and more..

A FAREWELL TO THE OLD WAYS

The following is an attempt to describe the end of the wooden yacht era. It covers the now lost art of yachting as it was in the 1950's. I was the 18 year old skipper of the 56-foot gaff headed schooner Samarang *described below.*

A light mist rose from the still, gray harbor water as the three young men pulled an old rope against the counterweight that held the long skiff clear of the breakwater rocks. As they scrambled in, Bob, the skipper, took up a long oar, fitted it into a well worn groove in the transom, squared his feet on the floorboards and began the twisting motion of the oar that quickly accelerated the skiff away from the rocks just as the sun began to burn away the mist, promising another perfect Santa Barbara day in 1955.

Samarang loomed large out of the dissipating mist as the skiff coasted nearer. Built in the 1930's, her tall Marconi-rigged mainmast stood high above the gaff-rigged foremast. The long bowsprit extended the fine lines of the hull and balanced the cantilevered boom that reached far aft of the ornate teak transom. The eyes of the three young professionals took in her functional beauty with renewed pride as they again deemed themselves fortunate to work on the best and fastest schooner in the harbor.

As the skiff slipped alongside, Bob hoisted himself over the gunwale while the two crewmembers, David and Larry, tied alongside. He tossed down two chamois and the two crewmembers began the daily ritual of wiping down the gleaming white topsides of the salty remains of the night mist. Meanwhile, Bob attacked the seemingly endlessly varnished teak rails, house, skylights, and trim. Larry soon pulled himself over the rail and took up a mop to dry the newly bleached teak decks and the bright white waterways.

By now the warm California summer sun was completing the drying of *Samarang* as the three crewmembers, stripped to the waist, continued their daily readiness of the sleek schooner. David tossed brass polish and rags to the others to begin the least inspiring part of the day. *Samarang* sported no chrome and every fitting on deck and below had to be polished as bright as the doors on the banks uptown.

The drudgery of polishing over, the three pursued final readiness of the schooner. David began removing sail covers and rigging sheets and lines. Larry used a small vacuum to clean and raise the nap just right on the deep red carpets that so richly contrasted with the deep teak wood below. Galley and heads had been cleaned the night before, so all was now ready for another day at sea.

Engine fluids having been checked, the skipper started the powerful diesel engine. David released the twin mooring lines at the bow and hauled on the spring line to ease the bow away from the large forward mooring can. Bob shifted the engine into forward and Larry dropped the stern line well away from the turning prop. *Samarang's* heavy wooden hull began to pick up speed as the yacht knifed through the calm harbor waters toward the City Float. *Samarang* was solid underfoot as she moved forward, and the only sound was the deep whisper of the engine and the periodic whoosh of cooling water coming from the exhaust pipe below the stern counter.

Seamanship was everything in the 1950's. Standing and sculling nonchalantly in the long skiffs, line handling, maintenance - but the ultimate among the pros was the backing in to the large multi-masted yachts at the City Float in front of tourists, friends, and rivals. *Samarang* had a large, three bladed, feathering prop that was offset to make the maneuvering equation more difficult. Hours of practice had taught Bob to approach the dock at just the right angle and then hit reverse with low revs as he put the wheel hard over. This time, he had to slip between two sixty-footers already hanging stern-to with about eighteen feet between, so *Samarang's* turning had to be a good distance from the dock. He let her swing past the backing line and then gently put throttle to the slowly turning prop. As the large propeller blades grabbed water, the schooner slowed its rotation and began to back. The prop offset came into play and the schooner began to swing out of line. At that moment, he shifted into neutral and the great rudder took over directional control. The schooner slipped between the two sixty footers, and only a slight touch of forward gear was necessary to stop backward progress just inches from the dock just as David casually stepped ashore and "threw a hitch" around the bollard. A small crowd had gathered to watch the great schooner arrive, but the three crewmembers acted out the ritual that no great thing had taken place.

Cockpit cushions were positioned, along with a last minute inspection to ensure that all was as a true yacht demanded. Now, the wait for the owner and his party to arrive – conversation with other skippers and crew, a nervous recoiling of a line that was not quite right, an exchange of looks with a pretty tourist, and another look of pride at the ready schooner.

First to arrive was the owner's butler with food and drink. Larry helped with the stowing while Bob pulled *Samarang* closer to the dock as the owner and his party arrived. Mr. Caspers gave his usual handshake and greeting to his skipper and David and introduced his guests. This time it was the chairman of the board of Mercedes Benz, his wife, and two twin and attractive teenage German daughters. Looks passed between the young crew. This would be one of the better sails on *Samarang*.

When all were placed comfortably in the cockpit, Bob fired the engine, David released the dock line, and the schooner moved smoothly away from her sisters down the main channel towards Stearns Wharf and the open sea.

Samarang's high bow plunged into the wide swells as the great schooner cleared the end of Stearns Wharf and entered open seas propelled by her powerful diesel.

Her guests were comfortably settled on cockpit cushions as Bob headed her into the wind for the hoisting of sails. David and Larry worked their way forward, easing fore and main sheets and running backs. The halyards had been hooked in before leaving the dock so, with Larry tailing, David began grinding the main halyard winch to start the large marconi mainsail on its way aloft. As it peaked, Bob lowered the main gallows and the mainsail was ready for its work.

The gaff-rigged foresail was next, and this time each crewman manned a halyard - David on the peak and Larry on the throat. Per tradition, they hoisted the gaff parallel to the sea until the throat was taut before peaking it at its upwardly raked angle. No winches on the foremast, so each helped the other override their halyard before "throwing a coil" to the pin rail.

Bob began to swing *Samarang's* head away from the wind and the powerful sails began to fill, slowly pulling the large yacht forward. The club-footed staysail was hoisted next. The genoa had been hanked on the forestay at the end of the long bowsprit before departure, and provided a final surge of acceleration as David sheeted it in after hoisting.

Samarang's lee rail dipped into foaming seas now rushing past, and the newly bleached decks turned golden with spray under the summer sun. The "Kenyon" showed seven and a half knots as the helm was eased and the crew trimmed sails for a broad reach down the coast. Discipline and tradition ensured that each sail was trimmed exactly and each line and coil "made up" to perfection. To ensure that the draft of each sail was right, trimming was always from bow to stern on a multi-sailed schooner.

Bob called for a jibe. The foresail and staysail were self tending, so Larry worked the genoa sheets around and David and Bob worked wheel, mainsheet, and running backs as the large overhanging boom swung across the cockpit stopping abruptly at the mainsheet's limit.

The sleek white schooner swept down the Pacific swells at eight and a half knots as Bob turned the helm over to Mr. Caspers in order to go forward to help rig the fisherman, a four-cornered sail that would soon fill the area between masts above and behind the gaff rigged foresail. What seemed spaghetti of lines and sailcloth immediately took form as the crew pulled the main and fore halyards while the sail slid up the foremast track as high as its downhaul line would allow. The main halyard was adjusted in concert with the sheet as *Samarang* heeled and accelerated up to a steady ten knots with twelve knot run outs down the white, foaming seas.

This was just a cruising day with owner, guests and butler. The three young professionals wished for a Saturday in such a wind, along with a full crew to set the giant "gollywobbler" and spinnaker instead of just the fisherman and genoa. Schooners regularly won many of the races in the fifties. Their giant spread of canvas was frequently too much for the sleek sloops, despite their superior upwind performance. Ninety-six foot *Morning Star* had just set a Transpac record as a schooner, although rumors were that she might soon be rerigged as a ketch. (She was, and set a new record in 1955.)

Bob took the helm once again as the butler began serving food and beverages to owner and guests. David and Larry stayed forward in deference to the tradition of the sea that crew came aft only on invitation and then only to do the boat's work. After the lunch items were cleared, the crew close-hauled the five sails as *Samarang* began to claw to weather on starboard tack with buried rail. The twin daughters of the owner's guests became restless with the comfort of the cushioned cockpit and were soon helped by Larry to the end of the long bowsprit to experience the dramatic view aft as *Samarang's* bow rose high over the oncoming seas to suddenly fall, parting tons of steel grey water to each side of the powerful hull.

Bob consulted his watch and judged that it was time to head for the harbor. One final tack and *Samarang* powered toward the speck of Stearns Wharf on the horizon. The high mountains formed a deep purple frame above Santa Barbara's white and red Moorish architecture, while the sparkling blue sea laced with whitecaps formed its base.

As the schooner rushed past the wharf, David and Larry dropped the two headsails simultaneously. With diesel now on, Bob put the helm over and headed up the wide harbor channel as the crew dropped the foresail and main as one to demonstrate what separated professionals from amateurs.

A parting handshake from the well-satisfied owner and guests, and *Samarang* was on her way to her mooring to be "put away" in readiness for another such sail the next day. Later, in the dusk, the three young professionals sculled to the skiff line, thinking that there may be a better job, but not knowing what it might be.

SEA TERMS
- GROG –18th Century. A mixture of rum and water. Named after Admiral Vernon who wore jackets made of a material called grogram. That resulted in his crew creating the nickname Old Grog. When he established a regulation

that caused the sailors rum ration to be diluted with water, they called it Grog.

- MOTHER CAREY'S CHICKENS –18th Century. A sailor's name for stormy petrels (far at-sea bird). The name is believed to be a corruption of the Latin *mater cara,* tender mother, referring to the Virgin Mary. Sailors believed that these little sea birds were under her special care, due to their hardiness, beauty, size, and skill in flight. If you have seen them "in weather" at sea, you may be a believer.
- SNUG – 17th century - Now a word in general use, this is another sailor's word that came ashore. It meant neat, trim, or compact, also tight. The word may have come from early Danish "snyg" of the same general meaning.

THE FLEISCHMANN YEARS

Many readers have responded with emails, and I thank you all. The following letter from Suzanne Farwell, Director of Communications for the Santa Barbara Foundation is worth sharing. The Santa Barbara Foundation is one of Santa Barbara's treasures. It "exists to enrich the lives of the people of Santa Barbara by bringing together groups who need assistance and those who are able to give." Suzanne wrote:

I read with interest of your account of the adventures of the Samarang. *It reminded me of the story of the* Haida I, *whose owner Max Fleischmann had an enormous impact on Santa Barbara. Heir to the Fleischmann gin and yeast fortune, Major Max came to Santa Barbara in the 1920. With nowhere to berth his 110 ft. yacht, he donated $500,000 for construction of the breakwater. (Max purchased a succession of 22 yachts, with most of them named* Haida!) *An avid polo player, he built the polo field in 1927. In addition to a host of other philanthropic activities (financing a surgical wing for Cottage Hospital, restoration of the Mission after the 1925 earthquake, several buildings for the Museum of Natural History), he decided to spice up the lives of the local people by funding free band concerts in the local parks. In order to assure the future of the Santa Barbara Band, he established the Santa Barbara Foundation on October 16, 1928.*

We all know what happened the following October [The Great Depression] . . . . *The scope of the Santa Barbara Foundation rapidly expanded to help feed hungry children and the thousands who found themselves unemployed. Seventy-nine years later, the Foundation sails on with a favorable wind, funding nonprofits throughout Santa Barbara County. It seems that yachting can lead to big things!*

NOT ALWAYS A BOWL OF CHERRIES

Word from friends cruising the South Pacific: "Along with other cruising boats, we're still waiting in Tonga for a weather window to cross to Fiji. The winds outside have been topping 35 knots constantly and the seas are reported at 15 to 18 feet. We need to be in Vanuatu in time for the Rally to Bundaberg on the Australian east coast, so we will probably step out in the morning anyway - with plenty of reefs in the mainsail." Also word from *Traveler*, whose event-filled passage from California to Hawaii was reported in an earlier *Scuttlebutt*. They are now cruising the Hawaiian Islands while waiting for the weather to allow them to make a break for Tahiti and beyond. It's tough being stuck in Hawaii. We'll follow their progress.

DISCOVERING SAN MIGUEL ISLAND– AGAIN

For 37 years John Olguin, 87 and director emeritus of Cabrillo Marine Aquarium, has led an annual reenactment of the historic 1542 landing of Juan Rodriques Cabrillo and crew on San Miguel Island at the west end of Santa Barbara Channel. Participants don period costumes complete with armor and metal helmets and make the 700 foot climb from Cuyler Harbor up Nidever Canyon to pay homage to Cabrillo at the site of the monument erected in 1937 by the Cabrillo Civics Club. It has long been believed that Cabrillo was buried on San Miguel Island, but his grave has never been found and no one knows for sure whether or not he was buried there.

THE UNPAID HAND

Ah, the romance of racing a sleek yacht with white sails filled by a warm breeze, colorful spinnakers ballooning ahead, whitecaps scattered across the deep blue sea - all part of gentlemanly competition for the silver trophy awaiting the winner at the yacht club.

Not so. Today sailboat racing at the upper levels is tough, athletic, injurious, hard fought, and shows no quarter among its contestants. It pulls the latest materials and aero/hydro dynamics technology from leading edge sciences to create racing machines made of carbon fiber, titanium, and anything else that is lighter and stronger than before. The rules of engagement are studied more closely than the U.S. Constitution in order to take instant advantage of all encounters on the race course. And the specifications setting the limits of design parameters in the various classes of boats are taken to their limits to achieve maximum speed and maneuverability. At the highest levels of the America's Cup, expenditures for a contestant can be in the tens of millions of dollars.

I am describing the limits that the sport of yacht racing has reached. Just as with professional and amateur golf and most other sports, there is plenty of room for the weekend amateur to compete at a comfortable, lower intensity level. Santa Barbara's racing scene ranges from the low intensity upward into the middle portion of the high intensity range. No America's Cup syndicates here yet.

Racing a sailboat is an art. No other sport I am aware of has so many variables that must be brought together for success. Every aspect of moving a sailboat through the water is a constantly changing variable: wind force and direction; the movement of the ocean waves, currents, and tides; the constant adjustment of equipment to accommodate the variables; and the war of wits against multiple competitors who use every trick in the book to cause your failure and their success.

But with all this advanced technology and equipment, perhaps the most important of all cannot be created on the drawing board – the racing crew. Even with on-board computers, nothing has yet replaced the knowledge, experience, physical strength, endurance, sensitivity, and intuition of the people who operate as a team to create a successful racing yacht. The owners and skippers may get the glory and trophies, but this success could not have happened without their crew. After "putting away" their racing machine following a hard fought victory, these men and women, perhaps limping a bit as they inspect their hands and arms for cuts and bruises, look forward to getting into dry clothing before a beer or two and tall tales at the crowded yacht club bar.

The following is a fine testimonial to the crewmember at all levels of yacht racing. I have never found out who wrote it or when, but it has been around for a long time and is as applicable to yacht racing today as 150 years ago.

THE UNPAID HAND
I doff my hand to the unsung crew
Who do the things they're told to do.
That hardy, loyal and faithful band,
The toiling throng… the unpaid hand.
The unpaid hand in his dungarees,
Rough and ready and aiming to please,
A-pulling the sheets and cleating them fast,
So the little ship won't finish last.
The unpaid hand who boils and burns
On a windless day when the buoy turns,
Are tough to handle and hard to make
In the sizzling sun that's hard to take.
The unpaid hand in the gale of wind
Soaked to the bone, his knuckles skinned,
Setting the spinnaker…taking it in,
Hoisting the Genny…swearing like sin.
Hurrying to weather to trim the boat,

Sailing like Hades to keep afloat,
Hauling the backstay…trimming the main,
Over, and over, and over again.
And when the races have all been run,
And the boat he crewed on is the boat that won.
And the lucky skipper is stepping up
To get his flags and the silver cup.
Back in the corner, feeling so grand,
With a nice stiff drink,
Is the unpaid hand…!

SEA TERM
- *CREW* –17th Century – Broadly, a ship's people other than the captain and officers. The word came, via Middle English and Old French, from the Latin *crescere,* to increase or grow. The significance of this is simply that most ships for several centuries had only skeleton crews as regulars, and "filled out" for voyages by various forms of recruitment (not always gentle).

SANTA BARBARA YACHT CLUB – POSTWAR YEARS

Founded in 1872, Santa Barbara Yacht Club (SBYC) is the second oldest yacht club in California after the 1869 San Francisco Yacht Club, now located in Belvedere. SBYC has a long and varied history, and carries a fine reputation world-wide. It's a well rounded club that appeals to the formal yachtsperson as well as the athletic racer who prefers to walk in wet and cold from a rugged contest to the comfort and camaraderie of the bar.

As a young boy, I first came in contact with SBYC just after the Second World War, when my father joined to continue his love for sailboat racing that began on Lake Michigan. Not the most prestigious time for the venerable club, its facilities during the war had been a room at the old California Hotel at the foot of State Street. I remember many fine trophies, paintings, and memorabilia stored in closets and around the single room that club groups used for meetings.

Despite its humble accommodations, it was an active club in the late 40's with a number of yachts registered and two active small boat racing fleets of 18 foot Mercury and Flattie sailboats. My father joined the latter, and I began crewing in races that were started and finished off Stearns Wharf. The missing ingredient was a place to go after the races for camaraderie and the telling of tall tales including why the trophy should have gone to the speaker rather than to another racer who actually crossed the finish line first. Because it was family racing, a local bar would not do, so the racers began meeting Mondays for lunch at the old 101 Restaurant to resail the events of the weekend. This began a tradition that became the very well attended Monday luncheons held at SBYC today that feature a variety of notable speakers in lieu of the tall tales told by members of yesteryear.

As Santa Barbara continued to grow, the desire for a clubhouse increased, and some members began working toward that goal. In January 1950 they opened negotiations with the City for use of a portion of beach for a clubhouse location. This was accomplished, and in July 1950, a SBYC member who was a Union Oil Company manager arranged for the acquisition of an old corrugated iron oilfield office to become the new clubhouse. It was not much, but the members rolled up their sleeves and began prying the rusted metal off the outside and replacing it with wood siding. The same was true with the interior of old seasick green thin planking. I remember digging holes in the sand to accommodate 55 gallon drums with ends removed that were then filled with concrete to hold wooden pilings to support the clubhouse above the sand to protect it from incoming tides and storm waves.

For the next fifteen years, it was the tradition of the club that the commodore for the year would organize additions and improvements to the clubhouse, mostly done with the free labor of the members. This included interior improvements, additions to the outside decking, and new rooms. Over time, it became a good sized building that the members could be proud of. During that same period, the Harbor was growing and the boat mooring cans were beginning to be replaced with marinas with walkways and slips for the boats. Today, all vessels are moored in slips and the Harbor has grown from a little over 100 mooring cans just after the war to the present 1200 slips.

The membership of SBYC also grew substantially, and in the early 1960's plans began to replace the present clubhouse with one that was larger and which represented an overall planned design rather than one designed from year to year. This was accomplished in 1966, and the new building has grown with periodic additions to the present day.

There are now over 700 members of various categories including flag, junior, life, Corinthian, non-resident, honorary, and temporary. The club is very active in supporting charitable and non-profit groups and events. All improvements on the sand beach that is leased from the City have been installed and paid for by SBYC. The club also pays monthly rent to the City.

SEA SHELLS

A giant wave swung towards me. I yelled to Steve across the water, "Let's take it!" I pushed the tiller over, sheeted in *Little Spook's* single sail and began surging ahead as I steered for the best angle to ride the oncoming giant now rising taller and taller above as it was pushed upward by the shallow bottom at the beginning of Santa Barbara Harbor's breakwater sandbar. My eight foot, one sail, flat bowed Sea Shell dropped its bow, accelerated down the wave, and then lifted and surfed forward at a speed its designer had never even dreamed of. As I worked the tiller and mainsheet to swing the bow to the proper angle, *Spook* stayed on the wave all the way to the end of the bar where the wave then slowly disappeared into the deep waters of the harbor. My tiny yacht again moved at a normal speed dictated by wind alone. As Steve and I began tacking up the harbor channel to put our boats away, I wondered what my parents would think if they knew what wild rides their twelve year old son was having.

Over the years, the Sea Shell dinghy sailing and racing program probably has had more impact on the overall population of Santa Barbara than any other boating activity. It all began on a rainy afternoon in 1948 when my father Ray Kieding took his two sons to Bill Smart's small ship's chandlery at the harbor to collect a large cardboard box that he had ordered several weeks before. That weekend, we began screwing and gluing together the plywood and wood pieces that came from the Haggerty Company in New England. They would become Santa Barbara's first Sea Shell sailing dinghy, the forerunner of hundreds to come over the next 49 years to the present day.

My father was an organizer, so his enthusiasm soon caused others to order Sea Shell kits. A small fleet developed, and racing began. Most of the new owners were adults, and the local fleet initially had only a few youngsters like me. By that time, our family had two Sea Shells, and my brother and I honed our racing skills in contests primarily against oldsters by using our light weight and greater agility to advantage. Soon, it seemed an extravagance to pay an expensive ninety-nine dollars plus shipping costs for kits that could just as well be duplicated and built locally. My father's good friend Northrup Ellis was very good with tools and soon made templates so the wood could be purchased and cut in Santa Barbara. Years later, a professional builder began selling completed Sea Shells. In recent years, wooden Sea Shells have outlived their efficiency, and the fleet has changed over to the professionally manufactured fiberglass Sabot prams that are in use today. But the fleet still retains its original name of Santa Barbara Sea Shell Fleet.

Over the years, Sea Shells have become strictly for juniors with one brilliant exception. During the spring to fall sailing season, you can visit "Sea Shell Beach" between Stearns Wharf and the harbor marinas and see dozens of multi-colored sails as youngsters race off the harbor shore. Parents and families watch from the beach, with some calling advice while their sons and daughters compete offshore at a variety of levels of intensity and skills. It's a lot to ask of a parent to miss Sunday football on television or other activities and chores in order to sit on the beach watching a bunch of kids racing tiny sailboats. But wait. No doubt, the adults are there to be good parents, but there's another reason that has been a key to the long success of the Sea Shell Fleet – the last race of the day is sailed by adults. Now mom or dad can demonstrate if their sage advice to Junior is as good as given. But win or lose, the adult race has served as an incentive that has resulted in more boats on the beach than might have otherwise occurred. Fifty years of success is an unprecedented record for a sailing fleet, and there is no end in sight for Santa Barbara's Sea Shells.

Today, around 20 boats show up on a Sunday for racing. Some are stored in racks on Sea Shell Beach, and others are easily transported to the harbor on car roof racks or small trailers for multiple Sea Shell families. Racing starts at 1:00 PM, and usually ends around 4:00 PM. The average Sea Sheller is between 8 and 13 years old. Fleet information is available on www:sbssa.org. Each season starts with practice races in April and official racing beginning in May. Some fleet events are held out of town as with the annual trips to Lake Lopez and to San Diego's Mission Bay. Each fall, the Fleet sponsors its always advanced sellout Wine Tasting and Yacht Tour to raise funds for this worthy junior program which gives Santa Barbarans the opportunity to taste fine wines while boarding and experiencing fine local yachts.

Many Sea Shellers enter the program with no personal or family sailing experience. Some go on to become accomplished yachtspersons and others never sail again. However, I have never run into a past Sea Sheller who has not enthusiastically expressed how important that experience was in their life. For example, a past sailor now living in Sacramento recently emailed, "My younger sister and our parents were involved in the Santa Barbara Sea Shell Association for about a half-dozen years in the 1960s. What a great time we had with other young families, and what great memories we still have!" Others have told me that they felt that their Sea Shell experience helped them stay on a productive track in school and had a major influence on their success in later life. I have grandchildren who have participated in the program, so our family can claim the sole title of having four continuous generations of Sea Shellers with the fifth soon to come.

SEA TERM
• Sea Shell – A shell of an offshore mollusk. Or, an eight foot sailing pram with a single mainsail, dagger-type centerboard, and transom mounted rudder piloted by a smiling youth off Santa Barbara's waters.

GRAVEYARD OF THE PACIFIC

The fog was thick with visibility less than a quarter of a mile as the 96-foot sailing ketch *Morning Star* surged down steep grey seas with run outs of over 14 knots. We hadn't seen sun or stars in over a week and had been relying on dead reckoning navigation for too long. Without an accurate position by sextant sighting for over seven days, the crew's nerves were starting to show as the large racing yacht continued its rush towards California's ominous *Graveyard of the Pacific* at Point Conception somewhere ahead. But with hundreds of miles of strong winds and currents behind us, we weren't sure exactly if, where, or when we'd sight the Point or better yet, its 26 mile light.

Our navigator was tops, but this was 1955 and well before exact satellite positioning with GPS or affordable collision avoiding radar. So we were relying on plotting estimated speed and direction on chart for many days. It was now dusk, and the skipper was preparing to "heave to" for the night and let *Morning Star* drift slowly until we again had some sort of visibility to safely sail onward the next morning. If we didn't stop soon, we might join the many ships, boats, and yachts that had been lost in the *Graveyard* over the last 140 years. But if we turned down the coast too early, we might meet our end on the unforgiving rocky shores of San Miguel Island.

But wait! Was that a flash of light ahead? All hands strained to see through the rapidly darkening fog. And then a call, "I see it!" We counted the seconds between flashes to identify the light. "Thirty seconds! It's Conception!" And just in time. With great relief, we made our turn down coast. The off-watch crew then rushed below to break out food and water that had been strictly rationed due to the uncertainties of the length of our trip home from Hawaii. *Morning Star* had once again broken the record for the Los Angeles to Honolulu Transpac race, but she did it with her engine's propeller removed to reduce drag for faster speed under sail. So we were bringing her home by sail power only with no use of the engine.

The next day, in contrast to the wild weather at Point Conception, we drifted in a dead calm off Anacapa Island, frustrated, and waiting for the slightest breath of wind to push us toward Los Angeles Harbor and then home. We had made it safely past the *Graveyard* in the largest yacht in the 1955 Transpac, but a few days later, we were saddened to learn that *Suomi,* the smallest yacht in the race, hadn't made it. She was rammed and sunk by the Swedish ship *Parramatta* in the fog off Point Conception with all five crewmembers going to the bottom with her. The *Graveyard of the Pacific* claimed more victims.

Why is it a graveyard? Looking at a map of North America, you will see that the western coastline runs approximately north to south. But forty-five miles above Santa Barbara, the coastline takes a unique turn to nearly east to west. This creates a dynamic transition in the area of Points Arguello and Conception. High winds, strong currents, and deep fogs predominate to create one of the most difficult and dangerous areas to navigate on the entire western coast. Over seventy-five vessels have run aground or been in collisions, and many lives have been lost.

The most dramatic occurrence was the grounding and loss of six of fourteen United States Navy destroyers en route on a training exercise from San Francisco to San Diego. On the morning of September 8, 1923, they were steaming in formation at a speed of 20 knots with just 250 yards separating each vessel. Visibility was close to zero, and the command ship's navigator's dead reckoning calculations indicated that they were past Point Conception and it was safe to turn to enter Santa Barbara Channel. But he ship's new radio direction finder indicated they were not yet past the Graveyard! This information was ignored as being the inaccurate input of a newfangled and unreliable electrical instrument. The direction finder was correct, and the dead reckoning was wrong. So when the fleet commander ordered the change of course, all six leading destroyers were lost in "the jaws of Honda" and twenty-three of the sailors aboard went to their deaths.

Of the over seventy-five vessels lost at sea or ashore, most resulted from the need to navigate by dead reckoning due to poor visibility in an area of strong winds, treacherous currents, high waves and rocky shores. Guestimated positions were marked on charts, but the actual positions of the vessels were often far from their estimated chart plottings. Only in recent years, when radar and GPS have become widely available, have captains became confident that they truly knew their vessel's position in relation to the dangerous shores of Conception, Arguello and San Miguel Island. Today, it is still essential to know the status of the weather at the *Graveyard of the Pacific.* For smaller vessels, it is still wise to anchor in a protected cove until the time is right to make the passage around the points under the best possible weather conditions. However, with radar and GPS, no longer does a captain have to wonder where his actual position is in relation to the treacherous points and beaches of the *Graveyard of the Pacific.*

WHERE NOT TO BUILD A HARBOR

Leaving Santa Barbara "sent a thrill of pleasure through the heart of every one in the boat. We pulled off with a will, saying to ourselves (I can speak for myself, at least), 'Goodbye Santa Barbara! This is the last pull here. No more duckings in your breakers, and slipping from your cursed southeasters!'... Each one was taking his last look at the Mission, the town, the breakers on the beach, and swearing that no money would make him ship to see them again." From *Two Years Before The Mast*, by Richard Henry Dana, about his voyage on the sailing ship *Pilgrim* from 1834 to 1836.

Then and for many years to follow, Santa Barbara had no safe anchorage or harbor. Soldiers and priests, but not seafaring men, founded the town in 1782. Goods and materials were brought overland, and there was no planning for the anchoring and off-loading of vessels. Santa Barbara had no natural headland to create a safe anchorage, and mariners dreaded the exposed roadstead so much that they would anchor a mile or two off-shore to allow room to up-anchor and claw away from Santa Barbara's pounding surf in a dreaded southeast storm.

A chart from the late 1800's shows a very different waterfront from the present. Today's sands of Ledbetter Beach and La Playa Stadium did not exist, and breakers beat against the cliffs below what is now City College. Just east of the present breakwater was the promontory of Castle Rock, long since removed in favor of a widened Cabrillo Boulevard. A narrow beach ran from Castle Rock down to today's cemetery. Inland from State and Milpas Streets were salt-water marshes - very different from the firm landfill that now supports hotels, businesses, roads, and commercial buildings. As the town grew, the need for ships to transport goods and passengers grew with

it. But many years would pass before a railroad and practical roads became available.

The early beginning of Santa Barbara's first harbor was a large sycamore tree with a hanging lantern that could be seen from a ship seeking to anchor in the saltwater roads during the early 1800's. The tree existed in 1976 when a plaque was installed at the northeast corner of Milpas and Quinientos Streets. Sadly, the five hundred year old tree is now gone, but you can view the plaque there. Years later, a formal lighthouse was built on the Mesa in 1856. The 1925 earthquake destroyed it, and an automated light which is still in operation replaced it.

A series of piers were build over the years in an attempt to handle arriving ships. In 1868, a pier was built at the foot of Chapala Street, but it was not sufficiently long to permit deep draft vessels to tie alongside. In 1872, 1500 foot long Stearns Wharf was built at the foot of State Street, and it successfully handled goods and passengers for many years. Stearns Wharf did not solve the need for a harbor, and was severely damaged many times by the same southeast storms that Dana cursed. The Edison Company built a pleasure pier near the present swimming pool in 1895. In 1887, the railroad finally reached Santa Barbara. Passenger traffic fell, but freight continued by ship until it was finally overtaken by trucks and automobiles.

Plans to build a true harbor began in the early 1900's. In the early 1920's, an engineering study was conducted to determine the best location. The studies included experiments of setting sawdust and empty jugs in the ocean off Hope Ranch to study current behavior. There were two conclusions that resulted from the tests: 1) don't locate a harbor near West Beach because prevailing currents would immediately shoal a moorage basin with sand while denuding beaches to bedrock further to the east, and 2) the most feasible and economical solution would be to widen the natural inlet at the present Bird Refuge, install jetties, and create a completely landlocked anchorage that would be safe in any weather year around.

So, why was the Harbor built where it is? There were other possibilities, and most were more supportable. But, as with all of history, events usually include a combination of necessity, power, politics, timing, money and more of the vast array of factors that manipulate human civilization. Santa Barbara's Harbor was no exception.

In 1926, Major Max C. Fleischman offered to donate $200,000 to build a breakwater if the City would match his funds. The Major was looking for a safe anchorage for his 250-foot yacht *Haida*. Santa Barbara's voters approved a matching bond issue for $200,000 in 1927, and barges immediately began carrying rocks quarried on Santa Cruz Island for the construction of the new breakwater. The initial work was completed in 1929, and a 600-foot extension was soon added. As engineers predicted, sand began building up at the western end, so the breakwater was then connected to the shore.

Over time, massive sand deposits built up to create today's Ledbetter Beach. The sand then continued to drift along the length of the breakwater and to drop into the quiet waters of the new harbor. The US Army Corps of Engineers began dredging this sand out of the harbor every three years. Total harbor dredging became impractical when the marinas were built, so dredging then took place primarily at the end of the breakwater every year to prevent further filling of the inner harbor. As more boats and slips were added, additional storm protection was needed. To provide increased storm protection, the sand spit at the end of the breakwater became somewhat permanent when sheet piling was driven into the sand to create yet another breakwater extension.

Winter closures of the harbor occur periodically when shallow, sand-filled waters combine with high, storm-driven southeast waves. Santa Barbara was embarrassed internationally in 1983 when the Queen of England's yacht *Britainia's* launch could not enter our harbor, forcing Queen Elizabeth and President Regan to drive from Oxnard to the Regan Ranch rather than enter our city in style.

The end of the breakwater and harbor is now dredged every fall and winter in order to move the sand to East Beach where it can continue its journey down the coast. Each year, the US Army Corps of Engineers spends approximately $2,000,000 on dredging. Hopefully, the U.S. Government will continue to pay the bill rather than Santa Barbara. In hindsight, the many millions of past dredging dollars could have been used to build a well-engineered harbor at the Bird Refuge, Goleta Slough, Carpenteria Slough, or to build an easterly breakwater to protect the present harbor from southeast storms. However; present social, political, and environmental conditions make any of these approaches infeasible at this time. Today, Santa Barbara is defined by its harbor and waterfront. It would not be Santa Barbara without them.

ALERT OFF SANTA BARBARA

On January 22, 1840, the 398 ton, three-masted, square rigged sailing ship *Alert* departed Boston, bound for Alta California and arrived in Monterey on June 27. *Alert* then spent many months sailing the waters between San Francisco and San Diego collecting cattle hides until it departed for Boston on December 30, 1842 with over 40,000 hides aboard. Captain William Dane Phelps' final entry in his ships journal of the voyage was on May 4, 1843. Theirs was a voyage of over three years. His May 3rd 1843 entry read:

Nauselt Light bore NW distance about 12 miles. At 7PM the sun set in splendor behind Yankee Land, a sight we have not seen for years. Of course, all on-board are in high glee at the prospect of being in Boston Bay tomorrow morning, which we shall be if the breeze continues (please God).

The journal and observations of Captain Phelps make fascinating reading for Santa Barbarans interested in our maritime history. *Alert* anchored off Santa Barbara and Refugio Beach numerous times as it plied its quest for hides. Santa Barbara is mentioned over fifty times in the journal and the Refugio landing more than ten times.

Thursday, Nov 4th. Owing to very light & variable winds, we did not arrive at Santa Barbara until this afternoon. Anchored in 10 fathoms, and prepared for a slip. [A slip is having the anchor ready to let loose in the face of bad weather.] *Yesterday, we were becalmed off the Island of Anacapa. Took the boat and went near the Island to fish and met with fine luck. Caught about 30 fine large rock fish, some of them, weighing 12 & 15 lbs.*

A captain's journal differs greatly from the ships log. A log is very cryptic and includes weather, ship's position, ship's activities, and matters of commerce related to the ship's mission. In a journal, however, a captain has full license to express his thoughts and observations. Captain Phelps does this well in his journal, with extended descriptions of Santa Barbara, the Mission, the Presidio, the ships encountered, the population, day to day experiences, and, of course, the business of trading for hides.

Friday Nov 5th. Light variable winds in the forenoon, and strong westerly winds in the afternoon & evening. Crew employed watering. Today heard of two more murders, one of them at the Refugio. A fellow who has frequently been employed by our agent to travel with him and take care of his horses in a jealous fit shot his wife dead. He ran to the next house and told the people that his wife had shot herself but she was yet alive when they reached the house and was able to tell the particulars. The murdering villain is in prison at this place, but will probably go unpunished, because he is "extensively connected". The particulars of this affair and the history of the parties concerned are too disgusting to relate. Sufficient to say, it presents one of those dark tales of vice, victimization, and degradation which but seldom occur. It is indeed lamentable that the laws of the country are so often violated, and that the stupidness of the executive winks at such outrages as are now frequently committed.

Captain Phelps' journal goes on to describe its forty-month voyage from New England to California and return. Also included in the journal are observations such as California prices at the time; for example, quill 1 cent, shoes $2.50, pick ax $1.00, file 35 cents, cloth pants $15.00.

The journal was published by Arthur H. Clark Company in 1983 under the title *Alta California, 1840-1842: The Journal and Observations of William Dane Phelps, Master of the Ship "Alert."* It is out of print, but can be purchased on www.abebooks.com .

WORLD'S OLDEST ANIMAL

A 3.5-inch Arctica Islandia clam, dredged from the seabed north of Iceland by a team of scientific researchers, was found to be 405 years old, making it the oldest live animal yet to be discovered. While the clam was alive when it was collected at a depth of about 274 feet, it died after being hauled in, according to researchers from Bangor University School of Ocean Sciences in Wales. The clam's age was determined by counting the rings on its shell. One wonders how many years longer it would have lived if it had not been recovered for science.

QUARTER CENTURY OF SATELLITE RESCUES

Since 1982, COSPAS-SARSAT, the international satellite search and rescue system, has been credited with saving the lives of more than 22,000 boaters, aviators and hikers worldwide, including nearly 6,000 in the United States and its surrounding waters.

DANGEROUS WINDS

"Let's get out of here!" was the decision of seasoned skipper Ralph Hazard while anchored at the Channel Islands upon deciding that weather conditions might be bringing a dreaded Santa Ana wind storm. Ralph fished our waters for over sixty years and gave the following advice: "A Northeaster [Santa Ana] gives boaters the biggest problem, because it comes so damn fast and there's no warning at all. It usually catches boaters after midnight, when probably ninety-nine percent of them are already in the sack. When the boat starts to bounce a little bit, they say, 'Oh, jeez, we're going to roll tonight!' Then, all of a sudden, BOOM! Here comes the white water and the wind! The bump [waves] comes first. That bump is always ahead of the wind. The wind will be anywhere from, I'd say, half an hour to an hour later. By the time the white water comes, you'd better be off the beach and on your way! The way I look for a Santa Ana is, if the weather clears up and gets beautiful, I can stand in Scorpion Anchorage and watch Hueneme's lights and all the lights down the line. But if it gets a little bit warm, uh oh! I don't go to bed. I watch and wait. Pretty soon, if a little bump comes in . . . . 'Let's get out of here!'

Santa Anas are the most dangerous winds encountered off Southern California's shores. But they bring on-shore danger as well, as Santa Ana winds often accelerate many destructive brush fires from Santa Barbara to San Diego. Santa Anas usually occur about a dozen times a year. They are extremely turbulent, with gusts often exceeding sustained winds by 60% and more. These winds arrive suddenly and then quickly build to maximum strength. Although they generally blow for four to six hours, they can sometimes continue for days. Most Channel Island anchorages are uninhabitable in a Santa Ana.

This "Perfect Wind" occurs when a large air mass moves over the high desert and encounters elevated mountains. The air is pushed upwards to clear the passes, causing it to cool below the dew point and lose moisture. Next, it flows down the mountain slope on the far side, warming due to compression as it descends — about 5°F per thousand feet of drop. Since the air loses less heat on its ascent than it gains during its descent, and since it also loses moisture during its ascent, it usually arrives at the bottom of the mountains as a hot, dry wind. Hot Santa Anas are usually localized at coastal waters below passes and canyons; however, if the air is very cold before its descent and it arrives at the coast cooler than the surrounding air, it will push the coastal air up or aside and deliver the stronger punch we associate with cold Santa Ana winds. It is cold Santa Anas that often reach our Channel Islands, sometimes with disastrous results.

Santa Anas can wreak dangerous havoc. In November of 1976, at least 100 persons were rescued by Coast Guard and Navy boats and helicopters off Santa Cruz and Anacapa islands. Forty boats needed assistance. Some sunk, some were missing and presumed sunk, and some took on water or were otherwise seriously damaged. Winds blew steadily at 70 miles per hour Saturday morning with gusts over 90 miles per hour.

A mariner must know the warning signs of a Santa Ana, and how to act quickly to avoid risk of serious losses. What are the signals?

- Weather maps showing high barometric pressure over the Great Basin between the Rockies on the east and the Sierra Nevada on the west. A pressure over 1035 millibars in the Great Basin will usually suffice. On the day of an onset of a Santa Ana, the pressure along the coast must be at least 10 to 12 millibars lower than that at the center of the Great Basin high. The likelihood of a Santa Ana is even greater if the high pressure air is cold.
- There is no haze or fog aloft. The air above is clear and stars shine with unusual brilliance. Usually, lights on the horizon appear as sharp pin points.

- The air is usually dry and often warm. Decks may be covered with salt crystals. Wet clothing dries completely. Lines formerly containing salt water are hard and stiff. The humidity is often below 20%.

A knowledgeable skipper will monitor his marine weather radio, as well as internet weather reports. The forecaster may not explicitly mention either Santa Anas or the islands. In fact, you may only hear reports of light and variable winds at Point Conception because a common part of the drama is the diminishing of normal northwest winds. An innocent forecast of "gusts below passes and coastal canyons" is another signal, as are warnings for motorists "driving high profile or light vehicles." You will get one last signal: "Swell from the northeast." Like hurricanes, Santa Anas send waves before them as heralds of their approach. Once the swell arrives from the northeast or east, strong winds have already crossed the coast. When the swell arrives, you must leave exposed anchorages immediately. Do not hesitate. Santa Ana winds are imminent.

When the fine weather of Santa Ana conditions beckons, professional and experienced mariners will still go to the islands, but they 1) carry heavy duty ground tackle, 2) go to the western end of Santa Cruz Island or even farther west where the force of the Santa Ana will be less, 3) anchor in a large anchorage using only one anchor – not in a snug cove requiring two anchors, 4) clear their decks, and 5) have rehearsed a contingency plan for evacuation.

If you are not confident of your seamanship or just don't want to expose your boat and crew to a Santa Ana, stay home whenever you see a large high pressure center over the Great Basin. Enjoy a great ballgame on television. " Life's too short."

CHRISTMAS AT SEA

Christmas at sea can be wonderful -- if you are among your loved ones. But if you are alone at sea, or working at sea away from your family, it can be a very lonely experience. Few landlubbers realize just how thickly populated the seven seas and our inland rivers are. In addition to all the U.S. Navy personnel out there, millions of Americans work on thousands of ships all over the world as merchant mariners, and more are aboard privately owned vessels that are plying all of the seven seas.

The Christmas-at-Sea program of the Seamen's Church Institute brings hospitality and love to deep-sea and river mariners with Christmas gifts containing handmade scarves, caps, vests, helmets or socks, as well as other useful items such as stationery kits, sewing kits, magnifying lenses, mirrors, combs, and more. These items are knitted, crocheted, or collected by more than 3,500 volunteers across the country. The program was started in 1898. Each year, more than 16,000 gifts are distributed. You can learn more and possibly participate by visiting www.seamanschurch.org.

The following is a typical letter of thanks from sailors who could not be home last Christmas: *"At our last call at New York, you delivered to us 26 plastic bags with gifts for my men and me. I'd like to thank you and all diligent knitters for these unexpected presents and for their prayers for our safety as well as for your good wishes for the year to come. On December 24th, we celebrated our Christmas Eve with all our crew. At that time, we were inside the Malacca strait, one of the places in the world most haunted by pirates. But we sailed under a good star and passed safely. We are all wishing you and all the persons who were caring and praying for us as well as your families some peaceful Christmas days and a happy year with best health and God's blessing.*" Capt. W. Koehler and the crew of CMV "Antwerpen Express" - December 2006. Note: The Malacca Straight is part of Indonesia near the Philippians where pirates board modern ships, capture or kill the crew, and abscond with valuables aboard.

"Christmas At Sea" by Robert Louis Stevenson (1850-1894). (He only lived 44 years, but in those short years, what he accomplished!)

The sheets were frozen hard, and they cut the naked hand;
The decks were like a slide, where a seaman scarce could stand;
The wind was a nor'wester, blowing squally off the sea;
And cliffs and spouting breakers were the only things a-lee.

They heard the surf a-roaring before the break of day;
But 'twas only with the peep of light we saw how ill we lay.
We tumbled every hand on deck instanter, with a shout,
And we gave her the maintops'l, and stood by to go about.

All day we tacked and tacked between the South Head and the North;
All day we hauled the frozen sheets, and got no further forth;
All day as cold as charity, in bitter pain and dread,
For very life and nature we tacked from head to head.

We gave the South a wider berth, for there the tide-race roared;
But every tack we made we brought the North Head close aboard:
So's we saw the cliffs and houses, and the breakers running high,
And the coastguard in his garden, with his glass against his eye.

The frost was on the village roofs as white as ocean foam;
The good red fires were burning bright in every 'long-shore home;
The windows sparkled clear, and the chimneys volleyed out;
And I vow we sniffed the victuals as the vessel went about.

The bells upon the church were rung with a mighty jovial cheer;
For it's just that I should tell you how (of all days in the year)
This day of our adversity was blessed Christmas morn,
And the house above the coastguard's was the house where I was born.

O well I saw the pleasant room, the pleasant faces there,
My mother's silver spectacles, my father's silver hair;
And well I saw the firelight, like a flight of homely elves,
Go dancing round the china-plates that stand upon the shelves.

And well I knew the talk they had, the talk that was of me,
Of the shadow on the household and the son that went to sea;
And O the wicked fool I seemed, in every kind of way,
To be here and hauling frozen ropes on blessed Christmas Day.

They lit the high sea-light, and the dark began to fall.
"All hands to loose topgallant sails," I heard the captain call.
"By the Lord, she'll never stand it," our first mate Jackson, cried.
"It's the one way or the other, Mr. Jackson," he replied.

She staggered to her bearings, but the sails were new and good,
And the ship smelt up to windward just as though she understood.
As the winter's day was ending, in the entry of the night,
We cleared the weary headland, and passed below the light.

And they heaved a mighty breath, every soul on board but me,
As they saw her nose again pointing handsome out to sea;
But all that I could think of, in the darkness and the cold,
Was just that I was leaving home and my folks were growing old.

SEA TERMS

- Sheet - A controlling line to a sail (13th century).
- About – To "come about" is to change course so the wind fills the sails on the opposite side of the boat. (16th century)
- Tack – To turn a sailing craft "through the wind" to take the wind to her other side. See "about" above. (15th century French)

CURRENT EVENTS

Sometimes knowledge comes from unexpected events. On May 27, 1990, the container vessel *Hansa Carrier* was enroute from Korea to the United States Pacific Northwest when it encountered a severe storm that caused twenty one of its 40-foot containers to be lost overboard in the mid-North Pacific Ocean. Five of the lost containers held approximately 80,000 athletic shoes. After six months, thousands of the shoes began washing ashore from along the southern Oregon coast and north to the Queen Charlotte Islands in British Columbia.

Oceanographer Dr. Curtis C. Ebbesmeyer of Seattle (my cousin) was so intrigued with reports of so many shoes coming ashore on the northwest beaches that he began contacting those who had found the shoes. He also began advertising for information on other findings of the shoes. He was assisted by a creative entrepreneur who recorded who had what models, sizes and left or right foot so he could hold swap meets to marry up pairs. With a bit of cleaning, the shoes were little worse for wear from up to a year at sea and could be sold to bargain hunters.

But Dr. Ebbesmeyer was more interested in the scientific results from the shoe spill than finding homes for separated pairs of sneakers. 80,000 floating objects released from a knownlocation at a known time was a scientific windfall that couldn't be missed. In the past, scientists had released 33,869 research bottles in the Northeast Pacific to help learn more about the currents that had been bringing items from Japan to North America for thousands of years. But the shoes were a giant sample that presented a chance of a lifetime opportunity to learn more, and they did. Results showed that given time, an object set afloat off Japan could follow the North Pacific Gyre through its component currents (Kuroshio, Subarctic, California, North Equatorial), circumnavigate the Pacific to Canada, the mainland United States, Hawaii, the Philippine Islands and back to Japan in four to six years.

Later, another major spill consisted of toy rubber ducks. "The ducks went around the North Pacific in three years - all the way from the spill site to Alaska, over to Japan and back to North America," said Dr. Ebbesmeyer, now retired. "This was twice as fast as the water at the surface - so I began to call them hyper-ducks." Thousands of the floating ducks washed up, battered and bleached by their journey through the waters of the Arctic, the Pacific and the Atlantic Oceans. It took ten years for some to reach the Atlantic Ocean. During their voyage, some of the ducks broke away and headed for Europe – others surfaced in Hawaii. Some may eventually make it all the way around the world.

Since the Great North Pacific Shoe Spill and the North Pacific Toy Spill, many more spills have helped scientists study the ocean currents of the world.

Based on comparisons of ceramic pottery found in both Ecuador and Japan, derelict vessels disabled by storms have probably been transported from Japan to the Americas by prevailing winds and ocean currents since at least 5000 years ago, Approximately twenty-percent of abandoned Japanese whaling vessels lost off Japan in the early 1800's drifted all the way to North America. The drift took about fifteen months and, in some cases, a few sailors aboard actually survived the trip.

If you wait long enough, things may come your way. The Chumash Indians of our coast found that redwood was the best material to construct of their Tomol canoes. They would wait patiently for the currents to bring this material to them from the north so they could build their next Tomol. You can see one that was built by contemporary members of the Chumash tribe at the Santa Barbara Maritime Museum.

WANDERER

Wham! Suddenly I landed in a heap against the wooden rail, feeling the stinging beginnings of a very sore back. "That'll teach you to keep an eye out!" from the tall captain as he strained heavily against the massive tiller to bring the heavy ketch about off Santa Barbara. I needed that "eye" to keep clear of the *Oscar's* thrashing loose-footed foresail as it came across the deck to fill once again on the new tack.

As a young teenager, I often crewed on the 1890's Norwegian life saving ship *Oscar Tybring*, then owned by sailor, movie actor, author, kidnapper, nomad, and what have you, Sterling Hayden, who had just given me his usual dose of sympathy. The *Oscar* was a cumbersome, double ended, gaff-rigged, wooden ketch that was built heavily to withstand fierce winds and icy seas while stationed off the coast of Norway as a rescue vessel. She performed that task well over the years, tallying a record of saving 329 lives and 102 boats while often operating in the arctic winter under appalling conditions.

Oscar Tybring was far from being a Santa Barbara "sailing yacht" and that suited Hayden perfectly. They were both loners, strongly built, and never duplicated. Hayden was a genuine adventurer and man of action, similar to many of his movie parts. He ran away to sea as a ship's boy at 17. Hayden soon sailed and fished waters off Newfoundland on some of the last of the true commercial sailing vessels. Fast schooners like *Bluenose* and *Gertrude L. Thebaud* raced from the Grand Banks to Boston, not for trophies, but to reach the docks first and win the highest price for their catch. Hayden was awarded his first command at 19, and soon made several voyages around the world. When I began sailing with him, Hayden was a movie actor who had played many roles, but he often professed distaste for film acting, claiming he did it mainly to pay for his ships and voyages.

Hayden sold the *Oscar*, but returned a few years later in another much larger 1890's vessel – the 150 plus foot San Francisco pilot schooner *Gracie S*, which he renamed *Wanderer*. She too was built sturdily in order to carry a knowledgeable ship's pilot off-shore to board a sailing ship and guide her through the currents, tides, and fogs that make San Francisco Bay a challenge for any mariner. (This was shown recently when a pilot erred and the tanker he was commanding hit the Bay Bridge in fog, spilling considerable oil into San Francisco Bay.) Many of us were waiting on Santa Barbara's breakwater for a first view of *Wanderer* rounding Ledbetter Point on her way to her new home. And then, there she was, under full sail and moving close along the shore to give Santa Barbarans a good look at a real sailing ship. She even fired a salute to the town with her single cannon. Upon boarding her later, we saw that the cannon had been both mischarged and misaligned, for a large chunk had been blown out of *Wanderer's* rail when the salute was fired.

Several of us local "water rats" had the good luck sailing with Sterling Hayden on the two vessels that he brought to Santa Barbara. Our captain loved to sail in the worst and roughest weather, and it was an unforgettable experience to work a true sailing ship – especially when sent high aloft to use "one hand for yourself and one for the ship" as she pitched and crashed through giant seas.

But the nomadic sailor/actor eventually moved on from Santa Barbara to new adventures and travails. He continued to act, wrote his 1890's sea novel *Voyage*, his autobiography *Wanderer*, and, whenever possible, to sail. Just as he approached the peak of his career as a movie star, Hayden suddenly abandoned Hollywood, walked out on a shattered marriage, defied the courts, and set sail with his four children aboard the schooner *Wanderer*. A broke outlaw, he escaped to the South Seas.

I think the following quotation from his 1963 autobiography best summarizes Sterling Hayden, the man:

To be truly challenging, a voyage, like a life, must rest on a firm foundation of financial unrest. Otherwise, you are doomed to a routine

*traverse, the kind known to yachtsmen who play with their boats at sea...
cruising, it is called. Voyaging belongs to seamen, and to the wanderers of
the world who cannot, or will not, fit in. If you are contemplating a voyage
and you have the means, abandon the venture until your fortunes change.
Only then will you know what the sea is all about. "I've always wanted to
sail to the South Seas, but I can't afford it." What these men can't afford is
not to go. They are enmeshed in the cancerous discipline of security. And in
the worship of security we fling our lives beneath the wheels of routine - and
before we know it our lives are gone. What does a man need - really need? A
few pounds of food each day, heat and shelter, six feet to lie down in - and
some form of working activity that will yield a sense of accomplishment.
That's all - in the material sense, and we know it. But we are brainwashed
by our economic system until we end up in a tomb beneath a pyramid of
time payments, mortgages, preposterous gadgetry, playthings that divert
our attention for the sheer idiocy of the charade. The years thunder by.
The dreams of youth grow dim where they lie caked in dust on the shelves
of patience. Before we know it, the tomb is sealed. Where, then, lies the
answer? In choice. Which shall it be: bankruptcy of purse or bankruptcy
of life?*

Sterling Hayden died of prostate cancer at the age of 70 at Sausalito,
California in 1986. He would have preferred to have lived one hundred
years earlier when men of iron sailed the seven seas in great ships of
wood.

SEA TERMS

- Come About, Tack – To change course with the bow of the
  vessel crossing the direction of the wind. 16th Century.
- Tiller – A bar which serves as a lever to turn the rudder.
  Anglo-Norse origin.
- Ketch – A two-masted sailing vessel with the second mast
  shorter and at the stern, but not behind the waterline.
  Origin debatable.
- Schooner – A two masted sailing vessel with the forward
  mast equal or shorter than the main mast. Or, any vessel of
  more than two masts. Origin debatable.

MILLION DOLLAR CLOCK

For countless centuries before 1700, thousands of lives, ships, and fortunes had been lost under the waters and against the rocks of the world's oceans because ship captains did not have the means to determine their ship's exact location. They knew how to locate their north-south position (latitude), but not their east-west position (longitude). England, the most powerful sea nation in the world at that time, was desperate to solve this problem.

A ship's captain was able to locate his north-south position (latitude) using a sighting instrument to calculate the angle between the horizon and the sun or other celestial body. But, that process would not work to locate his east-west position (longitude) unless the captain also knew the precise time of the day down to the second at the instant he made his celestial sighting. In the 1700's, a clock had not yet been invented that was accurate enough and portable enough to take to sea to help locate longitude. [A bit more technical information about this process is at the end of this column.]

After over 200 years of scientific failure, the English Parliament in 1714 offered a kings ransom of 20,000 British pounds (worth millions today) for a "practical and useful" means for determining longitude. A highly bureaucratic "Longitude Board" was formed to evaluate submittals of possible solutions. Scientists of the day pursued mapping the heavens as the answer, but more practical contestants sought to come up with a precise clock that could be carried on ships at sea. The competition required determining longitude to an accuracy of 30 miles.

This would require a clock that would keep time within two seconds each day.

John Harrison, a gifted young English clockmaker and craftsman, was making fine clocks of wood at the time the competition began. He and his brother toiled for six years, and then submitted their metal clock H-1 to the Board to be tested at sea on a voyage from England to Lisbon, Portugal. The clock worked well and the Harrisons felt they had met the rules and specifications of the competition. But, the finicky Board turned their clock down as not conforming to their requirements. The brothers, strapped for money, asked for and received the first of several requests for funds to continue their work. In 1739, they completed a revised clock H-2, but it weighed over 100 pounds. Knowing that the Board would do almost anything to avoid awarding the prize which would cause them to disband their lucrative positions, Harrison elected not to submit the H-2 version, but decided to solicit more funds to continue work on a lighter, more portable version. His discouraged brother left for another trade, and John Harrison spent the next 19 years working on clock version H-3. (Remember, he was working to win the equivalent of millions of dollars.) He finished 70 pound H-3, but was also working on H-4, which was only 5 ½ inches in diameter and weighed but a few pounds. When completed, the H-4 "sea watch" was a masterpiece.

In 1761, Harrison and several inspectors departed on a sailing ship to voyage to Jamaica to test H-4. Poor weather allowed only one sighting to test the clock. The results showed that it lost only 5 ½ seconds during the entire voyage and allowed longitude to be determined within one mile accuracy. This was far within the requirements of the competition, and Harrison knew he had finally become a millionaire. But the Longitude Board yet again decreed that they were not satisfied. They agreed that the results were astounding, but "reasoned" that the results could have been arrived at by the combination of several possible errors. They enticed poor Harrison to continue his work by giving him a partial award of 1500 pounds of the 20,000 prize. By declaring the competition not yet over, the Longitude Board were able to keep their lucrative and prestigious government appointed jobs for decades – now approaching 40 years! Yet another sea trial of H-4 was made to the Barbados Islands, but this time the Board had appointed one of the scientists who were pursuing the "map the heavens" solution as an evaluator of Harrison's clock. The evaluator's obvious conflict of interest resulted in H-4 being rejected once again, despite clearly meeting the competition specifications.

His health and eyesight failing, Harrison was now in his 70's, living on the financial edge, and working on a new clock, version H-5. Finally, the Board reluctantly agreed that H-4 met the specifications, but then piled on more requirements beyond those specified for the competition so many years before. Harrison, now in his 80's, was devastated. In desperation, he petitioned King George III for payment of the balance of his prize money. The King was convinced and instructed Parliament to investigate the matter. Finally, Parliament, but not the Longitude Board, awarded the funds. John Harrison died a millionaire just three years later. So ends the true story of inventive genius, tenacity, and the permanence of government agencies.

MORE ON CALCULATING LONGITUDE

Half of the problem of locating your position on earth had already been solved centuries before the 1700's. If you look at a map of the world, you will see horizontal lines. These lines show "latitude" which lets you know how far you are north or south of the equator. Latitude is expressed in degrees of a 90 degree angle. Zero degrees latitude would be on the equator, and 90 degrees latitude would be at the north or South Pole. Latitude is commonly determined by means of a sextant or other instrument that measures the angle between the horizon and the sun or another celestial body, such as the North Star. Using the angle, the latitude is then found by means of tables that give the position of the sun and other bodies for that date and hour.

Your map also has vertical lines running from north to south, which add up to 360 degrees, a full circle, and are called longitude. England decided that the start of the east-west circle should be at Greenwich England. Thus, any location on earth can be described by indicating its longitude and latitude where the horizontal and vertical lines cross each other. Santa Barbara's location is approximately 34 degrees north Latitude and 119 degrees west Longitude. By breaking the degrees into smaller parts, a location can be more precise. The precise location of the entrance to Santa Barbara Harbor is 34 24.47 degrees north latitude and 119 41.07 degrees west longitude.

Or, you can purchase a modern Global Positioning System (GPS) for a couple of hundred dollars and instantly know where you are within a few feet.

INLAND WATERS

Steve and I stretched painfully outboard to our physical limits with just a scant few inches of the ends of our feet remaining in the hiking straps to restrain us from suddenly flipping backwards off our surging sloop and into the cold waves and waters of the lake. We were sailing by the dam where winds blow their strongest, and the windward racing mark was coming up fast. I pulled the tiller extension roughly toward me while letting the mainsheet sheet fly as Steve and I wrenched ourselves back onto the deck. The mainsail boom slammed across in a flying jibe as *Intrepid* spun around the mark while simultaneously picking up a wave to begin surfing on a spray flying, screaming reach across the lake toward the next mark. This was as good as it gets for a pair of waterlogged teenagers racing our 18 foot Flattie sailboat against twelve others on arguably the best sailing lake in California.

Years later as our car climbed over a crest, my wife Joan and I were treated to a view of the lake's whitecap frosted waters that extended to the steep cliffs that rose vertically toward the high mountain peaks that seemed to almost reach the white cumulous clouds above. The seven-mile long lake has 42 miles of shoreline bays and coves. Depths reach 200 feet of cold darkness. Twenty-knot winds sculpt steep waves in the unprotected areas, while coves provide warmth and a quiet oasis from the lake's afternoon power. A true paradise, and well worth the twisting drive through the mountains.

Joan and I began anticipating the many possibilities to enjoy this mountain framed paradise – sailing, boat fishing, shore fishing, hiking, camping, visiting the nature center, touring, nature walks, pool swimming, taking nature tours afloat, horseback riding, picnicing, or just hanging out to enjoy the spectacular weather and out-of-doors.

The drive was worth it – all of twenty minutes from Santa Barbara. For this was Lake Cachuma, a mountain paradise annually enjoyed by over a million visitors, but which is almost unknown to many close-by Santa Barbarans, who either never or rarely visit it.

The statistics are overwhelming. Over two hundred twenty species of birds are listed as visiting the lake each year. Fishermen land a wide variety of freshwater fish. Roaming mammals include black-tailed deer, mountain lions, bobcats, deer, American brown bears, coyotes, foxes, skunks, gophers, rats, California ground squirrels, western grey squirrels and mice. Reptiles found in the area are western fence lizards and others, garter snakes, king snakes, rattlesnakes and more. Amphibians include frogs, toads, and salamanders. Arthropods variously include spiders and insects, and crayfish. Gastropods include several species of snails and even clams, introduced to the lake in 1964 to clear the water.

Although it was destined to become a recreational paradise, Cachuma Lake was created in 1953 as a solution to ever-growing Santa Barbara's water needs. The project was not without controversy, as the News-Press issues at the time reported the often bitter battles between some Santa Ynez landowners and Santa Barbara County water interests. But finally, Bradbury Dam was constructed, using 6,695,000 cubic yards of earth and rock fill. Its 23,000 acre feet capacity was first exceeded during a storm in February 1958. Water from the lake reaches Santa Barbara through 6.4 mile long Tecalote Tunnel, which was drilled through the mountains from 1950 to 1956. The seven foot diameter tunnel drops three inches every 1000 feet for gravity flow, and has a capacity of 100 cubic feet of water per second. Bradbury Dam cost $14,000,000 and Tecalote Tunnel cost $14,500,000.

Most Santa Barbarans watch the lake level carefully each year in hopes that a drought will be avoided. You can check this each day in the News-Press weather section. The lake spills at a water elevation of 750 feet. Through the years the up and down lake elevations seem to range from a high of 750 feet down to around 725 feet. The lake loses about 1 ½ inches a month due to evaporation in the winter and about 10 inches per month in the summer. Since most silt is captured at upstream Gibraltar Dam, Lake Cachuma has lost only around ten percent of its capacity in over forty years. Santa Barbara's water supply comes from the Santa Ynez River through three tunnels, from wells, and from the State of California aqueduct system fed from the High Sierra Mountains. During one extremely dry period, Santa Barbara built a desalination plant to convert sea water into drinking water. The basic plant and seaward piping still exists, but it would take more equipment and renovation to put it back in service. This seems unlikely due to the present availability of State water.

But back to recreation at this wonderful lake. A visitor can take advantage of services offered or be independent. The following activities are available at quite nominal fees – rowboats, pedal boats, patio deck boats, outboard motor boats, fishing gear, individual camp sites, group camp sites, Yurt cabins, central coast cabins, horseback riding, 2 hour eagle and wildlife tours on the 45 passenger *Osprey,* pool swimming, Junior Rangers program, and boat launching. The following activities are free (except for the park vehicle entry fee) – hiking, organized nature walks, Nature Center, andpicnicking. Go to the web at www.sbparks. org and click on "Locate a Park" to see comprehensive information on the lake and park.

The Lake Cachuma Recreational Area is owned and operated by Santa Barbara County. Entry and camping are on a first come first served basis, and there are not reservations. This is a big plus for Santa Barbara locals. State parks like Refugio beach take reservations which often prevents locals from spontaneously deciding to visit a park on short notice during the busy season. I am hopeful our county leaders will continue the no reservation program at Lake Cachuma. Much of the year, it is quite easy to get a camping spot. In the busy summer, I go up on a Thursday to sign up for a spot through the weekend. The fees are so reasonable that this works very well.

A WHALE OF A TRIP

One of the problems with my boating occupation is that periodically I have to take a large, multimillion dollar yacht to sea. Sigh, but someone has to do it.

In this case, I needed to make a 100 mile run to test the engines on a 72 foot motor yacht. I needed a crewmember, and called one of my experienced boating friends. Later, while discussing the pending trip at a BBQ, two more of my salty friends joined up. A large storm system was predicted, but it looked like we would be able to get the job done just before it hit.

We met at 7 AM on a Monday and drove to board the vessel at Ventura Harbor. I performed the normal procedure of checking engine fluids and turning on various electrical switches and panels to activate lights, pumps, trim tabs, and stabilizers. Then I initiated the electronics – radar, GPS, chart plotters, speed and depth instruments, and autopilot. Finally, it was time to fire up the two mammoth, thousand horsepower main engines. Their built-in computer system flashed more data on twin screens than I could ever use, but the key numbers looked good. After the warm-up, I activated the two slow-speed switches to reduce the engine's idle speed of 600 RPM's down to 550. I had some tight maneuvering to get out of the docking area and would need to do it slowly and carefully. The yacht's speed is 6 knots at standard idle and 5 knots at slow idle. The maximum speed allowed in the harbor is 5 knots - another reason to run at 550.

My crew/friends pulled aboard the dock lines and rubber fenders as I began backing away from the dock by momentarily engaging the shift levers in and out of reverse. A tight turn was required, and this was accomplished by rudder hard over, periodic momentary engagement of the engines with one in forward and one in reverse and additional help from the bow thruster. A bow thruster is a propeller located at the bow that pushes the bow right or left when a joy stick located at the helm is engaged.

When we had backed into the harbor turning basin, I rotated the yacht a tight 180 degrees so we could begin our forward progress towards the harbor entrance. After we cleared the harbor jetty, I deactivated the slow speed switches, adjusted the shift levers to synchronize mode, and began accelerating upward to reach 1900 RPM's as required for the test. In the synchronize mode, both engines run at identical RPM's, using just one rather than two control levers.

Despite the dire weather prediction, it was a beautiful day. Large, sun gilded clouds framed all horizons. The ocean was smooth and deep blue. Our global positioning system indicated we were making a speed of 18.5 knots over the bottom (20.8 miles per hour). With uncertain weather predicted later in the day, we discussed our routing options to accomplish the 100 mile objective. Possible choices included runs to and from Santa Barbara Island, Catalina Island, Marina del Rey, along the coast, or around part of Santa Barbara's Channel Islands. We decided to do a close-in circumnavigation of Anacapa Island, then to head westward along the outside of Santa Cruz Island, around its west end through the Santa Cruz Channel, and finally across the Santa Barbara Channel and back to Ventura Harbor.

Anacapa, our first objective, is a rugged island with marginal anchoring at Frenchy's Cove, Cat Rock, East Fish Camp, Cathedral, and access to the Coast Guard light and station by two long steel ladders at the eastern end. We saw many birds, seals, and sea lions as we viewed the forbidding cliffs and reefs during our island circumnavigation.

The backside of twenty-two mile long Santa Cruz Island features several good anchorages, rugged mountain peaks, and plentiful sea life. Coches Prietos is a lovely place to anchor and features one of the few sandy beaches on the island. We slowed to move in for a closer look at this cove that had provided us with so much enjoyment in past summers.

Moving westward up the island, we turned outward to clear tiny Gull Island. As we approached, Jack called out, "Whales ahead!" He was pointing to seaward of Gull Island. Suddenly, we all saw a number of telltale spouts of ranging from close-in almost to the horizon. I slowed the yacht to a near stop, and we began enjoying one of Santa Barbara's unique events – the great annual migration of whales from as far north as Alaska on their way to Mexican waters and the warm Sea of Cortez.

Based on the repeated spouts we spotted, there seemed to be between twelve and fifteen whales in the area. Four were very close by. I gently maneuvered the yacht to position just behind their leisurely progress along the island waters. Soon, we were within just a few yards from these giant regents of the seas. The four moved slowly along in tight formation, repeatedly surfacing to take in air before passing again beneath the ocean's surface. We were transfixed as each whale surfaced, blew, and then curved downward to show us their backs as their tails rose above the surface before sinking out of sight into the sea. Of course, none of us had thought to bring a camera, but the memories of these stately Grey Whales will stay with us for years to come.

After more than a half hour, we reluctantly turned away and were soon on our way to Santa Cruz's west end. The water was still smooth, but the sky and clouds were telling us of harsh weather to come. Passing through the Santa Cruz Channel and the often rough Potato Patch, we could see the vast sand dunes rising above Santa Rosa Island's eastern shores. I recalled when I worked as a teenager on the Vail family's yachts when they owned the island before it was acquired by the National Park Service.

The final run down and across the channel to Ventura Harbor was pleasant and beautiful. We secured the yacht, washed it down, and headed back to Santa Barbara as the darkening, cloud covered sky signaled its approaching wrath. Whenever I ran into one of my three crew friends in the weeks after the run, he would declare how much we all enjoyed our unique trip around Santa Barbara's matchless islands barely ahead of the jaws of a major winter storm.

"DEAD" RECKONING

At age sixteen, I was hired to travel to Los Angeles Harbor to meet a powerboat owner and take him on his 28 foot powerboat to Santa Barbara. I had been on a number of such boat deliveries in the past, but this would be the first on my own.

I arrived on time so we could get plenty of miles behind us before darkness, but the owner arrived very late which meant we would be getting off near the end of the day. I had already checked the boat and all seemed well. I suggested that we leave early the next morning, but the owner insisted we leave right away. In later years, I would have insisted that, as captain, it was my decision – but not at age sixteen.

There were no electronic navigation devices on recreational boats in those days, so navigation would depend on using only a compass, a chart, and knowledge of the boat's speed under power. I would be using "dead reckoning" navigation by recording the average compass heading we had steered every hour along with the average speed of the boat during that period. This would allow me to mark a penciled "X" on the chart to show where I estimated we were at that time. Dead reckoning coastal navigation had been used for countless centuries - ever since charts had been first invented. To work well, it is essential that the compass and estimated boat speed be as accurate as possible.

After leaving the dock, I made a run between two harbor buoys and compared the powerboat's compass heading with that shown on the chart. The compass seemed reasonably accurate, at least in that one direction. I would have liked to make test runs in other directions, but I wanted to as far at sea before darkness set in. With no speedometer, I was relying on the owner's statement of how fast the boat went under power. This was a mistake, as I later learned. I should have made a timed run between two buoys to be sure.

So off we went. The wind was blowing about 20 knots with a steep chop, but my experience was that this was LA Harbor's usual accelerated flow over the Palos Verdes hills, and that it would calm down once we got off-shore. I plotted a course up the coast that would keep us safely off-shore, and yet keep us out of the major shipping lanes where giant tankers and cargo ships charged along at over 18 knots speed. At appropriate points, I plotted changes of course on the chart that would take us safely around the various headlands on our way to Santa Barbara Harbor.

After a couple of hours, darkness set in, and we were fully dependent on steering accuracy and accurate chart plotting. The owner had told me the boat went 12 knots in normal conditions. We were still in chop, so to be conservative I used 10 knots in my navigation calculations before making changes of course. This way, if there was an error in estimating speed, we would be more safely further away rather than closer to shore. Three more hours of steering, and I was getting really tired. I asked the owner if he would steer for a while. He did, but had no skill in keeping a straight course, and the boat wandered in wide arcs from right to left. So, I had to take the helm again and try to stay awake and alert.

The wind and waves continued to stay fresh, but we then lost visibility as heavy fog began setting in. After an hour of straining to see ahead, I was startled when we passed a tall piling that had no reason being there. I hoped it was a deep-water buoy, because my calculations showed us to be well off-shore. But this event raised doubt and concern about the owner's claim regarding the speed of the boat. Just to be safe, I steered further out to sea, making careful note so I could record it on the chart and determine our approximate position. We ran all night in darkness and fog, and I continued to make X's on the chart that showed our calculated progress. More and more frequently, I felt myself beginning to collapse from fatigue, and I was forced to ask the owner totake over for a few minutes despite his wild gyrations at the helm.

Dawn finally arrived. We were enveloped in proverbial pea soup fog with visibility less than 100 yards. I studied the chart and the marks I had made throughout the night that estimated our hourly positions. I reasoned we had come far enough to begin working our way towards shore to try to visually determine our exact location. My calculations plus intuitive adjustments for current and wind indicated that we should be off the shores of Carpenteria. With almost no visibility, I guided the boat very slowly as we both stained to first see the approaching shore. Suddenly, a line of white spread from right to left ahead of our bow. It was the surf line, but the fog was so thick that we couldn't see land beyond. I carefully edged closer and then turned to parallel the coast to try to locate a landmark that might tell us where we were. At long last, we spotted a buoy and noted its color and markings so I could check the chart to see what and where it might be. I couldn't believe it! We had only come as far as Ventura, some fifteen miles short of my dead reckoning calculations. Either we had had a major current against us all night, or the boat did not go the speed the owner claimed, or both. It was the latter, and I had learned a lifelong navigation lesson – never rely only on someone's word or opinion without verifying it.

Finally, we made it to Santa Barbara and I let out a fatigued sigh of relief as we tied up at the City Float. The owner didn't have a clue as to the danger he had put us in, and merrily departed for home while I started to wash down the boat before running it out to its mooring can. As the shore boat ran me ashore, I realized I had learned a lot on this short but dangerous trip that would pay off greatly on future voyages.

Today, with the advent of electronic navigation, this story wouldn't have happened. For a couple of hundred dollars you can have a portable Global Positioning System (GPS) that will tell you where you are within fifteen feet. For two hundred more, a GPS will show your location on an electric map, and even talk to you about getting to your destination. But I still make marks on a chart, - just in case my GPS loses power and I'm on my own. But to avoid that, I also carry an inexpensive portable GPS as back-up. Dead reckoning is becoming a lost art, but I still get pleasure out of a historic and often intuitive process that uses all information available – speed, direction, chart, wave shapes, water color, sound, temperature, and anything else that may confirm your particular spot on the ocean.

EXPLOSIVE CATCHES

The crew of the Spanish fishing boat *Pedro y Loli* had a 2200 pound surprise catch while fishing the waters off Cabo de Palos. When they brought up their surprisingly heavy net, instead of fish they found an 11 foot long torpedo. The torpedo was tightly tangled in the net and couldn't be easily removed, so the nervous crew headed back to port, contacted local authorities for help, and hoped for the best.

A military bomb squad from Cartagena cautiously cut the torpedo loose while members of the Guarda Civil cut off public access to the fishing port. The torpedo was cautiously removed from the vessel for careful examination before being disarmed. The weathered weapon was discovered to be German-made and possibly dating back to 1914, although similar torpedoes were used in World War I, the Spanish Civil War and World War II. *Pedro y Loli's* relieved crewmembers were glad to have survived their close encounter with a catch that might have more than bitten back.

GITANA 13 SETS RECORD

The giant 110-ft twin hulled high speed catamaran *Gitana 13* with its 10 person crew departed in mid-January to attempt to break the sailing record from New York to San Francisco around Cape Horn. The clipper ship *Flying Cloud* held the record for over one hundred years – an 89 day 8 hour passage made in 1854. But in recent years, the record has been attacked by several syndicates with the current record now 63 days 5 hours 55 minutes held by *France's Ecureuil Poitou Charentes*.

Baron Benjamin de Rothschild's *Gitana 13* crossed the Equator from New York in 6.5 days, an average of just under 500 miles a day for the first 3,200 miles of the 13,945 mile voyage. But *Gitana 13* had to wait out two big 55 to 70 knot weather systems for five days before rounding treacherous Cape Horn. She still has a long way to go with doldrums (areas of no wind), and probable storms to work her way through. At the present rate, she has a good chance, but all sailors know not to take anything for granted at sea.

There are many sailing time records on the books. The 21,760 mile non-stop around the world record for a crewed sailing vessel is currently held by France's *Orange II* with a passage of 50 days 16 hours 20 minutes and 4 seconds. The non-stop single-handed record is 57 days 13 hours 34 minutes and 6 seconds. As you read this, a lone sailor is in the mid-pacific attempting to break that record.

Sailing records over the world originally were set by fast cargo ships whose captains risked life and ship to be the first to reach markets before their competitors. Instead of a trophy, first-in prize was top selling price for their cargo, which often made fortunes for the ship's owners and investors.

UPDATE - The giant 110-ft catamaran *Gitana 13* crossed under San Francisco's Golden Gate Bridge to end her record-setting 14,000-mile record sail from New York. In light breeze, she passed under the bridge at precisely 08:31:29 February 28 for an elapsed time of 43 days, 38 minutes (subject to ratification by the World Sailing Speed Record Council). That beats the old 1998 record of 57 days by more than two full weeks. Highlights of *Gitana*'s record run included a day's run of 640 miles, a top speed burst of 40.3 knots and several sustained speeds in the 30s.

SEA TERMS

- Cranky – Any craft of low or poor stability. 17th Century England from *cringan*, meaning weak or delicate.
- Forecastle – Often spelled and pronounced Fo'c'sl. Today's meaning is the foredeck (forward deck) of a boat or ship. Originally, it meant a raised platform at the bow, often armored, for archers and musketeers. 13th Century. Today it is usually an area under the foredeck used for crew's quarters. Since there is a lot of bow wave noise and up and down motion, it is not the best place on a ship to sleep. An old timer once quirked, "… and it ain't no castle."

VARIABLES

Picture yourself racing a sailboat off Santa Barbara. As you steer your boat on a warm, sunny day with picturesque whitecaps scattered across the deep blue sea, you concentrate on reaching the next racing mark ahead of your competitors. Your crewmembers chat over the events of the week, and how relaxing it is to race on a pleasant day with Santa Barbara's majestic mountains in the background. All look forward to a beverage and camaraderie discussion of the race with other competitors at the yacht club after the race.

In reality, cold waves throw spray into your face as you operate high tech winches and equipment to constantly adjust sails, rigging, hull trim, and a myriad of other gear and equipment while being ready to instantly change course to optimize speed or ward off your competitor's aggressive attacks. You're wet to the skin, cold, and suffering from bruises and bleeding hands as your skipper calls for even faster action and better results. At the yacht club after the race, cold stares or designed taunts can be expected from your competitors as they explain why you were lucky if you won, or how smart and fast they were if they finished ahead of you. But this really_is fun, and you wouldn't exchange it for anything!

Racing a sailboat requires dealing with more variables than any other sport that I know of. The dictionary defines a variable as *"Apt or likely to change or vary; changeable, inconsistent, fickle fluctuating, etc."* Every aspect of sailboat competition is a constantly changing variable – the surface you travel across, the forces of propulsion, the direction of travel, the adjustments of equipment, the actions of competitors, and many more. Literally, there are no constant factors in sailboat racing – none.

Sailboats are propelled by wind and waves. Wind never ceases changing in intensity and direction because of varying atmospheric pressure, air and sea temperatures, wave action, water depth, effects from land masses. Sailors must constantly change steering direction, sail shape, and heel (tilt) angle of their boat to maximize its speed and directional performance. If steering toward the waves, a helmsman must constantly sail a careful zigzagging course to reduce the negative affect of the waves and to optimize the speed of the boat. When the waves are coming from behind, the boat must be aggressively steered to get maximum push from the wave, and with larger waves to actually get up onto a wild surfing run out. This takes constant steering changes along with an agile crew and skipper who must move their weight inward and outward with only their feet in hiking straps to prevent tumbling backwards into the turbulent sea.

Ever changing wind speed and direction throughout the race requires both skipper and crew to continually change the shape of their sails. This is accomplished by using several adjustment devices attached to the sails, by changing the angle and bend of the mast, and by removing and replacing individual sails as the race progresses and wind and sea conditions change. Different sails are used to get the most speed during a particular wind speed and boat direction. For example, very lightweight sails are used when wind speeds are low, and much heavier and stronger sails are used in high wind conditions. When the wind direction is behind the boat, colorful parachute like spinnakers are launched. A well sailed racing boat's crew never stops constantly adjusting their sails during a race.

Winning sailboat races involves more than just boat speed. It is an adversarial sport, and contestants must use competitive and aggressive tactics to sail faster than their rivals and to maneuver their opponents into situations where they can control their opponent's actions and slow their progress. Because of the aggressive nature of sailboat racing, contests are conducted under very complete and complex written rules that establish which boat has rights over another during every instant of the race. As the boats maneuver over the racecourse, rights constantly transfer many times from one to another and then back again. If a competitor violates a rule and fouls another boat, a protest flag is flown. After the race, a meeting is held so the protest committee can decide if the violator should be penalized or ruled out of the race. Some violations can be undone during the race by the infringer executing a time consuming maneuver.

Perhaps the most difficult variables in sailboat racing are boat to boat confrontations within the allowable racing rules. As with chess, a skipper often plans several tacks (turns) ahead in order to be in a position to control his opponent or to have rights over him when he most needs them. He must also be concerned with other boats in the race who want to win by doing him harm within the rules. Often, there is bluffing and verbal shouts for maneuvering rights that are not deserved.

So sailboat racing involves the use and understanding of the variables of wind, tide, moon, temperature, sea depths, land masses, current, tactics, bluffing, physical strength, pain, the correct use of sophisticated equipment and electronics, and much more - all which must constantly be adjusted or responded to in order to win a tin cup and bragging rights at the bar. Not a tranquil, relaxing pastime.

SEA TERMS

- Tack – To turn into the wind from one board to another (starboard tack to port tack and vice versa. Also the lower aft corner of a sail. Also a general term for food – like tasty hard tack.
- Heel – To list under sail.
- Hike – To lean out to the weather side of a sailboat to keep it from heeling excessively.
- Racing Rules – In the United States, the rules set forth by the North American Yacht Racing Union. A competitor must also conform to rules set forth for the racing class of boat he is racing, and the yacht club that is conducting the races he is sailing in.
- Bar – A place to lick wounds incurred while racing a sailboat.

BOAT NAMES

Each year, the boat owners' organization Boat US releases its annual "top 10" list of the nation's most popular boat names. Top picks include names inspired by motion pictures, music, a love of freedom and a sense of humor.

The latest No. 1 pick, *Black Pearl*, came straight from the "Pirates of the Caribbean" movie, and evokes images of adventure at sea. *Liberty*, at No. 2, exemplifies patriotism and a love of freedom. *Second Wind*, at No. 3, conveys the idea that no matter how bad a day you've had on land, a boat gives you a second chance at a good experience. Other top names in order included *Amazing Grace, Aquaholic, Knot on Call, Second Chance, Wanderlust* and *The Dog House*. There was a tie at No. 10 – *Carpe Diem* and *Seas the Day*; both of which make it clear that boat owners really know how to enjoy life to the fullest.

CREATING A SANTA BARBARA TREASURE

In the 1990's, Santa Barbara was in the process of acquiring the massive Naval Reserve Building at Santa Barbara Harbor. Many local Santa Barbarans trained and prepared in the Reserve Building before heading to the war zones of World War II. After the war, many such properties and buildings were turned over by our Federal government to various communities across the nation at no charge. Not Santa Barbara. Our city was charged a substantial price to recoup the property. Unfair, but still a good investment. The waterfront is the front steps of Santa Barbara, and the City was wise to invest in keeping them pristine. Acquisition of the Naval Reserve property was essential in this regard. But what to do with it? The City cogitated, and requested suggestions from the public. A small group of boating citizens felt that this was an opportunity for a Santa Barbara maritime museum waterfront location that would never occur again. It was essential to preserve and protect the maritime history of Santa Barbara and this had not yet been done. A lot of meetings and politics took place before the Santa Barbara City Council made the strategically correct decision to allocate a significant portion of the Naval Reserve Building to save Santa Barbara's long maritime history for present and future generations.

Many strategic milestones took place to convert the dream into reality. It began with a handful of diverse individuals – a wooden boat builder, a sailing director, a computer expert, a ship's chandler, a marine researcher, and a property developer met frequently in a small meeting room at Santa Barbara Harbor to discuss the pros and cons of attempting to start a museum about the Central Coast's maritime history. There were no historians present, and the group's knowledge of local maritime history was far from complete. But they knew enough to be concerned that what was known would soon be lost if it wasn't collected and preserved. Old timers were passing from the scene, rare artifacts were slowly being lost over time, and information was slowly eroding. So the group readily agreed that preservation was an urgent matter – before it was too late.

All were astounded that no local museum had collected our marine history. Santa Barbara has been a maritime community since its first habitation. The Chumash had fished and navigated the Channel since before recorded time. Ships brought Spanish explorers and missionaries along with most of the supplies for the Presidio and Mission; the Yankee traders; the lumber that built the Victorian homes that grace our town today; and most of the town's settlers before 1900. Then came the visit of the Great White Fleet, the growth of the commercial fishing industry, the worst peacetime naval disaster in our nation's history with the sinking of seven US destroyers and the loss of twenty-two sailors at Point Honda, the single flight of Lockheed's giant flying boat, major chapters in the world's diving history, millionaire's grand yachts, the shelling of our coast by an enemy submarine during World War ll, ocean environmental crisis, undersea research, revelations in undersea oil technology, and much more.

And so, it was agreed that there would be a Santa Barbara Maritime Museum. Where, how to finance it, and how to organize it weren't yet known to this fledgling and diverse group. But weekly meetings were held in the cramped conference room at The Chandlery to wrestle with the myriad of details. More volunteers came aboard, bringing new skills and enthusiasm as necessary ways and means were debated. And strangely, a pattern of very good luck began to emerge that has continued to the present day. The City purchased the Naval Reserve Building at water's edge and needed a good use; talented volunteers came forward with exactly the right skills and contacts; a visionary City Council and staff were receptive to housing the museum; farsighted donors came forward at a critical time: and the community embraced the idea of preserving and presenting their largely untold and unique maritime history. This "luck" has been built on a foundation of thousands of hours of hard work by many dozens of volunteers.

Along the way, the final cornerstone of the museum philosophy was laid - interactivity. The founders wanted to have an exciting museum that would meet the high technological excitement of today's world rather than the static "cobweb" exhibits found in traditional museums of the past. On countless occasions, the founders explained "interactivity" to Santa Barbarans by using the example of the rattlesnake tail that is operated by a well-worn button at the Santa Barbara Museum of Natural History. Immediately, there was a nodding of understanding. As a result, Santa Barbara's maritime museum continues toward the goal of interactivity by using virtual reality, computerization, and other technological means to make the visitor a participant rather than a spectator. At the same time, the museum is sensitive to using conventional means where appropriate to provide a well-rounded experience for the public.

The museum opened in 2000, and has proven to be a great asset and attraction for Santa Barbarans and visitors alike.

SEA TERMS

- Maritime – Almost anything to do with the water. The word probably comes from Old French, and goes back to the Latin *Maritimus,* near to or of the sea. 15th Century.
- Great White Fleet – The Great White Fleet was made up of sixteen United States Battleships along with many support vessels that President Theodore Roosevelt sent around the world to show the nations of the world that the United States had become a major power to be reckoned with. It arrived in Santa Barbara in 1903.

DANGEROUS WAVES

High surf from major storms can pound Santa Barbara's waterfront during the winter months. An extreme example occurred when three viewers watching the dramatic breakers from the western corner of the breakwater were swept off the walkway, hurled them against the railing which broke, and then washed the three tourists downward into the harbor waters. About the same time, a woman was swept away by giant surf at Lime Kiln State Park thirty miles north of Cambria while trying to save her dog. Six years ago, NOAA's research vessel *Balena* was operating in calm seas near Point Arguello when, without warning, a giant wall of breaking water came from nowhere and rolled the vessel over and into the rocks. It was completely destroyed, but the four crewmembers survived.

The oceans and many of the lakes of the world are in constant motion, possibly generating the largest natural energy occurring at any given time on our planet. I was once becalmed for two days a thousand miles off California on a 96 foot steel sailing ketch. Just two days later, we were surfing down giant waves of such size and force that an ocean tanker was broken in half a few miles from us. Storm waves can be gigantic, but rogue waves like the one that wrecked "Balena" can be even more dramatic.

As described in *Science Daily News*, these giant waves have been talked about by sailors for centuries – often being attributed to the unexplained disappearances of ships at sea. But most never quite believed them. Rogue waves were considered merely a myth until recently when new studies using technological developments like instrument buoys, radar and satellites scientifically proved their existence. And, it has been found that they exist in much higher numbers than was previously expected. Rogue waves have caused many tragic accidents at sea, not only because of their immense power and heights that reach over 90 feet, but also due to their unpredictable nature – they can suddenly and without warning emerge from calm seas as unexpected giant walls of towering water as was the case with *Balena*.

So enjoy the usually safe pastime of watching our often dramatic surf, but also stand back to avoid a sudden surprise from a frequent "ninth wave" or a from a rare rogue wave.

YOU'VE COME A LONG WAY, HARBOR

Until the 20th century, it was very tough getting to Santa Barbara. The Mission and Presidio had to be supplied by sailing vessels from Mexico during the 1700's and 1800's. Gaviota Pass was so narrow that wagons had to be unloaded and disassembled on one side and then reassembled and reloaded on the other. The stagecoach ride over San Marcos Pass was long and sometimes perilous. A road was not feasible because of the crashing surf against the bluffs south of the town.

Thus, for many years the most viable means to travel to Santa Barbara was by sea. But there was no natural harbor, and the surf was large and forbidding. Richard Henry Dana recalled landing here in 1835 in his classic narrative *Two Years Before The Mast*. "This wind is the bane of the coast of California. Between the months of November and April, you are never safe from it, and vessels are obliged to lie at anchor at a distance of three miles from the shore with slip-ropes on their cables, ready to slip and go to sea at a moment's warning." He recalled the breaking of loud and high "combers" upon the beach, and when rowing ashore "...the sea had got hold of us, and was carrying us in with the speed of a race-horse. We threw the oars as far from the boat as we could, and took hold of the gunwales, ready to spring out and seize her when she struck."

Piers began to be constructed in the late 1800's at the foot of Castillo and Chapala Streets. Then in 1872, much longer Stearns Wharf was built at the foot of State Street. Landings became more practical and the town grew rapidly. Today, when you pass by one of our many Victorian homes, remember that they were built in the 1800's with lumber that was floated ashore from lumber schooners or unloaded onto one of the old piers.

But the piers were exposed to severe storms and didn't provide the protection needed for reliable commerce and travel. Investigations into the feasibility of building a harbor at Santa Barbara began in the 1880's. In the ensuing years, the natural lagoons at Devereaux, Goleta, and what is now the Bird Refuge were considered. These would have been better natural sites than the present harbor location, but a desire for closer proximity to Santa Barbara along with local politics prevailed. So in 1929 construction of our present harbor began. Two thirds of the funds were furnished by Major Max Fleischmann and one third by the City, Fleischmann was a major benefactor who funded may substantial community projects. A strong reason for his support of the harbor was to provide proper protection for his 250 foot yacht *Haida* (now a luxury yacht in the Mediterranean under the name *Rosenkavalier).*

If you sail into Frys Harbor on Santa Cruz Island, you can see where a hillside was blasted away to provide the large rocks used to create our harbor's breakwater. The rocks were transported across the channel on large barges. The original harbor was constructed with a detached breakwater that did not reach the land. But very soon it was clear that the protected waters were filling with sand, so a section was added to join the breakwater with the shore. The breakwater was completed in 1932, and for many years it was used for anchored and moored boats, many well over one hundred feet in length. In the late 1930's, the Naval Reserve Building was constructed along with the Navy Pier. There were rope lines in front of the present harbormaster's office to tie up skiffs that were used to row out to the moored boats. It cost ten cents a foot per month to moor a boat in the harbor, and a shore boat would take you to your moored boat also for a dime.

As our town grew, there was a need for more mooring space and added convenience. Harry Chanson and a group of investors approached the Harbor Commission, then chaired by my father, Ray Kieding, to get permission to build a marina. What is now Marina 2 was built with telephone poles as floats and wood planks as walkways. Chanson, Ken Elmes, Rod White, and others later constructed the Marine Center Building and the boat yard. Meanwhile, Jack Wright built the first phase of what is now The Chandlery Building. Then came construction by the City of what are now Marinas 1, 3 and 4.

It didn't take long to realize that the harbor had become a sand trap that captured the constant flow of sand along the coastline. For years, US Army Corps of Engineers has poured millions of dollars into the annual dredging of the harbor. The protected lagoon locations would have been better site choices for the harbor, and that would have dramatically changed the history of Santa Barbara. Until the 1960's, the Corps would completely dredge the harbor every three years, including the sand spit. As the harbor became more congested, it was decided to turn the sandpit into a breakwater extension by piling rocks onto it.

In the 1990's the urge to add that sixth pound to the infamous "five pound container" prevailed, and a new extension to Marina I was added. It seems that no more can be done, but can it? Will the eastern breakwater so studied in the twentieth century be constructed in the twenty-first? Inconceivable now, but who knows what the future might hold?

SHIPWRECK DIARY

Winfield Scott survivor Asa Cyrus Call was a passenger and survivor aboard the side-wheel steamer *Winfield Scott* during the California Gold Rush. The *Winfield Scott* ran aground on Anacapa Island, and it was eight days until they were picked up by the Pacific Mail Steamship Company's side-wheel steamer *California*. Here are exerts from Call's diary (slightly edited). There is an excellent exhibit at the Santa Barbara Maritime Museum.

Monday, Dec. 5th, 1853 – A rock in the Pacific, 20 miles from the coast –

I embarked on the Steamer *Winfield Scott* last Thursday, and at 12 o'clock we left Vally's St. Wharf for Panama. We had fine weather 'till Friday evening when it became foggy. One of the boilers had been leaking through the day which had retarded our progress, and the *Sierra Nevada* had

passed us, but it was repaired on Friday afternoon, and we were running about twelve miles an hour when I went to bed on Friday night. This was about 9 o'clock. I had just got to sleep when I was awakened by a tremendous shock. I knew we had struck a rock and hurrying on a part of my clothes, I hurried up on deck where I found a general panic, but the steamer was backed off and with the assurance that all was right most of the passengers retired again to their rooms. But I didn't believe she could have struck a rock with such force without sustaining some injury, and not knowing what the upshot of the matter might be, I went down to my stateroom and put my money and all other valuables in my trunk into my saddle bags, and went into the upper saloon intending

83

to be ready for what was to come next. I had hardly taken a seat when the steamer struck again, and with such force that it seemed as if the ship was breaking into a thousand fragments. I again hurried on deck, and went forward to see if I could see land. It was so dark I could see nothing, but I could distinctly hear the roar of the breakers ahead and on the larboard side. The steamer was unmanageable, and the order was given to let off the steam and to extinguish the fires to prevent

the ship's taking fire. The decks were densely crowded but considering the circumstances the people behaved remarkably well. It was a perfect jam. And all I could distinguish was an occasional small shriek as the ship lurched to one side giving evidence that she was sinking. About ten minutes after we last struck, the long boat was lowered, and I heard the Captain call for the ladies to go aboard. Some men pressed towards the boat but the Captain's orders were "knock the first man overboard that attempts to get into the boat". Meanwhile some life preservers were got up and were being distributed among the passengers. There was now a great breach in the steamer and the water was pouring in like a river. Our only hope was that she might not sink entirely, as we could feel her sliding down the side of a ledge of rocks. Pretty soon the fog began to break away a little and we could see the light in the long boat as she was coasting along in search of a landing. We could also see the top of a high peak just ahead of the ship and pretty near, but it seemed perpendicular and the white foam and the roar showed that we could never hope to land there. As soon as the life preservers were distributed, the other ships boats (five) were lowered, and filled with passengers. They all held about one hundred and fifty, and there were five hundred and twenty on board. After being gone about half an hour the long boat returned, having found a landing. And in about two hours all hands were taken off, and were landed on a rock about fifty yards long by twenty five wide. The next day, we came to a larger rock or island, about half a mile long by 100 yards wide. We have succeeded in getting provisions and water enough from the wreck to do us so far. The sea has been quite smooth, or we should have been all lost. A boat went off to the mainland day before yesterday and returned last eve. An express has been sent to San Francisco and I shall look for a steamer in three or four days. Robbery and plunder has been the order of the day since the wreck. But today we appointed a committee of investigation and have had everything searched. A good deal of property has come to light, and two thieves have been flogged. I have recovered a pair of revolvers, a Bowie knife, and some clothing, but I am a good deal out of pocket yet. But probably my other things never came ashore. We are on short allowance, but I today shot a seal with my pistol, and we shall have a luscious dinner. We are expecting a schooner from the mainland with supplies of water and provisions.

December 9th 7 p.m.

The old steamer California came to our rock sometime in the night last night and made her presence known by firing cannon. We climbed to the top of the rock and made a large fire of weeds, which is the only fuel we have on the rock. The sea was very rough which made it dangerous getting on board, but we finally accomplished it without any very serious accident.

It is now supposed that there were one or two men lost when we were wrecked, as they have never been seen since. One was a Mr. Underwood, a butcher by trade.

A STAR OF A BOAT

One of the most amazing stories in yacht racing is the hundred year saga of the Starboat. In this age of rapidly changing technology, it defies reason that a racing class that began in 1908 is still one of the classes that competes the Olympics. Granted, the 1908 version looked quite different from today's version, but the basic hull design is still very close to the original.

The Star is approximately twenty-two feet eight inches long on deck, fifteen and a half feet long at its water line, and five feet eight inches in beam. It has a very sleek hull with a weighted keel to prevent it from capsizing. Its tall, slender mast and streamlined form exude a sense of speed.

A skipper and one crewmember operate the very physically and mentally demanding Starboat. When sailing to weather in a blow, both skipper and crew must stretch out past the windward rail with only their bent knees, calves and feet on the boat's deck, while their thighs drop downward against the exterior side of the boat. While in this awkward posture, the two racers gain some support from hiking straps that support their weight and keep them from falling into the sea. When coming about, both must wrench themselves upward, down into the cockpit, under the long boom that is just a few inches above the deck, and out into the hiking straps on the other side – all while trimming the sails and steering a perfect turn so not a smidgeon of speed is lost. And all this takes place with competitors just a few feet away who are aggressively trying to pass or cause your boat to foul out of the race. Starboat sailors are large and tough, and pride themselves on dripping water and sometimes drops of blood on the yacht club bar's floor after the race as they perform the time honored post race pastime of explaining why their win was due to skill or their competitor's win was due to luck.

Yacht racers constantly strive to use the very latest of all applicable technology. This technology draws heavily from aeronautical design as well as the very latest developments in materials. Original Stars were made of wood. Today's boats are of fiberglass with a composite carbon mast and boom. Cotton sails have been replaced by Mylar, and many of the numerous fittings and lines derive from space age materials and technology.

How can a racing class almost a hundred years old still be competing at the Olympic level? First, the basic design was inspired far beyond any other racing sailboat in the early 1900's. From its beginning and to the present time, the Star has been one of the finest performing sailboats. I first sailed a Star after I had been racing other racing sailboats for over twenty years. I was overwhelmed by its feel and performance. It was as if I had never really sailed before. Soon after, I bought my first Star because I wanted to race in the best class against many of the top racing sailors in the world.

A second success factor was that Star design specifications allowed builders some latitude to incorporate innovative improvements. Some one-design classes require that all boats be exactly alike in order to have success based strictly on sailing skills and not on technology. The Star rules allow innovation, and this has resulted in an already exceptional boat that has kept up with changing technology for one hundred years.

One of the most important factors in the longevity and success of the Star Class has been that it has attracted many of the world's top racing sailors throughout its long history. The list reads like Who's Who in yachting. They brought prestige and innovation to the class. Some built on their Starboat experience to become skippers in the oldest continuous sporting competition in history – The America's Cup. Starboater Dennis Conner won the America's Cup in 1980, then lost the Cup for the first time in America's history, but then won it again in the next two competitions.

Sailing first became an Olympic sport in the 1896 Olympics in Greece. The USA first competed in Olympic sailing in 1900, but not again until 1928. The Star was first chosen as an Olympic class for the 1932 Olympics, which was won by the United States. Since then, Stars have been one of the sailing classes in all subsequent Olympics except 1976.

In 1923, Santa Barbara Yacht Club began its annual sponsorship of one of the world's premier Star racing events - the Lipton Cup. Each year, the winner's name is engraved on the ornate silver trophy that was donated by well-known yachtsman and tea magnet Sir Thomas Lipton. Over the past eighty-five years, some of the most famous names in yachting have competed for Santa Barbara's prestigious trophy. Four Santa Barbarans have won the cup – Niels Martin in 1934 and 1936 in *Phar Lap*; Bill Gerard in 1970, 1980, and 1997 sailing *Conqueror* and *Quest 80*; Bob Kieding in 1974 sailing *Liberty*; and Fred Hayward in 1976 in *Relampago*. The priceless cup is permanently on display at Santa Barbara Yacht Club.

There is no other sailboat racing class that has competed in so many countries of the world, over so many years, by so many top sailors, and in so many Olympic competitions. Truly the Starboat is the queen of one-design sailing. The Star Class web site is www.starclass.org.

SEA TERMS

- Beam – the width of a boat.
- To Sail To Weather – A sailboat on a course closest to the direction of the wind.
- To Come About – To turn a boat from its course past the direction of the wind and onto a new course

CHANNEL SWIMMER

David Yudovin likes sailing and swimming. And I mean swimming. He has swum many places around the world. And I mean around the world. The miles he has covered in the water during his many channel swims equal several trips around the world. Locally, he has swum to the California coast from Catalina Island, Anacapa Island, Santa Cruz Island, and several swims from South Coronado Island to the coast of Mexico. Further away, he has swum the English Channel, Morocco to Gibraltar, between Japanese islands, the Sunda Strait from Java to Sumatra, a number of swims between various Hawaiian Islands, the Cook Strait from the North Island to the South Island of New Zealand, and many more. To get a feel for times, an English Channel swim from England to France took 13 hours 37 minutes. He was the first person ever to accomplish many of his swims. His first ever swim from Santa Cruz Island to Santa Barbara took 15 hours 15 minutes. David has done channel swimming for many years, but hasn't retired yet. He continues to seek another first ever swim.

WRECKAGE ON OUR COAST

Hundreds of ships and boats have foundered on the Santa Barbara coastline and off-shore Channel Islands. The following news articles unveil the interlocking sequence of events surrounding the loss of two vessels. There were many commercial vessels operating in this area in the late 1800's, despite the arrival of the railroad in 1877. The Santa Barbara Maritime has an excellent exhibit of local shipwrecks. [Bracketed words have been inserted for clarity.]

MONDAY JANUARY 1, 1894 The wreck of the *Gosford* cost other people besides its Glasgow owner's money. Speckles Bros. of San Francisco have spent $10,000 in a vain endeavor to raise the steel hull. After five days of a southeaster wind in Cojo Bay [*near Point Conception*], where the *Gosford* lies in forty feet of water, the wreckers have given up the attempt to raise it intact. It will be broken up and sold for old iron. Four hours longer and the ship would have been raised, but on December 24 the storm began, and the engines, pumps and boilers of the wreck, which were on the *Gosford's* decks, were washed off by huge waves. The cofferdam surrounding it broke to pieces and the bulwarks were also broken. Diver Martin of the Union Iron Works was brought down from San Francisco by Captain Haskell of the tug *Fearless*. He discovered that the *Gosford* listed four feet to starboard and the main-deck beams were broken in the middle and hung down inside the hull. The storm carried the vessel out further than before, and it is now in forty-four feet of water and eight feet underwater, instead of four feet as formerly.

90

'We have abandoned all hopes of raising her," said Captain Haskell, "and have even lost all of our pumps and boilers, excepting one engine which was recovered from the sand by the diver. The vessel will probably be blown up with dynamite, as the *Golden Horn* has been."

On Tuesday morning, at 4 o'clock, the *San Pedro* [*wreck recovery boat*] had a narrow escape from going ashore near the wreck. The wind was blowing furiously, and the old wrecking boat gradually drifted in until she was in the breakers. Captain Scott of the tug *Pellet* shot a lifeline over the *San Pedro* with a Lyall wrecking gun, and for five hours the tug strained trying to get the boat out of danger. Captain Perry of the lighthouse said that he thought both vessels were lost. Finally, the *San Pedro* was got out of danger.

MONDAY, NOVEMBER 5, 1894 The steamer *Santa Cruz* was in port this morning and took on the remainder of the *Winfield Scott* wreckers on-board. She then moved a buoy for the [*Stearns*] wharf company, after which she sailed for San Francisco.

SAN FRANCISCO, Nov. 5. Word reached here today that the steam wrecker *San Pedro* was burned on Sunday night in Cojo Harbor. A private dispatch was received by Henry Rogers of the California Iron and Wrecking Company from Captain McKenna, dated Gaviota. Very few particulars were given regarding the matter, save that the vessel caught fire while McKenna was away and that there was a boat with four men in it missing.

Rogers immediately telegraphed to McKenna to get a tug and go in search of the missing men. The extent of the damage is not known, but on account of the solidity of the wrecker, Rogers is inclined to believe that it will be alright.

THURSDAY, NOVEMBER 8, 1894 On Monday night's stage, Captain Macgum and three seamen arrived from Gaviota and reported the total loss of the wrecking scow *San Pedro* at Cojo Bay Sunday night. The wrecker was raising the coal from the sunken ship *Gosford*, and had on-board several tons of it beside about thirty tons of wreckage. They were working short-handed, and on Sunday Captain Macgum, Seaman Andrew Uden, Diver John Lawrence and Captain Juliu of this city, who acts as pilot in the channel and among the islands, started for Gaviota to engage more help. They returned in the night or toward morning Monday and found the scow burned almost to the water's edge. The crew had left and was nowhere to be seen. They had been unable to quench the flames, so put off for land in a small boat. Captain Macgum even at this late hour thought there might be a chance to save her machinery, and made an effort to scuttle her, but to no purpose. At daylight they started back to Gaviota and boarded the stage, arriving here last night. The wrecking scow was the property of Rogers & Co., San Francisco, and was valued at $12,000 and insured for $6,000. She has been working recently on the wrecks of the *Newburn, Golden Horn, Winfield Scott,* and *Gosford,* and intended in a short time to work on the *Yankee Blade.* Captain Macgum with Uden and Lawrence will leave for San Francisco on the *Corona* this evening.

SATURDAY, NOVEMBER 10, 1894 The officers of the steamer *Queen* which arrived here yesterday afternoon, said that as they passed Cojo Bay they could see the masts of the wrecker *San Pedro* close beside those of the sunken *Gosford.* The men who were left on board the scow by Captain Macgum when he left for Gaviota are in the city. They left the scow in a small boat, and the next morning the lighthouse keeper showed them where to land.

SEA TERMS
- Cofferdam – A watertight enclosure.
- Bulwarks – A solid rail, usually consisting of extensions of the vessel's frames above deck-level and planked over. (15th Century)
- Scuttle – To sink a vessel by opening her seacocks or by cutting through the bottom. (15th Century)
- Seacock - A thru hull valve located below a vessel's waterline. (16th Century)
- Scow – A square-ended, flat bottomed craft. (18th Century)

FOLLOW YOUR DREAMS

The dream of sailing over the horizon is almost universal; intoxicating multi-billionaires to those whose only shot at the dream is to sign on as a deck hand for "three hots and a flop". My job through the years has frequently been to help make the illusive dream come true.

I recently received a call from a gentleman who wanted to see a Catalina 36 sailboat that we had advertised for sale. He said he'd be coming to Santa Barbara by train, so I offered to pick him up. Asked how I could recognize him, he answered, "I'm grey haired, six foot four, and look like a prison guard." Later, as I watched the off-loading passengers at the train station, I recognized him immediately. He did look like a prison guard, although I don't think I had ever met one before.

He was friendly, but clearly one who kept to himself. We spent more time than most as he carefully went through every compartment on the boat. He had many questions, and it soon became apparent that he was new to boating, but determined to make a good decision. As we talked, his story slowly developed. He had raised his son who was now on his own; his marriage was ended; and he had left his job with enough cash to chase his dream of sailing over that elusive horizon. And, by golly, he had spent his career as a guard at a maximum security prison.

He had saved carefully, allocating a portion of his funds to purchase a boat, a portion to get it ready, a portion for food and supplies during his dream cruise, and a portion to keep him going after the cruise until he could get a job and income to live on for a few years until his retirement checks began arriving. Somehow, I didn't think his next job would be as a prison guard.

I have followed with interest the dreams of many boaters through the years. As with life in general, some work out and some don't. I recall one that was very short. Four enthusiasts bought an old ketch and spent a year preparing it for their legendary dream – to sail her around the world. A grand bon voyage party was held on-board for their many friends who later watched the dream begin as the ketch passed slowly over the horizon. A few weeks later, I sailed into Ensenada Bay and sighted their ketch swinging at anchor, wondered why they hadn't covered much more ground by that time. After anchoring, I rowed over to say "Hi" and see how things were going. Only one was onboard, and he told me there had been a serious falling out among the crew and the cruise was over. This was an example that the mechanical preparation of a vessel is not necessarily the most important. Close quarters, rough weather, damp, cold, damage, and fear can sometimes transform a popular personality into someone you just don't want to be with. It's always wise for distance cruisers to take a few short trips to "shake down" both the boat and the crew to see if there are any problems to resolve before setting out.

On the other hand, I have seen many very successful cruises that have lasted for years. Those sailors have returned to Santa Barbara with wonderful tales of adventure, adversity, and paradise. I periodically reported in this column on the progress 47-foot "Traveler" as she made her way across the Pacific in pursuit of her owner's dream. She completed her voyage safely after three years in 2010. Skipper Michael Lawler quoted the following from Mark Twain - "*Twenty years from now you will be more disappointed by the things that you didn't do, than by the ones you did do. So throw off the bowlines. Sail away from the safe harbor. Catch the trade winds in your sails. Explore. Dream. Discover!*"

I wish the prison guard well, and, as with the many others, hope his dream will be fulfilled.

IS GOLETA DRAKE'S BAY?

Sir Francis Drake (1545-1596), slave trader, privateer in the service of England, mayor of Plymouth, and naval officer against the Spanish Armada was one of the western world's most outstanding figures during the reign of Queen Elizabeth I. Drake led the second expedition (after Magellan) to sail around the world in a voyage lasting from 1577 to 1580. Unlike Magellan, he sailed north as far as what is now California, secretly claiming the northern lands for England.

Drake spent several weeks at a California bay doing needed repairs on his ship *Golden Hind*. According to many text and history books, a bay now named after Sir Francis Drake near Point Reyes approximately 30 miles northwest of San Francisco at approximately 38 degrees north latitude has long been considered Drake's most likely landing spot on the west coast of North America.

Have textbooks about Sir Francis Drake studied by generations of students been wrong? Local historian and author Justin Ruhge presents a strong case in his recent book *Sir Francis Drake in Central California 1579* that Drake actually landed at the large, natural harbor that is now Santa Barbara's airport and the remains of the Goleta slough. Ruhge spent years of research examining many of the countless publications and documents published over the last 400 years. *Sir Francis Drake in Central California 1579* is like reading a detective novel as 400 year old clues are logically merged into a logical conclusion. Hundreds of years after the fact, there may never be decisive proof, but Ruhge's research and analysis presents a very strong case for the reader to conclude that Drake's bay was indeed the Goleta site.

In evaluating the historic clues, it is first necessary to know what the Goleta coastline was like during the late 1500's. What now remains as the Goleta Slough was once a very large bay that was first discovered by Europeans in 1542 by the Cabrillo expedition. The bay opened to the ocean with sufficient depth to allow substantial sailing vessels to enter and anchor. Several thousand Chumash lived on the bluffs on each side, around the perimeter of the bay, and on approximately 64 acre Mescaltitlan Island. Over the centuries, the bay slowly began filling with silt from mountain streams and sediment from the inflowing tides. In the 1930's Santa Barbara began filling a portion of the bay in order to construct an airport. With the advent of World War II, the Marine Corps built an air base and filled in even greater areas of the bay. The Marines bulldozed much of Mescaltitlan Island for landfill. Today, only a portion of the bay remains as Goleta Slough.

In studying the two possible locations of Drake's "Good Baye," the author lists clues and, one by one, compares them against features and history of the two possible sites. Some of the clues come from three anonymous narratives, three maps, and a drawing. Each source provides insight, but none alone provide decisive evidence.

The strongest evidence in favor of the area above San Francisco is that its latitude (distance from the equator) was reported as from 42 to 48 degrees north. The Point Reyes location is approximately 40 degrees north and the Goleta location is 34 degrees north. The reported latitude range could be in error due to a transposition error or due to the inaccuracy of the wooden navigational sighting devices used at the time.

The author evaluates eighteen descriptive phrases from the historic documents that relate to the location of Drake's landing location. He matches each criterion to the two locations, and the increasing "scorecard" begins to weigh heavily towards Goleta Bay. For example, the phrase "thick stinking fog" at first impression reminds of northern California fogs. But heavy fog is also found at the Goleta area. Further, the adjective "stinking" does not seem to relate to the northern location, but the Goleta slough vicinity is noted for oil seepage both on land and from adjacent ocean waters.

Other investigatory phrases include " low hills covered with snow," "Indian in a canoe," "islands off the harbor," "reed bowls that hold water," "poles and baskets of feathers," and "barren hills." Another clue source was testimony from Drake's brother when he was tortured during the Spanish Inquisition. I was fascinated to see evidence building for each site, but as I read on I slowly became more and more convinced that the weight was building in favor of Goleta. See what you conclude.

Sir Francis Drake in Central California 1579 is a captivating read that is made even more so with its inclusion the discovery of the five Goleta cannons near the entrance of Goleta Bay where the *Golden Hinde* may have swung at anchor four hundred years ago.

EAR TO THE WATER

The Santa Barbara Channel and islands encompass many diverse activities – fishing, shipping, research, yachting, resource extraction, and many more. One operation not well known by the public is underwater acoustic research.

Underwater acoustics include the process of monitoring or using undersea sound for a variety of applications. The sound can be natural or created. During the Cold War and after, underwater acoustics projects were a significant activity that took place on the back side of Santa Cruz Island. General Motors followed by its successor Maripro conducted a variety of operations that ranged from top secret defense to those of pure academic interest.

Many of us were captivated by the film *In Search Of Red October*, an exciting cold-war yarn about the search for a dangerous Soviet spy submarine. The tracking technology in the film was based on using hydrophones (underwater microphones). This was the same cornerstone technology used at the Santa Cruz Island acoustic facility. Basically, the Santa Cruz Island range consisted of a number of submerged hydrophones, located at considerable depth, and connected by cables running ashore to computers that accumulated data for a variety of uses.

There were several reasons for collecting underwater sound data. The most dramatic was the "Red October" mission. Underwater sound monitoring systems located at various strategic locations in the oceans of the world were used to track Soviet submarines and warships to determine their location and what mischief they might be up to. Despite great care to minimize it, all submarines and ships generate a unique acoustic "signature" that allows identification. It is assumed that the Soviets were also monitoring U.S. vessels.

A second use of underwater acoustics for defense purposes is to try to make your own vessels as immune as possible to identification and detection by other nations. This was a major activity at the Santa Cruz Island facility. U.S. submarines were driven through the acoustic range, and data was evaluated to determine if they were as "quiet" as possible or if they had tell-tale signatures. With tracking range data, the vessels could then be modified to reduce any problems. I can recall a number of cases where the entire 22 mile back side of Santa Cruz Island was declared off-limits to all vessels because a super secret U.S. submarine was being run through the range.

Another major application of underwater acoustic tracking is for weapons testing and evaluation. The primary location for such activities is AUTEC (Atlantic Test and Evaluation Center) which is located near the Bahamas Islands. It can evaluate both in-air and underwater weapons using above-water technologies such as radar and photography as well as underwater acoustic tracking arrays. A classic application would be to have an aircraft fly down range and launch a weapon that would fly a portion of its mission and then enter the ocean as a torpedo type delivery system. The Santa Cruz Island tracking range did underwater, but not in-air testing and evaluation.

The Santa Cruz range also operated two unique vehicles. One was POP (for Perpendicular Ocean Platform). This was a long, tubular ship over 100 feet in length. When partially filled with seawater, POP would sink at one end until it was in a vertical position with only a portion above water level. With almost a hundred feet of POP under water, the above water portion was as steady as a rock–even in rough winds and seas. This made it an ideal at-sea scientific platform for the conduct of motion sensitive projects. One night, POP came loose from its mooring and was carried up the island by ocean currents. The Coast Guard was radioed the next day that there was a vessel aground in the channel between Santa Cruz and Santa Rosa Islands. The position given indicated the vessel was in ninety feet of water. This seemed impossible until they learned that POP in its vertical position had a draft of over ninety feet.

The second unique vehicle was DOWB (for Deep Ocean Work Boat). DOWB was a two person, deep water submarine that was capable of operating over a mile beneath the ocean. It had remote controlled "arms" to perform underwater tasks, and was used at various locations around the world in addition to the more than 2000 foot depths off the back side of Santa Cruz Island.

In addition to defense related applications, the Santa Cruz Island range was also used for scientific research. Sound is continually being generated in the sea by a number of sources such as wildlife, weather, geological, and other sources. Much pure science was studied and evaluated on the range in addition to defense projects.

The Santa Cruz Island facility was closed down several years ago. It was dismantled with great care to ensure that both the island and its surrounding waters were returned to their original condition. That is not to say that underwater acoustics in no longer a prime activity elsewhere. Our government continues to operate several acoustic ranges for defense and scientific applications. Technology is ever-changing, and our oceans continue to be one of the major areas where new science and discoveries occur.

SEA TERMS

- Hydrophone – An underwater microphone that has been designed to be immune to damage from water and extreme underwater pressure.
- Acoustic – Pertaining to the hearing, to sound and its transmission; worked by sound or echoes.
- Acoustics - a branch of physics that studies sound.
- Draft – The distance from the waterline to the bottom of a boat. Important to know when operating in shallow water to avoid running aground.

DON'T OPEN THE BOX!

Many of us have heard the warning, *"Don't open Pandora's Box!"* Most of us take it as kind of "mind your own business" advice and, like many sayings, don't know its source. It originated from ancient Greek mythology, but took on grave nautical meaning in the late 1700's.

In Greek mythology, Pandora was the first woman on Earth. Each god helped create her by giving unique gifts. Zeus ordered Hephaestus to mould her out of Earth as part of the punishment of mankind for Prometheus' theft of the secret of fire, and all the gods joined in offering seductive gifts to this "beautiful evil". According to the myth, Pandora had a jar which she was not to open under any circumstances. But her curiosity was too great, and she opened the jar, which in modern accounts is referred to as "Pandora's box", releasing all the evils of mankind - Greed, Vanity, Slander, Envy, Pining - leaving only Hope inside once she had closed the jar again. The myth of Pandora first appeared in writings over 2800 years ago but it probably originated long before. There have been many variations, but all address the question of why there is evil in the world.

Now jump ahead three thousand years to the tragic South Pacific voyage of the *Bounty* in the late 1700's. Captain William Bligh's severe treatment of his crew resulted in mutiny by part of the crew. Bligh and eighteen officers and seamen who stood by him were set adrift by the mutineers in a longboat with their future survival in serious doubt. Mutiny leader Fletcher Christian, conscious of the British Admiralty's long reach, cut the anchor cable and sailed the *Bounty* into the night away from Tahiti. With eight shipmates, Tahitian women, and some

Polynesian men, Christian finally settled on distant, unknown, and uninhabited Pitcairn Island, but returned for a time to Tahiti for supplies. Bligh, meanwhile, navigated his longboat three thousand miles through open seas to what was then Dutch Timor where he managed to negotiate passages home to England on various Dutch ships.

A little more than a year after the mutiny, the Admiralty Lords commanded Captain Edwards to set sail on the ship *Pandora* to find, capture, and return the mutineers to justice. The *Pandora* left Portsmouth in November 1790, rounded the Cape and put into Matavai Bay, Tahiti, in March 1791. It didn't take Edwards long to track down the fourteen *Bounty* crewmen who had remained on Tahiti. The rest had decamped with Christian and their Tahitian wives to Pitcairn Island, a spot so remote that even Polynesian sailors were uncertain as to its whereabouts. Despite the wailing of their wives on-shore, the fourteen manacled prisoners were held aboard *Pandora,* where the "box" awaited them - a cell built on the quarterdeck and open to the searing tropical sun and torrential rains.

Pandora sought *Bounty* among the South Sea isles for three months without success, and finally turned its way toward England. The fourteen prisoners by then were severely sun damaged, frenzied and it had become dangerous to approach Pandora's box. After more weeks of hot equatorial sun, all aboard *Pandora* were cautioned, *"Don't open Pandora's Box!"*

On August 29th, 1791, as the *Pandora* slid through the darkening waters of the outer reef off the tip of Australia, she struck a submerged outcrop of coral and began to take water. As the ship sank, the prisoners begged to be freed. Seamen William Moulter took pity and, with great apprehension, unbolted *Pandora's* box. In the end, ten of the fourteen mutineers survived, along with eighty-nine of the ship's company. They were rescued and eventually the mutineers were sent to trial. Four were acquitted, three hanged, two pardoned and one freed on a technicality. Whatever remains of the wreck of the *H.M.S. Pandora* and her infamous "Box" lie about three miles northwest of Australia's Moulter's Cay, 120km east of Cape York.

BRASS MONKEY

A good supply of cannon balls was needed next to each gun on old war ships. The best storage method was to stack them as a square-based pyramid, with one ball on top, resting on four, resting on nine, which rested on sixteen at the bottom of the pyramid. This provided a supply of 30 cannon balls stacked in a small area next to each cannon ready for action.

But, how to prevent the bottom layer of cannon balls from rolling out from under the others as the ship pitched and rolled? After much trial and error, the solution was to build a metal plate with 16 round indentations to capture the bottom layer of cannon balls. Sailors named the plate a "monkey". But if the "monkey" were made of iron, the iron cannon balls would soon rust to it. The solution to the problem was to make the "monkey" of brass, which doesn't rust.

But, in cold weather brass contracts much more and much faster than iron. When the temperature dropped too far, the brass indentations in a "monkey" shrunk so much that the iron cannon balls rolled off and the pyramid collapsed. Thus, quite literally, it was cold enough to freeze the balls off a "brass monkey".

POSH

"Port Out, Starboard Home" is a phrase popularly believed to provide the etymology for the word "posh." According to this belief, Port Out and Starboard Home were the most desirable cabin locations on ships traveling to and from British colonies in the Far East, because they were shaded from the sun in both directions. But an extensive search of shipping company records and tickets from that period failed to reveal any evidence for explicit "Port Outbound, Starboard Home" reservations or other use of the phrase.

The true origin of the word "posh" is obscure. It appears in 1890 in *A Dictionary of Slang, Jargon & Cant,* as a "modern term for money, originally used for a halfpenny or small coin. From the gypsy pash or posh, a half." A second definition in that publication was a Dandy. The first widely published use of the word "posh" was in the British satirical magazine *Punch* in1918.

WINDY GULCH

Most of us think of the coast of California running from north to south, but it really doesn't. It actually runs in a north westerly to south easterly direction. You can have fun with your friends betting that Reno, Nevada is further west than Santa Barbara. You will win. Reno's longitude is 119 degrees 47 minutes West and Santa Barbara's is 119 degrees 41 minutes West.

But what happens 45 miles north of Santa Barbara at rugged Point Conception is surprising to many, and results in the phenomena of Windy Gulch as well as Santa Barbara's unique Mediterranean climate. At Point Conception the coast turns from south easterly to almost west to east. When you look straight out to sea from Santa Barbara, you are looking towards the South Pole!

There are generally strong winds, high seas and frequent dense fog at Point Conception with the historic result of numerous shipwrecks and the area's well earned reputation as "The Graveyard of the Pacific". But with the coast then turning dramatically towards the east, these winds and seas don't bend as sharply as the turn of the coastline and therefore run down the outer Santa Barbara Channel leaving Santa Barbara itself sheltered from the prevailing high winds and seas of the upper coast.

The Santa Barbara Channel is approximately twenty-two miles wide from the mainland to the four islands that border the channel. From east to west, these are San Miguel, Santa Rosa, Santa Cruz, and Anacapa. Point Conception's high winds and seas run down the outer channel waters in an eight to ten mile band along the islands. This harsh stretch has justifiably earned the name of "Windy Gulch," and has been a major challenge to mariners since the Chumash first landed on the islands.

The conditions in Windy Gulch can be very uncomfortable for recreational sized boats, and some sizes and designs should not attempt the passage. At peak conditions, the waves can reach substantial heights, but their steepness is even more challenging. But with a properly designed and outfitted boat, there are a number of ways to make successful and relatively comfortable crossings.

First, Windy Gulch is not always rough. You can check weather reports with the Santa Barbara Harbormaster's office or on the internet to determine what conditions are at Pont Conception and at the channel weather buoys, along with the forecast for the next few days. You may find that the channel is mild and not of concern. If the winds are up, you can make an early morning departure and arrive at the islands before the afternoon winds peak. I frequently leave about five in the morning for an easy crossing and a full first day at the islands. The trip over on a sailboat is close to the wind, but the return is generally a reach and a fun sail in high winds.

Since the Windy Gulch conditions generally begin about ten to twelve miles from Santa Barbara Harbor, the first part of the crossing is usually quite comfortable. You can reduce the impact of the Gulch by making your initial course more towards Point Conception, and then ease off easterly when you reach the large seas and winds. This results in your boat meeting the steep seas at a more comfortable angle. With a GPS navigator, it is relatively easy to follow a curved course to the islands and end up exactly where you planned. If yours is a sailboat, you can have a great power reach with sails eased and the impact of seas much diminished.

Further down the channel, Windy Gulch winds and seas lessen. San Miguel is almost opposite Point Conception, and it therefore takes the full force of the point's winds, seas, and fog. At the other end of the channel Anacapa experiences considerably less impact, but its waters can still be plenty rough at times. I strongly recommend careful planning if San Miguel is your destination. It is a great place to visit, anchor, fish, surf, hike, and more, but it's more enjoyable in clear weather.

The return to Santa Barbara is an easier trip because the direction of the wind and waves is further aft. Turning more easterly for a few miles diminishes their impact. Then turn back towards Santa Barbara for a pleasant voyage home.

But by all means, visit the Channel Islands. They are one of the most unique areas of the world, and just a few miles from Santa Barbara. If you are not a boater, there are several charter services that can take visitors, kayakers, and fishermen to the islands. These are sizable vessels with professional captain and crew that know our waters well. Too many Santa Barbarans spend a lifetime here without ever seeing the true wonders of our Channel Islands.

SEA TERMS

- Longitude - A measure of relative position east or west on the Earth's surface, given in degrees from a certain meridian, usually the prime meridian at Greenwich, England, which has a longitude of 0°. The distance of a degree of longitude is about 69 statute miles or 60 nautical miles (111 km) at the equator, decreasing to zero at the poles. Longitude and latitude are the coordinates used to identify any point on the Earth's surface. Latitude is used to identify a position north or south of the equator on Earth's surface. Units can be decimal or in degrees, minutes, and seconds.

- Web Weather – www.weather.gov/om/marine/home.htn - then click on "Los Angeles" and then click the area of interest on the map

- Sheet – A controlling line to a sail. 13th Century from old English "skeatline" and possibly also from Old Norse "skaut."

- Close To The Wind – A point of sailing on which the sheets are tightened all the way in so the boat can sail near to the direction of the wind.

- Reach – A point of sailing on which the sheets are eased, roughly with the wind abeam (toward the side of the boat). 17th Century from Anglo-Saxon "raecen" reach. Power reach – Adjusting the sails and helm on the reach to maximize speed from wind and waves.

- High – High pressure area – a region where the atmospheric pressure is greater than surrounding areas - frequently associated with light winds.

- Shroud – A major side stay (usually wire) to support a mast. 16th Century Old Norse.
- Heel – For a vessel to lean over from the force of the wind. 16th Century Anglo Saxon.
- Bilge – The lower part of the interior of the hull, usually below the floors. 15th Century French.

SANTA BARBARA PIONEER

Our town has been populated by many interesting citizens through the years. One of particular interest was George Nidever. Born in Tennessee in 1802, George Nidever was a frontiersman, mountain man, trapper, rancher, and sailor. In 1830, he joined a hunting and trapping party at Fort Smith, Arkansas, and after a year of adventuring from Missouri to Texas, the core of the party reached Taos, New Mexico. That fall, after setting out for the headwaters of the Arkansas River in Colorado, Nidever found himself and his rough group of mountain men battling Indians at Pierre's Hole. In 1834, Nidever crossed into California with the Walker party, the first group to cross the Sierra Nevada into California. Finally, he worked his way to the Pacific coast and Santa Barbara.

George Nidever made many sea otter hunting trips to the Channel Islands. He wrote, "… eight or ten days after I arrived here, Sills and I went to Santa Rosa Island. We had no boats, so we were obliged to hunt from land. We went over about May of 1835. Two weeks later Sills was taken sick and returned to Santa Barbara. I remained about six weeks longer and killed in all eight or ten otters – Sills having got none. I had with me a Kanaka Indian, employed to swim out for the otter killed, at $16 a month."

Also in 1835, the few remaining Nicoleño Indians from San Nicolas Island were relocated to the mainland. Eighteen years later it was discovered that one Indian woman had been left on island, and that somehow she may have survived. Father Gonzáles of Mission Santa Barbara paid Thomas Jeffries $200 to find her, but he was unsuccessful.

Nidever became interested and began his own search. In 1853, after two unsuccessful attempts, one of Nidever's men, Carl Dittman, discovered human footprints on the beach along with pieces of seal blubber which had been left out to dry. Further searching led to her discovery. She was living in a crude hut partially constructed of whale bones, and was wearing a dress made of greenish cormorant bird feathers. Nidever brought her back to his Santa Barbara home. She spoke a language of sorts, but was unable to communicate with anyone, even the local Chumash. A Santa Barbara Mission priest gave her the Spanish name of Juana Maria. After miraculously surviving alone on the island for eighteen years, she died within just a few weeks at Santa Barbara – perhaps from dysentery caused by her change in diet. Today, she is remembered as "The Lone Woman of San Nicolas Island." Her life was chronicled with very heavy artistic liberty in the classic children's novel *Island of the Blue Dolphins*. To this day the location of her grave is unknown. A plaque was placed in her honor on a wall within the Mission garden in the early 20th century.

In 1840, Nidever bought a large and conspicuous waterfront home on Burton Mound (Mason Street at Burton Circle). In 1842, as an adult, he was baptized at the Santa Barbara Mission. Soon after, he married María Sinforosa Ramona Sanchez (1812-1892), whose family owned the 14,000 acre Rancho Santa Clara Rio del Norte. Nidever ranched on San Miguel Island for two decades (1850-1870) where he built an adobe house 400 feet above Cuyler's Harbor. Using his fishing boat *Cora,* he rescued some of the stranded passengers after side-wheeler *Winfield Scott* wrecked on Anacapa Island in 1853.

Pioneer otter hunter George Nidever died March 27, 1883. His wife, Sinforosa, died in 1892. They were originally buried elsewhere, probably in the old Santa Barbara Catholic Cemetery on Cieneguitas Street, but in 1912 they were moved to unmarked graves in a family plot in Santa Barbara at Calvary Cemetery. The Santa Cruz Island Foundation, with help from volunteer Alex Grzywacki, recently located the two lost graves and those of two of their six children, Marcos "Mark" (1842-1909) and Jacob "Jake" (1848-1913).

The Foundation successfully petitioned the Los Angeles Archdiocese for permission to erect a suitable monument. Santa Cruz Island Foundation Advisory Council member, Osi DaRos, researched and chose an appropriate stone and design as would have been used in 1883. Civil Engineer Robin Gauss donated his services in designing the monument's base. Jed A. Hendrickson of Santa Barbara Monumental carved the stone's faces into which set portraits of both George and Sinforosa Nidever. Permission was granted by the closest living Nidever descendants. To this end, George Nidever's great grand daughters were located - Margaret Smith, of Santa Barbara, and her younger sister, Helen Shapero of Los Gatos.

A LIVELY BEACH

Late one Friday afternoon, I took a half-hour break at the yacht club before transitioning from an electronics installer into a yacht broker and showing a multi-million dollar yacht to a potential buyer. As I transitioned, I reflected on how many years I had watched the waves breaking against the turn of the breakwater. Then I began surveying the panoramic view of Ledbetter Beach from its western headland across to the breakwater and harbor. I noticed how many activities were taking place on this short stretch of Santa Barbara. Six kite-boarders were streaking back and forth with their multi-colored kits flying high above. Two windsurfers were taking advantage of the waves up the beach by Ledbetter Point. I spied a couple of conventional surfers as well. A kayaker was paddling past the yacht club on his way down the coast.

It now struck me that this was indeed a busy and unique locale, and I began making a list to contemplate the full impact. I recorded the beach walker as he strolled by, the cruising sailboats, the tourists, the sun bathers, the swimmers, and a sport fishing boat. I was running out of space on my scrap of paper, and found another to continue the chronicling.

Commercial fishing boats were returning with a catch that would soon reach Santa Barbara dining tables. Fast urchin diving boats also rushed towards the harbor, loaded down with delicacies so valued in Japan and other distant countries. A lone surf fisher waited patiently for his catch.

Tourists sampled the sand and touched our surprisingly cool waters. A beachcomber walked along the high tide line to see if any treasures came ashore with the kelp. And, of course, there were locals walking their dogs along the surf line.

On the horizon I could see the oil platforms, and envisioned their massive structures from the many times I have sailed close-by. And I spied a group of children playing in the surf with two watching supervisors – a summer day camp expedition.

The two flagged buoys in front of the yacht club reminded me of the sail racing activities on Wet Wednesdays and weekends. With its many programs and activities, the club itself is a major occurrence on the beach. Sporting catamarans rest on the sand above high water, ready to be pulled into the surf for an exciting day of hull-flying sport. Behind them is the yacht club's small boat storage yard, full of trailer boats ready for class or Wet Wednesday racing. Further down, the Shoreline Beach Cafe provides a good reason for locals and visitors to experience this dynamic stretch of Santa Barbara. And don't forget the many that park their cars and enjoy the view without debarking.

My reverie was forced to end. I finished my refreshment and headed to meet my customer. Perhaps he would complete my day by purchasing a fine yacht. He did!

SEA TERM
- "Starboard" refers to the right side of a ship as one faces the bow. It comes from Old English stéorbord and is a combination of *stéor*, meaning steer, and *bord*, meaning the side of a ship. On old ships, the rudder or steering paddle would be on the right side of the ship. Hence the term. Starboard is found as early as c.893 when it appears in Alfred's translation of "Orosius" - "Let him ealne weg þæt weste land on ðæt steorbord, & þa widsæ on ðæt bæcbord þrie dagas." (Let him keep the west land on the starboard, & the ocean on the left for three days.)

MOMENT OF WHAT?

Racing and cruising sailors don't speak the same language. Racers talk of "lifts," "headers" and "VMG," while cruisers are talking about "amps," how much they "burn per hour," and the best "anchor scope." Most of the subjects apply to both types of sailing, but the two types of sailors either may not be aware of it or don't care about that particular aspect of boating.

One invisible phenomenon critically affects both racing and cruising, but is not generally understood by either – "Moment of Inertia." Moment of Inertia has a major impact on a boat every time it goes to sea. It affects speed, comfort, and even safety. You can't touch it or see it, but it definitely influences the performance of both racing and cruising boats.

Many of us struggled in school to understand the meaning of The Law of Inertia, and why it was important to us: *A body at rest remains at rest, and a body in motion moves in a uniformly straight course, unless some force acts on it from the outside.*

OK. Maybe we finally have a reason why it's important if it makes you go faster, point higher, heel less, stay dryer, and ride smoother. Well, why didn't your high school teacher say that? You might have paid more attention.

Because of inertia, some outside force must always be supplied to produce or arrest motion. The heavier the body, the greater must be the force. And herein we get to practical boating. A boat will start heeling with a puff of wind, but a boat with a lighter mast and rigging will not heel as far, will begin recovering sooner, and will transfer more energy from the wind into forward motion (the object of the game) than a boat with a heavier mast and rigging. Now you know why the racing boats have light mast and rigging. And now you know why the best cruising boats are now sporting lighter carbon fiber masts. The new 3/42 has an optional carbon mast which is like putting two 250 pound gorillas on the windward rail. It doesn't heel as much!

The "classic" cruising boat is very solid and heavy, and at first blush, this seems like a good idea for heavy weather sailing. But, enter Mr. Moment of Inertia. A boat that is heavier in "the ends" (bow, stern and rig) will dive deeper and longer as it confronts waves than a light boat. The lighter boat rides over the waves while the heavier boat goes through or under them. And again, there is more energy left to convert into forward motion so you can reach that tropic isle quicker and more comfortably or you can be a bit faster on the racecourse if you are a racer. And now you know why racing boat hulls and the best cruising boat hulls are not solid glass but have cored interiors, which, by the way, are also stronger, but that's another subject.

If you are still a doubter, try this simple experiment. Tie a hammer or similar object to a piece of string and jerk your hand up quickly. The string will break. But if you pull steadily and slowly, you can lift the weight without breaking the string.

There are a number of ways to improve your cruising or racing boat's performance without major surgery or replacement. "Get the weight out of the ends." High test rather than standard anchor chain, Mylar sails rather than Dacron, lighter halyards, lighter radar reflector, storing heavy gear more to the center of the boat, leaving unnecessary gear at home, and more.

So next time you are sitting around with your cruising or racing buddies, start talking about how you have been doing some "Moment of Inertia" work on your boat and enjoy the blank stares.

Postscript: Many of us followed swimmer Michael Phelps's successful quest to break Mark Spitz's record of seven gold medals in a single Olympics. Spitz's career was a tough act to follow. Between 1968 and 1972, he won nine Olympic gold medals, one silver, and one bronze; five Pan American golds; 31 National U.S. Amateur Athletic Union titles; eight U.S. National Collegiate Athletic Association Championships; and set 33 world records.

My son Ken and I met Mark some years later when he became interested in sailing. We ended up selling him a J/35 sailboat. Being the competitor that he was, he decided to enter his boat in the Los Angeles to Honolulu TRANSPAC race. Ken went with him on the 2250 mile race. They did fair, and could have done better if Mark had understood the importance of Moment of Inertia. Against Ken's recommendation, Mark insisted on loading the boat down with a vast and heavy supply of soft drinks. This, when other competitors were taking every possible ounce of weight off of their boats.

BIG SWIM

There's more than one way to cross Santa Barbara's challenging channel — sailing, power boating, rowing, flying, waterskiing, windsurfing, kite boarding, and more. I have done several, but there is one I will never try and that's swimming.

Channel swimming has fascinated the public for over a century and none more captivating than crossing the English Channel. Captain Mathew Webb, who made the crossing in 21 hours and 45 minutes, first accomplished this in 1875. Christof Wandratsch who crossed in 7 hours 3 minutes 52 seconds in 2005 holds the current record. To put such a demanding accomplishment into perspective, at the end of the 2007 climbing season there had been 3679 successful assents to the summit of Mount Everest, while by 2005 there had been only 982 successful crossings of the English Channel. One woman, Alison Streeter, has swum it 43 times and is still counting.

Santa Barbara's challenging channel has been conquered a number of times by marathon swimmers. Cindy Cleveland, who swam fourteen miles from the mainland to Anacapa Island, made the first crossing in 1978. Since that time, eighteen more channel crossings have been made, excluding multi-swimmer relays. The longest to date was from Santa Rosa Island to Coal Oil Point near Goleta by Marc Lewis, who took 15 hours and thirty-six minutes for the thirty-mile crossing. Crossings have been made from Anacapa, Santa Cruz, and Santa Rosa Islands. So far, no individual swimmers have made the crossing from desolate San Miguel Island at the west end of the channel.

An exceptional swimmer from this area is David Yudovin of Cambrla. David has crossed from the mainland to Anacapa Island, and was the first to swim from Santa Cruz Island, completing the crossing in 15 hours 15 minutes. His long list of world swims include Java to Sumatra, Morocco to Gibraltar, several inter-island Hawaiian swims, Honchu Island to Kokkaido Island in Japan, the English Channel, numerous Catalina Island crossings, and more.

SEA TERMS

The relationship between mankind and the sea goes back almost to the origin of humans. With most of the earth covered by water, our early ancestors had to learn to travel across the vast waters for survival, trade, and prosperity. Water covers 70 percent of our planet, and 97 percent of that water is in the oceans. So it is little wonder that there is an extremely old and almost complete language associated with the sea. A landlubber (land lver) is often completely confused when he hears even modern sailors talking their nautical language. Here are some interesting sea terms. All are still in contemporary use.

- Mayday – the word mayday is the mariner's distress call. It comes from the French words "help me" or "m'aidez". It is only to be used when a person or a vessel is in grace and imminent danger and requires immediate assistance. "Pan Pan" (pronounced pahn pahn) is another important radio call that mariners use to transmit urgent messages and warnings to other sailors and rescue personnel, but it is used for situations that are serious but not life threatening.

- As The Crow Flies – Crows are landlubbers. Sailors long ago used crows as navigational tools. When the fog rolled in or the weather was foul (or should we say "fowl"), mariners would release a crow from its cage and note the dire5ion it flew, which was sure to be straight toward the closest land. Today we describe how far away something is "as the crow flies" to mean the shortest distance to it regardless of where the road is or what might be in the way.

- Fathom (Noun) – The length of outstretched arms or a nautical of 6 feet. (Verb) To measure to the bottom with a pole or line; to understand completely. Before we had rulers and tape measures, people measured things with what was fairly consistent and always nearby . . . their bodies. Horses are measured in hand; distance is measured by the foot. The fathom, used on nautical charts and by mariners, is six feet. Today, when we find ourselves a measuring tool handy and a good estimate will do, we can still use our bodies to approximate measurements. If you stretch your arms out from side to side, it will approximate your height. Since most men are somewhere around six feet tall, they can measure one fathom of length in fathoms with outstretched arms. Need a quick way of measuring how much line you've got tied to your anchor before you throw it overboard? Use your armspan to measure it in fathoms. Overestimate if you are vertically challenged.

- Aboard – On or in a vessel. As it has two sources, one Latin (*bordure*) and the other Anglo-Saxon (*bord*), both meaning side, this word suggests the wonderful wanderings of early navigators, such as the Danes to Greek shores and the Romans to the Baltic, Northern Europe, and British Isles. 14th Century.

- Bitter End – Bitt is a strong vertical structural timber or metal post, used to make fast (secure) heavy lines; usually in pairs, ergo *bitts*. The term comes from Dutch, Old Norse, and Latin. Bitter End is the inboard (closest to the ship) of a line. Quoting Captain John Smith (1627), "The part of the cable (line) that doth stay within board, the bitter being that part actually on the bitts." Author's note based on experience: The Bitter End is also a great watering hole (tavern) located on Virgin Gorda in the British Virgin Isles.

CLUES FROM THE PAST

For centuries, sailing ships have anchored off Santa Barbara's shores. Captain Juan Bautista de Anza sailed here in 1769, and Captain George Vancouver anchored off West Beach in 1774. And the Chumash have rowed their tomol plank canoes off Santa Barbara's barren shores since pre-Columbian times. But it wasn't until the late 1920's that Santa Barbara could offer more than a hazardous place to anchor. Because of the threat of dangerous southeast storms, captains were wise to anchor at least a mile off-shore in order to have time and room to up-anchor and claw away from the rocks and pounding surf along Santa Barbara's shoreline. Construction of the Chapala Street pier in 1868 and Stearns Wharf in 1872 did not provide safe refuge for craft.

Finally, construction began in 1927 on a rock breakwater to provide shelter for anchored vessels. By 1929, a thousand foot breakwater lay parallel to Cabrillo Boulevard just west of Stearns Wharf. This was soon followed by a 600 foot extension. But the breakwater restrained the natural flow of sand along the coast, and soon the protected waters became too shallow for anchored vessels. More rocks were barged in from Santa Cruz Island to connect the breakwater with the shore to keep out the sand.

Thus, our harbor is only about eighty years old and quite young when compared with Santa Barbara's long history. Since the first rocks were dropped off-shore in 1927, the waterfront has developed substantially and only a few clues remain to distinguish the early years of the harbor.

Clue One – If you travel to Frys Harbor, about half way up the channel side of Santa Cruz Island, you will see the remains of the large quarry where breakwater rocks were blasted from the hillside and loaded onto barges for their trip to Santa Barbara. The quarry is quite large, and it is clear that a great deal of rock was extracted. Rusting machinery and cables still remain as reminders of the work that was done there to help create Santa Barbara's new harbor.

Clue Two – Before 1927, Ledbetter Beach did not exist. A rocky shoreline ran along the base of the Mesa cliffs with almost no sand. When the new breakwater was extended out from the shore, it stopped the natural flow of sand along the coastline. Santa Barbara soon gained an impressive stretch of valuable beach.

Clue Three – The largest building at the harbor is now named the Santa Barbara Waterfront Center. It was constructed by the U.S. Navy in 1943 for operations associated with World War II - port security, mine sweeper training, Coast Guard vessel maintenance, and later for Naval Reserve training functions. The Center was designated as a City Landmark in 1999. Today, it houses the Santa Barbara Maritime Museum and a large restaurant. More clues of the early harbor can be found inside. A brass plaque from 1930 honors Major Max C. Fleischmann for his support and funding to help construct the breakwater. A second plaque lists the members of the Santa Barbara Harbor Commission that were in office at the time of construction of the Navy building. In the hallway to your left after entering the building, you will find a number of fascinating historic photographs showing the construction of the breakwater and the early years of the harbor.

Clue Four – During the construction of the large Navy building, a substantial number of smaller wood buildings were built to accommodate additional wartime activities. One still remains at the foot of the Navy Pier. Today, it houses the two cafes and several shops. The building has had new siding and roofing installed, so there is little evidence of its original construction

Clue Five – For many years, there were no slips to tie up boats at the harbor. All boats hung on mooring cans, and owners needed a rowing skiff to reach them. A row of pilings were driven in the harbor waters in front of the present yacht club, and circular lines with pulleys were installed between the pilings and the breakwater rocks. This allowed boat owners to pull their skiffs away from the rocks when not in use. When they needed to board their skiff, they would pull their skiff in and board it from the rocks. Today, you can still see many of the steel eyes that attached the pulleys to the breakwater rocks.

Clue Six – After the war, the city installed a large float next to the skiff lines. This made loading of food, gear, and passengers into the skiffs much easier, and also allowed boats to come in from their mooring cans and tie up at the float. Later, a second float was added. If you walk down the ramp in front of the yacht club that leads to present day Marina One, you will see the Santa Barbara Yacht Club Youth Foundation's floating facility. The large float at the center of the facility is the old City Float. It has deteriorated with age such that it is no longer practical to try to keep it from leaking. But it was constructed of massive wood timbers, and floats very solidly even with its interior full of sea water. Over the years, countless youngsters have launched the Foundation's small sailboats off the float as they learned to become competent sailors.

Clue Seven – Finally, you can see the dredge moored out near the harbor's entrance. Ever since the construction of the breakwater and the resultant creation of Ledbetter Beach, sand progresses along the breakwater's outside rocks and drops into the harbor's quieter waters. This sand must be dredged and sent on down the coast in order to maintain the harbor at an operational depth. Many millions of dollars have been spent moving sand through the years.

It may have been wiser and far less expensive to have built the harbor at the Goleta slough or where the bird refuge is today, but Santa Barbarans love their harbor at its unique location directly in front of their town. Come down to see the clues that reveal your harbor's past - except, perhaps, the quarry on Santa Cruz Island.

SIGHT AT SEA

Dense fog enveloped fifty-three foot La Serina, as Chuck and I cleared Santa Barbara Harbor on our way to haul out at Ventura Harbor Boat Yard. We could barely see 50 feet ahead, and were more than thankful for the 24-mile radar mounted at the helm that was showing land and sea obstructions on its screen. Better yet, the radar was interfaced with our global positioning system (GPS) which placed a line on the screen that showed our course to Ventura Harbor and even an "X" at our destination.

We initially set the radar at close range to detect other boats and any objects to avoid. Santa Barbara's off-shore oil towers showed clearly on the screen, as we safely slipped past them. After two and a half hours, the screen showed we were approaching Ventura Harbor. We switched to the electronic chart screen which showed two buoys just off the harbor entrance. It also showed that any miscalculation would put us hard on the breakwater rocks or on the beach, so we double and triple checked that we were heading for the outer buoy.

We reduced our speed down to two knots as we both strained to sight the buoy through the thick fog. At the very last moment, the buoy emerged from the fog so close that we had to quickly alter course to avoid collision. Then, a quick turn towards the beach to search for the next buoy. The radar showed it clearly, and after about four minutes, it too materialized out of the heavy fog. Identifying the harbor entrance on the radar screen was more difficult, because radar images only show what the signals hit and then reflect back. Two breakwaters and a beach don't look like pictures on a road map, so we continued to move ahead very cautiously. Again, at the last moment, a corner of one of the breakwaters emerged from the mist. After studying the radar screen, we decided it must be the outer breakwater. We put the helm over in a sharp but careful turn, and suddenly *La Serina* had crossed into the protected waters of Ventura Harbor.

Visibility was still near zero, but periodic channel buoys appeared on the screen to help us reach the boat yard. We both felt relief as we secured "La Serina" to the dock. Hopefully, the trip back to Santa Barbara the next day would be in clear weather. It was, and we were able to observe the harbor's intricate entrance and buoys. We couldn't have safely entered in such a fog without radar.

The history of radar began in the early 1900s with the invention of simple uni-directional ranging devices. The technique improved during the 1920s and 1930s and led to the introduction of the first early warning radar networks just before the beginning of World War II. Progress during the war was rapid, and today's radar systems are compact and affordable for recreational boats. Radar is in use all around us, although it is normally invisible. Air traffic controllers use radar to track planes both on the ground and in the air, and to guide them in for smooth landings. Police use radar to detect the speed of passing motorists. NASA uses radar to map the Earth and other planets, to track satellites and space debris, and to help with activities like docking and maneuvering. The military uses it to detect the enemy and to guide weapons. And, of course, radar is essential for boats and ships at sea.

The basic idea behind radar is straightforward – a signal is transmitted, it bounces off an object and is received by an electronic device. The process is similar to a sound echoing off a wall; however; radars don't use sound as a signal. Instead, they transmit electromagnetic waves called radio waves and microwaves. The name radar comes from *R*adio *D*etection *A*nd *R*anging.

ADVENTURES AT SEA

We have all read and heard tales of exciting adventures at sea - shipwrecks, dismastings, running aground, severe storms, gear failure, engine failure, injuries, sickness, being lost, lack of food, and more. But have you ever considered that most "hair raising" experiences seem to have happened to the least qualified and least prepared boaters? When you pick up a book about real-life adventures at sea, more often than not you discover that the author or main characters knew very little about boating and the sea, and that they found themselves in situations that could have been avoided if they had been more knowledgeable. They didn't take proper steps to prepare their boat, to learn to navigate, to check immediate and long term weather, to learn sound seamanship, and to prepare contingency plans. If they had taken those measures, they probably wouldn't have had the material to write an adventure book.

It's great fun to read about such adventures, and even better to read than experience them yourself. The sea has too many surprises in store without volunteering for more by being unprepared. Whether on a long voyage or just a short race or day sail, the same principles and procedures apply. You, your crew, your vessel, and your plans must be prepared before in advance of starting out. Problems can be just as serious a half mile off Santa Barbara Harbor as off the stormy shores of Tierra Del Fuego.

Proper preparations for going to sea are similar to those of a pilot flying a plane. A good pilot continually plans for the unexpected. He has alternate landing locations in the event of emergency, and he has thought out and practiced corrective measures in the event of mechanical or electrical failure. His close attention to weather is well known by all.

A qualified sailor should act no differently. His contingency plans are no less important, although adversity usually comes upon a boat at a much slower pace than an airplane. Since formal training resulting in a license is not required for recreational boating, it is up to each boater to take steps to accumulate knowledge and experience to avoid unscheduled adventures at sea. Classes are offered by the Power Squadron, the Coast Guard Auxiliary, private institutions, and boat charter and rental operators. There are many good books and videos available.

But there is simply no substitute for experience. It is amazing how many major voyages are begun before the skipper and crew have worked together, checked out their boat, and developed contingency procedures. "Shaking down" is a historic tradition in boating. Before tackling an island trip, a good deal of coastal sailing should be done, including practice in anchoring, reefing to reduce sail area, navigation, ship's systems operation, and safety drills. Before cruising to distant ports, several island trips should be made in a variety of conditions to secure as much practical experience as possible and to learn the characteristics of your specific boat. Truly successful blue water sailors have years of experience before they sail beyond the horizons.

An understanding of all your ship's systems is essential. It is surprising how many boaters have sailed or powered for years without even a basic understanding of how the various systems on-board actually work. As a result, they are incapable of repairing them, frequently have not maintained them, and wouldn't know where to begin to deal with emergency procedures associated with them.

The first step toward preparedness is to collect operating manuals for your boat and all equipment on-board. Then file them in a plastic file box or a three ring binder for accessibility. Next, read them. If there are essential areas you don't understand, ask professionals for assistance or consult the internet. Make a list of key spare parts to keep on-board, and familiarize yourself so you can install them. Consider which systems could create major problems if failure occurs, and take steps to have the means to deal with them. Major systems of concern are rigging, propulsion, plumbing, electrical, anchor, floatation, pumping, fire protection, and safety.

An example is the raw water cooling pump for your engine. If the impeller fails, you cannot use your engine, so you should have a spare impeller on-board and the tools and know how to install it. The same goes for bleeding diesel engine fuel or trouble shooting the ignition system on a gasoline engine. Most boats have several thru-hull valves. Each should have a properly sized wood plug next to it for rapid plugging in the event of a thru-hull failure. A readily accessible spare anchor is essential, as well as a plan to deploy it under adverse conditions such as heavy seas at night. Think about these things now, not when you are being blown toward a rocky lee shore.

Navigation warrants special mention. You must know where you are and how to get to a safe destination under difficult conditions. Successful navigation depends on knowledge, common sense, and experience built over many voyages. Electronics and other devices help a great deal, but your experience and native instincts may be what keep you off the rocks in fog or on a dark night.

Maintain your boat and its systems. If you do it yourself, you will learn a great deal about your boat. If you have someone else do it, take the time to learn through discussions with your maintenance person. Finally, develop contingency plans – just like a pilot. Think about what could happen before it does, and plan what you would do to counter the situation. If you're moving into a narrow, shallow channel with a current running, plan what you would do if you lose power. Is an anchor handy for fast deployment? If you encounter unanticipated severe weather (in spite of your usual practice of carefully checking in advance), have alternate anchorages in mind. Your mind should be trained to plan ahead for contingencies on a continuing basis. And don't keep them a secret. Let your crew know. One of your plans should cover the absence or incapacity of the skipper.

It would take books of information to communicate all the knowledge that a successful boater should aspire to. If you are keyed to learn, plan, and take advanced preventative measures, you will probably not get rich from writing a book about your "adventures at sea."

CHINESE FISHERMEN OFF SANTA BARBARA

The first mention of Chinese fishermen operating in California was in an article in *Daily Alta California* which described a Chinese fishing village operating in South San Francisco Bay in 1853.

Beginning about 1860, Chinese fishermen were operating in the waters off Santa Barbara and the Channel Islands. They were pioneers in Santa Barbara's emerging commercial fishing industry, and continued their operations for over 60 years. Fishing activities increased until there were Chinese fishing villages operating from the Oregon border to deep into Baja California.

A wide variety of catches were conducted, with emphasis on shrimp, squid, and abalone. They were sold locally, shipped to Chinese communities throughout the west, and exported to China. Marketing and export transactions were usually handled through Chinese merchants in Chinatowns.

Santa Barbara County fishing operations in the 1800's included approximately 25 Chinese fishermen, although the exact number is not known. Some commercial fishing was conducted by individuals, but most of the fishing was conducted by fishermen that were employed by merchants in Santa Barbara's merchant community, who often provided fishing gear and sometimes fishing vessels.

The primary merchants involved in commercial fishing operations were Sing Chung and Company, Sun Lung and Company, and You Kee. Sing Chung and Company owned six fishing junks in 1885. The company was located in the Elizalde Adobe at 45 East Canon Perdido Street. It sold Chinese goods, silks, fans, and bric-a-brac. In 1893, Sun

Ling and Company was located at 36 East Canon Perdido Street. Their operation was primarily concerned with abalone, with an investment of $300,000 in boats and fishing tackle. Yee Kee was also heavily involved in the abalone fishery and was operating from 27 East Canon Perdido Street in 1906. His store sold Japanese and Chinese fancy goods in addition to fishing operations.

The Chinese fished for everything in a methodical and industrious manner including algae and various fish and sharks. But their greatest profits were from the sale of abalone and shells. A United States Commission of Fish and Fisheries reported that the Chinese had a monopoly in the abalone fishery, and harvested 238,463 pounds of abalone in Santa Barbara County in 1892.

Chinese fishermen operated at all of the Channel Islands. Today, you can visit some of the harbors and coves named by them – China Camp on Santa Rosa Island and Chinese Harbor on Santa Cruz Island are examples. Their earliest operations in the 1860's were on Santa Cruz Island at Forney's Cove, Prisoner's Harbor, Scorpion Anchorage, and China Harbor. Today, these anchorages are used by commercial fishermen as well as recreational boaters. Operations were generally between May and November when weather conditions were most favorable.

Transportation to the islands was by junks that operated off-shore. Those who owned junks were landed on the islands by other commercial vessels. Chinese fishermen and merchants had to make arrangements with the owners of the islands to conduct their operations. An arrangement between one fishing operation and the Caire Company of Santa Cruz Island provided for payment of 150 pounds of abalone out of every thousand pounds that were gathered of both meat and shells.

Historians have identified many island locations where the Chinese fishermen lived and operated.

Archeologists are exploring several sites on the islands to learn more from artifacts. The settlements frequently consisted of tents surrounded by piles of iridescent abalone shells, and with abalone meat set out to dry in the sun.

Three Chinese fishermen suffered a terrible ordeal in 1900 on San Nicolas Island. They had been dropped off by the schooner *Santa Rosa* for an extended stay. While gathering abalone, pirates stole their food and supplies. After nine months of limited rations, one died and the remaining two were near death when the schooner *Dawn* rescued them. Unaware of their plight, their employer had been trying for some time to hire a vessel to pick the fishermen up, but none were available from Los Angeles to San Francisco. Eventually, he was able to charter the *Dawn*.

Beginning in the 1870's, state and federal fisheries agencies began to become concerned that regulation of fisheries must be implemented in order to avoid the depletion of sea life that was occurring on the east coast of the United States due to pollution and overfishing. Sentiment turned against the Chinese operations, and eventually laws were passed that limited and eventually ended Chinese commercial fishing operations.

Chinese fishermen pursued their trade with tremendous success using traditional Chinese junks and fishing methods. They forged a legacy through hard work and determination and played an important role in California's maritime history.

SANTA ROSA ISLAND

Her bow rose to meet yet another steep oncoming wave, but *Selene's* lee rail remained buried in the turbulent seas as a fresh blast of wind held the sleek sloop over in an extreme heel. Then her bow plunged downward, again buried by the relentless wind and seas of Santa Barbara Channel's infamous "Windy Gulch." But, the end was in sight, and gradually the wind abated and the punishing seas began to decline. *Selene* had finally reached the protective lee of Santa Rosa Island's Carrington Point. We headed into Becher's Bay and prepared to anchor and dry out from our twenty-nine mile sail from Santa Barbara Harbor. Later, we relaxed in the cockpit, enjoyed a panoramic view of this historic island, and made plans for swimming, hiking, fishing and exploring.

That was in the 1950's, and I had one of the greatest jobs a sea struck teenager could ask for. Ed Vail, one of Santa Rosa Island's owners, had hired me to take care of his 46-foot PCC sloop *Selene*. Better yet, he allowed me to use the boat when he wasn't.

Santa Rosa Island is the second most westerly of the Channel Islands, lying between westernmost San Miguel and Santa Cruz to the east. The windswept island is approximately sixteen miles long, eight miles wide, and encompasses an area of about fifty-four thousand acres. It is the second largest of the eight Channel Islands. Fog often envelopes the island and gale winds of forty to fifty miles per hour blow across the ridgelines throughout most of the year.

The Chumash inhabited the island for many centuries, crossing the channel in their swift and seaworthy Tomol canoes. Santa Rosa was first discovered by Europeans when Juan Rodriguez CabriIlo passed through in the mid 1500's. The Spanish eventually removed the Chumash from the island in the mid 1800's and resettled them at Mission Santa Barbara where many died due to a lack of immunity to mainland diseases.

The island was first granted to Don Carlos and Don Jose Cabrillo in 1839. Their daughters Manuela and Francisca married John Jones and Alpheus Thompson, who took over management of the island, stocking it with cattle, horses, rams and ewes. Jones and Thompson did not get along well, and Thompson sold his interest at an auction in the 1850's to Alexander P. Moore, who eventually bought out Jones, and was the sole owner until his death in 1893. He ran it as a sheep ranch and took advantage of the high demand for wool to make uniforms during the Civil War. He is reported to have had up to 100,000 sheep on the island before the collapse of the wool market in the late 1800's, after which most of the sheep were slaughtered.

In 1901, Walter L. Vail and his business partner J.V. Vickers began purchasing shares of Santa Rosa Island from the estate of A. P. Moore. Vail and Vickers were major landowners in southeastern Arizona. They were involved in many business ventures, including Southern California real estate, the formation of the community of Huntington Beach and the discovery and development of its oil fields.

Walter Vail was reported to be a tough businessman and one that wouldn't be pushed around. In 1980, he was preparing to move 900 of his cattle from his Empire Ranch in Arizona to the Werner Ranch just outside of San Diego. The Southern Pacific Railroad suspiciously raised their rates to Vail by 25 percent, perhaps because of past business battles between them. In any event, an outraged Vail would not pay such an unreasonable rate and retaliated by driving his cattle overland from Arizona to Southern California, a feat never accomplished before. He saved over four dollars a head. Other ranchers planned to follow suit, so the railroad finally returned to their previous rates.

Walter Vail was killed in 1906, so he didn't have much time to deal with Santa Rosa Island. He left his holdings to seven children, and ownership of the island had to be legally divided between them and the Vickers family. By the early 1900's, the Vail Company controlled close to one million acres in Arizona and California. The Vail and Vickers ownership of Santa Rosa Island continues today, now in its fourth generation. The Vail members of the partnership have conducted the management of island operation through the years.

N.R. Vail managed Santa Rosa Island until his death in 1943. He was followed by his younger brother Ed Vail (owner of the sloop *Selene* that I sailed), and then by his nephew Al Vail in 1961. Over the years, the island's owners were supported by a series of very competent foremen.

Island logistics were very difficult. For most of the history of the ranch, equipment, supplies, personnel, and livestock had to be transported to and from the island by boat across frequently rough channel waters. Through the years, Vail and Vickers Company owned a variety of boats for this purpose. The first that was specifically designed to carry livestock was the *Vaquero I*, built in 1913. She was 130 feet long and could carry 100 tons, which today would be equivalent to about four truckloads of livestock. Senior Santa Barbarans may recall *Vaquero II* landing cattle and sheep into pens on Stearns Wharf, where they were then loaded onto trucks. They may also remember the Taylor Ranch just north of Ventura. Vast holding pens were constructed to receive cattle, including those from Santa Rosa Island. When the Ventura pier was damaged by winter storms or otherwise inaccessible, the cowhands had to exchange their horses for rowboats. The cattle were driven into the ocean from the cattle boat, swam ashore, and then were driven to the Taylor Ranch pens.

Over the years, many additional events took place at Santa Rosa Island, including shipwrecks, oil exploration, and installation of a station of the military's Distant Early Warning System.

The history of the island continues, but the Vail and Vickers era will soon end. In 1969, President Jimmy Carter signed into existence the Channel Islands National Park, which included Santa Rosa Island. The legislated terms require Vail and Vickers to cease all island operations by 2011. In 1998, after ninety-seven years of ranching, the last cattle were shipped off the island. Vail and Vickers continue to operate their hunting operation, but that must cease by 2011. Vail and Vickers brought mule deer and elk to the island many years ago, and will have to remove them in accordance with park service mandates. I recall when then Governor and later Supreme Court Chief Justice Earl Warren and party would pass through Santa Barbara Harbor the 1950's on their way to hunt on Santa Rosa Island.

Thus 2011 will end the private operation of the Santa Rosa Island. Some may wonder if the ranching and other commercial operations did damage to the island. Former Channel Islands National Park Superintendent Tim Setnicka wrote in an opinion piece in the Santa Barbara News-Press in 2006, "To this day, no one has shown that the ranching operation has permanently, significantly, or irreparably destroyed park service resources."

SIR THOMAS LIPTON

The life of Thomas Johnston Lipton of Great Britain provides history with a most outstanding icon in the field of yachting. Sir Thomas, who was knighted in 1898 by Queen Victoria, offered all yachtsmen an excellent example of a true sportsman in the broadest, highest and finest sense. He exemplified a keen contender and clean competitor. He was undaunted by defeat. He was aggressive and ambitious to the end.

Sir Thomas' race winnings – and there were many – were marked by his modesty in victory. In his defeats abroad or in American waters, he demonstrated how one can be a good loser – "the world's best loser" – and always be a truly great winner.

His role as loser referred to his quest to win the America's Cup, a trophy that was won the first time by the United States yacht *America* against England's *Magic* in 1851 in a race around England's Isle of Wight. When Sir Thomas entered the fray at age 48, the Royal Yacht Squadron, England's most exclusive club, had already made ten unsuccessful attempts to regain the prized trophy from its keepers at the New York Yacht Club. Sir Thomas Lipton unsuccessfully challenged America for the cup five times over a period of thirty-one years from 1899 to 1930. His last unsuccessful challenge was with what was probably the pinnacle of racing yachts, *Shamrock V,* a 120 foot J-Boat sloop. The United States went on to successfully defend "The Cup" until it was finally won by Australia in 1983 after 33 successful defenses by the United States – the longest defense in the history of all sports.

Thomas Johnston Lipton was born on May 10, 1850 in Glasgow, Scotland, and eventually became one of the world's great success stories. He went to work at an early age as an errand boy in a Glasgow bookstore. At the age of 15, he came to the United States as a steerage immigrant but never forgot his homeland. He first worked in a grocery store, then drove a mule streetcar in New Orleans, became a traveling portrait salesman, and finally worked on plantations in South Carolina and Virginia.

Sir Thomas returned to Glasgow at age 26 with enough money to open a small grocery store that packaged tea leaves for convenient sale. One story has him promoting his Lipton Tea by letting loose dozens of piglets throughout London, just before dawn, with signs attached to each reading "Drink Lipton Tea." As his business grew, he opened other stores – first in Scotland and then all over Ireland, Wales and England. To supply these stores, he acquired tea plantations in Ceylon, and also purchased coffee and cocoa plantations throughout the world. A global entrepreneur, Sir Thomas operated a large packing house in Chicago, and a bacon curing plant and bakeries in England. He had fruit orchards and factories for making jellies and jams. Within ten years, he was employing over 8,000 persons.

Sir Thomas' business empire grew, and his stores were in many lands. His name, known around the world associated with "Lipton's Tea," became a household word. At the age of 40, he was a millionaire. Although his business success was recognized for tea, he was also a man who knew how to crown a life of labor with a penchant for leisure.

Despite his America's Cup defeats, Sir Thomas was still aggressive and ambitious past age 80. In fact, in 1931 he decided to mount another challenge for the 1932 races. His efforts were delayed due to declining health, and his ambition was finally thwarted by death on October 2, 1931. Sir Thomas never married, but left behind a rich yachting and business heritage.

His legacy of great sportsmanship still lives. Sir Thomas was dedicated to promoting competition and sportsmanship in yachting as well as other sports. He donated many perpetual trophies to yachting organizations throughout the world. The trophies remain silver works of art, and today are among the most prestigious that are the ultimate quest of any serious yachtsman.

Santa Barbara is very fortunate to possess one of Sir Thomas Lipton's magnificent trophies. It resides at Santa Barbara Yacht Club, and has been competed for since 1921 by prestigious 22-foot Star Boats, which have been used in Olympic competition longer than any other class of boat. Each year, the Lipton Cup is fought for during Semana Nautica by world class entries. In eighty-seven years of competition at Santa Barbara only four local sailors have won the cup, including the author.

Sir Thomas Lipton accomplished much in his life, but many will remember him as an intense sporting competitor, a many time winner, but also as most gentlemanly in his losses. His contribution to furthering the standards of the sport of yachting project far into the future.

RULES OF THE ROAD

The courses of boats have intersected since before recorded time. Quite likely, primitive humans propelling log crafts occasionally met another and took steps to avoid impact. There were no rules other than a collision could ruin your whole day, so it was best to steer clear of the other log. Boats improved over the centuries – enhanced shape, multiple oars, sail power, then engine power, higher speed, and then even greater speed, until today there are countless fast moving boats and ships navigating the more than 139 million square miles of the world's seas and oceans.

For most of history, wooden sailing vessels were so slow that there was no need for much in the way of navigation rules. With the coming of steamships, collisions became more frequent, and this led to the gradual introduction of regulations in the early 1800's. In 1838, the United States Congress passed a law to "provide better security of the lives of passengers on-board of vessels propelled in whole or in part by steam" This included a requirement for steamboats operating between sunset and sunrise to carry one or more signal lights. The color, visibility and location were not addressed. In 1846, a British law required steam vessels to pass port to port (left side to left side). Then, in 1848, the British added a requirement for steam powered vessels to show a red and green light as well as a white masthead light. Over time, these rules were fine-tuned, and additional rules specified the use of whistle and sound signals, set forth different rules for inland waters verses the high seas, procedures for course changes, and more. The purpose of all was to avoiding collisions. Today, vessels are governed by navigation rules set by "The Convention On International Relations For Preventing Collisions At Sea."

The rules are very official and appear very clear on paper. But, enter the real world of life at sea. You are in a small sailboat, have been underway for over twelve hours, and are struggling to find your way in dense, pea soup fog. You don't have a Global Positioning System, and have only a vague idea of where you are. Suddenly, your ears are almost shattered by the huge blast of a large ship's horn. Where is he? Are you and your boat about to be demolished by a tanker or freighter? How can you deal with academic "right of way" rules under such circumstances? All you can do is hope the ship's radar is tracking you and its captain will take measures to avoid you. Praying may help.

So the lesson is – follow the rules of the road if you can, but take all possible measures to avoid having to need them.

For example, I was recently crossing from Santa Cruz Island to Santa Barbara, and the weather was foggy and visibility poor. I had the VHF radio set to call-distress Channel 16. Off to starboard (right), we sighted a large ship coming up fast. It is very difficult to determine whether a small vessel traveling six knots is on a collision course with a giant ship traveling 18 to 25 knots – three to four times faster – especially in poor visibility. So I took up our radio's handset and called on Channel 16, "Large ship heading west off Santa Cruz Island. We are the small sailboat off your port bow. Do you see us?" No answer to several calls as our two vessels continued to converge. Then, from another vessel, "We see the ship and its name is *Mitsui Maru*. Using the ship's name, I called again and finally a reply, "We see you, and will pass ahead of you." We all relaxed in relief. Right of way rules are great, but insurance is better.

Every day, countless commercial fishing vessels, sport fishers, yachts, day sailers, giant freighters and tankers travel Santa Barbara's Channel. All are governed by the rules of the road, but the commercial traffic has additional safeguards. Large ships passing through the channel are restricted to two lanes, just like a highway, but without signs or painted white lines. A chart of the area shows dotted lines indicating a northbound traffic lane and a second for southbound. Each lane is one mile wide and the chart shows a separation zone two miles wide in the center between them. Through the years, there have been vessel sinkings and groundings, but I don't recall a collision between two giant ships in our channel, thanks to good seamanship, rules of the road, and the ship traffic lanes.

There are rules of the road for most mobile activities throughout the world – automobiles, aircraft, and many more. When new types of vehicles are introduced, rules are created to avoid catastrophe. One special set of maritime rules deals with the special circumstances of sail yacht racing.

To the uninitiated, sailboat racing is assumed to be a lovely and passive competition between beautiful yachts sailing serenely over calm seas. On the contrary, sailboat racing is aggressive, physically punishing, and needs strict rules to avoid collisions or worse. Hence the founding of the International Yacht Racing Union (IYRU) in 1907 and the North American Racing Union in 1925. Today, racing boats from eight foot prams to giant circumnavigators are controlled by a complete and complex set of racing rules that cover every possible interface between yachts, whether on a local race course or a thousand mile competition. The rules themselves have become a key tool in planning and implementing racing strategy. A serious contestant will plan several tacks ahead and use the rules to gain a controlling position over a competitor.

Passengers and operators of boats and ships can take comfort, knowing that there are sound rules worldwide to ensure safe passage and orderly avoidance of collisions. But, it is always a good rule to assume the other vessel is being operated by complete idiots and to be alert at all times.

WHAT'S IN A NAME?

All boats have names. Their range can be very wide – stately descriptions of the boat, the sea, life, cleverness, humor, sick, and many more.

One sailor informed impressionable lady friends that he had named his boat "after you". What greater compliment could there be? When one of his so honored friends went to the harbor to see his namesake, he was amused, but this was not always the case, for painted on the boat's transom were the words *After You*.

The top ten boat names of 2007 in order were - *Black Pearl, Liberty, Second Wind, Amazing Grace, Aquaholic, Knot On-Call, Second Chance,) Wanderlust, The Dog House, Carpe Diem* and *Seas The Day*.

To see how times have changed, here are the top ten from 2000 - *Serenity, Irish Eyes, Island Time, Sea Spirit, Obsession, Time Out, Reel Time, Escapade, Southern Comfort,* and *Serendipity*.

Laniru seems a beautiful Polynesian word, unless you crack the code and spell it backwards. How about *Sail Bad The Sinner* to let the folks out there know what kind of seaman you are. Or inconsistent *Never Again ll*. Sometimes, sailors put very long names on very small boats. One name took up most of sides of a 14 foot Laser sailboat, *Rommel Drove Deeper Into Africa*. And some wives may feel *Aquaholic* is actually a serious disease rather than a clever name.

Boats I have owned were named *Hokatiki, Temptation, Little Spook, Liberty, Chaos, Breeze,* and some forgotten.

A few more – *A Loan Again, Berth Control, Boatrupt, Crewless, Dock Holiday, Fin & Tonic, For Sale By Owner, Knot Again, Marlin Monroe, Pier Pressure, Reel Deal, Sea's The Day, Sailing The High Cheese, Thank*

You Pain Weber, X-Ta-Sea, and on and on. Imagine sifting through the boat names of the membership of the 530,000 membership of the Boat Owner's Association.

SAILING WITH GREENOUGH

In my late teens, I worked summers and weekends doing yacht maintenance, deliveries, and paid skippering. "Hammy" Greenough hired me to take care of his 59 foot yawl *Sabrina*, and I frequently took his sons George and Bill on Southern California cruises. George was a talented craftsman and inventor, even as a teenager. He was fascinated with sharks, and would row his longboat off Santa Barbara and chum for them. The sharks sometimes suffered from his fascination with explosives.

George Greenough may be a "mechanical genius." As a teenager, he was constantly building things to accommodate his wide interests. He built a small craft that was no more than a box that he would kneel in and propel with a flat piece of wood covering each palm of his hand. He could make it surf a bit, but at that time was primarily interested in getting into island sea caves for fishing. I can recall being anchored at remote Santa Barbara Island, talking on the radio to his father, and reporting that all was well with his two boys as I watched George and his tiny craft being tossed about by the aggressive waves pounding into the sea cave. That little box-boat was the start of George becoming the world renowned surfer and designer that he is today.

When George became interested in photography, he soon decided that commercially available lenses were unsatisfactory. As the uniquely clad, long haired, sunburned, teenage George walked into one of Santa Barbara's two camera stores, the staff did not recognize his budding genius. They were reluctant to look at the specifications for the lens design he wished to have built. But soon recognized him for the genius he was, and the lens was built. George went on to film "The Innermost Limits of Pure Fun" which stunned the surfing world with the first ever movie shots of an Australian beach rom from inside a curling wave using his high technology, home-made camera as he surfed his tiny board toward shore. This was just the beginning.

But back to sailing. After George's father sold *Sabrina*, he purchased the 42-foot sloop *Marmetta*, and George, I and two others were to sail her to Santa Barbara from Newport. She was a trim wooden sloop, and we took off late one afternoon looking forward to a fun but uneventful voyage. But the boat yard had not told us that *Marmetta* had been out of the water for some time, which caused her planks to shrink a bit. At sea, we found we were taking on significant water, but were already committed and things seemed under control with periodic pumping. Then came serious winds and waves, and periodic pumping became a full time job as the four of us rotated every twenty minutes around the clock. By the time we sighted Anacapa Island, it had become too much, so we ran for a port. The closest was the Port Hueneme Navy Facility just south of Oxnard. *Marmetta* literally surfed through the jetty and slid into calm waters where we tied up to the nearest dock. Cold, wet, and exhausted, we were sighing our relief when an official looking government vehicle screeched to a halt and two uniformed military police strode toward us. They forcefully informed us that we had tied up in a deep secret classified area and must leave at once. They unsympathetically listened to our plight that we had been sinking. A compromise was reached and we were allowed to move to a less secret area on condition that we would leave instantly when the wind lessened.

George continued to surf and design improved versions of his short boards. One came in handy when *Marmetta* was anchored in Lady's Cove at Santa Cruz Island. It was time to leave, but the engine wouldn't start. Surf running into the cove, but there was little sailing wind because of the high, shielding cliffs. We managed to reach the wind line with a line ahead attached to George on his knee board as well as two crewmembers pulling as they swam. They all had to do a fast scramble aboard as the wind finally surged *Marmetta* ahead. A side note: George named one of the best surfing locations on the Channel Islands after *Marmetta*. Its location is not widely known.

Today, George is a living legend and unique icon in the surfing world. He is best known for innovative surf photography, surfboard design, and ingeniously conceived and constructed devices including everything from wind generators to hand-made air mattresses to blue water fishing boats. When George becomes fascinated by an idea or object, he frequently goes about re-inventing it. He has produced films, sailed the Pacific in a 39-foot yacht that he built in his back yard, and even built countless toys ranging from ultimately practical to amusingly whimsical. He is credited as being the best mat rider ever, and still surfs this unique wave riding craft. His most famous board is a foamless fiberglass spoon shaped kneeboard that he christened *Velo*. George is known as a genius level inventor and the master of fiberglass engineering, design, and construction that he has used to build surfboards, camera housings, boats, and more. He now resides in Byron Bay in N.S.W Australia.

But I choose to remember the sun-wind-and surf-bleached, mile-a-minute talking, ingenious and innovative youth that made me earn every dollar his father paid me to try to keep an eye on him at sea.

Sea Terms:

- Yawl – A two-masted sailboat with the main mast (tallest mast) forward and the shortest mast aft of the stern waterline.
- Longboat – A large rowing boat.
- Sloop – A one-masted sailboat carrying a jib forward and a mainsail aft.

ROGUE WAVES

Almost every year, well equipped and soundly constructed sailing vessels with proper safety gear and experienced crew disappear. Their loved ones are forever left wondering why and how – was it a whale, a floating container, a submerged reef, a violent storm, a rogue wave? Records show that severe weather sunk more than 200 supertankers and container ships in the past two decades, but what about so-called rogue waves?

In the past, most scientists wrote off rogue waves as rare or even mythology. But now data collected by European Space Agency's ERS satellites confirm what many ship captains have come to know ocean waves as tall as ten-story buildings are a leading cause of large ship sinkings. Two radar equipped ERS satellites carry out a world-wide rogue wave census. Without aerial, cloud-penetrating radar, scientists could not gather meaningful and accurate wave data except from off-shore oil platforms. The satellite-based radar instruments plot the height of individual waves in 3 by 6 mile patches of the sea. Three weeks of satellite data results in 30,000 patches, which are then evaluated to identify dangerous and extreme waves. During one study period, a scientific team identified more than ten giant waves more than 75 feet high at various points of the world.

Further confirmation of rogue waves comes from at sea events such as when the 965-foot ocean liner *Norwegian Dawn* sailing to New York from the Bahamas was struck by a rogue 70-foot wave on April 16, 2005. It smashed windows and sent furniture flying, but the ship survived and the crew lived to report the wave. A smaller boat faced with such a wave would have little chance of survival.

Giant waves can be formed when strong winds beat against an opposing ocean current, when waves from different storms join forces, or when swells interact in extraordinary ways with a particular seafloor configuration. Vijay Panchang and his associates at Texas A&M University report they can now accurately predict the daily height of waves anywhere off the coast of the United States for the next 48 hour period. A buoy off the coast of Alabama recently recorded an average wave height of 52 feet before its gauge broke. Since that figure was an average measurement of sea-state, the largest wave at that location was probably twice that size - about 100 feet. "There were oil platforms destroyed," said Panchang, who requires his wave mechanics students to read *The Perfect Storm*. "The sheer magnitude of these things amazes me."

There are a few things that long-range cruising sailors can do when setting off, apart from the obvious ones like never traveling during a cyclone season, taking particular note of existing currents, and watching the weather like your life depends on it - which it does. Stay away from areas where swells meet from different directions, especially where there are underwater mountains and ranges. These are locations where rogue waves are more likely to develop. Another area to avoid is where underwater cliffs occur close to coastlines. One of the most notorious areas is the Bay of Biscay, where the depths change in a short distance from thousands of feet to a few hundred.

SS CATALINA

"Twenty-six miles across the sea, Santa Catalina is waiting for me." These song lyrics lured countless of visitors to Santa Catalina Island for decades, and still do today. Most visitors sailed across the channel on "the Great White Ship" - 301-foot long *SS Catalina*. It ferried more than 25 million passengers between Los Angeles Harbor and Avalon during its heyday from 1924 to 1975. According to the Steamship Historical Society of America, that's more than have been carried by any other vessel, anywhere.

Steve Springer, Los Angeles Times Staff Writer, recalled that "As a boy, it was like a journey halfway around the world to some exotic port. The bottom deck was cut out to make space for its lifeboats, which allowed adventurous kids room to roam and explore and fantasize about cutthroat pirates and man-eating sharks, and supplied romantic adolescent's places to pair up and be alone. There was a clown on-board to entertain the youngsters among the 2,000 passengers. Those who wanted more adult entertainment found it one deck above in the bar and on the dance floor where top-quality music was supplied by the big bands of that period. Those bands were on their way over to perform at the Casino, the large circular building out on the point at the entrance to Avalon, Catalina Island's only town.

"Shortly before noon, as the boat approached the end of its trip, speedboats from the island would slowly circle the ship like an honor guard. The steamship's smokestack would answer the speedboats with a loud blast that would echo off the mountains, startling the roaming herds of buffalo, alerting the small craft in the area, mobilizing the locals on shore and inspiring the young divers on the rocks. As a youngster, I chose to believe I was arriving in the South Seas, a million miles from school and mundane West L.A. For me, my annual summer ticket on the Great White Steamship was better than an E-ticket ride at Disneyland."

Sadly, SS Catalina has been abandoned at Ensenada Harbor for years since her heyday. Her white sides have lost their luster, and rust permeates the once proud, listing vessel. After many years of decay, a decision has finally been made to bring an end to her misery. The United States has provided $650,000 to the Port of Ensenada to scrap the steamship. This will make room for a marina project inside the harbor. Juan Ochoa, the port's Trade Development Manager, stated, "Unfortunately, American groups trying to float or recover the ship back to the USA didn't have luck in these last eight years. We know that some of them will feel sad or angry with this port decision, but port projects must move forward in order to have better service and facilities." Thus ends a proud era.

COMMERCIAL FISHING

Commercial fishing has been a major factor in Santa Barbara since the Chinese began here in the 1860's fishing for shrimp, squid, and abalone. Today, many more species of fish are commercially harvested off our coast. The top species in order are sea urchin, squid, crab, shrimp, rockfish, sole, lobster and sea cucumber. Other major catches include shark, halibut, swordfish, tuna, salmon, sheepshead, sea bass, croaker, whelk, and skate.

At one time Santa Barbara had massive sardine catches, and I recall the giant purse seiners that would visit our harbor during the sardine season. But sardines come and go in cycles, and this major fishery has diminished substantially in recent years. The up periods typically last 20-150 years, followed by periods of scarcity lasting 20-200 years.

Abalone is a once-strong fishery that diminished due to overfishing, sea otter predation and disease. In the 1960's there was a large processing building at the end of Stearns Wharf. I can recall sailing by and watching endless abalone shells flying out the door onto a giant pile after the processors had scooped out their delicious meat. Abalone are now regulated and making a slow return. Meanwhile, abalone farms at Dos Pueblos and Cayucos thrive, raising abalone in saltwater "raceways," and selling them to markets around the world. You can watch local kelp-harvesting boats unloading the food for these animals at Santa Barbara Harbor's City Pier.

Thanks to the steady demand from Asia, sea urchins have become Santa Barbara's largest catch. An obscure cousin of the starfish, they were once regarded as "pests" because they feed on kelp and can quickly decimate a kelp bed. In the years since Santa Barbara's commercial urchin fishery was established in the 1970s to meet the steady demand from Asia, sea urchins have become California's largest export item from the ocean.

Sea urchins are a challenge to harvest. Walking along the breakwater in front of the Maritime Museum, you can see many small, high-speed powerboats with diving equipment mounted in their cockpits. These urchin boats are fast and seaworthy, and depart the harbor during pre-morning darkness in order to reach the island urchin beds by dawn. Two fishermen are usually aboard – a diver and a tender – though in these tough economic times, some divers work alone. Their day is long and hard. The diver works on the ocean floor loading spiny urchins into a collection net that is then hauled to the boat's deck when he signals to the tender above by jerking a line. Typically, the two fishermen try to harvest a load of 500-1,000 pounds before making a necessarily slower and less stable run back to Santa Barbara Harbor. They then off-load their catch onto waiting trucks with a small crane before darkness overtakes. It is a dangerous occupation, and not all survive it.

Squid is Santa Barbara's second largest fishery. They are cigar-shaped cephalopods that measure seven to twelve inches long and sport two triangular fins, eight arms and two feeding tentacles. The fins and a siphon propel the squid as it darts through the water. Traveling in large schools, squid can either camouflage themselves or achieve jet-propelled flight in any direction when alarmed. Like octopi, they squirt gobs of ink to confuse their enemies and conceal their escape. Squid often appear along the coast of Santa Barbara and Ventura counties. Santa Cruz and Santa Rosa Islands are also traditional squid "hot spots."

Commercial fishing boats deploy purse seine nets at night to capture squid. The boats use blinding 20,000-watt "light plants" to attract the squid to their nets. Crewmen then bunch (or "dry up") the net before pumping the squid aboard. The squid are then iced, brought to shore, pumped into totes or trucks and processed for fresh, frozen or canned sales.

Cooked squid are mild, sweet and tender. They are delicious fried, steamed, sautéed, baked or broiled.

Commercial fishing is one of the few remaining occupations where the return is in direct proportion to the hard work put in. It is a lonely occupation, with long hours, danger, and constant battle against the massive powers of weather and the frequently violent sea. I recall sailing off the west Channel Islands in heavy overcast, high winds, biting cold and steep grey seas. Our goal was to reach a safe harbor. Along the way, we watched lone fishing boats as their crew worked to recover their nets or traps, regardless of the wind and weather, only to deploy them once again for the next catch. That independence and their constant fight with the elements have caused many to call commercial fishermen "the last cowboys." Other catches will be described in future columns.

OUR NAVY

The United States Navy traces its origins to the Continental Navy which the Continental Congress established on October 13, 1775 by authorizing the procurement, fitting out, manning, and dispatch of two armed vessels to cruise in search of munitions ships supplying the British Army in America. The legislation also established a Naval Committee to supervise the work. All together, the Continental Navy numbered some fifty ships over the course of the war, with approximately twenty warships active at its maximum strength.

After the American War for Independence, Congress sold the surviving ships of the Continental Navy and released the seamen and officers. The Constitution of the United States, ratified in 1789, empowered Congress "to provide and maintain a navy." Acting on this authority, Congress in 1794 ordered the construction and manning of six frigates. The first three ships built were aptly named *United States, Constellation and Constitution*. The War Department administered naval affairs from 1794 until Congress established the Department of the Navy on April 30, 1798.

Today, the United States Navy is the largest and most powerful in the world. During World War II, the United States Navy passed the Royal Navy as the world's largest and has since consolidated its top position. The Soviet Navy has grown since the 1960s, and today its successor, the Russian Navy, is the second largest navy in the world. China's navy is rapidly growing and may soon be the largest.

In addition to size, there are many other criteria in evaluating a country's navy. Technology and weapons systems are infinitely complex, and a score sheet is needed to match up the potential effectiveness of each navy. The United States leads in most but not all categories. Significant long-term efforts are presently underway to develop several innovative naval prototypes, for example, an operational-scale electro-magnetic gun and free-electron lasers, super-conducting electric power systems, and the advanced surface "X-Craft." These initiatives, as well as new concepts for persistent, netted, littoral anti-submarine warfare, sea-basing, and the exploitation of space, represent revolutionary "gamechangers" for future naval warfare.

Many feel that our Navy is the United States' most important foreign policy tool. A vital element of our power projection overseas is the Navy's Aircraft Carrier Battle Groups. Former US President Bill Clinton once said: "When word of a crisis breaks out in Washington, it's no accident that the first question that comes to everyone's lips is: 'Where's the nearest carrier?'" Carrier Battle Groups, each with an Air Wing more powerful than most national air forces and with ships more powerful than many national navies are essential in ensuring the United States leading position in world policy.

In October 2008, 129 ships (46 percent of the fleet) were underway away from homeport. One hundred and four ships were deployed overseas, along with 61,092 personnel (double the number deployed in 2007). The total force includes 332,436 active duty personnel (including 51,477 officers and 276,511 enlisted) and 6,438 mobilized reservists. The Department of the Navy also includes 184,335 civilian employees. The fleet comprises a deployable battle force of 283 ships and submarines and more than 3,700 operational aircraft.

Recently, the United States Navy commissioned its most powerful weapon system to date – the new aircraft carrier USS George H. W. Bush (CVN-77), the tenth Nimitz Class super carrier of the United States Navy. Former President George H. W. Bush was a highly decorated naval aviator during World War II. The USS George H. W. Bush is the final Nimitz Class aircraft carrier to be constructed. The next carrier built will be the USS Gerald R. Ford, and the first of the new Ford Class (CVN-78) of super carriers.

Santa Barbarans are fortunate that our port is visited by US Navy warships each year, and that the ships can usually be boarded by the public. Our town has a well-deserved reputation for its hospitality to visiting officers and crew.

Sea Terms
• "X" Craft – The Navy's The 262 foot long, 950 ton displacement FSF-1 *Sea Fighter* experimental ship Frigate – In early sailing ship days, a fast mid-sized ship rigged warship with one or two gun decks (17th Century). Today, it designates a large destroyer or destroyer-leader.

ANACAPA ISLAND

Recent crystal clear winter air presented dazzling views of Santa Barbara's Channel Islands – even tiny Anacapa Island to the east. Anacapa Island is actually a chain of three small islands, and many feel that viewed from the mainland they resemble a railroad engine followed by a train of cars.

Excavated shell midden sites on the island offer evidence that Chumash people occupied the island more than ten thousand years ago. Europeans first discovered Anacapa in 1542 when Juan Rodriguez Cabrillo led the first expedition to explore what is now the west coast of the United States. In 1769, explorer Gaspar De Portola named the islands "Las Mesitas," meaning Little Tables in Spanish. Then in 1793, Captain George Vancouver rechristened the islands "Anacapa," which derived from the Chumash Indian word, "Ennepah," an island of deception or mirage.

Located twelve miles off the California coast (29 miles from Santa Barbara), Anacapa's three sections are linked together by reefs that are visible at low tide. The islets are appropriately named East, Middle and West Islands. West Island, largest island of the group, is two miles long by six tenths of a mile wide, and rises to a peak of 930 feet. Middle Island is one and a half miles long, a quarter of a mile wide and 325 feet at its highest point. East Island is a mile long, a quarter of a mile wide, and rises to an elevation of 250 feet. Just off East Island is a forty-foot high natural bridge named Arch Rock, which has become the graphic trademark for Anacapa and Channel Islands National Park. Steep sea cliffs drop to the water around most of the perimeter of the rugged island. Numerous lava tubes and air pockets reveal the island's volcanic origin, and rugged sea caves beg exploration.

Rich with some of Mother Nature's most colorful and interesting offerings, Anacapa hosts over 250 species of plants and seabirds, and is the largest Brown Pelican rookery in the United States. Seven other species of marine birds nest there, as well as 22 species of land birds. About 90 per cent of the Western Gulls in Southern California were born on Anacapa, and it is a migration ground for many other birds. Harbor seals and sea lions breed on its rocky beaches.

Past maritime tragedies made it necessary to construct a lighthouse on the eastern end of the island. At 11 p.m. December 2, 1853, the side-wheel steamer *Winfield Scott* ran aground on Middle Anacapa Island in dense fog, jarring its passengers awake. En route to Panama from San Francisco, *Winfield Scott's* passenger list included many miners who had struck it rich at California's gold rush. Although everyone made it safely to shore in the ship's lifeboats, the atmosphere immediately following the wreck was frenzied as "every one was for himself, with no thought of anything but saving his life and his (gold) dust." The ship was a total loss, and its remains still lie submerged just north of the island.

The notoriety of the grounding prompted President Franklin Pierce to issue an executive order that reserved Anacapa for lighthouse purposes. Staff from the U.S. Coast Survey visited the island in 1854 and concluded that although the island's position at the eastern entrance to the Santa Barbara Channel was a natural choice for a lighthouse, "it is inconceivable for a lighthouse to be constructed on this mass of volcanic rock, perpendicular on every face, with an ascent inaccessible by any natural means." So instead, a lighthouse was built in 1874 at Point Hueneme, the nearest point on the mainland from Anacapa Island. However, shipping in the Santa Barbara Channel increased to the extent that the Lighthouse Board finally decided to construct an unmanned acetylene lens lantern on a fifty-foot tower on Anacapa Island, requiring servicing just twice a year.

Then on February 28, 1921, the steamer *Liebre* ran aground on the east end of Anacapa Island in dense fog directly under the light. With approximately nine-tenths of all vessels trading up and down the Pacific Coast passing inside the islands of the Santa Barbara Channel, the American Association of Masters, Mates and Pilots petitioned for a proper fog sound signal on Anacapa. What turned out to be the last major light station built on the West Coast was constructed in late 1920s on Anacapa Island. A thirty-nine foot cylindrical tower and a fog signal were built near the highest point on the eastern end of the island, along with four Spanish-style, white stucco houses with red tile roofs to accommodate the keepers and their families. The Fresnel lens light was manufactured in England by Chance Brothers and first displayed on March 25, 1932.

In 1962, it was decided to convert the Coast Guard's Anacapa Island Station to unattended operation and to remove all lighthouse personnel from the island. The change was prompted by planned missile test firings from Point Mugu that would have required the island's residents to spend several hours each week in a shelter. In 1970, a cooperative agreement was signed between the US Coast Guard and the US National Park Service, which gave the Coast Guard responsibility for maintaining and operating the light and fog signal, while the National Park Service would maintain all other island buildings.

Today, Anacapa Island is a major attraction for sightseers, fishermen, nature lovers, and sport divers.

TALES FROM CHARTS

While trying to get organized, I came across an old chart of the Santa Barbara waterfront that I had forgotten I had. It was dated 1870 and reveals interesting comparisons with today.

Stearns Wharf's predecessor pier shows at the foot of Chapala Street. Constructed in 1868, it was only about one-third the length of Stearns Wharf. But the pier was not long enough to reach water deep enough for large vessels; so much cargo had to be off-loaded onto small boats. In the case of most of the lumber used to construct the beginnings of our town, it was lowered into the ocean and floated ashore, through the surf. No railroad spur to Stearns Wharf is shown on the chart. This is not too surprising, inasmuch as the first train arrived at Santa Barbara August 18, 1887 – 17 years after my chart was drawn. The railroad spur to the Wharf was constructed in August of 1888, to permit transport of freight from the anchored ships to the city's main train tracks and reverse. Today, the Sea Center is located on the remaining short section of the spur, and you can easily envision it extending to the shore.

A surprise to me was where the 1870 chart locates a planned breakwater for Santa Barbara's harbor. It is the same length as our present breakwater, but located almost a half-mile to the east. The designer probably intended that the new breakwater provide protection of Stearns Wharf from our severe south-east winter storms. Where finally built, the present breakwater does not offer such protection. Another surprise was that the chart shows the planned breakwater a half-mile farther to seaward that where it was finally built in 1928. The more seaward location would have made sense to the 1870 designer, and for good reason. At that time, most boats sheltered at Santa Barbara were sailing vessels, and many were sluggish commercial freighters. Santa Barbara's most serious weather usually comes from the southeast, with high winds and waves capable of driving moored vessels onto the beach. In the late 1800's vintage sailing craft needed substantial sea room to raise sails, up-anchor, and slowly gain speed to claw their course to sea and away from the dangerous booming surf. That is why the designer placed the planned breakwater twice as far to sea than where it was eventually constructed.

Neither my old chart nor the final construction of our breakwater took adequate consideration of the continual movement of sand along our coastline. Today's Leadbetter Beach did not even exist until the breakwater was constructed in 1928. Its rock structure interrupted normal ocean currents such that sand began dropping to the ocean bottom. This sand build-up has caused problems and many millions of dollars of dredging costs that continue to this day. In addition, large quantities of sand were passing through the spaces between the breakwater's giant rocks, and a major project had to be enacted to fill as many of the spaces as possible with concrete. As sand reached the eastern end of the breakwater, the ocean current slowed, creating a major sandbar that required frequent dredging at very substantial cost. With the recent increased demand for mooring space in the harbor, the city decided to give up fighting the relentless formation of the sandbar and convert it into an extension of the breakwater. Large rocks were placed on the sandbar in a line running toward Stearns Wharf to provide increased south-east storm protection. Still, substantial dredging is a continuing process that will have to go on forever unless there is a major redesign of the harbor.

My 1870 chart shows many changes to the waterfront over the past 139 years. It also shows many inland transformations as well. For example, the street plan of Santa Barbara is fractional in comparison with today. A "ruined village" is shown next to the Old Mission. The present Bird Refuge is labeled *Las Salinas*, which may indicate that it may have had a higher degree of salt content in 1870 than today. Present day Salinas Street did not exist at that time.

No one knows when the first nautical chart was drawn. Most probably, it was preceded by word-to-mouth communications, then notes in journals, then sketches, and finally progression to the paper and electronic charts we use today. A nautical chart depicts the nature and shape of the coast, water depths, general topography of the ocean floor, locations of navigational danger, the rise and fall of tides, and locations of human-made aids to navigation. Nautical charts are among the most fundamental tools available to mariners, who use them to plan their voyages and to navigate ships using the shortest, safest, and most economical route. The U.S. National Oceanographic and Atmospheric Administration (NOAA) and its predecessor agencies have been producing nautical charts for over 200 years, and NOAA's Office of Coast Survey continually updates its inventory of thousands of charts.

But I like the old ones. I have a chart dated 1853 that covers the coastline from San Francisco to San Diego. It has 17 fine drawings of various landmarks along the coast to assist the navigator in determining his position. Detailed text discusses some "hidden dangers" and informs that there were only three "true harbors" between San Francisco and San Diego – the southwest side of Catalina Island (now named the Isthmus), Cuylers Harbor on San Miguel Island, and Monterey Bay. Santa Barbara is represented as an "open roadstead and not safe during the winter, but entirely so during the summer.

SEEING EYE

Closing a pretty big but complicated deal involved selling a sixty-foot sailboat in Canada for cash plus the trade-in of a fifty-three foot sloop from Santa Barbara. The Canadian seller had come down to inspect and test the Santa Barbara sloop, and the two of us were motor sailing it to Ventura Harbor to have it hauled-out at a boatyard for below-waterline inspection – a fairly routine cruise – until Mother Nature stepped in.

We had started out early in the morning to try to complete the inspection and get back to Santa Barbara the same day. Both the buyer and I were experienced sailors and navigators, so we weren't concerned when fog started filling in. But it soon elevated to the "pea soup" category, and we were soon relying heavily on the yacht's compass and radar.

Radar works fine if you understand what you are seeing on the screen. Electronic signals are transmitted outward and then bounce back to the antenna when they encounter a solid object. These reflections show up as an image on the radar screen. The object can be a buoy, a wharf, a hill, another boat – anything that provides a good reflective surface. But the radar picture does not show what lies behind the object or what its shape and dimensions are if they extend away from you. For example, assume the radar detects a long railroad train that is heading exactly towards you. You would see only the profile of the front of the train and have no idea if there were any other cars behind the engine.

It is a good idea to practice with your radar in clear daylight weather so you can learn how various objects appear on the radar screen. For example, study what the Mesa looks like from down the coast. From that angle it looks very different than the profile you see when returning from the islands. It is also good to practice identifying the navigation buoys that direct you in and out of the harbor. Such practice will make you better able to find your way into the harbor on a dark night, in a heavy rainstorm, or in thick fog,

On our trip to the Ventura boat yard, I studied the chart to see what objects we needed to avoid. First, we had to clear seven off-shore oil rigs and their adjacent buoys. An oil platform comes under the heading of "immovable object," and a collision would result in the end of our trip and perhaps us. Clearing points of land along the coast and other major in-water obstacles would not a problem with the aid of radar. The crunch would come when we approached the entrance to Ventura Harbor. I had entered the harbor many times, but that knowledge made me even more careful. With almost zero visibility, we first had to find the marker buoy about 100 yards directly off the harbor entrance. Then, we would have to make a sharp left turn towards shore and try to find a much smaller buoy located very close to the breakwater's rocks and pounding surf.

Ventura Harbor's entrance is not like the front door to a house that you can drive directly into. It consists of two parallel rock jetties that extend from shore straight out to sea. To protect this harbor entrance from severe weather, a long rock breakwater was built to seaward of the jetties like the top of the letter "T". We needed to find the small buoy next to the end of the "T", go a few yards further, and then make a hard left turn to enter the water between the two jetties and the "T" breakwater. Then, a right turn to enter the harbor between the two jetties. It sounds easy, but if we made a mistake, we would quickly run aground in the pounding surf that hits the beaches on each side of the jetties.

We began maneuvering very slowly, searching for the buoy that is to seaward of the south end of the rocky "T". I felt we were on a good heading, but we had no visibility and were in great danger of running ashore if we missed our turn at the buoy. Seconds passed as I stared at the radar screen. The image showed us about to run into the buoy, but we still couldn't see it through the fog. We slowed the yacht almost to a halt, and just drifted forward as our tension increased. Suddenly, the white buoy emerged from the fog, almost close enough to touch. Step one was a success, but we had two more to go.

We brought the boat to a full stop, and searched the radar screen for the small buoy that marked the end of the breakwater's "T". The radar found it and we began moving carefully towards shore. Missing this next buoy would put us on the beach, so all our attention focused into the murky view ahead. The tension fell when the small buoy ghosted out of the thick fog. We were now almost home. Powering a few yards closer to shore, we could just see the swells breaking against the end of the "T." Then a hard left and we were suddenly and thankfully moving in the quiet and protected waters behind the breakwater.

It was still foggy when we reached the boatyard where a travel lift raised the sloop out of the water for hull inspection. Later, as we were eating a lunch of fish and chips, the sun finally burst through the rapidly diminishing fog. We would soon be able to head back to Santa Barbara with clear afternoon visibility.

The Canadian had never been to Ventura Harbor before, and as we headed out between the two jetties with their "T" protection, he suddenly looked very uncomfortable. For the first time, he was able to see where we had made our tight maneuvers as well as the treacherous rocks that could have caused the end of the sloop. I would never have tried to enter the harbor in such conditions without radar. With almost zero visibility, it would have been a foolhardy risk. Using a global positioning system (GPS) may have worked, but I don't think GPS accuracy is sufficient to risk all in such a dense fog. It is far better to delay a trip or change destination when encountering severe weather or visibility conditions. But sometimes that is not possible, so it is essential to seriously practice using radar in good weather in order to be prepared for the bad.

STRANGE ARTIFACT

Archeology is a fascinating subject. Scientists have discovered remnants from the past that allowed them to piece together a wealth of information about the lives and times of our distant past. But I know of a modern artifact that may mystify the archeologists of the future.

It was deposited in the depths of our channel in the early 1960's, and has never been viewed since. At that time, I was working in General Motor's Sea Operations Department at Goleta. One day, I was called into the boss's office and told to report to the airport, board a small plane, and operate as a spotter. There had been a serious accident, and all resources were being mobilized to try to locate survivors of a sinking in the channel.

Earlier that day, a cement truck had been loaded onto General Motor's World War II landing craft *Retriever*. The truck had a full load of concrete that was being taken to Santa Cruz Island for construction work at GM's underwater acoustic tracking range on the back side of the island. The plan was to ship the truck across the channel on *Retriever*, land it at Prisoners Harbor, and then drive it across the island to Valley Anchorage. A GM employee was captaining *Retriever*, and the cement truck was being driven and operated by an employee of the concrete company.

Retriever departed from Santa Barbara Harbor and all was fine until seas started building up in mid-channel. The landing craft was not riding well, so the captain decided to relocate the cement truck for better balance. That was a fateful decision. *Retriever* stopped and rolled in the building swells while the two crew members began their relocation task. The truck's mixing drum was slowly rotating to keep the cement pliable. The plan was to start the truck's engine, detach the chain binders attaching the truck to *Retriever's* inner deck, drive the truck aft to a better balance point, reattach the chain binders, shut off the engine, and then continue back on-course to the island.

The driver was in the truck's cab with the engine running as the captain released the chain binders. The truck had just begun to move when disaster struck. Increasing waves suddenly shifted the truck, and the whole rig began falling to one side. In moments, *Retriever* began capsizing and the truck fell into the ocean. The driver had no time to get out of the cab. *Retriever* remained afloat, and the captain radioed a "Mayday" distress call for help. I spent the whole day in the plane searching the sea for the truck driver through binoculars, but to no avail. Boats below did the same, but all without result. The search was finally cancelled.

Now almost fifty years later, the cement truck remains under about 1000 feet of water in mid Santa Barbara Channel – far too deep for practical access or recovery. Someday the truck may be rediscovered by a sophisticated underwater vehicle. Cement trucks may then be known only from history books. But the real question might be, How did it get there? How could an ancient cement truck find its way to the bottom of the ocean ten miles from shore? Future archeologists may come up with some very interesting and perhaps bizarre theories.

TRADITIONS OF THE SEA

Mankind has operated on the lakes and seas of the world for thousands of years. In doing so, various procedures and traditions were created – many of which survive to this day, some essential to the survival of ships at sea. Tradition is particularly important to the British Admiralty and their ships at sea. Our country adopted many of these as well as others that are now an integral part of our country's commercial and recreational maritime activities. Here are some of the more interesting traditions and terms, many still in use today.

TOASTS – Spoken each day as the "sun drops below the yardarm," and time for a tot of whiskey at sea (US Navy ships have moderate rules on alcohol consumption based on ensuring that the force stays combat ready.)

- Monday – Our ships at sea.
- Tuesday – Our Men
- Wednesday – Ourselves (as no one else is likely to concern themselves with our welfare).
- Thursday – A bloody war and quick promotion.
- Friday – A willing soul and sea room.
- Saturday – Sweethearts and wives, may they never meet.
- Sunday – Absent friends and those at sea.

Port And Starboard – The Norse used a single steering oar on the right or *steer board* side of their vessels. It was found awkward to put a vessel alongside a dock on the opposite side of this oar, so a plank was put across from the dock to the ship. This plank was called a *ladeboard* and later *larboard*. But there was much confusion over the use of the terms *larboard* and *starboard*. Relief came when the French, with their high ships' sides, devised a shortcut for handling cargo. They cut loading doors called *ports* in the sides of their ships. To mariners this became the *portside*. So "starboard" is the right and "port" is the left.

Limey – Captain Cook, on his second world voyage on H.M.S. Resolution (1772-1775), lost only one man to the disease of scurvy. In a document to the Admiralty, he attributed his good fortune to his crew's consumption of lime juice. This resulted in their adoption for general use in British ships, whose sailors are often referred to as *Limeys*.

Admiral – The prefix *vice* with *admiral* means *in place of*, and therefore is a lower rank than an admiral. At one time, it was considered most important to protect the head and rear of a fleet of ships, usually with two squadrons known as the *vanguard* and the *rearguard*. The admiral commanding the rearguard was *the admiral of the rear* or *rear-admiral*. The *admiral of the van* was next in seniority to the *admiral* and bore the rank of *vice-admiral*.

Punishment – (no longer in effect) The punishment for sleeping on watch, a very serious offence because it endangered the ship, was at first humiliating and then for repeated offences – brutal. A bucket of sea-water was poured over the head of a first offender. If a second time, the offender's hands were tied over his head and a bucket of water was poured down each sleeve. For a third offence, the man was tied to the mast with heavy gun chambers secured to his arms, and the captain could then order as much additional pain to be inflicted as he wished. The fourth offence was inevitably fatal; the offender was slung in a covered basket hung below the ship's bowsprit. Within this prison, he had a loaf of bread, a mug of ale and a sharp knife. An armed sentry ensured that he did not return aboard if he managed to escape from the basket. Two alternatives remained – starve to death or cut himself adrift to drown in the sea.

Wind – Being the primary means of propulsion of vessels for thousands of years, wind has always been a sailor's obsession. I once sailed on a long voyage where one of the crew was an ancient Latvian who has spent almost all his life at sea. Our 96-foot ketch had been becalmed for several days well over a thousand miles offshore. Each day, the Latvian ritually scratched the tall mainmast with his fingers, confident that it would bring wind. Then wind came, and he remained convinced. The phrase "whistle up a wind" comes from the sailors' superstition that a wind could be raised by whistling for it. But the meaning has long since been reversed on-shore, so today "whistling up a wind" means doing something that will produce nothing.

Dressing Down – Thin or worn sails were often treated with oil or wax to renew their effectiveness. This was called "dressing down." If an officer or sailor was reprimanded or scolded, he was said to have "received a dressing down."

She – Some objects are regarded as masculine. The sun, winter, and death are often personified in this way. Others are regarded as feminine, especially those things that are dear to us. The earth as Mother Earth is regarded as the common maternal parent of all life. In languages that use gender for common nouns, boats, ships, and other vehicles almost invariably use a feminine form. Likewise, early seafarers spoke of their ships in the feminine gender "she" to indicate the close dependence they had on their ships for life and sustenance.

Who Shines The Ship's Bell – An old Navy tradition has it that the ship's cook shines the ship's bell and the ship's bugler shines the ship's whistle. This tradition is still being observed on some of the ships of the modern Navy; however, in normal practice, the ship's bell is maintained by a man of the ship's division charged with the upkeep of that part of the ship where the bell is located.

Anchors Away – "Anchors Aweigh" was written in 1906 as a march for the US Naval Academy Class of 1907. The music was composed by Lt. Charles A. Zimmerman, bandmaster of the Naval Academy, and the lyrics were written by Midshipman Alfred H. Miles. "Anchors Aweigh" was first performed at the Army-Navy football game in Philadelphia in 1906 (Navy beat Army 10-0).

USS STOCKDALE

Santa Barbara has had strong ties with the sea and the United States Navy over many years. Our city has hosted many ships, including the massive aircraft carrier USS Ronald Reagan (CVN 76) which was officially "adopted" in June 2000 by the Santa Barbara Chapter of the United States Navy League.

The Santa Barbara Navy League recently sponsored the commissioning of the Navy's newest ship, the USS Stockdale DDG-106, an Arleigh Burke-class guided missile destroyer. The dramatic story the new ship's namesake, Admiral James Bond Stockdale, shows him to be one of our country's greatest military heroes and one who set an example few can approach.

James Stockdale was born on December 23, 1923 in Abingon, Illinois. He graduated from the Naval Academy in 1946, and attended flight training in Pensacola, Florida. In 1954 Admiral Stockdale was accepted to the Navy Test Pilot School where he quickly became a standout and served as an instructor for a brief time. He was the first pilot to amass more than one thousand hours flying the F-8U Crusader, then the navy's hottest fighter, and by the early 1960s he was at the very pinnacle of his profession as he took command of a navy fighter squadron.

In August 1964, Stockdale played a key role in the Gulf of Tonkin incident, which led the Johnson administration to initiate large-scale military action in Vietnam. Stockdale always maintained that he had not seen enemy vessels during the incident, but the next morning the

39 year old pilot was ordered to lead the first raid of the war against North Vietnam.

On September 9, 1965, at the age of 40, Stockdale, who had been promoted to Carrier Air Group Commander (CAG) was catapulted from the deck of the USS Oriskany for what would be his final mission. While returning from the target area, his A-4 Skyhawk was hit by anti-aircraft fire and Stockdale ejected, breaking a bone in his back. Landing in a small village, he badly dislocated his knee, which subsequently went untreated and eventually left him with a fused knee joint and a very distinctive gait.

Stockdale was imprisoned in Hoa Lo Prison, the infamous "Hanoi Hilton," where he spent the next seven and a half years as the highest-ranking naval officer and leader of American resistance against Vietnamese attempts to use prisoners for propaganda purposes. Despite being kept in solitary confinement for four years, in leg irons for two years, physically tortured more than 15 times, denied medical care, and malnourished, Stockdale organized a system of communication and developed a comprehensive set of rules governing prisoner behavior. These rules gave prisoners a sense of hope and empowerment, which many credited with their ability to endure the lengthy ordeal.

The climax of the struggle of wills between American POWs and their captors came in the spring of 1969. Told he was to be taken "downtown" and paraded in front of foreign journalists, Stockdale slashed his scalp with a razor and beat himself in the face with a wooden stool, knowing that his captors would not display a prisoner who was disfigured.

Later, after discovering that some prisoners had died during torture, he slashed his wrists to demonstrate to his captors that he preferred death to submission. This act so convinced the Vietnamese of his determination to die rather than cooperate that they ceased their torture of American prisoners and gradually improved their treatment of POWs. Released from prison in 1973, Stockdale's extraordinary heroism became widely known, and in 1976 he was awarded our nation's highest military honor, the Medal of Honor, by President Gerald Ford.

Stockdale is one of the most highly decorated officers in the history of the Navy, wearing twenty-six personal combat decorations, including two Distinguished Flying Crosses, three Distinguished Service Medals, two Purple Hearts, and four Silver Star medals in addition to the Medal of Honor. He is the only three-star admiral in the history of the Navy to wear both aviator wings and the Medal of Honor.

When asked what experiences he thought were essential to his survival and ultimate success in the prison, Admiral Stockdale referred to events early in his life – his childhood experiences in his mother's local drama productions which encouraged spontaneity, humor, and theatrical timing; the lessons of how to endure physical pain as a football player in high school and college; and his determination to live up to the promise he made to his father upon entering the Naval Academy – that he would be the best midshipmen he could be. Stockdale believed it was the uniquely American ability to improvise in tight situations that gave him the confidence that the US POWs could outwit their captors and return home with honor.

Stockdale retired from the Navy in 1978 after serving as president of the Naval War College. He then embarked on a distinguished academic career as a senior research fellow at the Hoover Institute of War. He wrote twelve books and numerous articles, and was awarded eleven honorary doctoral degrees. He lectured extensively on those character traits which serve one best when faced with adversity. The Secretary of the Navy established the Vice Admiral Stockdale Award for Inspirational Leadership that is presented annually in both the Pacific and Atlantic fleets. Admiral Stockdale was a member of the Navy's Carrier Hall of Fame, The Aviation Hall of Fame, and was an honorary fellow in the Society of Experimental Test Pilots. On August 30, 2007, the newly built main gate at Naval Air Station North Island in Coronado, California, was inaugurated and named after Vice Admiral James Stockdale. The headquarters building for the Pacific Fleet's Survival, Evasion, Resistance and Escape operation was also named in his honor, and in July 2008, a statue of him was erected at the Southeast entrance of Luce Hall at the US Naval Academy, which also houses the Vice Admiral James B. Stockdale Center for Ethical Leadership.

Gone but not forgotten, Vice Admiral Stockdale died at the age of 81. His namesake ship aptly has the motto "Return With Honor."

His memory will be preserved by one of the United States Navy's latest warships, 509-foot USS Stockdale DDG-106, a fast (over 30 knots) surface warship with multi-mission offensive and defensive capabilities that can operate independently or as part of carrier battle groups, surface action groups, amphibious ready groups, and underway replenishment groups.

The commissioning ceremony of the USS Stockdale took place at Naval Base Ventura County (NBVC) Port Hueneme in 2009, where many national leaders participated in honoring the Stockdale family, crew and legacy, as well as more than one hundred surviving POWs and Medal of Honor recipients.

The Santa Barbara Council of the Navy League of the United States continues to raise funds to support the USS Stockdale and the men and women who serve aboard her through a USS Stockdale Foundation to support morale, welfare and recreation programs for the crew, meet crew-member emergency needs, and to help finance scholarships for the children of crew members.

MY KINGDOM FOR A LEMON

For thousands of years, countless sailors were ravaged by the horrors of the dreaded disease, scurvy. Scurvy not only caused incalculable deaths at sea, but it has also devastated populations on land. It is now known to be caused by a lack of Vitamin C, but for centuries it was incorrectly attributed to other causes. Scurvy was probably first observed as a disease by Greek physician Hippocrates in the fourth century BC. Thirteenth century Crusaders frequently suffered from scurvy, as did soldiers in World War I. It occurs at some remote locations today where it is not yet understood.

It took many centuries for the true cause of scurvy to be discovered. The British civilian medical profession of 1614 knew that it was the acidic content of citrus fruit which was lacking, but they incorrectly concluded that any acid would work when ascorbic acid (Vitamin C) was unavailable. In 1614 John Woodall published *The Surgeon's Mate* as a handbook for apprentice surgeons aboard East India Company ships. In it, he incorrectly described scurvy as resulting from a dietary deficiency. His recommendation for its cure was fresh food or, if not available, oranges, lemons, limes and tamarinds, or as an incredible last resort, Oil of Vitriol (sulfuric acid).

In 1734, physician Johann Bachstrom published a book on scurvy in which he stated that "scurvy is solely owing to a total abstinence from fresh vegetable food, and greens, which is alone the primary cause of the disease." He therefore urged the use of fresh fruit and vegetables as a cure. In 1740, to cut down on its foulness, citrus juice (usually lemon or lime juice) was added to the recipe of a ship's traditional daily ration of watered-down rum, known as "grog." These sailors were healthier than the rest of the navy, due to unknowingly receiving daily doses of vitamin C. In 1747, James Lind conclusively proved that scurvy could be treated and prevented by supplementing the diet with citrus fruit such as limes or lemons. But still, the actual cause was unknown.

Captain James Cook sailed around the world from 1768 to 1771 in HM Bark Endeavour without losing a single man to scurvy. But his suggested methods, including a diet of sauerkraut and wort of malt, were of limited value. Sauerkraut was the only vegetable food that retained a reasonable amount of ascorbic acid in a pickled state, but it was boiled for preservation, and much of its Vitamin C content was lost. It was impractical to preserve citrus fruit for long sea voyages, so Cook's success against scurvy was due more to his regime of shipboard cleanliness and frequent replenishing of fresh food than from Vitamin C. Probably most important was Cook's disallowing the common practice of the crew eating fat scrubbed from the ship's copper pans, which reduced their ability to absorb Vitamin C.

British sailors continued to suffer from scurvy throughout the American Revolution. Then scurvy was substantially reduced during the Napoleonic Wars when the long-ignored prescription of fresh lemons was finally put to use. Other navies soon adopted this successful remedy, but the cause of scurvy was still not correctly known.

Entering the 1900's, it was still widely believed that scurvy was prevented by good hygiene, regular exercise, and crew morale rather than diet, so ships continued to be plagued by the disease. But at the same time, fresh meat was a used as a preventative for scurvy by civilian whalers and arctic explorers. When Robert Falcon Scott made his two expeditions to the Antarctic, he believed that scurvy was caused by "tainted" canned food. Arctic explorer Vilhjalmur Stefansson, who lived among the Eskimos, proved that the all-meat diet they consumed did not lead to vitamin deficiencies. He later participated in a study in New York's Bellevue Hospital in 1935, where he and a companion ate nothing but meat for a year and remained in good health. Shackleton's arctic expedition which relied heavily on native animal food products was also free of scurvy, but his Ross Sea party lost three men, all suffering from scurvy. Finally, in 1932, the connection between vitamin C and scurvy was established by American researcher Charles Glen King of the University of Pittsburgh.

Today, scurvy is now well-known to be caused by the lack of vitamin C. Scurvy is rarely found in modern western society adults, although infants and elderly people are sometimes affected. Vitamin C is destroyed by the process of pasteurization, so babies fed with ordinary bottled milk sometimes suffer from scurvy if they are not provided with adequate vitamin supplements. Virtually all commercially available baby formulas contain added vitamin C for this reason. Human breast milk contains sufficient vitamin C, if the mother has an adequate intake. Scurvy is one of the accompanying diseases of malnutrition. Unfortunately, it is still widespread in areas of the world that depend on external food aid.

TO MAKE A FLYING MOOR

Very explicit instructions from an old navy manual ...

"Make all necessary preparations for coming to; overhaul and bitt a double range of the weather cable, and bitt the lee one at the range to which she is to be moored. When approaching the anchorage, reduce sail to topsails, jib, and spanker, if moderate, but if fresh, to jib and spanker only; when near the berth of the first anchor, luff-to, stream the buoy, and when headway has nearly ceased, let go the weather anchor, up helm, stand on and veer away roundly, to prevent the range from checking her; when the full range is nearly out, hard down the helm, down jib, clew up the topsails, out spanker, and let her lay the range out taut; when taut, let go the lee anchor, furl sails, bring-to on the weather cable, reeving away on the lee one, and heave into the moorings. Moor taut, to allow for veering; clap on service, and veer it; if hemp cable square the yards, stop in the rigging, and clear up the decks."

A WHALE OF A TOOTH

I enjoy maritime history, and along the way have collected some interesting items. One of my favorites is a scrimshaw whale's tooth. Scrimshaw is the name given to handiwork created by whalers made from the byproducts of harvesting marine mammals. It is most commonly made out of the bones and teeth of Sperm Whales, the baleen of other whales, and the tusks of walruses. It takes the form of elaborate carvings in the form of pictures and lettering on the surface of the bone or tooth, with the engravings highlighted using a pigment. The making of scrimshaw began on whaling ships between 1817 to 1824 on the Pacific Ocean, and survived until the ban on commercial whaling. Today, the practice survives as a hobby and as a trade for commercial artisans. A maker of scrimshaw is known as a scrimshander.

Scrimshanders were generally ordinary seamen who did their craft to while away the many hours of a typical three-year whaling voyage. Some would copy elaborate drawings from magazines of the day, and others would make original carvings from their imagination. I have collected examples of both. The artwork on one tooth was clearly copied from a professional drawing of the time. It shows a square rigged ship in the background with a longboat in the foreground being attacked by a whale. On the other side of the tooth is carved, "A stove boat of the ship Ann Alexander — 1851. I did some research and found the story in the November 29, 1851 issue of The London Illustrated News as well as Herman Melville's quotation after his hearing of the sinking, "Ye Gods! What a commentator is this Ann Alexander whale. What he has to say is short & pithy & very much to the point. I wonder if my evil art has raised this monster." Melville's classic Moby Dick had just been published and he worried that his book might have created a monster whale.

The New Bedford whaler *Ann Alexander* was cruising the offshore sperm whaling grounds in the Pacific on the 20th of August 1851. Whales were sighted and two boats sent out. About noon the mate's boat struck a large bull sperm whale and was off on a "Nantucket sleigh ride." Suddenly, the whale stopped, turned on the boat and "chawed it up." The other whale boat with the ship's captain John S. Deblois in charge came to the rescue and the men were taken back to the ship.

The men went out again to search for the stricken whale, and once again the mate's boat made a strike and was smashed up, requiring another rescue by the captain. Back on the ship, they headed for the whale which at last sounded and headed rapidly towards the ship. As it came near, the ship headed into the wind and let it pass. They crew tried to get another chance to strike, but it was too late in the day and the chase was given up for the time being.

The *Ann Alexander* was making about five knots in the late afternoon, and the captain was at the rail when suddenly he saw the whale rushing at the ship at about three times her speed. There was no time to take any avoiding action, and the whale struck the ship which shuddered as if it had hit a rock. The whale had hit abreast of the foremast about two feet above the keel and had knocked a great hole through the bottom. Water rushed in and anchors, cables and anything that might help keep her from sinking were thrown overboard.

Finally, the captain ordered all hands into the two remaining whale boats while he jumped from the sinking ship into the sea and swam to the nearer boat. The ship lay on her beam ends (on her side) with topgallant yards of her masts under water. They waited by her all night, and the next day the captain boarded her – none of his crew would take the risk – and cut away the masts. She then righted herself, and they were able to retrieve some supplies and set out for land in the whaleboats. Surprisingly, they were rescued the next day in the open Pacific by a passing whaling ship and all eventually returned to New Bedford.

Five months later, the crew of the whaler Rebecca Sims harpooned and killed the whale. He was old and diseased. In his head they found buried large wood splinters. And embedded in the blubber on one side they discovered the metal heads of two harpoons, both bearing he initials of the whaling ship *Ann Alexander*.

OIL ON THE BEACHES

The fortieth anniversary of Santa Barbara's famed 1969 oil spill brought back memories. The harbor was full of oil, and all boats had black sides as high as waves had splashed. The method of removal was a surprise. Dozens of rowboats spread across the harbor waters, each with two individuals literally blotting up oil the same as ink at your desk. But in this case the blotter was farm straw pitched into the oily water, recovered by a pitchfork, and dropped into the rowboat bottom.

By that time, I had a "real" job at an aerospace company in Goleta, but I also had the full use of a 59 foot sailing yacht in return for having it maintained and keeping an eye on it for its out of town owner. All the boat owners in the harbor put in claims to Union Oil for reimbursement for the cleaning of their boats — except one, the yacht I was "yachtsitting." It was owned by a successful wildcat oilman, and he elected to pay for the cleaning himself.

BRINGING HER HOME

In the summer of 1955, Fred and I arrived in Honolulu after an 8 1/2 hour propeller-driven flight from LA. As our taxi sped away at six in the morning, and we began hiking across open fields to Ala Wai Yacht Harbor to try to sign on to crew on one of the recently arrived Transpac racing yachts on the long sail back to California. Deciding to start at the top, we waited patiently alongside ninety-six foot ketch *Morning Star*, which had just won first to finish honors for the third time – this time in the roughest winds since competition began in 1906.

Captain Bob Washkite, *Morning Star's* solemn and serious professional, looked over our letters of introduction two hours later, while we nervously prayed for a berth on this, the best of all of the deep sea racers. His gruff "OK, find bunks in the forepeak" was poetry to two sea struck teenagers.

Then followed a week in paradise – surfing in front of Waikiki's then three hotels, followed by instant prestige as we casually spread beach towels with *Morning Star's* monogram carefully arranged for all to see. At night, we would take dates to the palatial Moana Hotel. By entering from the beach and being careful not to sit down, we danced at no cost. On the night before *Morning Star* was to set sail for California, we sneaked onto a darkened field to collect thirty pineapples for the voyage.

We waved to our week-long Hawaiian friends as *Morning Star* was slowly towed from the dock toward open sea. (Her giant propeller had been removed to reduce drag for the race, so we would have to sail every inch of the way home.) All of the crew of 13 were under age 20 except the skipper, the sharp tongued German cook Johnny Flatkin, and an old Latvian professional who had sailed most of the world's seas and looked as old as Moses. Two of the young crewmembers were from Hawaii, seeking their first adventure to the Mainland.

It took ten of us to hoist *Morning Star's* giant mainsail. Then she showed us why she was the queen of offshore racing as she buried her 96-foot lee rail and clawed to weather doing over 15 knots through massive Pacific rollers that had formed far to the north in the distant Aleutians.

The wind increased substantially that night, and several of the crew paid miserably for their fine living ashore as they hung to the yacht's stern rail while returning their well-cooked dinners to the sea. Later, half the crew were wedged into their bunks trying to simultaneously keep from being hurled out, to sleep, and to rid themselves of vile feelings in their stomachs. Suddenly, the ketch lurched violently, and then a shout, "All hands on deck!" Dark, solid seas crashed across the deck as we discovered the reason for the hail. The huge mainsail that had powered *Morning Star* 2600 miles to victory had exploded from luff to leach, and her giant boom swung with dangerous violence from rail to rail. It was almost dawn by the time we removed the seemingly acres of wet salt- stiffened canvas from the spar and were able to tie the wild boom in place. Welcome to offshore yachting!

For the next nine days, we sailed hard on the wind with genoa jib and mizzen sail at bow and stern with a vast open space where the mainsail should have been. It was a unique thrill to steer rail-down *Morning Star* as she plunged ahead doing14 knots with just jib and mizzen flying. Our ancient Latvian mariner patiently sewed for hours and then days, while promising to have the mainsail flying again before the California coastline came into sight.

The clockwise-rotating Pacific high pressure area continued to move towards Alaska, so we had to sail close-hauled over 1100 miles north and slightly west to try to pass above to get into the easterly winds that would allow us a course toward home. Finally turning east, we still sailed into the windless center of the high and sat dead in the water for two days. Our discarded garbage made better time than we did. It was eerie to dive from *Morning Star's* high deck deep into the silent sea knowing the bottom was more than four miles below. What was down there? Meanwhile, our aged and superstitious Latvian scratched the mainmast to raise a wind.

Mainsail finally repaired and bent on, the giant ketch was soon moving well as the easterly wind finally filled-in. Filled-in was an understatement. The wind soon exceeded 60 knots, and the seas were more like mountains than waves. *Morning Star* surfed down the combers, and only the helmsman could survive on deck by being lashed to the mizzenmast. The rest of the crew remained on-call in the sheltered "dog house." Seas washed over each helmsman as if he were standing in the surf on a beach. But what a thrill to wrestle the six foot wheel as the giant ketch began driving faster and faster toward the trough as though her needle bow would plunge straight down to Davy Jones' inhospitable locker. Just then, her massive hull would begin to vibrate and the ketch would lift up and surf at a speed of over twenty knots while half her hull was lost from sight in roaring wind and spray. We knew we were in a blow when we heard a merchant ship's distress call. She had broken in half a few miles from our wild sleigh ride.

Morning Star sailed on in what turned out to be a 3100 mile voyage. The weather stayed nasty, and the skipper was able to make only three celestial sextant sights to determine our location. Our stale dead reckoning calculations told us we were approaching the mainland, so we kept a nervous and vigilant lookout to sight land before our keel found it first. Point Conception north of Santa Barbara was our landfall goal. Usually rough and foggy, it is not an area to take casually. Finally, we saw a point of light and then sighted land through the damp grey overcast. After three weeks, we were nearly home!

With no propeller for the engine, we hadn't known how long the voyage would take, so the cook had us on two cups of water a day and tight rations to ensure enough food until we docked. With land now in sight, we raided the ship's locker and stuffed ourselves with unaccustomed food delights. I found a box of raisins and rushed a fist-full into my mouth. It was my last. When I looked down my hand was alive with maggots. Shades of ancient marinering.

The wind lightened and the sun came out as we worked our way down the backside of Santa Barbara's Channel Islands. A few miles past Anacapa we became becalmed, so the Captain called out all hands to sand and varnish all of *Morning Star's* bright-work. In the '50's, a racer was still a yacht and it wasn't acceptable to tie up at LA in other than "Bristol" condition. A Navy plane flew over and radioed us to immediately leave the secret Pacific Missile Range. We replied that we would be happy to, but that the wind would not comply. They weren't amused.

Finally, after 21 days and many challenges, we set foot on land and reentered a world of hustle and bustle that for a few days seemed very strange.

Sea Terms-

- Ketch – Two masted sailing vessel with smaller mast aft of the stern waterline.
- Forepeak – Living or storage space in the bow of a sailing vessel.
- Luff – Front edge of a sail.
- Leach – Back edge of a sail.
- Spar – Any mast, boom, pole, on a boat.
- Genoa Jib – A very large jib (sail at the front of a sailing vessel).
- Mizzen Sail – A fore and aft (front to rear) sail hoisted on the back mast.
- Close Hauled – Sailing as close to the direction of the wind as possible.
- Sextant – A device that measures the angle between the horizon and the

sun, moon or specific stars to determine your position on earth.

- Bristol – In Bristol Condition is a vessel that is in perfect condition.

LEND A HAND

A freshening upper-twenties breeze was filling in as we pulled out from San Francisco's famous St. Francis Yacht Club to test sail a powerful 44-foot J Boat sloop. The sky was slate grey as a steep chop pushed against the outgoing tide. The cold penetrating wind cut its way through our light Southern California jackets.

We passed forbidding Alcatraz Island doing a good eleven knots on a run towards the Bay Bridge on our way to Alameda. The wind had shifted west, and a gybe to the port tack was in order. I began winching in the large mainsail in preparation for the maneuver. When all was ready, the helmsman swung the bow to port, a crewman grasped the slackening mainsheet and flung the boom across our stern. I was set to give a big ease of the mainsheet to help absorb the boom shock before trimming the mainsail for the new track. To handle the increasing wind speed, I put five turns on the winch to control the big mainsail as I did the ease.

The boom slammed across the stern, and instantly I was flying after it toward the new lee rail. My left hand had been lassoed by the flying mainsheet! My shoulder slammed against a stanchion as I was dragged over the lifeline toward the rushing water as the boom tried to pull me over the side and into the cold, churning bay. Twisting and pulling against over a ton of force, I had only a second or two before I would be in the water or, worse yet, being dragged behind the boat at eleven knots by my painfully extended arm.

I jerked free at the last moment and fell awkwardly backwards into the cockpit, sensing fierce pain and an awareness of torn flash and the cockpit seat covered in blood. "This is bad!" I cried, "Get me rags, fast!" Rebecca was quickly there and wrapped my hand to try to stop the bleeding. Dizziness began setting in as she helped me to a bunk below. Despite our eleven-knot sailing speed, Chuck fired up the engine for even more as we made a frantic run toward Alameda, the car, and a hospital.

Time seemed to stand still as blood continued to flow. An artery had clearly been cut. Rebecca frantically searched the unfamiliar boat for a first aid kit, but there was none on board. So it was more dirty rags and sail ties pulled tight to stem the bleeding.

After a seeming eternity, we reached the Oakland dock, and Chuck and Rebecca quickly tied up the large sloop. Then, a rush to the car, the hospital, paperwork, waiting, X-rays, waiting, consultation, waiting, stitches, waiting, and finally to the blissful peace of a hotel bed.

Three months later, the stitches were gone and I was in the midst of repeated physical therapy sessions with the goal to be able to pull a line and turn a winch handle again. In the meantime, it was one-handed computer typing, boat steering, and frustrating one-armed golf.

What had happened? Did I do a dumb thing? After weeks of pondering, I finally realized that it was a freak accident. As the boom slammed across the stern, the loose mainsheet flew across the cockpit and looped a hitch around my wrist like a cowboy's lasso, dragging me across the cockpit to the railing and almost into San Francisco's icy grey waters. Should I have done something different? No. It was a one in a million event. But, next time I will be sure to check for a first aid kit on any strange boat I'm on. And, I have boned up on my knowledge of first aid.

I hoped that my hand and wrist would someday get back to normal, but they haven't. Three bones in my wrist are still about twenty degrees out of line. The accident cost me five golf strokes and some other inconveniences, but it was well worth it that I didn't go into the Bay and lived to tell this story.

Sea Terms
- Gybe – Turning a sailboat with the wind behind sufficient to cause the wind to push on the opposite side of the sail. This requires the boom to cross the stern of the vessel to the opposite side.

- Boom – A pole attached to a mast that holds and stretches the bottom of a sail. (16th century)
- Mainsheet – A sheet is a line (rope) used to control a sail. The mainsheet controls the mainsail of a sailing boat. (from early Norse)
- Stanchion – One of several vertical supports for rails or lifelines. (from Anglo-Saxon period)
- Knot – When used as a measure of a boat's speed, it is a nautical mile per hour. A nautical mile is longer than the 5280 foot land mile we are most familiar with. A nautical mile is 1/60 of a degree of latitude which can vary from 6046 feet at the equator to 6092 feet at latitude 60 degrees. The origin of knot as a measure of boat speed was from the technique of tying knots in a line at measured intervals and then running it out from the stern of a ship and counting the number of knots passing when timed with a timeglass. The practice has been traced back to the 1400's, but probably occurred in some form much earlier.
- Sail Tie – A line to tie an unused sail in place. Also called gaskets and sail stops. (17th century)

SANTA BARBARA'S PIRATE

The subject of Somali pirates doing their evil deeds on the Indian Ocean is much in today's news. Here's the story of Santa Barbara's own seventeenth century pirate, Hippolyte de Bouchard.

Hippolyte de Bouchard was both a French and Argentine sailor who fought on varying sides for Argentina, Chile, and Peru. An accomplished mariner, he was the first Argentine to circumnavigate the world. During his first campaign as an Argentine corsair, he attacked the Spanish colonies of Chile and Peru. As an Argentine privateer, he occupied Monterey, California, and thus for a short time claimed a small portion of the future state of California. Sailing south, he raided Mission San Juan Capistrano. Toward the end of his voyage he attacked various Spanish ports in Central America. He is remembered as a hero and patriot in his second homeland of Central America, and several places are named in his honor.

Bouchard was born in Saint-Tropez around 1780. Initially, he worked in the French merchant fleet, and then served in the French Navy in their war against the English. After several campaigns in Egypt and Santo Domingo, young Bouchard became disillusioned with the way the French Revolution was going. He traveled to Argentina in 1809 to aid their May Revolution and became a part of the National Argentine Fleet. He was granted Argentine citizenship for his part in defending the City of Buenos Aires from a Spanish blockade and playing a key role in other battles. In 1815 Bouchard started a naval campaign under the command of Admiral William Brown wherein he attacked the fortress of El Callao and the Ecuadorian city of Guayaquil. On September 12,

1815 he was granted a corsair license to fight the Spanish aboard the French-built corvette *Halcon*.

Bouchard then decided to sail towards California to take advantage of the Spanish trade, but Spanish authorities learned of his intentions and Governor Pablo Vicente de Solá ordered all valuables taken away from Monterey and increased the gunpowder stock at all the military outposts. In November 1818, two Argentine ships were sighed off Monterey Bay and the Spanish governor ordered the cannon installations along the coastline and at the garrison to prepare for battle. Women, children, and men unfit to fight were sent to Soledad for safety.

Bouchard knew the bay very well because had already visited Monterey two times. Before dawn, he deployed 200 men to their small boats. 130 had guns and 70 had spears. They landed about four miles from the fort in a hidden creek. The fort posed very weak resistance, and after an hour of combat the Argentine flag was flying above it. The Argentines held the city for six days, stored their plunder, and then burned the fort, artillery headquarters, the governor's residence and the Spanish houses. The Creole population was not harmed.

At the end of November, Bouchard sailed from Monterey, passed Point Conception, and then anchored off of Refugio Canyon about twenty miles west of Santa Barbara where he and his troops went to the ranch of the Ortega family. Finding little resistance, the Argentines took food, killed cattle, and slit the throats of saddle horses in the corrals.

A small squadron of cavalry sent by José De la Guerra from the Santa Barbara Presidio waited quietly nearby until they had an opportunity to capture some stragglers. They arrested an officer and two sailors and brought them back to the Presidio in chains. Bouchard thought the men were lost and waited for them the whole day. Then he decided to go to Mission Santa Barbara, where the three men may have been taken as prisoners. Arriving at Santa Barbara, he saw that the town was heavily defended and decided an attack would be too dangerous, so he sent the Governor a message requesting a meeting. In reality, what Bouchard saw through his spyglass was the same small troop of cavalry that stopped and changed costume each time it passed behind a heavy clump of brush. This illusion made Bouchard think the garrison had many more troops than was the actual case. After the negotiation, the three captured men were returned to Bouchard's ship *Santa Rosa*.

On December 16, Bouchard's ships weighted anchor and headed for San Juan Capistrano. Upon arrival, he demanded food and ammunition from the Spanish garrison, but the Spanish officer in command refused, replying that he had enough gunpowder and cannonballs for a successful defense. Bouchard did not tolerate being threatened and sent one hundred men to take the town. After a short fight, the pirates pillaged valuables and burned Spanish houses. Then they then left for Vizcaíno Bay, where they repaired their two ships and rested. The California raids earned Bouchard the reputation as "California's only pirate," and he was thereafter often referred to as "Pirata Buchar" by California's Spanish population.

Next, Bouchard sailed to blockade San Blas in today's Mexico. During the blockade, a schooner was sighted and the pirate's two ships set to chase but failed to reach her. Bouchard's ships continued on to Acapulco, but found no significant ships to plunder and sailed on. Attacks were made in further down the west coast of the Americas with good success. Ransoms were collected, and captured ships were burned if negotiations for plunder failed. Bouchard's remaining career included a trial in Argentina from which he kept his ships but not his money, operations in Argentina, Peru, Columbia, and finally as part of Chilean Navy

When he finally retired, Bouchard decided to live on the properties that had been given to him by the Peruvian Government. He had lost contact with his family many years before, having lived with his wife only ten months before beginning his expedition around the world. He never learned of the birth of his daughter.

Throughout his career, Bouchard was known for his heated temper, a temper that led to incidents between him and his subordinates to whom he meted out terrible punishment whenever they disobeyed him. In retirement, he treated his field slaves as he had treated the sailors. Fed up of his punishments, one of his servants killed him on January 4, 1843.

In his adopted country of Argentina, Bouchard is revered as a patriot and several places are named in his honor. One of the warships used by Argentina in the Falklands War against the United Kingdom was briefly named *ARA Bouchard*. California memories differ.

Note: With the long passage of time and the scope and nature of Bouchard's activities, there are conflicting versions of his story.

DELIVERY

Some time ago, I was hired to take a 72-foot motor yacht to Ventura for a quick haul-out to have new prop nuts installed on the ends of her propeller shafts. I was very familiar with the yacht and had operated it many times in the past. But voyages are successful only when proper preparations are made in addition to constant surveillance during the passage, so I went aboard to check things out a few days before the trip.

First, I entered the engine room to inspect the two 1000 horse-powered Caterpillar diesel engines. Oil levels in engines and transmissions were correct, and a physical inspection showed no leaks or other problems. Next, I went to the lower helm station, switched on gages to check the condition of all twelve batteries aboard, and all had good readings. I then fired up both engines and let them warm up. Each engine has a digital control screen that indicate performance status. On a yacht this size, the information is overwhelming – coolant temperature, oil pressure, transmission pressure, transmission temperature, boost pressure, engine load, fuel consumption rate, battery voltage, engine speed, trip fuel consumed, trip engine hours, and engine idle hours. I scanned through them, and all were within acceptable limits. After shutting down the engines, I fired up the diesel generator to check its operation and output. The generator provides good insurance by creating electricity to charge the batteries and to get the engines started if battery power is too low.

With the propulsion systems checked out, the next concern was navigation. A full compliment of navigation electronics were located at both the lower and upper steering stations. Dual screens at each helm station could be programmed to show a variety of information. Various switch settings allowed the navigator to select any information desired and display it either as a single item or with as many as four windows on each screen. The most important readouts were global positioning system (GPS) vessel location, radar, chart plotter, and voice communications by long range single sideband radio (SSB) or very high frequency radio (VHF). I turned on all systems and verified their operation.

Then, a full inspection of the entire yacht inside and out, including electrical systems, bilge pumps, stowage, head (toilet) operation, fresh water systems and fuel supply. All were in good order.

Lastly, I laid out the planned course to Ventura Harbor on the GPS-chart plotter – heading 103 degrees and distance 22.7 nautical miles. I planned to run the engines at 1895 RPM's (revolutions per minute) which would create a speed of about 18 knots per hour. This would result in a passage of approximately an hour and a quarter. I needed a two person crew, and was pleased that two long-term friends and sailors said they would come. The plan was to pull away from the dock at 7 AM on the following Tuesday. The boatyard was expecting us between 8:30 and 9:00 at their haul-out dock. The advanced preparations had taken about two hours, but could have taken much longer if problems had been detected. I planned to monitor weather forecasts for the next few days.

The next Tuesday, I arrived at the yacht at 6:30 in the morning and went through a final checkout similar to that of a few days before. Then I fired up the engines, electrical systems, and navigation systems. I entered the 103 degrees course on the GPS chart plotter, and then listened to the most recent weather report on the VHF radio. A front was reported to be moving in with gale force winds (34 to 47 knots) predicted up-coast above and outside of San Miguel Island. These conditions could be expected to be substantially reduced on the inner coastline between Santa Barbara and Ventura, and should not be a problem for such a large and powerful yacht. Nonetheless, I took the forecast seriously and considered alternatives in case the conditions became too severe.

Charlie and Llew arrive about 6:50 AM, and we quickly let off lines and maneuvered the yacht away from the dock. To rotate the large vessel, I put one engine in forward idle and one in reverse. The rotation was made even tighter by the use of the bow thruster (a propeller mounted sideways in a tube in the bow of the yacht).

Pulling clear of Stearns Wharf and the breakwater, we encountered confused seas and significant chop. This verified the weather predicted for further west and out to sea, but the wind was low and the large yacht almost ignored the seas. With autopilot set for a course of 103 degrees, the chart plotter showing our progress on a line to Ventura, and all gages with good readings, we were on our way at 18 knots. Over time, the seas settled down and we enjoyed an event free passage. Hundreds of pelicans and far more seagulls seemed to be having a terrific day of fishing. Quite a change in population from the days when pelicans were endangered by DDT flowing down rivers and streams some years before. We passed the off-shore oil towers, and were soon off the city of Ventura heading for the navigation buoys at the harbor entrance. Our radar picked them up, confirming we were on a good course.

Arriving at Ventura Harbor's entrance, we paid close attention to the navigation buoys before entering the harbor. A hard left turn is required, and disaster if you wait too long. Even with radar aboard, I try to avoid night entries. I had recently entered in pea soup fog, and it was not fun. The Canadian boat buyer with me had turned white when he saw the entrance in clear weather as we returned to Santa Barbara the next day.

The boat yard's travel lift was waiting as we docked, and soon the stately yacht was rising out of the water supported by giant straps. I made arrangements with the yard office. Then Charlie, Llew and I took off to explore and have an early lunch while yard workers removed and replaced the prop nuts that held the yacht's two giant propellers on their shafts.

The yacht was ready to launch when we returned. As it settled in back in the water, I fired up the diesels and we were again on our way. The navigation was reversed to a 283 degree course heading, and shortly the oil rigs off Carpenteria came into view. We soon tied up at the yacht's Santa Barbara end tie slip, put things away, locked up, and washed her down with fresh water. A farewell beverage at the yacht club ended a long but enjoyable day. I was reminded of when I was about 18 and a wealthy yacht owner frequently said to me as I operated his sailing yacht , "Say Bob, I wonder what the poor people are doing today?" I was often tempted to reply, "They're running the yachts of rich people," but I never did.

"DEAD" RECKONING

As with aircraft pilots, boat skippers are vitally concerned with avoiding unscheduled landings - and for good reason. Off-shore ship sinkings are relatively rare when compared with the loss of vessels due to running aground. I recently read Justin Ruhge's book *Maritime Tragedies On the Santa Barbara Channel – A history of Shipwrecks In Fog and Storms from Point Sal to Point Mugu,* and added up ship groundings verses sinkings off-shore. Of a total of 146 ships lost between 1815 and 2000, only fourteen took place off-shore, of which only one was due to a World War II attack.

Santa Barbara's coastline has had more than its share of shipwrecks, but one area predominates. From Pt. Mugu to Gaviota there have been 34 wrecks. The Channel Islands have claimed 23, and 13 were lost on the stretch between Santa Barbara and Goleta. But 76 vessels met their doom along only 33 miles of coastline between Point Sal and Point Conception, which has been aptly named California's "Graveyard of the Pacific." But before you decide it is too dangerous to go to sea today, note that of 146 recorded losses, only 19 occurred between 1950 and 1980, and just four groundings and two collisions at sea since 1980. Today, with radar and global positioning systems, modern electronics have changed everything.

But in the past, when there was insufficient visibility to see landmarks or determine position from sextant sights of the sun, moon or stars, a captain had to use "dead reckoning" navigation to determine his approximate position. To navigate by dead reckoning, the navigator first marks his starting location on the chart. After each hour underway, he writes down his average compass heading and estimated speed. Since his boat is moving across a liquid (water) that is constantly affected by wind, tides and currents, he must estimate how far these forces have moved him off his planned course. He hopes his compass is accurate, but most are a few degrees off on some headings. All things considered, dead reckoning navigation is an educated guess, and some sailors are much better at it than others. Over the years, I learned to use every available tool in making a successful landfall using dead reckoning – the smell of the land, the color of the water, presence of birds, the shape of the waves, listening for identifiable sounds, and more. But it doesn't always work. Some years ago, a sea captain who ran aground in dense fog thought he had collided with San Miguel Island off Point Conception, but soon realized he was on the mainland when he heard a train whistle.

As a teenager, I was sent to Los Angeles to help a boat owner bring his 32-foot powerboat *Manana* to Santa Barbara. We were delayed driving from Santa Barbara, and thus departed San Pedro Harbor at the very end of the day – our first mistake. I should have insisted that we leave at dawn the next morning, but then ...I was just a teenager. The entire inventory of navigation equipment on-board *Manana* was only a compass and a chart. I knew enough to check the compass's accuracy by running *Manana* between two buoys and comparing its compass reading with what the chart said it should be. It was pretty close, so I felt I could use the plotted compass courses from the chart with a feeling of confidence. The second major element of dead reckoning navigation is knowing the speed you are traveling. I asked the boat owner, and he said *Manana* did nine knots at 2000 engine RPM's. Good. I knew the speed of the boat and had verified that its compass was fairly accurate. Next, I drew lines on the chart to show the various compass headings and distances required to navigate up the coast to Santa Barbara. I felt I was in good shape.

Off we went, but then things started to unravel. Thick fog set in, and I discovered that the boat owner didn't know how to steer an accurate course. At the wheel, he zigzaged all over. It looked like I would be steering all night without sleep. As we passed the harbor breakwater and entered open ocean, the wind picked up and *Manana* pitched into steepening waves. Our conservative compass heading was calculated to take us well off-shore to clear any obstacles and land masses. About 11

PM, I was startled to see a large piling loom out of the darkness. But we had to be several miles off-shore in water too deep for pilings! I assumed it must be floating and not driven into the sea bottom, but I began to get a bad feeling about things. Later, and completely exhausted, I asked the owner to steer so I could get just a few minutes of sleep. It was zigzags again, so back on the helm for me. A seeming eternity, and finally dawn filtered through the thick fog. My chart calculations showed that we should soon be approaching Santa Barbara Harbor, so I turned *Manana* towards shore, slowed her engine, and strained to see through the fog to find land and then home. Suddenly, a wall of white appeared just ahead – the surf line. I didn't know if I was just short or just past Santa Barbara, so I decided to run up-coast along the surf until I spotted a known landmark. We ran on for about fifteen minutes, and then the fog cleared just enough to identify . . . Carpenteria? That couldn't be! My dead reckoning navigation said we should have been miles further up the coast. Dumbfounded, I continued up coast, and then *Manana* finally and thankfully entered the protection of Santa Barbara Harbor.

But what had actually happened? Hindsight showed I had done the right thing making sure the compass was accurate; but I was wrong in accepting the boat owner's statement about the speed of his boat. He was way off. *Manana* could easily have been wrecked in the surf that night, and our lives possibly lost because of mistaken turns made in darkness and fog based on the owner's incorrect speed information. I don't know why we avoided disaster to this day. It was probably because I was over conservative in setting a route farther off-shore than usual. The boat's owner nonchalantly thanked me and happily departed for Los Angeles, completely unaware that his misinformation and my failure to double check it could very well have stowed us both neatly in "Davy Jones Locker." On the other hand, I took away lessons that would stead me well on future voyages, but hopefully not with this owner.

Sea Terms –

- Davy Jones Locker – The bottom of the sea. "Davy" is a legendary evil spirit of the sea. 17th Century.
- Pt. Sal to Pt. Conception – A rough stretch of coastline with severe wind and weather about 45 miles north of Santa Barbara.

- Dead reckoning – A procedure of navigation using speed, course, and drift data or estimates. The term is believed to be a corruption of "deduced reckoning". 18th Century

LANGUAGE OF THE SEA

The schooner's skipper took her head to wind while the crew heaved up the throat and followed with the peak halyard. Falls were attached to haul the last few inches as the skipper put helm down, and the classic schooner took off on a close reach with a bone in her teeth. Runners were eased, and the gaffed sails stayed protected from chafe by baggywrinkle on the shrouds. Further to weather, a sleek monohull clawed close-hauled as her muscular crew manned the coffee grinder to flatten the genoa to optimum shape. "Giver her an ease for a bit more twist," the skipper called, "and I need more beef on the rail. Call the steam gage."

When a landlubber gets on a boat, it is like visiting a strange country. Unfamiliar objects prevail, and the nautical vocabulary of skipper and crew sounds like a foreign language. There is evidence that the ancient Egyptian language contained nautical terms before 3500 BC – nearly 5500 years ago. With the major portion of our planet covered with water, logic would argue that humans must have communicated regarding nautical matters from almost the beginning of human language when boats were merely floating logs. As watercraft become a major source of transportation across the world for so many centuries, sailor's languages developed common terms that could be understood by mariners from many countries. Nautical terms and phrases became and remain today truly an international language.

New nautical terms continue being created to keep pace with growing marine technology. Where once wind and paddles propelled craft, today propellers and even jet propulsion move vessels across the seas. The availability of new space-age materials is resulting in even more changes.

Definitions of maritime terms and words are not as precise and consistent as those found in Webster's and other conventional dictionaries for more standard vocabulary. Sea terms are influenced by language, local pronunciation and geography. I have five terminology source books, and the definitions of identical words vary to a surprising extent.

Here are a few nautical terms and their historic derivation.

- Admiral – The highest ranking officer in most navies. Probably from the Arabic language around the year 1200.
- Bitter-End – The inboard (closest to the boat) end of a line. Captain John Smith was quoted in 1627, "the part of the cable that doth stay within board.." (By the way, the Bitter End is also a great place for food and beverage at the British Virgin Islands.)
- Boat – A general term for any small craft. Probably from Old Norse "beit" or "Bato" and appeared around the year 400.
- Baggywrinkle – Although it sounds like an ill-fitting pair of trousers, it appeared in the 1800's and means padding on a sailing ship's rigging to inhibit wear and chafe on the sails.
- Avast – As from "Avast you lubbers," spoken by many sea captains in pirate movies, "Avast" is a shipboard order to hold or stop hauling. The term appears to come from Old Dutch "bou'vest" from the 13th century, but could be related to the Portuguese word "abasta," meaning "enough" and could even go back to the Arabic centuries earlier.
- Navy – The first known "navy" was Assyrian around 700 BC, it described a fleet of ships with armed men aboard. Later, the term meant any gathering of ships, not necessarily armed (14th century); and yet later it came to mean armed ships (16th century). The derivation of the word is a bit vague, but it did come from Old French, "navie" (fleet – (800 – 1300 AD) and goes back to the Latin "navalis" for naval, perhaps as early as BC.

- Chart – A mariner's map. The term comes from the French "charte" and can be traced to Greek "khartes," and may be of Egyptian origin ((3500-1200 BC).

"KON TIKI"

Sixty-two years ago, the words Kon Tiki spread throughout the world and became a symbol of adventure and perseverance for young and old alike. But when I recently mentioned these magic words to several younger acquaintances I received only blank, unknowing stares.

On the April 27, 1947 a strange craft that was soon to play a major role in one of the great sea adventures of all time departed from Lima Peru. Archeologist Thor Heyerdahl along with five other Norwegians, one Swede, and a parrot were on their way to test Heyerdahl's not well accepted theory that the islands of the South Pacific were first settled by peoples from South America. Heyerdahl's reasoning was based on observations that some plants, trees, stone statues, pyramids and even legends found in South America resembled those he had seen on Easter Island as well as other Pacific islands. But Easter Island was 4,000 miles to the west of South America, and over 20,000 Pacific Islands lay thousands of miles further west. Could the islands have been settled by people who traveled on such an awkward means of transport as the raft Heyerdahl built and named Kon Tiki?

The design of Kon Tiki was similar to rafts built by the Conquistadores in South America during the 15th and 16th centuries. Constructed of balsa logs and lashed together with rope, the rafts were clumsy, slow moving and difficult to steer. To begin the project, Heyerdahl and his companions flew to the Ecuadorian capital of Quito which is at an elevation 9300 feet above sea level. There they cut down balsa trees for the base materials to construct the raft. After lashing the logs together they then rode them down the Palenque River to the sea where they were loaded onto a ship bound for Lima, Peru. At Lima, a 45 foot long central log was he central log of the raft was lashed to four shorter logs on each side creating an arrow shape. Then, smaller balsa logs were lashed crossways and overlaid with bamboo to form the deck. Finally, an eight foot by fourteen foot bamboo hut was constructed to provide limited shelter from the elements. A crude mast was constructed from two lengths of mangrove wood lashed together in the shape of an upside down "V". A simple rectangular sail that could be hoisted on a bamboo yard arm completed the rig.

The crude and clumsy raft didn't appear capable of crossing an ocean. At the last minute, the Peruvian navy, horrified by the ragged contraption, begged Heyerdahl to cancel the expedition. But he was unrepentant. "I knew all the time in my heart that a prehistoric civilization had been spread from Peru and across to the islands at a time when rafts like ours were the only vessels on the coast," he wrote. "and I drew the general conclusion that, if the balsa wood had floated and lashings held for Kon Tiki in A.D. 500, they would do the same for us now if we blindly made our raft an exact copy…"

On-board Kon Tiki at departure were food provisions for four months, a ham radio, and an inflatable dinghy with oars. Ahead lay open sea far from the safety of shipping routes. The raft was unproven, and the voyage ran against the mass opinion of scholars and sailors alike who believed that the raft would either become waterlogged or disintegrate long before it reached land. Most people thought the explorers were crazy. and most of today's sophisticated rescue tools did not exist in 1947.

The crew and raft were quickly put to the test when on the second day the worst storm of the entire voyage began building. Enormous waves soon engulfed the ungainly craft as two crewmen struggled with the steering oar in a vain attempt for control. Finally, after sixty hours of punishment the raft stalled with its bow pointing into the direction of the wind, and the exhausted crew were able to pull down the sail and ride out the storm. The ungainly craft's success was due to her great flexibility that allowed even the biggest seas to simply pass through her open structure "as through the prongs of a fork."

When the storm abated, Kon Tiki resumed her steady progress across the Pacific, logging a minimum of nine miles a day and once an impressive 71 mile run. The average for the entire crossing was 46.4 miles a day - just under two miles an hour.

The Humbolt Curent that carried them along also guaranteed that the explorers would never be hungry. Kon Tiki was always surrounded by plentiful sea life – bonito, flying fish, squid, tuna, pilot fish, sharks, and other tropical creatures. In addition to fishing with line and hooks, the crew devised a remarkable hands-on method of catching sharks by luring them close with bait, grabbing them by the tail as they passed by, and then dragging them on-board. On one particularly productive day, they captured nine sharks, two tuna, and several bonito. Heyerdahl observed, "To starve to death was impossible."

Finally, after ninety-three long and sometimes punishing days at sea, the weary crew sighted land. It was the island of Pukapuka, but the current pushed them too far north to make a landing. The same happened several times over next few days, until Kon Tiki was finally driven ashore on Raroia reef in the Tuamotu Islands, almost 550 miles from Tahiti.

After 101 arduous days at sea, Thor Heyerdahl and his exhausted crew had proven that man could successfully cross the Pacific by raft. The voyage attracted massive media interest and turned the bearded crew into celebrities. Hyerdahl's wrote *Kon Tike: Across The Pacific By Raft*, which was translated into sixty-five languages and sold over 20 million copies. His film of the voyage won the 1951 Oscar for best documentary.

But Heyerdahl's epic voyage failed to impress most archeologists who regarded his methods as "unscientific". Sixty years later, the question of how the South Pacific islands were settled was finally and decisively answered by a newer science. DNA studies showed that the migration to the Pacific islands began about 6000 years ago when humans first journeyed from China and Taiwan to the Philippines and New Zealand and then traveled onward to settle many of the thousands of South Pacific Islands. Some isolated colonists may have come from South America, but they did not impact the mainstream of settlement. Thor Heyerdahl is not remembered for his science, but rather as one of the world's great sea adventurers. Today, Kon Tiki can be seen at the Kon Tiki Museum at Oslo, Norway.

WHAT'S IN A NAME?

Boat names can reveal much about the personality, passion, or experiences of a boat owner. The Boat U.S. list of Top Ten List of Most Popular Boat Names is particularly revealing:

1. _Seas the Day_: While this boat owner may feel he has no control over his declining retirement account, he is completely in charge while boating and intends to get the most out of his boating lifestyle.

2. _Summer Daze_: A combination of warm weather and long days spent afloat on sunsplashed waterways may have put this boater into a dreamlike state.

3. _Second Chance:_ Perhaps this boat owner has had a life changing experience and feels his boat now gives him a second lease on life. "_Second Wind_" is the sailboat equivalent.

4. _Aqua-Holic:_ On the Top-Ten list for the last seven years, this boat name illustrates a boater's chronic love for the waterways.

5. _Wind Seeker:_ No doubt a true sailboat name for a wanderer or racer.

6. _Dream Weaver:_ Like the 1976 Gary Wright song that muses about an escape to dreamland, this boat owner may weave memories of good days spent on the water, sheltering them from the pressures of day-to-day life.

7. _Black Pearl_: The name of a fast, stealthy and intimidating fictional ship from the Disney _Pirates of the Caribbean_ films.

8. _Hydrotherapy:_ Takes into account the healing nature that boating provides this boat owner.

9. *The Salt Shaker:* If you know what a "Parrot head" is, you'll know what *The Salt Shaker* is for. On a Saturday night this boat and its owner could be the most popular in the marina.

10. *Sea Quest:* This boat owner likely grew up watching Jacques Cousteau TV specials and wants to explore the world with his boat.

The following names were voted by the editors of *Boat U.S. Magazine* to be the most humorous:

1. *What College Fund?* With three out of four boat-owning households making less than $100,000 a year, where else are you going to get the money?

2. *Stocks-N-Blonds:* Clearly someone still has a job on Wall Street.

3. *Anchor Management:* The calming effect that boating brings.

4. *Sweet Em-Ocean:* A floating love shack?

5. *Knotty Buoy:* The Johnnie Depp of boaters.

6. *Reel-e-Fish-ent:* Could teach Capt. Sig Hansen of the Discovery Channel series *Deadliest Catch* a thing or two about fishing.

7. *A-Frayed Knot:* Fearless in their ability to tie a bowline knot.

8. *O-Sea-D*: Obsessive, compulsive, and loving the ocean.

9. *A-Loan-Again:* Either cruising for a date or has purchased their boat on credit.

10. *Really Big Car:* Small boat complex?

Boat U.S. (Boat Owners Association of The United States) is the nation's leading advocate for recreational boaters, providing its 600,000 members with government representation, programs and money saving services.

WHAT'S IN A TOAST?

The term "toast" has its origin in sixteenth century England, where it was fashionable to add a small piece of toasted bread to drinks. The toast was a delicacy, somewhat like an olive in a martini. It thus became customary for the term "toast" to be applied to a drink, proposed in honor of a person during a meal, or at its conclusion. Although the bit of toast is no longer used, the term has survived to the present day.

Toasting is a means of expressing good will toward others on a social occasion. It may take place at receptions, dinners, wardrooms or wetting down parties.

Toasting first began with the English custom of flavoring wine with a piece of browned and spiced toast. In 1709 Sir Richard Steels wrote of a lady whose name was supposed to flavor a wine like spiced toast. Thus evolved the notion that the individual or institution honored with a toast would add flavor to the wine.

A Ship's Company today uses the past tradition to honor individuals or institutions by raising their glasses in a salute while expressing good wishes and drinking to that salute. Etiquette calls for all to participate in a toast. Even non-drinkers should at least raise the glass to their lips.

Those offering a toast should stand, raise the glass in a salute while uttering the expression of good will. Meanwhile, the individual(s) being toasted should remain seated, nod in acknowledgement, and refrain from drinking to one's own toast. Later, they may stand, thank the others, and offer a toast in return.

The one who initiates the toasting should be the host at a very formal occasion, or any guest when the occasion is very informal. The subject of the toast is always based upon the type of occasion. General toasts would be "To your health", or to "Success and happiness", while special occasions such as formal dinners ashore, captain's dinner aboard ship with a distinguished guest, and general wardroom gatherings would require toasts to be more specific in nature, such as "The Loyal Toast" or the traditional Wardroom toast of our period, both detailed below.

Life at sea on the old square riggers was long and lonely. Voyages from "civilization" to the distant reaches of the Western Pacific Ocean frequently exceeded three years in length. So a 'tot of rum as the sun set beneath the yardarm was an important time of the day, and the traditional toasts for each day brought nostalgic thoughts to those concerned. The Royal Navy of Great Britain memorialized the following after-dinner toasts to be spoken in the officers wardroom:

Monday – Our ships at sea

Tuesday – Our men.

Wednesday – Ourselves (for no one else is likely to concern themselves with our welfare).

Thursday – A bloody war and quick promotion.

Friday – A willing soul and sea room.

Saturday – Sweethearts and wives, may they never meet.

Sunday – Absent friends and those at sea.

But the standing toast that pleased the most was "The wind that blows, the ship that goes, and the lass that loved a sailor."

THE WRECK OF THE *YANKEE BLADE*

The steamer *Yankee Blade,* wrecked on the rocks in the desolate Point Conception-Point Arguello area approximately forty-five miles up the coast from Santa Barbara on September 30, 1854, is remembered as one of the Pacific Coast's classical tales of barratry (fraud on the part of a ship's officers or crew that results in loss to the ship's owners). Carrying gold bullion variously reported from more than $100,000 to nearly ten times that amount, the sailing ship was allegedly deliberately run ashore by criminals who had boarded her at San Francisco. The *Yankee Blade* had left San Francisco for the last time, in a race with the *Sonora* for a $5000 purse. It passed through the Golden Gate and headed south into the fog-covered Pacific and disaster.

The tragedy resulted in considerable loss of life. Survivors were rescued by the steamer *Goliah*, which landed them at San Diego first week of October. Among those rescued was C. F. Spearman, who later served as a major during the Civil War and then settled in Keosauqua, Iowa. His account of the wreck was recorded in the Pioneer Society files, and is of interest not only as a first-hand account, but because it differed considerably from previously published accounts of the reign of terror aboard the doomed vessel. The following accounts are from letters her wrote in reply to inquiries. (No corrections of form or spelling have been made, but some clarifications appear in brackets, and some punctuation has been inserted.)

"I was on the *Yankee Blade* when she was wrecked off the coast of Point Conception. About Sixty miles above Los Angeles About one mile from the Coast. It was about 12 o'clock. I was standing in my stateroom waiting for the dinner bell to ring when the ship struck the rock.

"I ran up on Deck and found out what had happened. I started back to my room for my satchel, but found I could not get to my room on account of the ship was filling with water. I went back on deck. There I found all the passengers (eleven hundred) crowded on the front part of the ship to keep out of the water. We were there from about 12 o'clock the first day until one the second day.

"About one o'clock during the night and day, the life boats were taking off the passengers. It was slow work for they [the passengers] had to go down the anchor chain. The sea between the ship and shore was full of breakers, so the life boats had to go quite a distance to get to the shore. The boats the women got into were overcome by breakers, and they were drowned. About one o'clock the second day we saw a ship anchor about one half mile away They sent their life boats to help us. We all got off by dark.

"It was a ship that ran from San Diego [the *Goliah*] to San Francisco. They took us to San Diego the third day. San Diego was a Mexican town. All the houses were of mud. It had a hotel that was run by an American. We had been three days without anything to eat except one cracker and a small piece of salt fish. There was a butcher shop where we landed. The boys soon cleaned it out. We went downtown and soon cleaned the town out of all they had to eat. Before night, the Mexicans in the country heard of us and brought in what they had to eat to feed us with. The next day we had an oversupply. Such as it was, we stayed there about ten days. Then when another ship came down from San Francisco and took us back to San Francisco. I was back to San Diego in 1910, fifty-four years afterwards. I went down to old San Diego. The mud houses were fallen down except two. The Hotel had been moved away. The town had been deserted. Five or six houses were all that was left and the post office. I still have my meal ticket that I had in my hand when the ship struck. Will send my Photo if this isn't satisfactory. Write and I'll try an answer any thing more." Major C. F. Spearman, Keosaukua, Iowa

In a subsequent letter, Major Spearman answered some questions. "The date of departure from San Francisco, Sept 28th 1854 I think. Think about 30 women on-board. All lost I understood. The cause of accident very foggy - struck a rock. There was not much wind. There was no looting or robbing of passengers to my knowledge. There was no investigation made, if so, didn't hear of it. Do not know the name of ship running from San Francisco to San Diego [the *Goliah*]. We landed at old town. Wharf was in good condition. The soldiers were at old town. There were many soldiers. The butcher shop was at old town. We remained in San Diego about 10 Days. All members left but one, as I remembered. I had no interview with any newspaper men in 1910."

The "San Diego Historical Society Quarterly" April 1959 published the following: "At 3:30 p.m., on October 1, 1854, the *Yankee Blade* struck a rock at Point Pedernales, which grounded the ship. Eye witness accounts attest to foggy conditions, stating the land was hardly visible. The sea between the grounded ship and the shore, which was less than a mile away, was rough. The Captain tried to reverse engines and back off the reef, but water was rushing in through a gash, one foot wide and thirty feet long. The ship was lost."

From the "Weekly Alta California," October 21, 1854: "Meeting of the *Yankee Blade's* Passengers on the Plaza: Yesterday afternoon a meeting of the shipwrecked passengers of the *Yankee Blade* took place on Portsmouth Square, for the purpose of adopting measures whereby their alleged wrongs could be redressed. 'Resolved, That after a careful investigation and by an unbiased judgment, we have come to the firm conclusion that sheer negligence upon the part of the managers of the *Yankee Blade*, in directing her course, and in running so near a coast well known to be dangerous, was the cause of the disastrous wreck."

The 30 or so passengers that died were either lost in the surf or buried in a common grave somewhere on the bluffs above Point Pedernales. No one has reported the location of this hasty grave. Captain Randall stood trial for his role in the disaster almost a year after the occurrence, and was acquitted of all charges by a panel of his peers. Though he undeniably later profited from the gold removed from the wreck, his reputation as a respected mariner was reinforced by his continued unblemished career at sea.

ANCHORING AT THE CHANNEL ISLANDS

One of the last refuges from the pressures and congestion of twentieth century America are Santa Barbara's Channel Islands. They remain almost untouched by commercialism, and although there are several commercial boats that visit the islands, some wish the flexibility and privacy of visiting the islands on a private boat. The twenty-two mile crossing frequently includes high winds and seas in the unprotected outer channel waters, and they create a significant challenge to reaching the rugged island paradise.

Another challenge after arrival is anchoring. There are no mooring cans or docks to tie up to. Many boaters miss the experience of visiting the Islands because they worry about successfully anchoring in one of the many beautiful but potentially treacherous coves. This is unfortunate, not only because they are missing inspiring scenery, hiking, fishing and diving, but also because they could learn to successfully anchor at the islands with reasonable preparation and understanding. Two elements are necessary for successful anchoring— proper equipment and proper technique. Combining both results in anchoring becoming a routine procedure rather than a frustrating and uncertain chore.

Equipment is of paramount importance. Because there are so many easy coves and anchorages throughout the United States, most boaters are able to get by with simple "lunch hook" anchoring by just dropping a small anchor without setting it properly. Many boaters are therefore under equipped for the serious anchoring required at our Channel Islands. The anchors and ground tackle provided by boat manufacturers are frequently undersized, and should be reassigned to become the stern rather than the bow anchoring system. The bow anchor should be much larger. Anchor, chain, and line sizing charts are available in catalogs, but they are generally one or two sizes too small for our Channel Island's challenging wind and wave conditions. The classic 7:1 scope assumed in anchor charts is unrealistic (anchor line to be 7 times longer than the water depth where anchoring). The limited space available in most Channel Islands coves does not allow for a ratio greater than 4 or 5 to 1. This is another reason for using substantially larger anchor and chain than the charts recommend.

Not all anchor designs have been successful at the Channel Islands. Short anchor line scope, mud, sand, rocks, and seagrass all impact the holding task of the anchor. The Danforth type anchor design has proven very successful over many years. It stows well on sailboats and powerboats, and is easy to handle. When pitted against rocks, the high tensile version's greater strength is preferable. But boaters should beware of the many bargain priced versions of this fine type of anchor and stick with the original.

Since it was first introduced in California, the Bruce Anchor has rapidly become one of the most popular anchors for use at the Channel Islands. It fits well in a sufficiently cantilevered bow roller, deploys easily, and rarely bends when locked in rocky conditions. As with most anchor designs, island grass can inhibit successful setting of the smaller sizes (22 lb. and under), so larger sizes are recommended.

Many boaters are strong advocates of plow anchors, which resemble the blade of a farmer's plow. Plow anchors have become traditional on many cruising sailboats throughout the world, and fit bow pulpits and rollers well. Their track record at the Channel Islands is good, but I have found it second in performance after the Danforth and Bruce designs.

Aluminum anchors have a poor performance record at the Islands. Their light weight prevents them from setting well in the grass and small bottom stones that are often encountered in island coves. Only the larger models have a good chance of setting properly, and then with at least 30 feet of galvanized chain.

Boaters frequently have undersized anchor chain and line that prevents successful anchoring at our islands. Chain has much lower strength than most expect. Its job is to provide strength, significant weight to help in setting the anchor, and to resist chaff from sharp bottom rocks. Line (rope) quickly loses strength when frayed by chaffing and needs to be sized to accept wear and tear over the years.

With proper gear and procedures, a boater can relax in a beautiful island cove, enjoying a beverage and watching ill-equipped and inexperienced boaters going through the unsuccessful "anchor drill" that frequently places undue strain on friendships and even marriages. You can learn more from one of several good books on the subject, or by hands-on training at a local boating school.

ALONE AROUND THE WORLD

Astounding adventures at sea began almost with the origin of mankind on earth. Ancient Chinese created sophisticated nautical charts and journals thousands of years BC. But, one of the greatest feats of all time was the first known single-handed circumnavigation of the world by sail. It was accomplished in the late 1800's by Joshua Slocum, a Canadian-American seaman whose story took the world by storm, and its impact has never diminished.

Slocum was born in 1844, within sight of the Bay of Fundy in Nova Scotia. As a boy, he yearned for a life of adventure at sea, away from his demanding father and an increasingly chaotic life at home among his many brothers and sisters. He made several attempts to run away from home, finally succeeding at age 14 when he signed-on as a cabin boy and cook on a northeast fishing schooner. By age 16, he had left home for good. Slocum and a friend signed-on at Halifax, Nova Scotia as ordinary seamen on a merchant ship bound for Dublin, Ireland.

From Dublin, he crossed to Liverpool as an ordinary seaman on the British merchant ship Tangier, bound for China. During the next two years, he rounded Cape Horn twice, landed at Batavia (now Jakarta) in the Dutch East Indies, as well as the Moluccas, Manila, Hong Kong, Saigon, Singapore, and San Francisco. When off-watch, he studied for the Board of Trade examination and received his certificate as a fully-qualified Second Mate at age 18. Slocum quickly rose through the ranks to become a chief mate on several British coal transport ships. His first blue-water command in 1869 was as captain of the bark Washington, which he sailed across the Pacific from San Francisco to Australia, and then home via Alaska. He then went on to command a number of vessels, meet and marry his first wife in Australia, survive a shipwreck, fight off pirates, remarry after the death of his first wife, and finally to began publishing accounts of his many adventures.

After his long and varied career, Joshua Slocum decided to attempt a sailing fete that no known person had accomplished before. In 1890, at Fairhaven, Massachusetts, he rebuilt the 36' 9" sloop-rigged fishing boat Spray, soon to become one of the most famous sailboats of all time. Slocum wrote, "I had resolved on a voyage around the world, and as the wind on the morning of April 24, 1895 was fair, I weighed anchor at noon, set sail, and filled away from Boston, where the Spray" had been moored snugly all winter. The twelve o'clock whistles were blowing just as the sloop shot ahead under full sail. A short board was made up the harbor on the port tack, then coming about she stood to seaward with her boom well off to port, and swung past the ferries with lively heels. A photographer on the outer pier of East Boston got a picture of her as she swept by, her flag at the peak throwing her folds clear. A thrilling pulse beat high in me. My step was light on deck in the crisp air. I felt there could be no turning back, and that I was engaging in an adventure the meaning of which I thoroughly understood."

Slocum sailed around the world using very crude navigation tools. His primary method to determine latitude (north-south position) was by dead reckoning, whereby he kept notes of his average compass course and estimated boat speed and then marked them on a chart. For longitude (east-west position), he relied on a cheap tin clock for approximate time and made noon-sun sights with a sextant.

He normally sailed Spray without touching the helm. Due to the length of its sail plan and long keel, Spray, unlike faster modern craft, was inherently capable of self-steering by adjusting or reefing the sails and lashing the helm in place. Slocum wrote that he manually steered Spray only when maneuvering or in an emergency. He was proud of the fact that at one point he had sailed 2,000 miles west across the Pacific without once touching the helm.

On June 27, 1898, more than three years after the start of his epic voyage, Joshua Slocum sighted Newport, Rhode Island, and became the first known mariner to circumnavigated the world - a distance of more than 46,000 miles. But Slocum's return went almost unnoticed.

The Spanish-American War, which had begun two months earlier, dominated the headlines. Later, after the end of major hostilities, many American newspapers published articles describing Slocum's amazing adventure.

In 1899, he published his account of the epic voyage in "Sailing Alone Around the World", first serialized in The Century magazine and then in several book-length editions. Reviewers received the slightly anachronistic age-of-sail adventure story enthusiastically. One went so far as to declare, "Boys who do not like this book ought to be drowned at once." In one review, Sir Edwin Arnold wrote, "I do not hesitate to call it the most extraordinary book ever published."

By 1901, Slocum's book revenues and income from public lectures provided him enough financial security to purchase a small farm on the island of Martha's Vineyard, seven miles off the coast of Massachusetts. But after a year and a half, the ardent adventurer found he could not adapt to a settled life. Soon Slocum was sailing "Spray" from port to port in the northeastern US during the summer and in the West Indies during the winter, lecturing and selling books wherever he could.

In November 1909, Joshua Slocum set sail for the West Indies on one of his usual winter voyages. He had begun planning his next adventure - exploring the Orinoco, Rio Negro and Amazon Rivers. He was never heard from again.

"Sailing Alone Around The World" is no longer in print, but you can find used and some reprint copies on the internet, as well as in e-book and audio book formats.

DEEP TRADITIONS

In 1872, fledgling Santa Barbara's State Street was a graded dirt thoroughfare with pedestrian boardwalks and gas lighting at night. America's Civil War had ended, and just seven years before the schooner America had soundly beaten sixteen English yachts. America's golden age of yachting had begun.

John B. Stearns had completed Santa Barbara's new wharf so cargo could be unloaded and visitors could walk to land instead of being rowed through the surf from sailing ships anchored off-shore. City promoters had decided that Santa Barbara should have a fine hotel, so in 1874 construction of the Arlington Hotel began a mile inland from the windy beaches. Visitors to Santa Barbara were transported to the hotel on a mule car line that was established for that purpose.

Without a harbor, there was no storm protection for moored yachts. Leadbetter beach had not yet formed, and the shoreline was a mixture of rocks and sand. But the Stearns organization and other commercial interests felt that Santa Barbara's image would attract more visitors if it had a yacht club, so the club's early membership consisted of a combination of boaters and real estate promoters. Santa Barbara's new club was the second yacht club in California. Metropolitan San Francisco's Yacht Club had formed just three years earlier in 1869.

Santa Barbara Yacht Club's first clubhouse was a single story, 35 x 20 foot building on the west side of the foot of Stearns Wharf. It had previously been the home of John Stearns while he constructed the wharf. The southeast corner of the small clubhouse was occupied by a galley with a wood stove. In the southwest corner was the head (toilet) with a pipe leading to the beach below. A battered piano stood in the northeast corner. The early club's membership was around fifty – some actually being boaters.

Boating was difficult without the protection of a true harbor. In 1921, yacht club members sponsored a survey to determine if and where it would be possible to locate a yacht harbor. The firm of Hill & Co. of San Francisco was hired and concluded that the best location would be where the Bird Refuge is located today. An alternative location in the report was by Castle Rock, (where the harbor is located today), but that location was rejected in the report because of probable shoaling – a wise conclusion in view of the millions of dollars that have since been spent dredging sand to keep the harbor open and functional.

In 1924, a southeast gale washed the early clubhouse out to sea. The following year, civic leaders Max Fleischman, T. M. Storke, Dwight Murphy and Seldon Spaulding started construction of a new building on Stearns Wharf and leased it to the yacht club. The new clubhouse opened in 1926 on the site where the Harbor Restaurant is located today.

At the same time, yeast king and yacht club member Major Max Fleischman offered Santa Barbara financial help to construct a suitable harbor. Despite the warnings in Hill & Co.'s report, the city decided to build the harbor in its present location. Voters approved a bond issue for $250,000 to build a 1,000 foot breakwater, and construction started in January 1927. When work was finally completed, the breakwater length had grown to 2,435 feet and the cost to $775,000.

The yacht club sponsored races and other yachting events through the 1920's. In 1925, the year of the Santa Barbara earthquake, the Southern California Yachting Association (SCYA) Regatta was scheduled to be held at Santa Barbara. The SCYA offered to call it off because of the earthquake damage, but the club said it was willing to put it on if the visitors didn't mind a few inconveniences. The regatta that year was the biggest and best to date.

Some of the yachts owned by the club members and moored within the new harbor were Haida 128 ft., Invader 135 ft., Faith 106 ft., Malibu 100 ft., Patolita 82 ft., Radio 110 ft., Westward 68 ft., Hafje 58 ft., Navigator 78 ft., Zingara 65 ft., Caprice 65 ft., and Wymitch and

Bayadere, each about 50 ft. In addition, there were four 8 meters, seven star boats and 12 large power yachts of various sizes.

The 1930's were a rocky period for the club. Prior to 1929, membership in the club was limited to not more than 100 members. Following the stock market crash and the onset of the depression, membership was thrown open to anyone, with the result that it jumped up to between 600 and 700 members, few of whom were yachtsmen.

Generally poor conduct on the part of a few members, however, threatened to collapse the club. In 1932, the yachtsmen who had dropped out were induced to come back, and the club was reorganized. Those not interested in yachting were for the most part dropped from the membership. 1937, however, saw a repeat of the 1932 problem by non-yachtsmen members, and the Stearns Wharf clubhouse was lost for non-payment of rent.

The club was again reorganized in March 1938 and renamed the "Channel Corinthian Yacht Club". The name "Santa Barbara Yacht Club" was readopted in 1940. The clubhouse was a one room shack on the east side of Stearns Wharf, opposite the previous yacht club building.

By 1940, the Club was again in sound financial condition, and the members began working towards property of their own. The city was in need of a civic auditorium, so plans were drawn for a building to be erected immediately west of the breakwater. The southern wing was to be the yacht club, the center an auditorium, and the northern wing for the US Naval Reserve. The city council appropriated $20,000, and the Federal Government's Works Project Administration (WPA) was to put up the balance. But World War II intervened while construction was well under way. The WPA was discontinued, and the city was stuck with a building less than a third complete. The building was acquired by the US Navy, and the harbor was closed for the duration of the war. But a "shadow" yacht club was held together by a few members.

Club activities began again in 1946. In 1947, the first regatta was held from the Naval Reserve Armory. Club meetings were held in various member's houses, and then the club leased a suite in the California Hotel. That was when my father joined the club. I can recall the hotel closet packed with some of the fine trophies that are now on display in the present clubhouse.

In 1950, negotiations were conducted with the city for the yacht club to lease a portion of beach next to the breakwater as a clubhouse location. Club member Wiley Cole worked for the Union Oil Company, and arranged for the acquisition of an old corrugated iron field office that could be used for a clubhouse. When club members pulled off the iron siding, they found severely rotted wood, much that had to be replaced. But, the clubhouse was completed and in use by December of 1951. Additions and improvements were added each year, and the humble shack became quite a fine clubhouse. Club members called the building "Mejor Que Nada" – better than nothing. In 1966, the building was removed and the current facility was constructed. The tradition of improvements continues.

Today, Santa Barbara Yacht Club has over 700 members, and conducts a broad program for all ages and interests, including racing, cruising and social events. The club sponsors the Santa Barbara Yacht Club Youth Foundation that performs sailing instruction and other youth related programs that are open to the public. The club also supports racing programs at local schools and UCSB. There is a strong program of women's activities that include contributions to youth activities, educational functions, and more. The yacht club also hosts the starting and finishing points for the Santa Barbara to King Harbor, Encinal to Santa Barbara, and Santa Cruz to Santa Barbara races. These events are estimated to bring 300 yachts and up to 5,000 people to Santa Barbara each year. The club also provides support for the Santa Barbara Harbor Festival and the visitation of US Naval Vessels. Each year funds are raised by the club's annual Charity Regatta to support Hospice Care. The club also conducts the program that flies the many flags along the length of the harbor's breakwater.

SNUG HARBOR

Brisk, cool, December winds swept across the deep blue channel waters, pushing white rolling surf onto bright, deserted beaches. The sky was clear, but the tops of billowing clouds appeared at intervals from behind the coastal mountains as a reminder of the changing season. Vivid in winter clarity, Santa Barbara's Channel Islands seemed much closer than twenty-two miles. To an experienced eye, there would be a price to pay in crossing to its safe anchorages— but it should be well worth it.

A thirty-two foot sloop powered out from the protection of Santa Barbara's harbor and headed into the freshening westerly breeze. The crewmember hoisted its mainsail. The helmsman then steered down a few degrees to catch the wind and begin forward motion. The jib was unfurled, sheets were tightened, and the sloop heeled and accelerated through crisp winter chop.

Two figures were working in the cockpit, one at the helm, and the other tending sheets. Each wore a snug sweater, foul weather gear and watertight boots. As the coastal mountains slowly faded behind, the brisk air and light spray felt invigorating as the tangled webs of life on shore began to clear. The sloop surged across the now white flecked, steel-blue waters on its way to Pelican Bay on Santa Cruz Island.

As the wind freshened, the skipper mentally reviewed his preparations and contingency plans. Satisfied that they were well-prepared for a blustery crossing, both were happy to "pay their dues" to traverse the channel on a winter's day. The challenges would make their destination much more rewarding, and limit the goal to just those sailors who qualified by thorough preparation and seasoned knowledge of the ever-changing and demanding winter winds and seas.

Santa Cruz Island slowly arose ahead, increasingly clear and distinct. Island greenery spawned by recent winter rains emerged, while tall pines contrasted in deeper and darker shades. Streams would be running briskly, and hiking would unveil limitless images to record on film or memory.

The sloop reached mid-channel, leaving behind the protective lee of Point Conception, forty five miles to weather. Winds and seas that had already traveled across thousands of miles of open winter ocean surged against and under the California sloop. Her lee rail was buried, and spray flew in almost continuous sheets. Her helm pulled hard against the helmsman's grip as the sloop climbed the steepening seas and then fell down the backs of the high Pacific rollers. Skipper and crew were cautious but at the same time exhilarated as they crossed the windswept and now quite deserted sea.

Sea, wind, sails, and vessel all merged, creating the sound of a low howl as the pitching and diving sloop surged onward. The crewmember wrestled open the companionway hatch and then quickly climbed downward to check things below deck. Bracing his body while reaching for handholds, he moved forward, checking the bilge, port holes, and any gear that may have come loose from the lurching motion of the small sloop. All seemed well. The comparative warmth felt good, but the physical and mental effects from the rapid motion in close quarters weighed heavily in favor of a quick return to deck and fresh air. But one more job. He checked the GPS (global positioning system) to get an updated course and distance to Pelican Bay, and to verify the visual dead reckoning being done at the helm above. Quickly, he marked their present position and time on the chart and then verified that the electronic answer conformed with logic and physical observations.

On deck above, the wind continued to strengthen, and the sloop pounded harder into steepening swells. The outer channel wind had swung a bit north, so jib sheets were eased, fairleads moved forward, and the jib furling line trimmed to reduced the area of the genoa to a smaller working jib size. The helm became easier and heeling decreased as the sloop accelerated down the dark seas.

Anticipating the increasing wind and seas of "Windy Gulch," the skipper had sailed a few degrees west of a direct rhumb line course to Pelican Bay so the sloop could "fall off" a few degrees when it encountered the rougher outer-channel waters. With updated course and destination information from the GPS, main and jib sheets could be eased and the sloop's bow turned more southerly to lessen the impact of the punishing winter seas. With waves now on the aft quarter, the sloop accelerated and began surfing down the giant Pacific rollers. The credible six knot speed when clawing to weather now turned into ten knot reaching run outs as the bow parted blue water into white froth and spray and the sloop surged ahead on a wet and wild California sleigh ride.

The island loomed ahead. Its pine-clad mountains seemed to drop dramatically into the turbulent waters. Gradually, the wind diminished and comparative silence fell as pastoral land aroma replaced the roar of sea and spray of just minutes before. The sloop slid quietly towards land under the warm and protected lee of Diablo Point. Pelican Bay lay a just a mile ahead. The sloop ran dead before a soft island breeze, still pushed by large but now diminishing seas.

Oilskin tops were shed as the two sailors readied anchors and the inflatable dinghy. As the sloop swung around the point and into the protection of Pelican Bay, they could see a Catalina 36 sloop from Santa Barbara tucked well into the bay's far corner beneath sheer cliffs. It would be tonight's only neighbor. Later, ritual sea stories and exaggerated wind estimates would be exchanged along with traditional toasts to the "sun sinking below the yardarm."

The harsh crossing was well worth it.

SEA TERMS

- Sloop – A sailboat with a single mast, a mainsail, and one or more jibs (front sail).
- Lee rail – The side of a boat furthest from the direction of the wind.
- Helm – Steering device. Either a steering wheel or, as in this case a, a long wooden bar.
- Bilge – The lowest area in a ship's hull where any water collects.

- Dead reckoning – Navigation by estimating boat speed, direction, and time.
- Fairlead – A pulley (block) that a line passes through.
- Genoa – a large jib.
- Rhumb line– A straight line course between two points.
- Companionway – The entrance from above deck to below deck.

LONE WOMAN OF SAN NICOLAS ISLAND

Remote San Nicolas Island, seventy miles off the coast of Southern California, has been occupied by people for hundreds of years. The native Indians called it Ghalas-hat. Food was plentiful from the sea and from hunting sea otters and seals. Traveling in boats made from driftwood that came ashore, the islanders were able to trade and communicate with the peoples of the mainland as well as from the other islands.

In the 1800's, Russians and Aleuts came down the coast from Alaska to kill seals and sea otters and sell their fur in Russia and Asia. They killed many Indians as well. Then Americans arrived from New England, bringing Kodiak Indians with them. The killings of the island natives continued, until there were only about twenty-five local Indians remaining.

The padres of Mission Santa Barbara called the island "San Nicolas," and its local Indians "Nicolenos." The padres seemed to be the only ones who cared about the few remaining inhabitants of San Nicolas Island, and in 1835 convinced an American sea captain to sail to the island to bring the remaining islanders to the mainland for safety.

But upon his arrival at the island, a great storm developed. The ship was in danger of being driven onto the rocks, so its captain had the Indians quickly pack their belongings and board the ship. One young woman thought her baby had been brought aboard the ship by others, but could not find it. She pleaded with the captain to return to shore, but he feared that could result in the lost of his ship and all aboard. He told the young mother that they would return the next day when the storm subsided.

But the young mother did not believe her baby could survive alone and threw herself into the heaving ocean to swim ashore. Due to increasing bad weather, the captain decided he had to leave to save his ship. They sailed to San Pedro with the rest of the Indians, vowing to return for the Indian mother. But the captain would not be returning. His employers sent him north to San Francisco where his ship was sunk in rough water as it entered San Francisco Bay.

Badly battered by the seas and surf, the young woman finally reached the shore, almost too tired and sore to stand. Forcing herself, she went to the spot where she had last seen her child. It was not there. Frantically, she began searching the beaches and canyons, but to no avail. Many exhausting hours later, she knew her baby would never be found alive. Now she was the only human on the island. Would the ship return for her? Only birds, seals, wild dogs and the young mother remained on San Nicolas Island.

The storm ended the next day, and the young woman searched the horizon for a sail. After many days, she gave up hope and now realized that she would have to use all her knowledge and resources to survive. Would it be possible? She would have to build a shelter and learn where she could find food. She would have to skin birds or animals to make clothes. If she wanted fire, she would have to learn how to start one herself – without matches.

Still no ship came. She had become the Lone Woman of Ghalas-hat. Over time, she learned all the places fresh water could be found. She located the best rocks and tide pools along the shore for abalone and other shell fish. Over time, she learned which plants were good for food.

Fire was essential not only for cooking and warmth, but to keep the wild dogs away from her camp. They had been left by earlier ships and over time became mean and wild. The young woman had watched elders from her tribe make fire. Using a sharp shell, she made a grove in a stick, placed dry grass close, and began rubbing the grove with another sharp stick. Her arms and muscles became sore, but on and on she rubbed. Finally, there was a whiff of smoke. Exhausted but elated, she gently blew on the smoke and finally a small a burst of flame appeared. She now had a fire, but would have to keep it going day in and day out as her most important tool for survival. This became one of her most important jobs.

Months and then years passed. The young women continued to improve her shelter and other survival skills. One day, she spied a ship passing the island, but she had no way to let them know she was there. She began planning to build a large fire when the next ship appeared, but then decided that it would not be wise. The sailors might be the ones who killed so many of her people and could do the same to her.

It had now been ten years since she had talked to another person. She had been about 18 years old when she swam back to the island looking for her baby. Over time, she had learned to build fire and shelter, where to find and store food, and how to make clothing. She even made friends with some pups whose mother had died.

More years passed. A few ships stopped at San Nicolas Island, and seamen found traces of the stranded mother – fire ashes, hidden food, primitive tools, and even footprints. But she remained hidden and was not found until one of the mission padres convinced Captain George Nidiver to sail to the island and search for her. Nidiver and a crew that including Indians went to the island to hunt seals and sea otters as well as to search for the woman. They hunted otters and seals for six weeks, but did not find the elusive woman. They discovered more footprints, but she remained hidden, listening to them talking in a language she could not understand. Finally, Charles Brown found her and took careful steps to assure her that he was a friend. Through sign language, she was urged to pack her belongings and join them on the ship. She had been alone on the island for eighteen years.

There were many sights at Santa Barbara that were exciting to the Indian woman. She had never seen a horse or a wagon or large homes. Numerous people, church bells, the music of singers, and almost all the features of civilization were new and strange to her. The padres gave her the name of Juana Maria. She lived with Captain Nidiver's family, but after a few weeks started to become weak. Eating her native foods did not help. She became increasingly ill, and finally died. She was buried at the Santa Barbara Mission.

Juana Maria never went to school. She spent all but a few weeks of her life on Ghalas-hat (San Nicolas Island). But she had learned her lessons well, and could take care of all her needs and became an example of what commitment and the love of a mother for her child should mean.

There is a bronze plaque placed on a wall at Santa Barbara Mission where Juana Maria is buried that reads, "Juana Maria – Indian woman abandoned on San Nicolas Island eighteen years and found and brought to Santa Barbara by Captain George Nidiver in 1853.

AMERICA

Probably the most famous yacht in racing history, the America was a 19th century racing yacht which gave its name to the international sailing trophy that was the first known as the Royal Yacht Squadron of England's "One Hundred Guinea Cup". America was designed for Commodore John Cox Stevens and a syndicate from the New York Yacht Club. On August 22, 1851, America won a challenge race against England over a 53 mile course around the Isle of Wight off the south coast of England. She finishing eight minutes ahead of the best yachts in the prestigious Royal Yacht Squadron.

America was designed by George Steers (1820-1856) whose schooner-rigged pilot boats were among the fastest and most seaworthy of their day. The vessels needed to be fast because harbor pilots competed with each other for business by being the first to reach an arriving ship. Pilot schooners also needed to be seaworthy in order to be able pilot inbound and outbound vessels in all kinds of weather. In addition to pilot boats, Steers also designed and built seventeen racing yachts, some which were favorites among the competitive members of New York Yacht Club.

America was captained by Richard Brown, a skilled member of the Sandy Hook Pilots who were renowned worldwide for their skill in maneuvering the challenging shoals around New York City. The pilots were extremely skilled competitors who raced to incoming ships that needed a knowledgeable pilot to get their cargos ashore first and thus gain the best prices. Brown sailed aboard a pilot boat designed by George Steers, who was also a personal friend.

America was crewed by Brown and eight professional sailors. George Steers his older brother James, and James' son George were passengers. The schooner left New York on June 21 and arrived at Le Harve, France on July 11. There they were joined there by America's owner John Cox Stevens. After America was dry docked and repainted, she departed for Cowes on England's Isle of Wight. The crew enjoyed the hospitality of the Royal Yacht Squadron while Stevens searched for someone who would race against his yacht for both fame and for money.

The British yachting community had followed the construction of the America with interest, and perhaps some trepidation. When America arrived at Cowes, there was one yacht, the Laverock, that agreed to an impromptu race. The accounts of the race were contradictory. A British newspaper reported that Lavrock held her own against America, but John Cox Stevens later reported that America had beaten her handily. Whichever the outcome, the report seemed to discourage other British yachtsmen from challenging America to a match. She didn't race again until the last day of the Royal Yacht Squadron's annual members-only regatta, after which it was customary for Queen Victoria to award the prize. Because of America's presence, a special provision was made to "open to all nations" a race of 53 miles 'round the Isle of Wight, with no handicap for the varying yacht designs." The race was to be for first to finish, and winner to take all.

At 10 AM on August 22, 1851, seven schooners and eight cutters started the race. America had a poor start due to a fouled anchor, and she was well behind when finally underway. But within just a half an hour she was in fifth place and still gaining.

The eastern shoals of the Isle of Wight are called the Nab Rocks. Traditionally, racers would sail around the east (seaward) side of a lightship that marked the edge of the shoal, but a knowledgeable skipper could sail a shorter distance between the lightship and the mainland if they had a good pilot. America had such a pilot, and he took her down the west (landward) side of the lightship. After the race, a contestant protested this action, but was overruled due to the fact that the official race rules did not specify which side of the lightship a yacht must pass. The result of this tactic put America in the lead, and she held onto it throughout the rest of the race. At one point, her jib boom broke, but it was quickly replaced. On the final leg of the race the yacht Aurora was gaining, but she was still eight minutes behind when the America crossed the finish line. Legend has it that while watching the race Queen Victoria asked who was in second place. With no other yachts in sight, she received the famous reply: "There is no second, your Majesty."

John Cox Stevens and his New York Yacht Club syndicate owned America from the time she was launched on May 3, 1851 until ten days after she won the English regatta that made her famous. On September 1, 1851, "America' was sold to John de Blaquiere, the 2nd Baron de Blaquiere, who raced her only a few times before selling her in 1856 to Henry Montagu Upton, 2nd Viscount Templetown. Upton renamed the yacht Camilla, but he failed to use or maintain her. In 1858, she was sold to Henry Sotheby Pitcher.

Pitcher, a shipbuilder in Gravesend, Kent, England, rebuilt Camilla and resold her in 1860 to Henry Edward Decie, who then sailed her back to the United States. Decie sold the schooner to the Confederate States of America that same year. The Confederates used the fast yacht as a blockade runner in the American Civil War. At that time, she may have been renamed "Memphis", but details are unclear. In 1862, the yacht was scuttled (deliberately sunk) at Jacksonville just before Union troops took the city.

Upon the northern army's occupation of Jacksonville, Camilia/Memphis was raised, repaired and renamed America by the Union. She then served as part of the Union's blockade for the remainder of the war. America was armed with three smooth bore bronze cannon that had been cast at the Washington Navy Yard. She carried a 12-pounder on her bow and two 24-pounders amidships. The larger 24-pounders had a bore diameter of 5.75 inches. Each 24-pounder weighed 1300 pounds, and had a range of 1140 yards. After the war, America was used as a training ship by the U. S. Naval Academy. On August 8, 1870, America was entered by the Navy in the America's Cup race at New York Harbor, where she finished fourth.

America remained in the U. S. Navy until 1873 when she was sold for $5,000 to Benjamin Franklin Butler, a former Civil War Commander. Butler raced and maintained the boat well. To keep the sleek schooner competitive, he commissioned a rebuild in 1875 and then a total refit of the rig in 1885. Upon the General's death in 1893, his son Paul inherited the schooner, but he had no serious interest in her. Paul Butler then gave the yacht to his nephew Butler Ames in 1897. Ames reconditioned America and used her occasionally for racing and casual sailing until 1901 whereupon she fell into disuse and disrepair.

In 1917, America was sold to a company headed by Charles H. W. Foster. Then in 1921, America was sold to the America Restoration Fund which donated her to the U. S. Naval Academy at Annapolis. Sadly, was not maintained there either, and by 1940 was in a seriously decayed state. On March 29, 1942, during a heavy snowstorm, the shed where the America was being stored collapsed. Three years later, in 1945, the remains of the shed and the ship were finally scrapped and burned.

America's memory lives on as probably the most famous racing yacht in history. The subsequent America's Cup competition is the world's longest running sporting competition. The United States successfully defended the Cup for one hundred thirty-two years. It was finally won by Australia in 1987. Since then, the competition has become less between countries that between syndicates. The most recent competition for the America's Cup was won by Switzerland in 2007. The winning skipper was Ed Baird, an American who was born in Florida. United States syndicates have challenged three of the five times since the first time the cup was first lost. The next competition will probably be in giant twin-hulled catamarans. A far cry from the famous schooner that gave the competition its name.

TOY BOATS

I collect a number of types of antiques, but mostly nautical. One of my favorite collection topics is toy boats. But the results of my research first surprised me but then made good sense. I assumed toys were a fairly recent development because early generations would have to work full time on their survival. Kids will be kids, and all kids come up with things that can be used as toys.

Most young mammals have been observed playing with whatever they can find, turning such things as pinecones, rocks, and food into toys, so it simply makes sense that toys have a history as old as human civilization itself. Toys and games have been unearthed from many sites of ancient civilizations. They have been written about in some of our oldest literature. Toys excavated from the Indus valley civilization (3000-1500 BCE) include small carts, whistles shaped like birds, and toy monkeys which could slide down a string.

The earliest toys were made from materials found in nature, such as rocks, sticks, and clay. Thousands of years ago, Egyptian children played with *dolls* that had wigs and movable limbs which were made from stone, pottery, and wood. In Ancient Greece and Ancient Rome, children played sticks, bows and arrows, yo-yos, and with dolls made of wax or terracotta. When Greek children, especially girls, came of age it was customary for them to sacrifice the toys of their childhood to the gods. On the eve of their wedding, young girls around fourteen would offer their dolls in a temple as a rite of passage into adulthood. Ancient Roman toys included several that would be familiar to children today, including dolls, dice, rattles, and toy dishes for playing house.

As technology changed and civilization progressed, toys also changed. Whereas ancient toys were made from materials found in nature like stone, wood, and grass, modern toys are generally constructed from plastic, cloth, and synthetic materials. Ancient toys were often made by the parents and family of the children who used them, or by the children themselves. Modern toys, in contrast, are generally mass-produced and sold in stores. The materials that toys are made from have changed, and what toys can do has changed. But the fact that children play with toys has not changed over the many centuries.

Tin toys were first made at the beginning of the Industrial Revolution in the early 1800's, and represented the first trains, steam engines, iron boats, and carriages of that period. These early toys were artisan creations but as the nineteenth century progressed and technology advanced, toy factories appeared so that by the turn of the century complex trains sets, stunning boats and cars were being produced in considerable quantity in both America and Europe.

As with other toys, toy boats were objects to be played with rather than looked at and consequently the vast majority were destroyed or damaged by their youthful owners. All Nineteenth Century and early twentieth century toys are now rare objects that many people today have never seen.

The Forbes family of "Forbes Magazine" fame have collected toy boats for many years. The collection exceeds over three hundred, and many are quite old and quite rare. Jaques Milet and Robert Forbs published *Toy Boats – 1870-1955 – A Pictorial History* which includes ocean liners, river boats, warships, submarines, speedboats, rowboats and floor boats. The book is out of print, but I have found copies for sale on the internet.

I own three antique toy boats. One is 12 inches long and seems to have been built by German toy boat maker Fleischmann and Company around 1900. It is an ocean liner and has a key operated motor that drives a propeller. It shows its age, but is a rare survivor of over one hundred years of exposure to the rough and tumble use of enthusiastic children.

A second ocean liner is 20 inches long and may have been built by Frenchman George Caratte, also around the turn of the 19th century.

Lifeboats line its upper rails, and it is also powered by a wind-up motor which drives a propeller.

The third toy boat is quite unique. It is also made of metal, but is powered by a steam driven motor. Alcohol is poured into a small container and slid under a boiler filled with water. When the alcohol is lit with a match, the heated water gives off steam that is routed to the motor which turns the propeller. I have been unable to determine the builder, but it seems to have been constructed in the early- to mid 19th century.

USS SANTA BARBARA

United State's Naval Ship *Santa Barbara's* keel was laid on 19 December 1966 at the Sparrow's Point Maryland shipyard of the Bethlehem Steel Corporation, and launched on 23 January 1968. The 564 foot *Santa Barbara* was commissioned and joined the Atlantic Fleet on 11 July 1970. Originally home ported in Davisville, Rhode Island, her home port was changed to Charleston, South Carolina, one of America's oldest and most historic cities.

The ship and crew of the *Santa Barbara* have earned an outstanding reputation as a professional and "can do" team. The ship's awards include Battle Efficiency "E" Awards won in 1979, 1980, 1989, and 1993 for exceptional performance from all departments, and superior overall ability. She was awarded the Meritorious Unit Commendation in 1973 for numerous records set replenishing at sea during the Vietnam Conflict, and again in 1988 for her performance during her Mediterranean deployment. In 1989, she earned the Golden Anchor Award for the best retention in her class, and was parent command for the 1989 Surface Forces Atlantic Sailor of the Year. Her latest awards are the Maritime Warfare Excellence Award, the Engineering/Survivability Excellence Award, the Command and Control Excellence Award, the Logistics Management Excellence Award, and the Meritorious Unit Commendation for her performance during her 1992 - 1993 Mediterranean deployment.

On 30 September 1998, "Santa Barbara" was decommissioned and transferred to the Military Sealift Command (MSC), Naval Fleet Auxiliary Force, where her hull number was changed to T-AE-28. She was finally retired on August 5, 2005. In 2006, the Santa Barbara was towed to Brownsville, Texas for scrapping.

OUR EARLY HARBOR

On February 23, 1942, not long after the outbreak of war in the Pacific, a Japanese submarine emerged from the ocean and lobbed 16 shells at the Elwood Oil Field about 10 miles west of Santa Barbara, the only direct attack on the U.S. mainland during the entire war, and the first wartime attack by an enemy power on U.S. soil since the War of 1812. Although the submarine gunners were terrible marksmen and only caused about $500 damage to a catwalk, panic was immediate. Many Santa Barbara residents fled, and land values plummeted to historic lows.

Our military quickly began operations in Santa Barbara County and throughout the country. In addition to the U.S. Marine Base at present-day UCSB and the U.S. Army base at Camp Cook, now Vandenberg Air Force Base, there was an active U.S. Navy presence at Santa Barbara Harbor. The Navy's harbor operations included port security, mine sweeper training, maintenance of U.S. Coast Guard vessels, and later U.S. Navy Reserve functions.

After the war, Santa Barbara Harbor quickly transformed to civilian operations. How did our post 1946 harbor compare with today's? There were no buildings or parking lots on East Beach between the base of the breakwater and Stearns Wharf, where now nearly half the distance is covered with parking lots. There were no slips in the harbor, but about 200 boats were tied to single mooring cans that allowed the fleet to swing in unison to face the varying direction of the wind. There are now 1100 slips, and just a handful of mooring cans remaining. Boaters park their cars and walk to their vessels along marina walkways. 1946 boaters generally kept rowing skiffs tied to continuous lines that ran to pilings about 40 feet from the breakwater's rocky edge. When walking along the breakwater in front of Santa Barbara Yacht Club today, you can look down and see some of the iron rings that attached the skiff lines to the shore.

The breakwater provided protection from storms and waves, but its present inward angled extension towards Stearns Wharf did not exist at war's end. The harbor entrance had to be dredged every three or four years to remove the endlessly growing sandbar from the constant flow of sand down the coast. Years later, it was decided to pile rocks on the ever-forming sandbar to provide additional storm protection as marinas were constructed within the harbor to accommodate more boats that could be accommodated on moorings. Millions upon millions of dollars have been spent to have the harbor located at the City's doorstep. Use of the natural estuaries at the bird refuge or the bay at Goleta would have avoided much of the sand problem, but clearly were not politically feasible.

Another 1940's means to get to a moored vessel was by shore boat. As thick, damp fog encompassed the harbor and not a boat could be seen from shore, echoing cries of "Shooore boat" could be heard repeated again and again. Upon his return from the war, Ken Elmes installed a float to accommodate the first fuel station at the western end of the harbor, along with a shore boat service and sailboat rentals. The shore boat was operated by "Duffy", and it cost ten cents a ride. The fuel float was attached to base of the Navy Pier on its seaward side. Today, a newer fuel float is located at the far end of the pier.

Two large floating platforms were installed along the breakwater to seaward of the Elmes operation so boats could tie along side to load passengers and gear. These floats were later replaced by the current accommodation dock. Commercial fishing boats now tie bow and stern to the breakwater where the skiff lines had been before. One of the original large floats was later used by the Santa Barbara Yacht Club Youth foundation to store its boats for its youth sail training program.

For a number of years after the war, the harbor's military buildings were used for a variety of civilian activities. Today, only the building at the foot of the Navy Pier remains. It accommodates a dive shop, city maintenance shops, a cafe, a fish market, a kayak business, and a chandlery. The stately Navy Building now accommodates a two-story restaurant, a museum shop, and the popular Santa Barbara Maritime Museum. The museum is located where the Navy had its drill area and basketball court. When entering the building, turn down the hallway to your left to view fascinating photographs of the Navy Building during the war. At war's end, other now gone wartime buildings were used as a coffee shop, a meeting facility, boaters storage lockers, a ships chandlery, and a boat brokerage office.

After the war, Santa Barbara Yacht Club's facility was a single room in the California Hotel. The venerable club was formed in 1872, and is the second oldest yacht club in California. I recall seeing a number of its very prestigious and historic trophies piled high in the hotel room's closet. Today they are properly displayed in fine cabinets at the current clubhouse. Through the many years, the club has occupied buildings on Stearns Wharf, on a yacht, a building near east beach, a room in the California Hotel, and finally several evolutions leading to the present building on Leadbetter Beach.

Today, the harbor is filled with as many boats as can fit, is administered by a large city department, has many commercial shops and service operations, an active commercial fishing fleet, a major maritime museum, fine restaurants, fishing and island charter boats, rental boats for local sailing, yacht brokers, two yachting clubs, and more. Today's harbor is unrecognizable from that at the end of the war.

UNPRECIDENTED DREAM

Hillary Lister has bestowed to the world a dramatic lesson about overcoming adversity. On August 31, she became the first quadriplegic to sail single-handed around Britain.

Born in 1972 at Kent, England, the 37 year old sailor suffers from progressive condition reflex sympathetic dystrophy. She was able-bodied until the age of 15 when the condition set in. By 1991, she had lost the use of her legs, but continued her studies in biochemistry at Jesus College, Oxford, and then in 1996 continued her studies and started work towards a PhD at the University of Kent. But her condition continued to deteriorate. She lost the use of her arms in 1999, and was unable to finish her doctorate, but has since been awarded an honorary doctorate by the university.

In 2003, Hillary was introduced to sailing. She says the experience gave her life "new meaning and purpose". This remarkable woman took on the challenge and inspiration of the sea. To overcome the problem of controlling a sailing vessel without the aid or arms and legs, a series of controls were developed that she could operate by sucking and plowing on a series of plastic tubes. She named her twenty-foot Artemis 20 sailboat "Me Too".

She soon to put her new skills to the test, and in August 2005 became the first quadriplegic to sail solo across the English Channel (in 6 hours and 13 minutes). In July 2007, she became the first female quadriplegic to sail solo around the Isle of Wight (in 11 hours 4 minutes). These fetes resulted in her being awarded the London Sunday Times Helen Rollason Award for Inspiration.

Hillary continued to set her sights high and on June 16, 2008 set off in an attempt to be the first quadriplegic to sail in stages solo around Britain. She departed at 3:00 PM from Dover on the first leg and arrived at Eastbourne at 11:55 PM, tired but happy to have completed the first leg of her journey.

The next day, she left for Brighton at 12:30 PM, arriving wet and cold and later than planned at 7:10 PM. It was decided to take a rest day as much for Hillary as her support team. The discovery of a failed boom fitting resulted in further days, and she was on her way on to Hayling on the sixth day of her venture. Weather prevented another day's departure, and she set off again on the eighth day of her journey bound for Limington. She arrived the next day, but sustained damage from severe weather.

England doesn't have the fine summer weather we experience at Santa Barbara. For the next seventeen days, weather and damage to the boat and it electronics prevented progress until she was finally able to depart on July and reached Portland on July 13, twenty-eight days after starting her overall venture. Then off to Brixham and on to Salcombe, arriving on the 33rd day of her trip. But severe weather, equipment problems, and then a structural problem with "Me Too's" keel resulted in further frustrating delays.

On forty-second day of the voyage, "Me Too" finally set sail from Salcombe and arrived at Mevagissey around noon on July 28. Then on to Newlyn, but more damage was sustained. Continued bad weather and technical problems led to the voyage being suspended on August 13. Hillary remained committed and determined to finish the voyage. But it would be another year before she could resume her quest.

The interim was spent repairing and improving "Me Too" and its equipment. Much had been learned, and all involved were optimistic that the next year's phase would result in Hillary Lister becoming the first quadriplegic to sail single-handed around Britain.

At 5:00 PM August 24, 2009, Hillary arrived at Harwich to an amazing welcome including pipes and drums. All England had learned of her valiant quest and her aim to show others that they could strive and succeed despite their disabilities. Then, fighting winds and weather most of the way, Hillary sailed on and finally arrived at Dover on August 30 at 5:45 PM to a MASS of welcomers.

The news media was upon her. "It is difficult to do all the press, my diaphragm is in a bad way and I get tired easily with the interviews. But I want people to know my story because it's important they realize disabled people can accomplish anything, given the right tools." She defined her aim as to help other disabled people feel empowered. to that end she set up her own charity, "Hillary's Dream Trust". The charity goal is to provide assistance to disabled and disadvantaged adults who dream of sailing.

Hilary sailed clockwise along the coasts of Cornwall, Wales, The East Coast of Ireland, Scotland, The Caledonian Canal, The East Coast of England and home to the finish line in Dover.

AN ANCIENT PRACTICE

Fishing is an ancient practice that dates back at least to the Upper Paleolithic period which began about 40,000 years ago. Isotopic analysis of the skeletal remains of Tianyuan man, a 40,000 year old modern human from eastern Asia, has shown that he regularly consumed freshwater fish. Archaeological features such as shell middens, discarded fish bones, and cave paintings indicate that sea foods were important for survival and were consumed in significant quantities. During this period, most people lived a hunter-gather lifestyle and were, of necessity, constantly on the move. However, where there are early examples of permanent settlements such as those at Serbia's ancient Lepenski Vir, they almost always show evidence of fish as a major source of food.

Spear fishing with barbed poles was widespread in Paleolithic times. Cosquer cave in Southern France contains cave art over 16,000 years old that includes drawings of seals that appear to have been harpooned. The Neolithic culture and technology spread worldwide between 4,000 and 8,000 years ago. Early hunters in India used harpoons with long cords for fishing since early times. The main fishing methods in use today came began at the time of early farming and pottery making.

The earliest known form of fishhook was called the gorge. The gorge was a relatively long, perhaps an inch or two, quite thin device constructed of wood, bone or stone. The ancients tied the gorge parallel to a baitfish and attached a handheld line just off-center of the gorge. When a larger fish swallowed the baitfish, the angler would tug on the line which would cause the gorge to position itself at right angles to the line and pierce the fish's throat. Gorges were crafted one at a time using whichever materials were available. In the era from 7500 to 3000 years ago, Native Americans of the California coast engaged in fishing with gorge hooks and line tackle. In addition, some tribes are known to have used plant toxins to induce numbness in stream fish to enable their capture.

The ancient river Nile was abundant with fish and provided staple food for much of the population. The Egyptians invented various implements and methods for fishing that are illustrated in tomb scenes, drawings, and papyrus documents. Simple reed boats were used for fishing. Woven nets, weir baskets made from willow branches, harpoons and hook and line were all in use. By the 12th dynasty, metal hooks with barbs were introduced. Nile perch, catfish and eels were among the most important fish. Some documents indicate that fishing may also have been pursued as a form of recreation.

Around 2800 - 2600 BC, traditional Chinese history begins with three semi-mystical and legendary individuals who taught the Chinese the arts of civilization. Of these, Fu Hsi was reputed to be the inventor of writing, hunting, trapping, and fishing.

There are numerous references to fishing in ancient literature, but in most cases the descriptions of nets and fishing gear do not go into detail. An early example from the Bible is Job 41:7: "Canst thou fill his skin with barbed irons? or his head with fish spears?"

Fishing scenes were rarely represented in ancient Greek culture, an indication of the low social status of fishing. The Museum of Fine Arts at Boston has a circa 500 BC wine cup on display that shows a boy crouched on a rock with a fishing rod in his right hand and a basket in his left. A similar basket with an opening on its top is shown in the water below – possibly a fish cage for keeping fish alive or a fish-trap. The Greek historian Polybius (circa 203 BC–120 BC), in his Histories, describes hunting for swordfish by using a harpoon with a barbed and detachable head.

Greek author Oppian of Corycus wrote a major treatise on sea fishing between 177 and 180 AD. He described various means of fishing including the use of nets cast from boats, scoop nets held open by a hoop, spears and tridents, and various traps "which work while their masters sleep". He explained fishing with a "motionless net" as follows: "The fishers set up very light nets of buoyant flax and wheel in a circle round about while they violently strike the surface of the sea with their oars and make a din with sweeping blow of poles. At the flashing of the swift oars and the noise the fish bound in terror and rush into the bosom of the net which stands at rest, thinking it to be a shelter: foolish fishes which, frightened by a noise, enter the gates of doom. Then the fishers on either side hasten with the ropes to draw the net ashore."

Pictorial Roman evidence comes from mosaics which show fishing from boats with rod and line as well as nets. Various species such as conger, lobster, sea urchin, octopus and cuttlefish are illustrated. In a reference to fishing, some Roman gladiators were armed with a trident and a casting-net, and would fight an opponent who carried a short sword and a helmet with the image of a fish on its front. The Greco-Roman sea god Neptune is depicted as wielding a fishing trident.

In another example of fishing in world history, pearl fishing was conducted in India as early as the 1st century BC. In Norse mythology the sea giantess Rán used a fish net to trap lost sailors. The Moche people of ancient Peru depicted fisherman on their ceramics.

The list goes on. Clearly fishing is one of the world's oldest avocations - at first for survival and sustenance and later adding recreation.

TALES FROM BOTTLES

In my small collection of maritime antiques, I have three ships in bottles. One of my goals has been to collect items made by legitimate and lonely sailors at sea who used their craftsmanship to pass the time on long and lonely days. Their abilities ranged from skilled to "nice try". Two of my models were made by craftsmen that were skilled to the extent that it is difficult to determine whether they were professionals or not. One is in a Haig Scotch bottle and the other in a decanter-styled bottle. The third was clearly made by an unskilled sailor, which makes it the easiest to judge as authentic. The model is in an old wine bottle; the ship is a crudely constructed three-masted square rigger; and the sea waves are crude and poorly painted. I love it! Whenever I examine it, I easily visualize its lonely builder doing his very best to duplicate his ship as he tried to fill the long hours as he crossed vast oceans and seas.

Ever since sailors began building models and cleverly sliding them into bottles, the world had held a fascination for these miniature ships, lovingly crafted by a seaman's callused hands during his off-watch hours. Over the years, these ships have turned up in the oddest places as sailors parted with their hard-earned keepsakes as gifts for their sweethearts, friends, and relatives, and often to pay for the debts they had ran up in port for entertainment, lodging, and a few tots at the bar.

But, when and where did the idea first occur of putting ships inside bottles? The history of ships in bottles parallels the development and improvement of clear glass bottles. As a result, it is usually by dating the bottle – using the shape and style of the bottle and the manufacturer's marks on the bottle – that the age of the model ship is determined.

However, this is at best an approximation, since the bottle may have been lying around for uncounted years in some dark corner before someone decided to bottle a ship. That aside, once manufacturing techniques progressed to the stage where glass bottles could be mass-produced that were clear enough to easily see through, sailors and others started putting ships, crucifixion scenes and other motifs inside them.

Author Jean Randier's *Nautical Antiques for the Collector* contains illustrations of the fine examples of ships in bottles displayed at the Musée de St. Malo in France. He concluded that early examples of bottled ships date from "not much earlier than the 1830's" since that was when dark, opaque bottle glass began being replaced with the clear glass made possible by the newer manufacturing processes developed at the dawn of the Industrial Revolution.

However, some earlier examples of ships in bottles are known to exist. The earliest found to date was built, and signed, by an Italian named Gioni Biondo in 1784. His model is in the Museum für Kunst - und Kulturgeschichte (Art and Cultural History Museum) in Lübeck, Germany. The date of this ship is unusually confirmed because the model builder was thoughtful enough to write the date on its sail. Whether this is the earliest example of the art remains unanswered.

"Patience Bottles'" – bottles with "Inside life" – depicting scenes of gold mining and smelting operations at what is now northern Hungary were made as early as 1700. While not ships in bottles, they confirm that the art of building inside bottles had already reached a high state by the mid 1700's.

The Dutch are famous for their ship models. The oldest known Dutch ship in a bottle is displayed in the Rotterdam Maritime Museum. It contains a model of a Netherlands Poon-schip – a small one- masted freighter with lee-boards (retractable boards on the side of a sailing ship to keep it from drifting sideways when underway). The ship hangs suspended from the bottle's stopper on two wires or threads and is dated 1795. The oldest American ship in bottle found to date is signed "Fire Island Lighthouse - E.J. Udall." Research indicates that Udall was the lighthouse keeper around 1886.

Over the years, our fascination with bottled items has lead many people to attempt building anything and everything inside bottles – buses, trains, fire engines, airplanes, houses, crucifixion scenes, a sailor sitting at a table building a ship in a tiny bottle, and even bar scenes complete with customers playing cards. Japanese bottlers added their own unique touch by building ships that sailed into the bottle, rather than the Western way of sailing out of the bottle towards the neck. Yet, despite all these various bottle topics, none seem to hold our fascination as much as old bottled ships.

There are many locations throughout the United States and the world to see ships in bottles and ship models. The maritime collections at Mystic Seaport Museum include more than a thousand full-rigged models, eight hundred ship builder's half-models, and seventy "models in bottles." Also included are forty shadowbox models and thirty tow tank models. The museum and seaport are a must to visit for anyone interested in the sea and its history.

The Ships-In-Bottles Association of America is one of several affiliated ships-in-bottles organizations throughout the world. All share the common goals of promoting the traditional nautical art of building ships-in-bottles through the exchange of ideas and the hope of advancing the cause of international good will by sharing mutual interests. Their journal *The Bottle Shipwright* is published quarterly and introduces ideas for ship-bottling. Go to www.shipsinbottles.org.

How do they get the ship models with their tall masts through the narrow neck of a bottle? First the ship model is constructed. Then the masts and sails are laid flat on-deck with all rigging attached to the hull with the exception of the forestay (line at the bow of the boat). The model is carefully slid through the bottle neck and into place in the bottle. Then a string attached to the forestay is pulled and the masts rise to their vertical position. The forestay is glued or attached in place and the operation is complete.

THE WRECK OF THE *WINDFIELD SCOTT*

California's gold rush was launched in 1848 with the discovery of gold at Sutter's Mill. This event marked one of the largest migrations in history, as people from around the world rushed to California seeking to strike it rich. The great gold rush created almost hysteric demand for ships to carry miners and goods to California. Many Easterners chose not to take the overland route across the United States, but sought sailing ships to make the 14,000-mile journey around Cape Horn to the isolated frontier called California. Eventually, shorter overland routes across Panama and Nicaragua allowed travelers to avoid rounding Cape Horn and to connect with steamers operating between Panama and San Francisco.

On October 20, 1850 the New York Herald announced, "Another new steamer of about two thousand tons will be launched from the shipyard of Westervelt & Makay on Tuesday morning at 10 o'clock. She is intended for the trade between Panama and San Francisco. We understand that no expense has been spared to secure strength, safety and speed, and she will bear the name of the gallant General in Chief of the US Army, Winfield Scott."

The Winfield Scott was built of wood with double iron bracing that included white oak, live oak, locust, cedar and Georgia yellow Ppine. Mounted to her round stern was an American eagle with a coat of arms and a bust carved in the likeness of General Winfield Scott. The steamer had accommodations for 165 cabin and 150 steerage passengers, although she would ultimately carry numbers exceeding 400. From her round bow to her straight stern, she had a registered length of 225 feet and a 45 foot beam.

The captain and clerk's offices and the kitchen were located on deck – all very commodious. Between decks aft was the general drawing room, with two-berth staterooms positioned on each side. The forward saloon was similarly arranged. Beneath the drawing room was the dinning saloon which could comfortably seat more than 100 persons. It also had staterooms at each side, all thoroughly ventilated and well lighted. Forward were the pantries and the main semi-circular staircase. Beneath the dining saloon was space for the steerage passengers, also very airy and light. Few vessels could boast of such excellence in the important necessaries for the comfort and health of her passengers.

The Winfield Scott was not immediately dispatched to the Pacific Coast, but was initially engaged in servicing the New York to New Orleans route under the flag of Davis, Brooks and Company. In 1852, ownership was transferred to the New York and San Francisco Steamship Company Line and the side wheel passenger steamer departed for San Francisco via Cape Horn, arriving on April 28, 1852. She was advertised as "doubled engined" with passengers to connect with the steamer United States for New York. The line changed its name in May 1853 to the New York and California Steamship Company, which retained ownership of the Winfield Scott until the company came to an end. Winfield Scott was then sold in July 1853 to the Pacific Mail Steamship Company. The steamer had become quite popular on the Panama-San Francisco route and provided not only popular passenger service but also carried important intelligence, mail, newspapers, and express freight, including gold mined from the mother-load returning east.

The Winfield Scott's early steam propulsion system was not without its problems as passenger Asa Cyrus Call noted in his diary on December 1, 1853. "I embarked on the Steamer 'Winfield Scott' last Thursday, and at 12 o'clock we left Vally's Street Wharf [San Francisco] for Panama. We had fine weather till Friday evening when it became foggy. One of the boilers had been leaking through the day which had retarded our progress, and the 'Sierra Nevada' had passed us, but it was repaired on Friday afternoon, and we were running about twelve miles an hour when I went to bed on Friday night."

Passenger Edward Bosqui recalls what happened later that night. "At midnight I was suddenly awakened from a sound sleep by a terrible jar and crashing of timbers. Tumbling out of my berth, I was confronted by the horror stricken visage of my toothless and baldheaded stateroom companion, who had not time to secure his wig and false teeth and was groping about to find them. Leaving him paralyzed with fear, I hurried out on deck, where my attention was fixed on a wall of towering cliffs, the tops of which were hidden by the fog and darkness and appeared about to fall and crush us. All around was the loud booming of angry breakers surging about invisible rocks."

Winfield Scott became a total loss at Anacapa Island, with over 400 passengers becoming stranded on the small island. On the following day, the side-wheel steamer California on her

northbound run to San Francisco from Panama with a full complement of passengers, arrived at

the island and took on some of the women and children and the cargo of gold bullion. After eight long days, the California returned well provisioned and rescued the remaining passengers and continued on to Panama. Some crewman stayed behind to recover what they could of the remaining mail and passenger baggage still submerged in the hull.

Today the submerged remains of the Winfield Scott lie off Anacapa Island, 27 nautical miles southeast of Santa Barbara, part of the NOAA Channel Islands National Marine Sanctuary and the Channel Islands National Park. The site continues to be studied by archaeologists representing both agencies, and assisted by the Coastal Maritime Archaeology Resources Organization. A number of salvage operations had been previously conducted on the wreck over the years, but many parts can still be found in about 30 feet of water. The major artifacts remaining are the paddle-wheel shaft and hub, the paddle-wheel shaft support, and portions of her side-lever machinery.

The underwater archaeology exhibit at the Santa Barbara Maritime Museum features a diorama of the shipwreck site. A simulated diver working from a model of the sanctuary research vessel Shearwater, tours the site stopping at various parts of the Winfield Scott. Actual underwater videotape footage runs consecutively on a monitor screen and provides an overview of the history of the wreck and work being performed by underwater archaeologists. Also included in the exhibit

are historic artifacts from the Winfield Scott as well as examples of
tools used by underwater archaeologists to record shipwreck data and
information.

SAN MIGUEL ISLAND

Cold steep seas crash against lonely Richardson's Rock and then race on to collide with fog-shrouded San Miguel Island off Central California's isolated ocean coast. Only the most stalwart of sailors reach this westernmost Channel Island when its winds are up and blustering.

Radiocarbon dating indicates there was human occupation on the island over ten thousand years ago. Archaeologists have mapped 542 Indian sites on the island, evidence that Indian settlement was more than temporary.

Portuguese explorer Juan Rodriguez Cabrillo was the first European to land on San Miguel Island, arriving on October 18, 1542. Cabrillo named the present-day islands of San Miguel and Santa Rosa "Islas de San Lucas." Later, he changed the name of San Miguel Island to "La Posesion," after one of his ships. The Chumash Indians called San Miguel Island "Tuqan."

While Cabrillo was wintering on San Miguel Island, he broke either an arm or a leg which soon became seriously infected. When he realized he was dying, Cabrillo turned his expedition over to his chief pilot Bartolome Ferrer. He died from his injury on January 3, 1543. It is generally believed he was buried on the island, although his grave has never been found. The explorer was honored in 1937 by the Cabrillo Civic Clubs of California who placed a monument to Cabrillo on a knoll on San Miguel Island overlooking Cuyler Harbor.

After Cabrillo's death, the island was renamed "Juan Rodrigues" and also "La Capitana" in his honor. It appeared on a map In 1748 as "San Bernardo" and the same on explorer Miguel Costanso's 1770 map. The name "San Miguel" became generally accepted when English explorer George Vancouver marked it as such on his charts in 1793.

In 1848, the Treaty of Guadalupe Hidalgo ceded mainland California to the U.S. Government, but the Channel Islands were not included. The treaty was redrawn a few years later, but San Miguel Island was again inadvertently omitted from the list of islands the United States was to acquire. In 1895, Great Britain intended to take advantage of this technicality in order to use the island as a ship coaling station on the route between Vancouver and the Hawaiian Islands. President Grover Cleveland must have heard of the threat, for in July 1896 local U.S. Marshall Nicholas Covarrubias was ordered to sail with a group of surveyors to record the property. The surveyors completed their work, and the island was claimed as a United States possession.

As on the other Channel Islands, squatters, fisherman and otter hunters lived and worked on San Miguel during these historic times. In the 18th and 19th centuries, sea mammal hunters were drawn to the island to capture its coveted fur bearing sea otters. Yankees, Russian sponsored Aleuts and Kanakas, and others were among those who came to hunt.

Ranching began on the island sometime around 1850. The early "owners" of the islands were not legal owners, but owners by possession only. The first record of a long-term resident on San Miguel Island was George Nidever, who purchased 6000 sheep, 125 head of cattle, 25 horses and "All the right, title, interest, claim and ownership..." to one half of the island. The sale was made by the Santa Barbara County Sheriff to settle the debts of Samuel C. Bruce. This was the first recorded deed for San Miguel Island. It is unknown how Samuel Bruce obtained his "interest."

The island was "bought and sold" several times over the next 18 years. Then, in 1887, one-half of the island was purchased for $10,000 by William G. Waters, a veteran of the Civil War who soon began ranching. Ten years later, Waters and his investors formed the San Miguel Island Company. In 1908, Waters and investor Elias Beckman became involved in a lawsuit which resulted in the U.S. government claiming its right of ownership of San Miguel.

Between 1911 and 1948, San Miguel Island saw its share of lessees with the U.S. Government. One was Robert Brooks who hired his long-time friend Herbert Lester to help manage the island. Lester was a World War I shell-shock victim who had spent several years in an Army hospital. Brooks felt the island would help him.

In 1930, the Lesters moved into the house originally built by Captain Waters. They seldom went to the mainland, and when it came time to educate their two daughters, Mrs. Lester taught them herself. Herbert Lester became quite proficient in obtaining unusual memorabilia from island shipwrecks and displayed them at his "Killer Whale Bar". He even proclaimed himself "King of San Miguel." Lester's endless charm and astonishingly likable personality together with Elizabeth Lister's humor and intellect served as a magnet to draw famous and plain people out to the island. In 1935, the film *Mutiny on the Bounty* was filmed at San Miugel.

Sadly, Herbert Lester, despondent over his health and ever tightening Navy restrictions, committed suicide in 1942. He was buried above Harris Point on San Miguel Island. His wife Elizabeth raised her children on the mainland. In 1974, Mrs. Lester published *The Legendary King of San Miguel Island*, a history of her family's life on the island. Elizabeth Lester died in 1981 and is buried next to her husband.

In 1948, the Navy revoked Robert Brook's lease and ordered him to be off the land within 72 hours. Brooks had to leave behind many of his belongings and livestock. He returned just once in 1950 on a short trip to collect some additional items, but he was never allowed to collect them all.

Sheep grazed undisturbed on San Miguel Island until the 1960s, when the Navy ordered their elimination. The island continued to be a central point for naval training well into the 1970's. Then San Miguel Island became part of both the Channel Islands National Park and the Channel Islands Marine Sanctuary and remains such today. The National Park extends one mile off-shore and the Marine Sanctuary extends from mean high-water and out six nautical miles.

DANGEROUS WATERS

It was a cold wintery night in 1872 as the 148-foot side-wheeler steamship Sacramento headed up the coast of Mexico bound for San Francisco. She was carrying her usual load of passengers and crew, but this time she was also laden with two million dollars in gold bullion and silver coin.

After leaving the lee of Cedros Island and crossing the Bay of Vizcaino, Sacramento's navigator attempted to make a land sighting of Punta Baja or Isla San Martin through the murky night. But suddenly he smelled the tell-tale tang of kelp and knew it was too late. The ship abruptly ran high upon what was to become known after the ill-fated ship as Sacramento Reef. It was also to become known as a "seething cauldron of Hell."

As the Sacramento rapidly disintegrated, her passengers and crew clung to the drifting wreckage. Finally, they made it to San Martin Island, cold, exhausted and frightened. They were later rescued, but what became of the fortune in gold and silver that was lost among these rocks is not known.

The survivors were stranded one hundred and fifty miles south of Ensenada. Large and lethal Sacramento Reef is steep with ocean depths ranging from twenty-eight to seventy-five feet close alongside. Barely submerged rocks spread beneath almost four square miles of sea surface, providing ideal grounds for dense, floating kelp. The reef is difficult to detect, as the slippery kelp fronds obscure the breaking seas and dampen their warning hiss.

Just twelve miles north of Sacramento Reef, the isolated headland of Punta Baja has claimed its own golden treasures and the lives of at least two other vessels. In 1851, the crew of the American steamship Union was celebrating the Fourth of July, perhaps with too many patriotic toasts. The ship struck Point Baja and sank. All the passengers were rescued, but not their luggage. For years afterward, gold and silver coins washed ashore along nearby beaches.

Hundreds of ships have been wrecked and sunk along Baja California's rugged coastline, ranging from 18th century whaling schooners, to 19th century steam-driven side-wheelers, to modern sloops and sportfishers. Some vessels like the Sacramento struck hidden reefs. Others were claimed by storms, fires and freak waves.

Many lives have been lost – miners returning from Gold Rush claims, passengers of the Victorian era, fishermen plying their ageless passion, and more. Some ships went to their murky graves laden with gold and jewels, while others bore nothing more than the last prayers of those aboard. Today, lavender wreathes of coral decorate the tilted decks and broken ribs that thrust from the sandy bottom, illuminated by shafts of sunlight filtering down. There is no doubt that these dangerous waters will claim more victims.

On the lighter side, the cargo of a thousand cases of Tecate beer washed ashore after the ship Noroeste wrecked on Punta Baja in 1978. It's reported that the local salvagers partied for a week consuming the free cerveza.

HOW HAPPY IS A CLAM?

During the mature period of their lives, only the most masochistic of molluscs could be expected to experience anything but a sense of imminent dread. Even the most comfortable of clams can hardly be called the life and soul of the party. All they can expect is a watery existence, and the likelihood that at any moment to be rudely interrupted by a man with a spade, followed by conveyance to a very hot place.

The saying "Happy as a Clam" is very definitely American and hardly known elsewhere. The fact is, we've lost its second half, which made everything clear. The full expression is "happy as a clam at high tide or happy as a clam at high water." Clam digging has to be done at low tide, when the digger stands the best chance of finding and extracting them. At high tide, clams are comfortably covered in water and able to feed comparatively at ease and free of the risk that some hunter will suddenly rip them from their sandy berths. That seems a good enough definition of "happy."

The saying in its shortened form was first recorded in the 1830s, although it is almost certainly much older.

LANGUAGE OF THE SEA

Etymology is the study of the history of words and how their form and meaning have changed over time. A number of years ago, etymologist Mario Pei wrote that someday soon there may be a truly international language – perhaps by the end of the twentieth century. It would seem that his prediction failed to occur, but on further reflection it can be argued that there is indeed an international language that works very well – the language of the sea.

With over seventy-one percent of the earth's surface under water, it is small wonder that the myriad number of seafarers and those along the shores had to develop a language that could be understood by millions around the world - regardless of nationality. Traders on-shore, encounters between ships, mixed international crews, ship to ship and ship to shore radio communications, navigational devices and aids, and many more all require common understanding by those who deal with the sea throughout the world. As a result, almost from the beginning of human history a common language of the sea began to develop, and it continues to this day as technology and the world changes.

Because of the long seafaring history of England and its colonies around the world, much of the language of the sea is English. If you step aboard a large merchant ship of almost any national flag, you will probably see the safety, operational, and principal compartment nameplates in two languages – English and the ship's own national language. For example, in the Red Sea, you might hear a Greek officer conversing with a Jordanian pilot, or in Le Havre a Danish captain talking with a French tugboat skipper in . . . English!

In the tenth century, the inhabitants of the British Isles were not seafarers to any extent, unlike their neighbors in Scandinavia who had been sailors since the fifth century. But the English had to take to the sea in order to defend against Viking raiders. In addition, a large number of Danes and Norwegians settled in Britain where they continued their maritime activities. The French language entered that of the sea when the Normans invasion of England of 1066, and their influence continued during recurring wars over the next 300 years.

The language of the sea continues to expand and change as nations, communications, and technology follow new paths. The following are samples of the unique language of the sea. (The approximate century of first use is indicated. Also shown is country or origin.)

- Aloft – Up the mast. As in the crew went aloft to work the sails. (12th – English)
- Baggywrinkle – Padding to prevent chafe (wear) aloft (14th – English)
- Bitter-End – The inboard (closest to the ship) end of a line. (15th English)
- Bootlegger – An old term for smuggler, revived in Prohibition days. Sailors smuggling goods ashore hid them in their seaboots. (18th English)
- Carronade – A special short, light, ship's cannon named of the Carron Iron Works of Scotland where it was first made in 1779.
- Cat-o'-Nine Tails – The terrible whip with which sailors were flogged. It is believed that its origin was from Egypt, where the cat was sacred, and even then was believed to have nine lives. The Egyptians were said to believe that by scourging with cat hide, good passed from the whip to the victim. It's dreaded nickname was "cat".
- Chantey – A shipboard song, sung while at a specific job, such as walking a capstan, hoisting a sail, etc. A "Chanteyman" would usually lead the singing, and the crew or work party would join in. From the 16th century French "chanter" – to sing.
- Chart – Well known to all as a map dealing with portions of the sea, but also very old. It traces back to the Greek

word for map "Khartes," but is probably from much earlier Egyptian origin – perhaps before 3000 B.C, more than 5000 years ago.

- Clean Bill of Health – A document indicating that a vessel has no serious illness on-board and is in a generally healthy condition. 18th Century England, and now used by the general population in addition to its maritime application.

- A collision at sea can ruin your whole day. – This simple statement, according to one naval historian, is attributed to Thucydides, a Greek seaman, adventurer, and statesman of the fourth century B. C.

- Eyes – The extreme bow (front) of a ship. It's origin is uncertain; it could refer to the eyes on the dragonheads usually seen on the bows of Viking ships of the tenth to twelfth centuries.

- Fathom – A mariner's unit of measure – 6 feet. The term came from the Anglo-Saxon word "foethm," meaning the space reached by the fully extended arms held out to each side. Probably 12th century England. As a side note, I used to measure rope lengths this way when I operated the ship's chandlery at Santa Barbara Harbor.

- Forecastle – (Often abbreviated to Fo'c's'l and pronounced that way.) Now the forward deck on a ship, originally a raised platform at the bow, often armored, for archers and, later, musketeers. Also, on many ships it was used for crew's quarters. One old timer was quoted as saying, ". . . and it wasn't no castle."

THE GOLETA CANNONS

Heavy storms and strong tides hit the Goleta coast in the winter of 1981. High waves scoured away over ten feet of sand, revealing bedrock and beach stretches that had not seen the light of day for decades. Jogging along bleak Goleta Beach, Nolan Harter was surprised to see several encrusted shapes partially uncovered from the sand. After a closer look, he decided they must be old cannons and took immediate steps to contact parties that would have the resources to salvage them before the Pacific buried them once again. The find was extraordinary – the only such recovery in California's history.

As it turned out, five heavily encrusted cannons were recovered and transported to the University of California at Santa Barbara where they were immediately placed in a special chemical bath to prevent rapid exfoliation which occurs when long-submerged iron objects are exposed to the air. Studies of the cannons would center around determining what the cannons were, where they came from, and how they came to be on Goleta Beach.

It will probably never be known exactly how the cannons arrived in the Santa Barbara Channel. There are, however, many theories. Early speculation suggested that Sir Francis Drake may have left the cannons behind during his 1578 visit to California. Research on the cannons has proved this to be unfeasible, as the cannons are of an 18th century design and there is no evidence that Drake actually entered the Santa Barbara Channel. Many believe that the cannons were thrown off a sailing ship as a result of a shipwreck or grounding. When vessels ran aground, heavy items (like cannons) were thrown overboard to raise the waterline to enable a grounded vessel to refloat. Based on the arrangement of the cannons along the shore, this theory is very possible. Local historian Justin Ruhge believes that the cannons may have come from the Santa Barbara schooner Dorotea, which foundered near the Goleta Slough around 1829 or 1830. The cannons may have been pushed overboard at this time. When Santa Barbara resident Jose de la Guerra purchased Dorotea, the ship's bill of sale listed the inclusion of five cannons like these found on Goleta beach.

Recent discovery of the cannons captivated local and distant audiences alike, and the restoration of these maritime treasures became truly a community effort. Hundreds of volunteers spent thousands of hours researching and restoring the cannons. A committee was established in 1984 to oversee the restoration process and to plan the cannons' future display. The committee included representatives from the University of California at Santa Barbara, Goleta Valley Historical Society, Santa Barbara Trust for Historic Preservation, Santa Barbara Historical Society, Courthouse Legacy Foundation and the County Board of Supervisors. Recognizing the importance of this maritime discovery, the participating organizations worked to present the cannon history to the public. Much discussion surrounded the future home for the cannons. Because the artifacts were unique to Goleta's maritime history, the committee decided in March of 1989 that custody of the cannons should be given to the Goleta Valley Historical Society; however, loan of the cannons for temporary display could be arranged, which resulted in two of the cannons now being on display at the Santa Barbara Maritime Museum.

Firing such weapons is no simple matter. A gun crew would generally consist of three to five men for each of the Goleta Cannons. The steps for firing were as follows:

1. <u>Worm the Gun</u> Using a long wooden rod with a metal screw scraper attached at one end, scrape any residual material from the inside of the barrel.
2. <u>Sponge the Gun</u> Run a wet cloth back and forth the length of the barrel to clean it and to extinguish any burning particles.
3. <u>Insert the Fuse</u> Place the fuse into the touch hole.
4. <u>Load the Gun</u> Place a charge of black powder and wadding into the barrel.

5. <u>Ram the Gun</u> Insert a long-handled rammer to tamp down the charge in the barrel.
6. <u>Load the Projectile</u> Insert a cannon ball into the barrel and ram it down.
7. <u>Prime the Gun</u> Pour a small amount of black powder into the vent hole of the cannon so the flame will reach the charge.
8. <u>Fire the Gun</u> Apply a slow-lit match to the fuse. When the powder ignites, the gun will fire.
9. <u>Hold Your Ears!!!</u>

There are a number of clues to the cannons' past. By comparing them with known cannon designs and markings, researchers were able to determine that the cannons were most likely made in Britain during the middle to late 1700's. At that time, the British were the primary builders of small ships' guns like the three and four pound projectile Goleta cannons.

There are several differences between the five cannons. Two were cast from the same pattern and two others from a different pattern. Four are four pounders, and the other is a three pounder. Trunnion markings (cylindrical projections on the sides of the barrel used to mount a cannon in its carriage) also provide valuable clues. One is date stamped 1778, and other markings indicate it was probably built by the Scottish Cannon Company. Two others have a raised "H" on their right trunnions, indicating likely construction by the Harrison Foundry between 1734 and 1746. Ages vary, as indicated by differences in firing provisions. Two cannons have touch holes and the other three were fired by later-invented vent field patches.

Lack of ornamentation indicates that the cannons were likely from a merchant ship rather than a royal or naval vessel. All merchant vessels carried cannons – primarily three to six pounders. Guns of this type were used for a variety of reasons including defense against enemy vessels, navigation through fog using the echo from firing to detect a nearby landmass, and alerting coastal towns of the ship's arrival.

RESCUE AT SEA

One of the roughest areas of the world's seas is along the rocky and storm-tossed coast of Norway. Incidents had been so numerous that the Norwegian Society for Sea Rescue (NSSR) was formed in 1891 to further boating safety and, when necessary, to conduct rescues. NSSR now has 53,000 individual members and operates 39 rescue vessels. Some of these are all-weather, medium endurance, high-seas capable craft, but there are also many all-weather lifeboats. Most of the lifeboat crews are paid and live aboard their boats for twenty-day periods, taking the next twenty days off. Since its founding, the NSSR has saved thousands of lives and rescued tens of thousands of vessels.

It took an evolution of design before lifeboats were developed that could withstand the severe off-shore weather and storms to conduct rescues and provide skilled local pilots to safely assist ships to quiet harbors. A Norwegian designer named Colin Archer put pen to paper in the late 1800's to create vessels that could perform for extended periods at sea in all weather conditions . For one of his early designs, he chose a double-ended shape that would part on-rushing seas at either end.

As word spread of Archer's revolutionary off-shore boat, his fame and business grew, which brought him to Norwegian physician Oscar Tybring. After a storm, Tybring had been walking along the shore when he discovered a wrecked ship with all the crew drowned. Realizing that the brutal Norwegian coast had no lifesaving service, he enlisted others to help form such an organization. When it came to building rescue vessels, Tybring asked several designers to compete, and Colin Archer won the task of creating a redningskoite, or rescue boat.

Archer designed a vessel with a double-ended shape that would be able to handle terrible sea conditions and still be maneuverable and capable of fighting off a lee shore. At around 47-feet, the first redningskoite, appropriately named Colin Archer, was launched in 1893. But it was a redningskoite launched in 1895 and named after Oscar Tybring that holds the record for saving 329 lives and 102 vessels in fearsome conditions.

Santa Barbara became exposed to the world of rescue at sea when a rugged, slow sailing, double-ended, ketch-rigged rescue boat named "Oscar Tybring" arrived in our harbor in the 1950's. Movie actor and life long sailor Sterling Hayden had purchased the very same historic Norwegian lifeboat that held the life saving record.

Hayden was a genuine adventurer and man of action, not dissimilar from many of his movie parts. He ran away to sea at 15, as a ship's boy. His first job was on a schooner en route to Balboa Beach, California from New London, Connecticut. Later, he was a fisherman on the Grand Banks of Newfoundland, ran a charter yacht, and served as a fireman on eleven trips to Cuba aboard a steamer. He skippered a trading schooner in the Caribbean after earning his master's license, and in 1937 served as mate on an around the world cruise on the schooner Yankee.

For most of his career as a leading man, Sterling Hayden specialized in westerns and film noir, such as *Johnny Guitar, The Asphalt Jungle* and *The Killing*. Later on, he became noted as a character actor for such roles as Gen. Jack D. Ripper in *Dr. Strangelove or: How I Learned to Stop Worrying and Love the Bomb* (1964). He also played the Irish policeman, Captain McCluskey, in Francis Ford Coppola's *The Godfather* in 1972.

As a teenager, I sailed as a crewmember on two of Hayden's boats. Sterling Hayden was a traditionalist, and scorned having an engine on a sailing ship. That made it tough getting the clumsily sailing Oscar Tybring back to her harbor mooring in little or no wind. We would lower a large dory over the side, attach a long line, and then man the oars to gradually tow the heavy rescue ship to her mooring can in the harbor. Another problem was that the "Oscar" had no boom (a long, wooden pole attached near the bottom of the mast which stretched the mainsail outward for proper sailing). When the "Oscar" was tacked and the mainsail flapped like an angry flag, you had to take care not to be the victim of a vicious whack on the head. This happened to me once, and I was thrown across the deck into a heap against the rail. I never let it happen again.

Sterling Hayden's next boat was a pilot ship I had first seen seven years before as the Gracie S. Hayden renamed it Wanderer, probably after his rocky lifetime. At one point, he escaped from his marital and other problems, "kidnapped" his children, and sailed for Tahiti on Wanderer. When he first sailed her to Santa Barbara, we all lined the breakwater to see the historic ship sail by. Hayden was up for the moment and fired a salute to Santa Barbara with the ship's cannon. When Wanderer tied up at the Navy Pier, we could all see his miscalculation – the cannon had been improperly aligned, and a portion of the ship's rail had blasted away.

Hayden was a large man. Standing 6-feet 5-inches tall, he was one of the tallest leading actors of all time. His rather high-pitched voice didn't match his great size. But he was very strong. I recall straining to tighten a halyard with another crewmember when Hayden suddenly appeared, and in his less than manly voice squeaked, "One side!" while he decisively wrenched the halyard downward to its proper setting.

In 1976, to address the needs of rescue organizations around the world to raise funds, exchange information and provide co-operation, a group of American professional seamen and business men formed the Association for Rescue at Sea (AFRAS). The Norwegian and United States organizations have recently embarked on a large program to modernize and standardize the rescue fleet.

In 1988, AFRAS contributed to the refitting of Hayden's earlier vessel Oscar Tybring. Later, the Oscar Tybring was refurbished and refitted by a dedicated group in California in honor of the Norsk Selskab Til Skibbrudnes Redning *(Norwegian Sea Rescue)* centennial in 1991. In 2004 the venerable old life ship was entered in the Classic Yacht Race at Channel Islands Harbor in California. After 115 years, the Oscar Tybring was still proudly sailing the seas.

HOLYSTONE

The use of sea terms began thousands of years ago, and their origin frequently can be interesting. One such term is "holystone."

A holystone is a soft and brittle sandstone that was used for scouring and whitening the wooden decks of ships as part of making them "bristol." (Bristol as a sailing term is from the 1500's and means shipshape and is derived from that fact that Bristol, England at that time was known for its well fashioned ships.) Holystone was used in the British and American Navies for scrubbing the decks of their sailing ships.

The term may have come from the fact that "holystoning the deck" was originally done on one's knees, as in prayer. Smaller holystones were called "prayer books" and larger ones "Bibles." Some English churches were constructed of sandstone that worked well in ship deck scrubbing. Such stones are said to have been taken from the ruined church of St. Helens on the Isle of Wight off the south of England. Tall square rigged sailing ships would often anchor in St. Helens Roads to take on fresh water before setting off on their journeys, and would collect holystones from St. Helens and may also have collected them from churches still in operation.

Holystoning is said to have been banned in the US Navy in 1931 because it wore down the decks the decks of the ships, but a photo on the US Navy's *Navsource* purports to show Navy midshipmen holystoning the deck of the battleship USS Missouri in 1951 in a standing position).

John Huston's 1956 film *Moby Dick*, and most recently Peter Weir's 2003 film *Master and Commander - The Far Side of the World*, show sailors scrubbing the decks with holystones.

Holystoning is referenced in Richard Henry Dana's diary which became the 1840 classic *Two Years Before the Mast* – perhaps when the brig *Pilgrim* visited Santa Barbara?

"Some officers have been so driven to find work for the crew in a ship ready for sea, that they have set them to pounding the anchors and scraping the chain cables. This kind of work, of course, is not kept up off Cape Horn, Cape of Good Hope, and in extreme north and south latitudes; but I have seen the decks washed down and scrubbed, when the water would have frozen if it had been fresh; and all hands kept at work upon the rigging, when we had on our pea-jackets, and our hands so numb that we could hardly hold our marline-spikes. Six days shalt thou labor and do all thou art able, and on the seventh—holystone the decks and scrape the cable."

The Iowa class battleships (*New Jersey, Wisconsin, Missouri,* and *Iowa*) all had wooden decks (over the steel decks) and were holystoned regularly until they variously came out of commission during the 1990s.

The Baltimore class of heavy cruisers all had wooden decking in the area around and near the quarterdeck, and extending fore and aft along the sides of the ship. The USS *Saint Paul* (CA73) was the last of this class left in commission, serving in the Vietnam War as Seventh Fleet flagship. It was decommissioned in 1971. Her "cruise books" have many photographs of the deck divisions holystoning the wooden decks.

Holystoning in the modern navy was not generally done on the knees but with a stick resting in a depression in the flat side of the stone and held under the arm and in the hands and moved back and forth with grain on each plank while standing – or sort of leaning over to put pressure on the stick driven stone.

THE MAN-O'-WAR'S MAN

The following is quoted from: *Seaman - Navy Training Course - 1951 - Indoctrination For New Sailors:*

"By this time you're a deep salt water man with probably a few miles of ocean travel behind you. You belong to an outfit that has never lost a war, and wear a uniform which has never been turned stern to the enemy. The guns you fire are a little more complicated than the broadside on the old Constitution, but World War II has proved that, although the Navy doesn't have wooden ships any more, it still has the same iron men.

The men of the white stripe branch, the seamen, are still the great backbone of the Navy. They still sail ships, fire the guns, and man the boats. You want to be not only a sailor, but a real seaman as well; a man who can pass a shell, fire a gun, throw a hitch, make a splice, get around in a boat, and perform all the duties of a true man-o'-war's man. Besides that, like the men who went before you, you want to be clean, square, and on the level with your shipmates, with your officers, with everybody".

These words are till true today, but now it's both men and women and more sophisticated weapons that comprise the best navy in the world.

LET THERE BE LIGHT

Giant storms at sea are dangerous, but far more boats and ships are lost against the shores of the world than in its depths. Often, vessels that have been abandoned by captain and crew are later found gently floating on after-storm swells. In many cases, it is far safer to stay onboard than to abandon ship. And the shores are far less forgiving than off-shore waters, and vessels break up at astounding speed when they meet rocks and beaches.

California has eight hundred and forty miles of coastline, ranging from pleasant sandy beaches to nearly vertical mountains that plunge straight down into the sea. Prevailing westerly winds tend to push vessels closer to the shore than intended - often with deadly results. Wise navigators regularly plot their course miles from the nearest landfall.

Prior to the middle of the 19th Century, California's coast was dark and largely uncharted. The area was so poorly understood that many mariners and chartmakers believed it to be an island. Some early explorers unsuccessfully endeavored to sail around the California "island," and many lost their lives and their ships in the attempt.

By the 1850's, the gold rush lured many ships and boats to our coastline bearing hopeful miners and settlers. To increase safe passage for the rapidly growing exodus of immigrants to California, the United States government began establishing a string of thirty powerful navigational lighthouses from San Diego in the south to Crescent City in the north. Their need was further emphasized when the lighthouse building contractor's ship *Oriole* was wrecked on a shoal near Cape

Disappointment and the Columbia River, the planned site for the fifth lighthouse.

For good reason, Santa Barbara's wind blown coastline was designated for five of the thirty planned lighthouses. Over one hundred years later strong winds, high seas, dense fog, and strong currents still cause seasoned mariners to take every advantage of seamanship and navigation to make successful passages through our channel.

The first lighthouse to protect Santa Barbara waters was established in 1874 at Point Hueneme. At that time, lighthouse design resembled a Victorian home with a wooden tower emerging from its center – in this case 52 feet high. Lighthouse keepers and their families resided in the home portion of the structure. They were on call twenty-four hours every day to ensure the constant reliability of these lifesaving sentinels. Each lighthouse light is timed to flash at a different interval and duration to allow mariners to determine which lighthouse it is. The original Point Hueneme lighthouse has been replaced with an automatic and unmanned light. The light flashes white every thirty seconds and has a range of twenty miles.

Next in line is the light on Anacapa Island at the eastern end of the Santa Barbara Channel. From a distance, the island appears placid, but its jagged rocks have torn apart more than its share of passing ships. In 1853, the side wheel steamer *Winfield Scott* slammed into the island, stranding 250 passengers for several days without food or shelter. But it wasn't until 1912 that construction of the lighthouse began. Equipped with an automated, acetylene lamp on a steel tower, it is located near the very spot that the *Winfield Scott* had driven into the rocks nearly sixty years earlier. In 1932, the structure was replaced with a masonry tower 277 feet above the sea. The lighthouse is now part of Channel Islands National Park, and has a modern lens that flashes twice every sixty seconds with a range of twenty miles. Even today, sighting Anacapa light is extremely important to up-coast bound vessels to ensure they are passing safely into the narrow eastern entry of Santa Barbara Channel.

The lighthouse at Santa Barbara was built in 1856. Its first keeper was Albert Williams, but he soon tired of the routine and returned to farming. His wife Julia took over as the keeper after Albert's replacement left. She went on to run the lighthouse for the next forty years, and became one of our country's most famous lighthouse keepers. In all that time, Julia Williams spent only two nights away from the station – to attend the weddings of two of her sons. The lighthouse was destroyed in Santa Barbara's 1925 earthquake. Today, it is a modern, unstaffed automatic beacon located on the cliffs of the Mesa near Meigs Road. It flashes white every ten seconds and has a range of twenty-five miles.

In my opinion, the most ominous waters off California are those from Point Conception up-coast and past Point Arguello. There are just fifteen miles between the two points, but over the years churning seas and gale force winds have claimed dozens of vessels ranging from eighteenth century Spanish sailing ships to twentieth century yachts and steamers. On the first of October in 1854, four hundred and fifteen people perished when the steamship Yankee Blade rammed into the rocks close to shore. She carried a fortune in gold bullion which has since been recovered.

Another major tragedy took place on the evening of September 8, 1925 when seven U.S. Navy destroyers slammed into the fog-shrouded coast at nearby Honda Point, despite the close proximity of the Point Arguello lighthouse and its radio beacon. Twenty-two men were lost in what has been designated as the U.S. Navy's worst peacetime disaster. Nonetheless, the Point Arguello lighthouse has saved countless other ships since its construction in 1901. Because of its remote location, it was one of the first California lighthouses to be automated. It was decommissioned in 1934 and replaced with an aero-marine beacon on an iron-skeleton tower.

Over the course of many years, I have gratefully used all the Santa Barbara area lights described above. Today, mariners have access to global positioning systems (GPS), radar, and other navigational aids to reduce unintentional groundings, but weather and high seas still take their toll. All warning devices are welcome to a mariner at sea, and I have come to value every one. Lighthouses and their automated successors are high on my list. There is great comfort in physical sight in addition to relying on electrons performing on a screen.

ROBOTS TO THE DEEP

A shipwreck is a catastrophe for sailors and owners, but it is also an opportunity for historians and archaeologists to learn more of the past. Wrecks provide insight and evidence of not just nautical technology, but also information of the economy, trade, culture, and even warfare of past times. There are an estimated three million shipwrecks at the bottoms of the world's oceans, seas, rivers, and lakes. Most are out of reach due to inaccessible depths and locations. Recent underwater archeology has been done mainly by scuba diving that essentially limits projects to 150 feet of depth and excludes almost ninety-eight percent of the sea floors from inspection. Further, shallow water wrecks are more susceptible to damage from storms, seaweed, coral, amateur sport divers, and salvagers than are more inaccessible deep water wrecks. True, most trading vessels have been coastal rather than ocean-going ships, but there is vast untapped information to be derived from deeper water wrecks.

Marine archeologists have sometimes been able to gain access to manned and unmanned small submarines to explore deeper waters, but such expeditions are very expensive with costs sometimes exceeding a million dollars. Often such expeditions are privately financed speculative ventures and are more treasure hunts than archeology.

Modern robotic technology is changing things, as more comparatively inexpensive automatic underwater vehicles (AUV's) are beginning to become operational. Until the development of AUVS, mini-subs have had to be guided by signals passing down cables from a mother-ship operating on the sea surface above. This requires mother-ships to be specially fitted out at substantial cost. By contrast, an AUV can be launched into the sea and operated independently with no cable to a ship above. This allows a wider range of ships and boats that can support underwater archeological operations at substantially reduced expenditure.

AUV's have been used to explore a promising area of seabed off the coast of Egypt to locate and explore wrecks known to be there. The area is off the coast where the ancient port of Marsa Matruh was located. This Bronze Age port was frequently used by vessels from the historic sites of the Nile River, Crete, the Aegean Sea, and the eastern Mediterranean Sea. The area includes regions near Zawiyet Umm el-Rakham (meaning "the rest house of the mother of vultures"), a Bronze Age fortress-temple built by Ramesses II about 1280 BC, and which would have been the focus of a great deal or marine traffic. Any shipwrecks dating from that time would be the oldest seagoing vessels ever discovered.

The underwater robot for the project is approximately seventy-nine inches long, eight inches in diameter, and weighs eighty-one pounds. It is equipped with cameras and sonar devices to record the sea floor's topography. Other sensors record the water's salinity, temperature and chemistry. These measurements will determine how biologically active the sea area being examined is, and will indicate the likely state of preservation of wrecks in the area. If all goes according to plan, the wrecks will be initially located by sonar. Once a promising site is identified, the AUV vehicle will move in for a closer look and a detailed evaluation will begin.

Although the scientists hope to find many more, they already know of one wreck within the target area. It is a Roman ship that was discovered by divers last year near Bagoush, approximately 180 miles west of Alexandria Egypt. It is undergoing careful research and analysis similar to that applied to a cargo vessel recently discovered off the island port of Chios. In that case, an earlier model of Automatic Underwater Vehicle named "Sea Bed" was guided over the wreck to take photos on a grid of eight-foot squares. The wreck is approximately seventy feet long, twenty-six feet wide, and five feet deep – similar to a sailing barge. Approximately 350 amphoras (a type of ceramic vase with two handles and a long neck narrower than its body) were located near the surface of the silt on which the vessel rests. They probably had contained olive oil and aromatic resins. About half of the amphoras are intact, and hundreds more are expected to be located. The amphoras were not scattered, and there is no evidence of fire or trails of debris that would suggest that the crew were trying to lighten the ship's load to stop it from sinking. Therefore, it's likely that it went down suddenly and unexpectedly, probably sunk by one of the area's notorious, unpredictable and violent downdrafts of wind.

The advancing development of AUV automatic underwater vehicles will allow researchers to discover many of the countless undiscovered shipwrecks around the world. AUV's will allow studies to take place without damage to these ancient artifacts, and will certainly cause substantial rewriting of history as more and more new facts are collected. Additiional areas of the historic Mediterranean are planned for operations, including Cyprus, Algeria, and Libya. Such underwater access was once thought possible only in science fiction. Author Arthur Clark in his novel "Rendezvous With Rama" suggested that mankind would eventually have to drain the Mediterranean in order to study its archeology. Fortunately, with the advent of AUV's, there will be no such need.

SHIPS' RECORDS

The ship's log book was originally created to record readings from its log. A log was a method to determine the speed of a boat at a specific time. A chip of wood was tossed off the bow and then timed to determine how long it would take to reach the stern of the boat. With the length of the boat known, along with the time for the chip to move that distance, a calculation could be made to determine the speed of the boat. The date, time, and speed were recorded in a "chip book," and also marked on a chart. With repeated recordings, the approximate position of the boat could be determined to a reasonable degree of accuracy. Over time, the book became named as the "ship's log" and eventually "the log." No one knows when the first logbook was written, but it would have been centuries ago.

Today, ship's logs have expanded to contain many additional types of information, including a record of operational data such as weather conditions, times of routine events, significant incidents, crew complement, what ports were docked at and when, and much more. The logbook is still essential to traditional navigation, and must be filled in at least daily.

Most national shipping authorities and admiralties require that logbooks be kept to provide a record of events, and to help crews navigate should their radio, radar or Global Positioning System (GPS) fail. Examination of the detail in a ship's log is often an important part of the investigative process for official maritime inquiries in much the same way as an electronic "black box" recorder is used on airplanes.

Logbook entries are frequently of great importance in resolving legal cases involving maritime commercial disputes.

The term "logbook" has spread to a wide variety of other endeavors, and logbooks are widely used for complex machines like nuclear power plants or particle accelerators. The paper versions are rapidly converting to become electronic computer generated logbooks. In military terms, a logbook is a series of official and legally binding documents. Each document (usually arranged by date) is marked with the time of an event or action of significance.

Commercial ships and naval vessels often keep a "rough log," or "scrap log," - a preliminary draft of the ship's course, speed, location, and other data, which is later transcribed as the "smooth log" or "official log" - the final version of the ship's record. Changes may be made to the rough log, but the smooth log is considered permanent and no erasures are permitted. Alterations or corrections in an official logbook must be initialed by the authorized keeper of the logbook, and the original data entries which have been cancelled or corrected must remain legible.

The following is an example of an actual ship's logbook entry from H.M.S. Swiftsure on Wednesday, June 27, 1888 while on a course from St. Vincent to Rio de Janeiro. All entries were by hand, and abbreviations were used. I have owned this logbook for several years. It also includes handmade maps and watercolor sketches of locations where the ship made stops.

Latitude (dead reckoning): 19 degrees 30 minutes South/ 36 degrees 35 minutes West Time: 02:28 Wind Direction: Southwest Wind Force: 4.6 (miles per hour) Barometer: 30.29/70 Remarks: Set topmast staysail and fore and main trysails.

A ship's journal differs from the ship's log in that it is usually a narrative description of events, reflections, information and other subjective inputs compared to the more formal recording of the ship's position, performance, and other legally based entries found in the ship's logbook. It usually makes for more interesting reading.

The following is an example of an actual ship's journal entry. Captain Davis and his crew from the American sealing ship, Cecilia, claimed to have landed at Hughes Bay (64°01'S) looking for seals. These men were the first recorded humans who claimed to have set foot on the newly discovered continent of Antarctica. The ships journal entry reads:

Commences with open cloudy weather and light winds a standing for a large body of band in the direction SE at 10A.M. Close in with it our boat and sent her on-shore to look for seal at 11A.M. The boat returned but find no sign of seal at noon. Our Latitude was 64°01' South. Stood up a large bay, the land high and covered entirely with snow. The wind coming round to the north and eastward with thick weather. Tacked ship and headed off-shore. At 4P.M. fresh gale and thick weather with snow. Ends with strong gales at ENE. Concluded to make the best of our way for the ship. I think this southern land to be a continent.

The Davis Sea, part of the Southern Ocean, was named after Captain Davis. Also, the coastal strip where the men were alleged to have gone ashore is called Davis Coast.

NOT AROUND MY NECK!

A giant bird that flies hundreds and even thousands of miles off-shore has become far more than one of earth's magnificent creatures. The wandering albatross (Diomedea exulans) has the largest wingspan of any living bird. This makes it is an expert glider and capable of remaining in the air for several hours at a time without beating its wings. It has even been known to sleep while it flies. I recall seeing these giant birds soaring just a few inches above breaking seas in heavy overcast, rain and strong winds as we clawed our way toward home from Hawaii on the 96-foot ketch Morning Star. The largest measured albatross was captured in the Tasman Sea in 1965. It had a wingspan of eleven feet eleven inches. That compares to the giant South American teratoron (Argentavis magnificens) which lived over six million years ago and had a wingspan of over twenty-five feet.

Through the ages, the giant albatross has been regarded by sailors as both an omen of good but also of bad luck. In Samuel Taylor Coleridge's 1798 poem, The Rime of the Ancient Mariner, an albatross is described following a ship, which was generally considered to be an omen of good luck. But then an imprudent crew member shoots the albatross with a crossbow, an act that was known to bring a curse upon the ship. To punish the mariner and to try to stave off the bad luck, his anxious shipmates forced him to wear the dead albatross around his neck.

Ah ! well a-day ! what evil looks
Had I from old and young !
Instead of the cross as the Mariner's story progresses hung.

Before first appearing in a dictionary, the word albatross and its severe consequences also appeared in Mary Shelley's 1818 novel on Frankenstein in which Robert Walton speaking to his sister states, "... but I shall kill no albatross..."- Another early reference was in Charles Baudelaire's collection of poems, Les Fleurs du mal, in a poem entitled L'Albatros about men on ships who catch albatrosses for sport. The final stanza compares poets to the lonely birds— exiled from the skies and then weighed down by their giant wings, till death. This sense of pending doom was first catalogued in the Oxford English Dictionary in 1936, but didn't enter general usage in the 1960s.

Coleridge's The Rime of the Ancient Mariner relates the events experienced by a mariner who had just returned from a long sea voyage. The Mariner stops a man who is on the way to a wedding ceremony and begins to recite a story. As the Mariner's story progresses, the wedding guest's reaction turns from bemusement to impatience and then to fascination and fear. The Mariner's tale begins with his ship departing on its journey. Despite initial good fortune, the ship is driven south and off-course by a storm and eventually reaches Antarctica. An albatross appears and leads them out of the Antarctic. But, as the albatross is praised by the ship's crew, the Mariner shoots the bird with a cross-bow. The crew becomes very angry with the Mariner, believing the albatross had brought the south wind that led them out of the Antarctic. The sailors change their minds when the weather becomes warmer and the mist disappears, but the crime has aroused the wrath of spirits who then pursue the ship "from the land of mist and snow" and send it into uncharted waters, where it is becalmed.

Day after day, day after day,
We stuck, nor breath nor motion;
As idle as a painted ship
Upon a painted ocean.
Water, water, everywhere,
And all the boards did shrink;
Water, water, everywhere,
Nor any drop to drink.

The sailors change their minds again and blame the Mariner for the torment of their thirst. In anger, the crew force the Mariner to wear the dead albatross about his neck as punishment. Eventually, in an eerie passage, the ship encounters a ghostly vessel. On-board are Death (a skeleton) and the "Night-mare Life-in-Death" (a deathly-pale woman), who are playing dice for the souls of the crew. With a roll of the dice, Death wins the lives of the crew members and Life-in-Death wins the life of the Mariner. Her name is a clue to the Mariner's destiny; he will endure a fate worse than death as punishment for killing of the albatross.

One by one, all of the crew members die. But the Mariner lives on, night and day seeing his curse in the eyes of the crew's corpses. Eventually, the Mariner's curse is lifted when he manages to pray. The albatross falls from his neck - his guilt partially expiated. The bodies of the crew then become possessed by good spirits, rise again, and steer the ship back home, where it suddenly sinks in a whirlpool, leaving only the Mariner behind. As penance for shooting the albatross, the Mariner is forced to wander the earth, telling his story, and teaching his lesson to those he meets.

Be Kind To Animals Week is usually held in May, but the Mariner recommends celebrating it year around.

WHERE DID THEY COME FROM?

Humans have dealt with and traveled the seas for thousands of years. Not surprisingly, a language of the sea developed and many of its words and phrases have entered our everyday English language. Here are a few.

BETWEEN THE DEVIL AND THE DEEP BLUE SEA - In wooden ships, the "devil" was the longest seam of the ship. It ran from the bow to the stern. When at sea and the "devil" had to be caulked, the sailor sat in a bo'sun's chair to do so. He was suspended between the "devil" and the sea — the "deep" — a very precarious position, especially when the ship was underway.

CHEWING THE FAT - "God made the vittles but the devil made the cook," was a popular saying used by seafaring men in the 19th century when salted beef was staple diet aboard ship. This tough cured beef, suitable only for long voyages when nothing else was cheap or would keep as well (remember, there was no refrigeration), required prolonged chewing to make it edible. Men often chewed one chunk for hours, just as if it were chewing gum, and referred to this practice as "chewing the fat."

CROW'S NEST - The raven, or crow, was an essential part of the Vikings' navigation equipment. These land-lubbing birds were carried aboard to help the ship's navigator determine where the closest land lay when weather prevented sighting the shore. In cases of poor visibility, a crow was released and the navigator plotted a course corresponding to the bird's flight path because the crow invariably headed towards land. The Norsemen carried the birds in a cage secured to the top of the mast. Later on, as ships grew and the lookout stood his watch in a tub located high on the main mast, the name "crow's nest" was given to this tub. While today's Navy still uses lookouts in addition to radar, etc., the crow's nest is a thing of the past.

CUP OF JOE – Josephus Daniels (1862 - 1948) was appointed Secretary of the Navy by President Woodrow Wilson in 1913. Among his reforms of the Navy were inaugurating the practice of making 100 sailors from the fleet eligible for entrance into the Naval Academy, the introduction of women into the service, and the abolishment of the officers' wine mess. From that time on, the strongest drink aboard Navy ships could only be coffee. Over the years, a cup of coffee became known as "a cup of Joe."

MAYDAY – "Mayday" is the internationally recognized voice radio signal for ships and people in serious trouble at sea. Made official in 1948, it is an anglicizing of the French *m'aidez*, "help me."

PORT HOLE – The word "port hole" originated during the reign of King Henry VI of England in the late 1400's. King Henry insisted on mounting guns too large for his ships and the traditional methods of securing these weapons on the forecastle and aftcastle could not be used. A French shipbuilder named James Baker was commissioned to solve the problem. He put small doors in the side of the ships and mounted the cannons inside the ships. These doors protected the cannons from weather and were opened when the cannons were to be used. The French word for "door" is "porte" which was later Anglicized to "port" and later went on to mean any opening in the ship's side, whether for cannon or not.

THE WHITE FLYERS

In 1907, two identical luxury ships were launched and immediately became famous for their speed, luxury and grace. The *Yale* and the *Harvard* were among the first American ships to be powered by steam turbine engines that used oil instead of coal for fuel. Each ship had three propellers and twelve thousand horsepower which propelled them at sustained speeds of over twenty knots as they transported thousands of passengers between major ports on both the eastern and western seaboards of the United States.

The 407-foot *Yale* had a long career that included service in both world wars, finally being scrapped in California in 1949. But the *Yale's* sister ship *Harvard* was destined to a tragic end in 1931 upon a rocky California shore, taking her place on the long list of great shipwrecks of the Pacific Coast.

The *Yale* and *Harvard* each contained 987 berths in 311 staterooms – forty of them deluxe suites with parlors and thirty with private bathrooms. Descriptions were lavish – "The interior decoration and fittings of the ships strike a new note, and it is safe to say that in no other American steamer yet built has there been so elaborate and beautiful embellishments incorporated in the design." The owner of the shipping line had given orders that his new vessels were to be "the fastest, safest and most luxuriously fitted ships in the country."

Their first service was between Boston and New York. Each ship would depart from opposite ends of the route at 5 PM and arrive at their destinations at 8 o'clock the following morning with their passengers fresh from a comfortable night's sleep en route. The two liners were players in an ongoing commercial war between the owners of the New Haven Railroad and those of the Metropolitan Steamship Line for dominance of the lucrative Boston-New York routes. To compete with the steamship company, the railroad cut its overnight fare down to $3.65. The battle waged on, and then the ships were finally moved from the competitive chaos of the east to begin service in California.

The two ships tied up at the East San Pedro wharf on Terminal Island in December 1910. The white speedsters immediately began making four 18 ½ hour runs a week between Los Angeles and San Francisco, and also runs to San Diego. The fare from Los Angeles to San Francisco was $8.35. A sleeping berth cost an additional fifty cents or a dollar depending on location. Rooms cost between one dollar and four dollars depending on facilities. Deluxe cabins with private baths cost six and eight dollars.

With the advent of World War l, both ships were commandeered into the U.S. Navy for troop carrier service. The *Harvard* made sixty round trips across the Atlantic and transported a total of 157,384 personnel during the war period. In 1920, both the *Harvard* and *Yale* were released from military service and sailed for California, this time through the Panama Canal rather than around South America as before. The white flyers then began five sailings a week between Los Angeles and San Francisco.

On May 29, 1931, the two ships made simultaneous departures as was their practice. The *Harvard* steamed from San Francisco's Embarcadero and out through the Golden Gate on her 972nd California voyage. It was to be her last. During that night, the two ships passed near each other on opposing northwest-southwest courses between Point Sur and Point Arguello about 45 miles up the coast from Santa Barbara. Captain Frank A. Johnson, veteran master of the *Yale*, noted that the Harvard was passing more than 2 ½ miles inside her normal southbound route, a course that would ultimately take her onto the rocky coastline. The *Yale's* captain did not contact the *Harvard*, assuming that its veteran Captain Hillsinger knew what he was doing.

DON'T LEAVE PORT WITHOUT THEM

Many people envision that the greatest dangers at sea are severe storms with towering waves far offshore from the protection of land. In fact, the two greatest hazards to navigation are grounding in shallow water and colliding with rocks, wrecks, and obstacles that damage or sink a ship. Today, most mariners rely on electronic navigation devices to ensure safe passage. Radar and Global Positioning Systems (GPS) have reduced many dangers at sea, but far from all. A prudent skipper operates on the basis that there may be an electrical failure or other circumstances that will render his electronic devices inoperable. The back-up system to today's modern electronics probably began evolving over three thousand years ago – the paper chart.

Nautical charts as we know them today have evolved over the last eight hundred years. The earliest navigators had to rely on whatever information they could collect. Notes and sketches were made of courses, obstacles, landmarks, and other essential information so they could be recalled or shared with others. Over time, this information began to be converted into standard presentations. Portolan charts of the Mediterranean Sea were created in the late 13th century. The first atlas of nautical charts was produced by the Dutch seaman and cartographer Lucas Janszoon Waghenaer in 1584. The process continued as technology improved.

But until recently, knowledge of the paths and hazards of the oceans and seas was often kept as secret as details of today's modern nuclear weapons. Such navigational information, if kept confidential, could provide great advantage to nations at war or between fierce commercial competitors. Charts and journals were locked or hidden away from ship's crews as well as external competitors or enemies.

President Thomas Jefferson realized the importance of nautical charts to commerce and the security of the young United States, and ordered a "survey of the coast" in 1807. The Survey of the Coast was the organization established to carry out Jefferson's vision, and it has been the official chart maker of the United States for the past 200 years. Collecting underlying data began in 1816 with geodetic surveys in New Jersey and New York, and in 1835 with hydrographic surveys of New York Harbor. The Survey of the Coast published its first nautical chart in 1844.

In 1970, the then-named Coast and Geodetic Survey was incorporated into the United States National Oceanic and Atmospheric Administration (NOAA), which today continues to produce nautical charts, predict the tides, monitor the magnetic field of the earth and solar system, and maintain the geodetic network upon which all precise positioning on the North American continent is based. Today's charts depict coastlines, islands, rivers, harbors, and features of navigational interest such as water depth, hazards, and aids to navigation.

With the recent advent of modern communications and satellite imaging, previously secret sea routes and hidden refuges are now widely known. Some secrets may still exist, but probably just a handful. Today, you can walk into any ship's chandlery or surf the internet to secure detailed information and charts of the world, typically for only $23.95.

The Santa Barbara Maritime Museum has a collection of nautical charts on display ranging from a rare chart made by artist James McNeil Whistler in 1705 when it was believed that California was an island, to a modern navigational chart of our Santa Barbara channel and its off-shore islands.

It is essential that the navigator look ahead along the intended path of a ship to ensure that the

ocean depth exceeds the boat draft and that there are no rocks, wrecks, or obstacles which lie above the needed draft of the boat or appear in close proximity to the intended path. Electronic or paper charts are essential for the safety of vessels at sea. It is a prudent captain that has a full set of charts and a full understanding of how to read and understand them.

ANACAPA ISLAND

Anacapa, the smallest of Southern California's off-shore islands, lies twelve miles off the coast between Santa Barbara and Ventura. The island is actually composed of three islets - East Island, Middle Island and West Island.

The origin of Anacapa's name is not known for certain. In 1770, Spanish explorer Gaspar de Portola mistook West Anacapa for the sail of a distant ship. When he learned of his mistake, he named the islet Velo Falsa, false sail, and the adjoining islands Las Mesitas, or small tablelands. Four years later, Spanish explorer Juan Perez renamed them "Isletas de Santa Tomas." In the last decade of the 1700's, English Explorer George Vancouver called all three islands "Eneeapah," but mistakenly spelled it "Enecapa" on his maps. Years later, a 19th century map showed it as "Encapa." Finally, in 1852, the U.S. Coast Survey set it down on their charts the island as "Anacapa" and the name remained.

The Indian influence on the Northern Channel Islands may date as far back as ten thousand years. It is not known if Chumash Indians lived year around in permanent settlements on Anacapa Island, but they did occupy all three islets at least seasonally. There is evidence of at least twenty-three kitchen midden areas on the island. Lack of a dependable supply of fresh water was a deterrent, but the intertidal areas were rich in their nutritional offerings for these maritime people. There are no written Spanish accounts of people living on the island, however.

During the 19th century, seasonal fisherman used Anacapa Island as a base. A logbook of the U.S. Coast and Geodetic Survey dated September 1853 mentions an old house on the south end of Middle

Anacapa. Captain George Nidever was one of the first persons to have interests on Anacapa Island after the collapse of Chumash Indian culture. He raised sheep, even though it was on government owned property. During the next forty years, Anacapa Island was bought and sold by several parties, most notably the Pacific Wool Growing Company. It was not until 1902 that the U.S. Government resumed an active role as land owner when it leased the island to Louis Le Mesnager for the grazing of sheep. Le Mesnager held the lease until 1907 when Heaman Webster took over and increased the sheep operation to 500 head. Webster lived on Middle Anacapa Island for ten years with his wife and two sons. The children were educated on the island by a tutor in a tent school erected by Webster.

In 1917, Webster tried to renew his lease for 25 years instead of the usual term of 5 years. But that would require an Act of Congress, and since Congress was occupied with the war in Europe they had no time for such a small matter. Webster eventually lost his lease to Captain Ira Eaton who assumed the lease for the next ten years. Captain Eaton had a resort operation on Santa Cruz Island and used Anacapa as a storage place during prohibition for bootlegged liquor. Eaton later sublet the island to the Santa Barbara Fish Company which placed fishermen on the island.

No lessee was recorded between 1927 and 1932; however, in 1928 Raymond "Frenchy" LaDreau settled on West Anacapa Island where he lived a hermit-like existence for the next 28 years. He became the unofficial Park Service representative, reporting on acts of vandalism and island activities. Well-known among fisherman from Monterey to Ensenada, Frenchy enjoyed periodic company, but lived with only his cats in a cabin built in a cove that now bears his name – Frenchy's Cove. He left the island in 1956 at the age of eighty.

In 1932, C. Fay Chaffe was awarded the island lease and attempted to develop a sport fishing camp as well as subleasing. In 1937, the U.S. Government decided that no further leasing would be allowed.

There have been over a dozen major shipwrecks on Anacapa Island, the most famous of which was the *S.S. General Winfield Scott* on December 2, 1853. The 225-foot steam-powered paddle wheeler was enroute from San Francisco to Panama with passengers, mail, supplies and nearly $2,000,000 in bullion. In dense fog and under full steam about midnight while most of the passengers were asleep, the *Winfield Scott* ran aground on the north side of Middle Anacapa. Fortunately, the ship struck a slanting ledge of rocks and not the ominous vertical rock wall just 200 feet in front of her. This allowed the passengers and crew to safely abandon ship and salvage much of her cargo before she sank.

Sighting a distress signal the following day, the steamship *California* turned to aid the stricken ship. Although heavily laden, the *California* was able to take some of the stranded passengers aboard and on to San Francisco. Captain Le Roy of the *Winfield Scott* sent some members of the crew to Santa Barbara to notify the Pacific Mail Steamship Company of their fate. Dispatches were sent 350 miles by rider, and assistance arrived at the survivor's island camp eight days later. By then, provisions and water had been exhausted and the situation had become desperate. The remaining passengers and crew were rescued and sailed on for Panama on the rescue ship.

Shortly after the wreck of the *Winfield Scott*, the Coast Survey Project identified the need for a permanent lighthouse facility on Anacapa Island. But it was not until 1911 that funds became available. A fifty-foot tower was constructed on the extreme eastern end of the island for the light. Today's lighthouse was activated for manned operation in 1932. The site included a 30,000 square foot concrete pad for collecting rain water, a water tank, a light tower, a powerhouse, a fog signal building, and several lighthouse keepers' dwellings. The light was automated for unmanned operation in 1968. Before that time, the light was tended around the clock by rotating crews of Coast Guard personnel. Today, perched at an elevation of 277 feet, the light is visible for 24 miles and the foghorn can be heard on the nearby mainland.

Anacapa Island is now a National Park, although certain areas are reserved by the Coast Guard. Island Packers Company regularly takes visitors by boat from Channel Islands Harbor to East Anacapa Island. Travel time is just under one hour.

NOAH'S ARK

Perhaps the most famous vessel in the history of western civilization as described in the Bible was the ark built by Noah. Genesis, Chapter 6 described to it as follows: (Modern terms are shown in parenthesis.)

- 6:14 Make for yourself a coffer (box) of pitch trees (cypress); nests shall you make in the coffer, and you will cover it inside and outside with a covering (pitch).
- 6:15 And thus you shall make it; three hundred cubits (~450 ft.) the length, fifty cubits (~75 ft.) its breadth, and thirty cubits (~45 ft.) its height.
- 6:16 A light you will make to the coffer, and to a cubit you shall finish it above; and the opening to the coffer you will place in its side; with lower, second, and third floors you will do it.

So, the ark had the following specifications:

- A box-shaped vessel
- Made of wood from pitch trees, today called cypress trees
- Seams (spaces between the planks) caulked with pitch from the trees
- Length about 450 feet
- Width (beam) about 75 feet
- Height of about 45 feet, but it is not clear if this was the height above the water or the total height above and below the water
- An exterior deck and two lower interior decks

We don't have blueprints of the ark, so let's see what it may have looked like -

The ark was probably constructed of wood from cypress trees that were native to the Mediterranean region. Cypress is a symmetrical evergreen that often reaches a height of more than 90 feet. It is a close-grained yellow or reddish wood that is so resinous that it resists rotting even after prolonged submersion in water.

An axe to cut and prepare the logs would have been desirable, but not necessary. Sharpened hand stones could have been used for log preparation. Construction of a two-layer log raft would have required about 450 two-foot diameter logs, each seventy-five feet long. If Noah didn't want to cut down trees, he could have appropriated those harvested by beavers. Beavers usually select trees between two and eight inches in diameter, but can fell trees with diameters as large as thirty inches.

Noah may have studied beavers to learn other useful techniques. Colonies of beavers often dig canals from a grove of trees to a pond. The canals are up to three feet wide and are often several hundred yards long. Noah could have been floated his timber down beaver canals to his building site, or built his own canals.

Thatching the logs into a single hull would have been a big job. It would have required gathering prairie grass or vines, drying, weaving them into rope, and then tying the framework together. To make the arc watertight, its seams would have been sealed with pitch from the cypress trees. Remains of pitch-covered reed boats used on the Euphrates River as far back as 3800 BC have been discovered in modern times. Using a two-layer hull design with one layer longitudinal and the other cross ways would have provided good stability and strength in both directions.

The upper part of the ark may have been constructed of cypress poles with thatch covering the sides and the top. Thatch roofs have been known to withstand winds of up to 100 miles an hour and to last from forty to sixty years.

The reference to the light is difficult to envision. Some have interpreted it as a sort of cupola along the top center line of the arc. Others visualize a side covering to within one cubit (about 18 inches) of the top of the cupola to create an all-around opening for light and ventilation. Some imagine an opening in the side of the arc as a combined door and entrance ramp for loading all the animals and their food.

Now as to the Bible's passages for the passengers -

- 6:19 And from every living thing of all flesh, two of all to come into the coffer, to keep alive with you; male and female they will be,
- 6:20 From the flying creature after their kind, and from the cattle after their kind, from every creeping thing of the earth after its kind, two from all will come to you to keep alive.
- 6:21 And you take for yourself of all eatable that is eaten, and you will gather to yourself; and let it be for you and for them for eating.
- 7:2 From every creature clean will you take to yourself seven *by* seven, a man and his woman; and the creature that not clean it by two , a man and his woman;
- 7:3 Of the flying creature of the skies seven *by* seven, a male and his female, to keep alive seed upon the face of all the earth.

A big order to load such a crowd onto the ark! Viewing the situation from a nautical perspective, the logical loading would be to put all the large and heavy animals on the bottom floor and the smaller animals on the two upper stories of the ark. The humans would seem to be destined to spend most of their time on the lower floor taking care of the feeding and cleaning up chores.

Additional space would be required because the ark would also have to serve as a warehouse with room for food storage for over a year. In addition, stored food would be needed while new vegetation began growing after the flood waters receded.

In summary, Noah's ark probably would have been a very large vessel with special provisions for storage and accommodations for its very unusual passengers.

Note: This article does not attempt to interpret the Bible. It is an exercise in envisioning what the arc might have been like from a nautical standpoint.

THE GRAFFITI THAT HAD TO BE SAVED

A poignant exhibit has been traveling to various museums across America that brings home the impact of war on those who served in Vietnam. In unprecedented format, the thoughts and feelings of American soldiers and marines were recorded as letters and art sketched on the canvas of their shipboard pipe berths as the troopship *General Nelson M. Walker* steamed toward Vietnam. Each canvas bunk, four-high and eight to a unit, contained a bright orange life vest. Many of the bunk undersides were signed with names and hometowns. The soldiers wrote personal messages of homesickness, politics, humor, family, bravado, and anxiety. Some made drawings that revealed the minds of American soldiers on their way to war.

After the war, the 600-foot long, P-2 class *General Nelson M. Walker* was placed into mothball storage and eventually scheduled to be scrapped in Texas. The seasoned warship was a veteran of World War II, the Korean War and Vietnam. Of the over three million men and women who served in Southeast Asia and offshore, it is estimated that a half-million went there by ship. *General Nelson M. Walker* therefore was a veritable time capsule. Canvas bunks remained intact with mattresses, sheets, pillows and blankets. Compartment bulletin boards showed troop notices dated 1967. Dirty dishes were stacked in the galley. The troops were long gone but their presence still remained.

When the *Walker* was inspected, its Vietnam graffiti was rediscovered and its unique importance was recognized. Its graffiti was a historic record, and it had to be saved. Stories from every bunk of the musty troopship needed to be uncovered and shared.

The Vietnam Graffiti Project of Keswick, Virginia took the lead to preserve the ship's unique art and record of the war. Soldiers and sailors that were on the ship were located and related their individual experiences. Vietnam helicopter pilot Jim Reeder told of leaving for war aboard the *Walker*. Navy Chaplain Charles Van Frank remembered how he had offered moral support to young officers on the ship before they arrived in Southeast Asia. Many more came forward with tales of their voyage.

The exhibit provides an opportunity for visitors to inspect a complete eight-man bunk unit with the original pillows, sheets and life vests recovered from the ship. Many who have seen the exhibit smiled at graffiti humor of wall-displayed bunk canvases and recognized the familiar town names inscribed by California soldiers. Visitors may use their cell phones to hear former *Walker* troop passengers share their personal voyage stories.

Santa Barbara Maritime Museum curator Abbey Chamberlain explained, "It was the human stories that drove our decision to host the traveling Vietnam graffiti exhibition, which has attracted a more diverse audience than many of our exhibits. The raw emotion conveyed through the canvases and the authentic voices in the audio tour have struck a chord with the local community, leading to some wonderful collaboration in the exhibit's marketing and educational programming."

The graffiti inscriptions provide a unique insight into American history during the turbulent times of the 1960's. As University of Virginia Institute for Public History scholar Dr. Phyllis K. Leffler observed, "The graffiti, which constitutes new primary artifacts, provide identity markers for the soldiers. Their personalities, relationships, regional connections, and fears come alive through their drawings. This is a meaningful way to juxtapose the public and official face of war with the personal and private one."

As part of the research project, many who had left graffiti aboard the *Walker* were located. Most were in their early sixties. Almost every soldier who wrote his name on the bunks also inscribed his hometown, which made tracing them easier. Each *Walker* veteran located was provided with a questionnaire asking about his voyage. His or her recollections were then recorded during a follow-up interview. The researchers wanted to learn what each soldier did and how he felt during the voyage. They wanted their stories.

Some of the soldiers and Marines had carried inexpensive, Kodak *Instamatic* cameras aboard the ship. Photos taken during their voyage were copied, along with letters written on the ship. These intimate keepsakes personalized the graffiti. Uncensored letters offered more insight into their thoughts and emotions. Several veterans shared their Super-8 movie film taken during the voyage, along with audio tapes of the original 1960's music that was piped into the ship's troop compartments.

University of Virginia Institute for Public History scholar Dr. Phyllis K. Leffler observed, "As a historian of the United States who has specialized for more than twenty-five years on the American War in Vietnam, I have rarely encountered a project that so successfully recovers the wartime feelings and attitudes of young Americans on the brink of war."

Second Squadron Cavalry member Jerry Barker recalls the graffiti left on the ship. "I think man is obsessed with his mortality, and we all want to leave a piece of us behind. It was just a point in time when they were being carried away on this journey. They wanted to leave a little piece of them, a little piece of their heart, a little piece of their soul. That insignificant gesture has really wound up to be quite significant."

Mike Brinkley, a member of the Army's 51st Maintenance Company had been a construction worker before enlisting, and on the troopship he had a feeling that he might not return from the war. "I recall lying in my rack, just letting my mind go where it wanted to, mostly thoughts of home and thoughts of my friends and all my loved ones that I'd left behind," he said. "And I thought, well I might not make it back. Here I am, eighteen going on nineteen, going to Vietnam to teach the Communists a better way of life, make sure that they wear their Levi blue jeans and drive Chevy pick-ups. I thought well, gee whiz, this may be the last thing that I see or the last thing that I possibly leave on this earth that would indicate I was even here."

Among the more poignant graffiti was that left by an African-American soldier from Clover, South Carolina. During his August, 1967 voyage, newly-married draftee Zeb Armstrong wrote his name, hometown, and "Billie Armstrong My Dear Wife." Not knowing his future, he also wrote, at the end, "Will I Return???" adding emphasis to the comment with three question marks. He did return.

In addition to graffiti, the weary ship contained other artifacts – soap bars, scouring pads, paper cups, life vests, pillows, sheets, blankets, whistles, signal mirrors and a variety of personal items left in the bunks by the last group of troops to leave the ship. Empty cigarette packs, candy bar wrappers, peanut shells, whiskey bottles, pain relief packages, magazines and Walker newspapers help to tell the story.

Upon completion of the graffiti exhibit, University of Virginia scholar Dr. Phyllis K. Leffler, who worked on the project observed, "When my executive director and I walked into the auditorium and saw the canvases, we became speechless. As we looked at the drawings and read the words, we both turned to each other with tears in our eyes. Since both of us had lived through the Vietnam War, we realized that this was our war—our history—not our parents, not World War II, not Korea, but us. The canvases were from a ship that carried our very young warriors to Vietnam. We were fascinated with the stories."

NAVIGATING THROUGH HISTORY

Communicating navigational information has been essential for successful navigation since the earliest historic times. As humans began traveling across the earth, they needed to know what others had learned before them – geography, routes, dangers, and other information that would make their travels as safe and efficient as possible. The methods of communicating such essential information have changed significantly over the centuries, beginning with person-to-person exchanges, then to transportable paper drawings or charts, and finally to today's high-speed internet transmissions that can flow directly into a ship's electronic navigation and steering systems. Not withstanding modern technology, the required information has remained unchanged: Where am I? Where is my destination? What obstacles are in my path? What course shall I follow?

The earliest known sea charts were called "portolans," and the oldest known portolan is the "Carte Pisane," which was probably drawn in 1296. Portolan charts, drawn on vellum, showed coastal outlines, inlets, rivers, and other such details. They were used in conjunction with written sailing directions, and were initially drawn of the Mediterranean Sea. Later charts extended further afield to include new lands discovered during the Age of Discovery.

Genoa and Venice were the first centers for the production of portolan charts. Later, Catalan mapmakers, particularly in Majorca, began making outstanding charts. " Knowledge is power," and the information on their portolan charts was considered to be state secrets by Portugal and Spain. Their descriptions of the Atlantic and Indian coastlines would have been very valuable to newcomer English and Dutch raiding ships.

The earliest surviving portolan chart, the *Carte Pisane*, was drawn about 1290 and is now located in the Bibliothèque Nationale Library in Paris. Its maker is not known, but most scholars believe it was made in Genoa. The writing on the chart is in several languages, which was not unusual for those times. But the mystery is that the chart has no known ancestors. The *Carte Pisane* seems to have emerged full-blown from the seas it describes. It has the grid pattern based on circles and compass directions that later portolan charts have, and its portrayal of the Mediterranean is startling in its accuracy. But where are the earlier charts showing the development of this form of mapping? To add a further touch of mystery, the depiction of Italy on the *Carte Pisane* is not nearly as accurate as that found on the portolan charts that immediately followed it (and the *Carte Pisane* is supposed to have been made in Italy). Also, the portrayal of the Atlantic areas "is deplorable looking" in the words of a major scholar of this and other early portolan charts, James E. Kelley, Jr. What sources were used in making the *Carte Pisane*? No one knows. Was it compiled from many earlier charts like putting together a jigsaw puzzle, or did one cartographer simply create it entirely as his own work? With its details of names and coastlines, the *Carte Pisane* seems to reflect the results of many voyages and the use of many earlier charts. But no earlier charts are known...

The first printed sailing guide that included charts and written descriptions was Lucas Waghenaer's *Spieghel der Zeevaerdt*, published in 1584 in Leiden in the Netherlands. Its publication prompted others, and sea atlases and charts soon became readily available for merchant as well as naval captains. In 1588, an English translation of Waghenaer's work, *The Mariner's Mirror*, appeared and became immediately popular among English seamen, so much so that soon any practical navigation volume which included charts came to be called a "waggoner."

The Dutch dominated the chart publishing market through the 1600's. New charts were regularly added, but the old charts were mostly reused without updating – a dangerous practice. English publishers soon began producing their own series of sea atlases, but the French came to dominate this trade by the late seventeenth century.

France formed the first governmental mapping agency Dépôt des Cartes et Plans de la Marine in 1720. This was followed in 1795 by the Hydrographic Office of the British Admiralty, and by the United States Coastal Survey in 1811. While the government agencies had the advantage of more funds for production and access to first-hand surveys, privately published charts still remained in demand by merchants and other private mariners. For most of the century, British Admiralty charts were regarded as specialist charts for the British Royal Navy.

Near the end of the eighteenth century, a major change took place in the nature of published sea charts. By that time, charts were based on the Mercator projection that allowed a straight line on a chart to follow a straight compass bearing, thus avoiding the need to struggle with accommodating the curvature of the earth. That, combined with advancements in marine survey techniques and position fixings, made it practical to plot a ship's course directly onto a sea chart. Awkward atlas books of charts were eliminated in favor of individual charts that could be laid flat to work on with navigational tools.

These working charts needed to display a great deal of detail and show a wide enough area of the earth to be of practical use. Thus, charts tended to be fairly large and were typically rolled for storage and ease of spreading out on a ship's chart table. Official charts, such as those issued by the British Admiralty, were printed on thick, expensive paper in order to survive the rigors of sea conditions on-board a ship at sea. Private publishers, who couldn't afford costly paper, gave their charts added strength by backing them with blue manila paper that was in common use for wrapping unbound pamphlets. Thus, the term "blueback charts" was applied to privately published sea charts to distinguish them from officially produced government charts.

Individually printed sea charts are historically of great significance, as it was these charts which allowed commercial, private and military ships to successfully navigate the seas and oceans of the world up to the mid-nineteenth century when electronic means became available. These were the charts that were used by explorers, merchantmen, and naval captains who opened world frontiers that oiled the wheels of history.

There is a great scarcity of historic sea charts for two main reasons. First, any sheet of paper being used on-board a ship at sea was often subjected to damage and destruction during its use in adverse weather conditions. Secondly, incorrect information on an out-of-date chart could be extremely dangerous for ship and crew, so many were destroyed as soon as updated charts became available.

The Santa Barbara Maritime Museum has on display some very interesting historic charts – a late 18th century chart of the world; a 1705 chart of California when it was thought to be an island; an 1853 hand-colored chart of Vancouver's West Coast Reconnaissance; a very rare 1854 engraved copper plate made by famed artist James Abbot McNeil Whistler of a chart/drawing of Anacapa Island; a U.S Coast Survey chart showing Vancouver's reconnaissance of Prisoner's Harbor, Cuyler Harbor, and San Clemente Harbor in 1852; a photograph of a painting of the U.S. Survey vessels *Active* and *Ewing* anchored at Cuyler Harbor at San Miguel Island; a modern chart of Santa Barbara's coastline and the Channel Islands; and a contemporary three-dimensional chart of the Channel Islands Marine Sanctuary showing the underwater mountains and canyons off the coast of Santa Barbara.

GUARDING OUR COAST

Immediately after the American Revolutionary War (1775–1783), the brand-new United States was struggling to stay financially afloat. National income was desperately needed, and a great deal of this income came from tariffs on imported goods. Rampant smuggling reduced the country's income, so there was an urgent need for protection of our waters as well as for strong enforcement of tariff laws. On August 4, 1790 the United States Congress, urged on by Secretary of the Treasury Alexander Hamilton, created the Revenue-Marine Service, later renamed the Revenue Cutter Service. The new Service was assigned the responsible to enforce all United States maritime laws. In 1832, this mission was expanded to have the revenue cutters assist mariners in distress. The Service was merged with the United States Life-Saving Service In 1915 to form today's United States Coast Guard (USCG). Thus, the U.S. Coast guard can lay claim to being the United States' oldest continuous seagoing service.

To describe the operations of the USCG over the past two hundred and ten years would require a book, but here are some of the highlights.

- During the Quasi-War with France in 1798–1801, the Revenue-Marine fought alongside the Navy, assisting in the capture of 20 French ships.
- After 1794, the Revenue-Marine began intercepting slave ships that were illegally importing slaves into the United States, freeing hundreds of would-be slaves.

- Revenue Cutters were assigned to enforce the very unpopular Embargo Act of 1807, which outlawed nearly all European trade, import and export, through American ports.
- In the War of 1812 against Britain, the Revenue Cutter USRC *Jefferson* made the first American capture of an enemy ship, the brig *Patriot*, in June 1812.
- Revenue-Marine cutters again served under command of the U.S. Navy in the Mexican-American War of 1846–1848. The cutters were crucial for shallow-water amphibious assaults.
- On April 11, 1861, the USRC *Harriet Lane* fired the first maritime shots of the American Civil War. The cutter fired a shot across the bow of the Confederate steamship *Nashville* as it tried to enter Charleston Harbor during the bombardment of Fort Sumter.
- Revenue Cutters assisted Navy operations throughout the Civil War. When Lincoln was assassinated on April 15, 1865, Revenue Cutters were ordered to search all ships for any assassins that might be trying to escape.
- With the outbreak of the Spanish-American War in 1898, the Revenue Cutter Service saw much action.

In 1915, President Woodrow Wilson signed into law an act to combine the Revenue Cutter Service with the Lifesaving Service Act to Create the United States Coast Guard. This and formed the new United States Coast Guard. Gradually the Coast Guard would grow to incorporate the United States Lighthouse Service in 1939 and the Navigation and Steamboat Inspection Service in 1942.

In 1990, the United States Coast Guard created a military award known as the Coast Guard Bicentennial Unit Commendation which commemorated the original founding of the Revenue Cutter Service.

Today, the United States Coast Guard is a branch of the United States Armed Forces, and is one of our seven uniformed services. The USCG is a maritime, military, multi-mission service that is unique among the military branches in having a maritime law enforcement mission with jurisdiction in both domestically and international waters as well as a federal regulatory agency mission. The USCG operates under the Department of Homeland Security during peacetime, but can be transferred to the Department of the Navy by the President or Congress during time of war. As of August 2009, the Coast Guard had approximately 42,000 men and women on active duty, 7,500 reservists, 29,000 auxiliarists, and 7,700 full-time civilian employees.

The motto of the Coast Guard is *Semper Paratus*, Latin for Always Ready or Always Prepared.

Because of its distinctive blend of military, humanitarian, and civilian law-enforcement capabilities, the USCG is able to provide the following unique benefits to the nation:

- Maritime Safety – Eliminate deaths, injuries, and property damage associated with maritime transportation, fishing, and recreational boating. The Coast Guard's motto is "*Semper Paratus*" (Latin for "Always Ready", and the service is always ready to respond to calls for help at sea.

- Maritime Security – Protect America's maritime borders from all intrusions by halting the flow of illegal drugs, aliens, and contraband into the United States through maritime routes, preventing illegal fishing, and suppressing violations of federal law in the maritime arena.

- Maritime Mobility – Facilitate maritime commerce and eliminate interruptions and impediments to the efficient and economical movement of goods and people, while maximizing recreational access to and enjoyment of the water.

- National Defense – Defend the nation as one of the five U.S. armed services. Enhance regional stability in support of the National Security Strategy, utilizing the Coast Guard's unique and relevant maritime capabilities.

- Protection of Natural Resources – Eliminate environmental damage and the degradation of natural resources associated with maritime transportation, fishing, and recreational boating.

During the undeclared Quasi-War with France in 1798–1801, the U.S. Navy was formed and the Revenue-Marine fought alongside the Navy, capturing or assisting in the capture of 20 French ships. After 1794, the Revenue-Marine began intercepting slave ships illegally importing slaves into the United States. Many slave ships were seized and hundreds of would-be slaves were freed.

Revenue Cutters were assigned to enforce the very unpopular Embargo Act of 1807, which outlawed nearly all European trade, import and export, through American ports. The Act was enforced until it was repealed in 1808. In the War of 1812 against Britain, a Revenue Cutter made the first American capture of an enemy ship. USRC *Jefferson* was the first to capture a British merchantman, the brig Patriot, in June 1812.

Revenue-Marine cutters again served under command of the U.S. Navy in the Mexican-American War of 1846–1848. The cutters were crucial for shallow-water amphibious assaults.

On April 11, 1861, the USRC *Harriet Lane* fired the first shots of the maritime conflict in the American Civil War of 1861-1865. The cutter fired a shot across the bow of the Confederate steamship *Nashville* as it tried to enter Charleston Harbor during the bombardment of Fort Sumter. Revenue Cutters assisted Navy operations throughout the war. When Lincoln was assassinated on April 15, 1865, Revenue Cutters were ordered to search all ships for any assassins that might be trying to escape.

With the outbreak of the Spanish-American War in 1898, the Revenue Cutter Service again saw plenty of action.

President Woodrow Wilson signed into law the Act to Create the Coast Guard on January 28, 1915. This act effectively combined the Revenue Cutter Service with the Lifesaving Service and formed the new United States Coast Guard. Gradually the Coast Guard would grow to incorporate the United States Lighthouse Service in 1939 and the Navigation and Steamboat Inspection Service in 1942.

In 1990, the United States Coast Guard created a military award known as the Coast Guard Bicentennial Unit Commendation which commemorated the original founding of the Revenue Cutter Service.

The USCG maintains offices at Santa Barbara Harbor and operates USCG Cutter Blackfin which is moored at the harbor's Navy Pier. The newly designed 87-foot Coastal Patrol Boat has several enhancements including improved mission sea keeping abilities, significantly upgraded habitability, and compliance with all current and projected environmental protection laws. It also employs an innovative stern launch and recovery system using an aluminum hulled inboard diesel powered waterjet small boat. The vastly larger pilot house is equipped with an integrated bridge system including an electronic chart display system (ECDIS) which interfaces with the USCG's new surface search radar. SWIII computers along with a fiber optic network allow the crew to access the vessel's CD-ROM technical publications and drawings.

TWO YEARS BEFORE THE MAST

Santa Barbara is uniquely connected with one of history's most famous and influential authors, politicians and sailors – Richard Henry Dana, Jr. Most know Dana as the young man whose experiences at sea in the 1800's resulted in his writing one of the world's most famous books, *Two Years Before The Mast* which included descriptions of Dana's visits to Santa Barbara while a seaman on the brig *Pilgrim*.

Richard Henry Dana was born in Cambridge, Massachusetts on August 1, 1815 into a family that had first settled in colonial America in 1640. His father was both a poet and a literary critic, which strongly impacted young Dana's later career. As a boy, he studied in Cambridgeport under a strict schoolmaster named Samuel Barrett. Barrett was infamous as a disciplinarian who punished his students for almost any infraction by flogging. He frequently pulled students by their ears, and once nearly pulled one of Dana's ear off, causing young Dana's father to protest so strongly that the practice was abolished

In 1825, Dana enrolled in a private school that was overseen by historic essayist, philosopher, and poet Ralph Waldo Emerson, whom Dana later mildly praised as "a very pleasant instructor", though he lacked a "system or discipline enough to insure regular and vigorous study." In 1831, young Dana enrolled at Harvard College, but his support of a student protest in his freshman year soon cost him a six month suspension. In his junior year, he contracted measles which led to ophthalmia which seriously reduced his eyesight.

Fatefully, Dana's worsening vision inspired him to take a sea voyage while he was still physically able. But rather than going on a fashionable

Grand Tour of Europe and despite his high-class birth, Dana elected to enlist as a merchant seaman. He departed Boston in 1834 aboard the brig *Pilgrim* bound for California, which was still a part of Mexico. The voyage took Dana to a number of settlements in California, including Monterey, San Pedro, San Juan Capistrano, San Diego, Santa Barbara, Santa Clara, and San Francisco. The arduous voyage was far from a vacation. After witnessing a bloody flogging of a fellow sailor, he vowed to try to help improve the miserable lot of the common seaman of the time.

Pilgrim's stay at Santa Barbara was a pleasant break for the young seaman, and he included great detail of the festivities surrounding the marriage of Dona Anita de la Guerra de Noriego y Corillo in the journal of his voyage.

The *Pilgrim's* mission was to collect cow hides for shipment back to Boston, so Dana spent much of his time in California tanning hides and loading them onto the ship. The work was back-breaking, and the young man soon decided to return home earlier than his ship's schedule. He signed on as a crewman on the ship *Alert* for the voyage home.

Alert arrived in Massachusetts in the fall of 1836, and Dana quickly enrolled at Harvard Law School to learn the necessary skills to follow his quest to help oppressed seamen. He graduated in 1837 and was admitted to the legal bar in 1840. Specializing in maritime law, Dana successfully defended many common seamen in court. During that period, he wrote *The Seaman's Friend*, which became a standard reference on the legal rights and responsibilities of sailors.

Richard Henry Dana had kept a diary during his voyages, and published it as a memoir in 1840. *Two Years Before the Mast* made a strong and vivid case against the poor treatment of oppressed seamen. The term, "before the mast" refers to the common sailors' quarters that were located in the forecastle in the ship's pounding bow. Officers' quarters were comfortably located near the stern where the motion of the ship was far more pleasant. When the California Gold Rush began, *Two Years Before the Mast* was highly sought after as one of the few sources of information about California, but when it was first published, Dana was paid only $250 along with twenty-four complimentary copies.

Continuing his quest to defend the oppressed, Dana became a prominent abolitionist, helped to found the anti-slavery Free Soil Party, and represented a number of apprehended fugitive slaves during the late 1840's. In 1859, while the U.S. Senate was considering whether the United States should try to annex the Spanish possession of Cuba, Dana traveled there and visited Havana, a sugar plantation, a bullfight, and various churches, hospitals, schools, and prisons. He documented the trip in his book *To Cuba and Back.*

During the American Civil War, Dana served as a United States Attorney and successfully argued before the Supreme Court that the United States Government could rightfully blockade Confederate ports. After the war, he became a member of the Massachusetts legislature, and also served as a U.S. Counsel in the trial of Confederate President Jefferson Davis.

Richard Henry Dana died of influenza in Rome, and he is buried in that city's Protestant Cemetery. His son, Richard Henry Dana III, married Edith Longfellow, daughter of famed author Henry Wadsworth Longfellow.

Two Years Before The Mast was Dana's greatest legacy, and it remains a best seller 170 years later. Today, there is a hide-thrower sculpture dedicated to Dana and all the other hide throwers at Dana Point, California. A reproduction of the brigantine *Pilgrim* was built and sailed around Cape Horn to California. It is now on display at the Orange County Marine Institute. Several schools are named in Dana's honor.

Selected works by Richard Henry Dana include *Two Years Before the Mast, The Seaman's Friend: Containing a Treatise on Practical Seamanship, Cruelty to Seamen, An Autobiographical Sketch -1815-1842, To Cuba and Back, Journal of a Voyage Round the World -1859-1860,* and *Twenty-Four Years After.*

MASSIVE FORCE

Ocean currents are one of the largest forces on Earth. Currents support the life of nearly fifty percent of all species on Earth. They provide twenty percent of the animal protein and five percent of the total protein consumed in our human diet. One of every six jobs in the United States is marine-related, and over one-third of the U.S. Gross National Product originates in coastal areas.

For centuries, mariners have known that ocean currents flow along generally consistent paths. For example, Spanish galleons transporting gold and silver from Mexico to Spain made use of the Gulf Stream to help them return home. In 1772, Benjamin Franklin used information from ships' log books to draw a map of the Gulf Stream. Since then, scientists and mariners have gained much more information on both where currents flow and their effect on many of our planet's systems including climate and weather.

Knowledge of surface ocean currents is vital in reducing costs of shipping, since proper route selection can substantially lower fuel costs. Captains steer into currents that provide an extra push toward their destination, but try to avoid those that impede their progress. Such knowledge was even more essential during the era of sailing ships. A good example was the Agulhas Current which long prevented Portuguese sailors from efficiently reaching India. Even today, around-the-world sailing competitors utilize surface currents to make the fastest possible passages.

Ocean currents also affect temperatures and climate throughout the world. For example, the current that flows warm water up the north

Atlantic Ocean to northwest Europe prevents ice from forming by the shores which could otherwise block ships from entering and exiting ports. Currents are also very important in the dispersal of many life forms throughout the world.

An ocean current is a continuous, directed movement of ocean water generated by forces such as breaking waves, wind, Coriolis force, temperature and salinity differences, along with tides caused by the gravitational pull of the moon and sun. Depth contours, shoreline configurations and interaction with other currents influence a current's direction and strength.

Ocean currents can stream for great distances, and together they create a global conveyor belt which plays a dominant part in determining the climate of many of the Earth's regions. Perhaps the most striking example is the Gulf Stream, which makes northwest Europe much more temperate than any other region at the same latitude. Another example is the Hawaiian Islands, where the effects of the cool California Current result in a sub-tropical rather than a tropical climate as found at other locations of the same latitude.

Currents exist at all depths in the ocean; in some regions, two or more currents flow in different directions at different depths. Although the current system is complex, ocean currents are primarily driven by two forces: the gravitational pull of the sun and the rotation of the Earth.

Surface currents make up about 10% of all the water in the ocean, and are generally restricted to the upper 1,300 feet of the ocean. They are generally wind driven, and develop clockwise rotation in the northern hemisphere and counter-clockwise rotation in the southern hemisphere. The areas of surface ocean currents move somewhat with the seasons, most notably the equatorial currents.

Deep ocean currents are driven by water density, temperature gradients and gravity. They flow far below the surface like submarine rivers. They are now being researched by a fleet of underwater robots called "Argo." Density-driven deep ocean currents act as the ocean's "conveyor belt," moving sea life and other objects across the globe.

Ocean currents are measured in Sverdrup (Sv), where 1Sv is equivalent to a volume flow rate of 1,000,000 m³ (35,000,000 cu ft) per second.

As described in a previous column, the distribution and identification of the origin of debris throughout the oceans has importance in identifying and studying ocean currents.

In 2005, the California State Coastal Conservancy and the State Water Resources Control Board invested $21 million from voter-approved Propositions 40 and 50 funds to build an infrastructure to map ocean surface currents. The California Coastal Ocean Currents Monitoring Program (COCMP) uses a suite of technologies, high-frequency radar in particular, to track ocean surface currents in near real-time. Fifty-four land-based stations now span the California coastline, providing anyone with access to the Internet the ability to track past and near real-time movement of California's coastal waters, including floating pollutants. COCMP was formed to better manage California's ocean and coastal resources and to ensure a healthy ocean environment for current and future generations.

High-frequency radar (HF radar) systems measure radio waves that are reflected off the surface of the ocean. Each land-based HF radar installation is sited near the coastline and includes two antennas: the first transmits a radio signal out across the ocean's surface about ninety miles, while a second listens for the reflected radio signal after it has bounced off the ocean's waves. By measuring and processing the change in frequency of the radio signal that returns, the system determines how fast the water is moving toward or away from the antenna. Data from neighboring antennas are processed and displayed as surface current maps in near real-time. The system utilizes minimal energy, comparable to the power of a household light bulb.

The movement of the surface waters can be viewed in near real-time in a Google Maps interface or at web pages developed for specific users. If an oil spill occurs, these maps and products can be used to track where the oil is moving, even at night or in dense fog and extreme weather. Similar maps and websites allow city environmental managers to follow the trajectory of coastal discharges—like sewage spills or coastal runoff after heavy rains—so that only the affected beaches are targeted for water safety testing and subsequent closures to protect our health. Sailors use HF radar model predictions to find the fastest currents in a race. Marine biologists use COCMP data to track the movement of marine organisms to establish marine sanctuaries.

A wide variety of users, including local, state and federal agencies, resource managers, industry, policy makers, educators, scientists and the general public use COCMP web-based products. These tools all them to track oil and other pollutants, manage marine fisheries, improve coastal water quality and reduce human exposure to pollutants, and to design marine parks and conservation areas. They also allow them to improve efforts to restore endangered salmon and steelhead runs, increase efficiency and safety of maritime shipping, aid Coast Guard search and rescue operations, track planned and unplanned coastal discharges, plot routes for recreational sailing and boating, and assess the potential of ocean energy.

As long term time-series of surface currents are established, these data will contribute to our ability to monitor climate change, assess the impacts of climate change on coastal habitats, increase precision in weather and climate forecasts, predict storm surge, and mitigate coastal erosion.

JUAN RODRIGUEZ CABRILLO

On June 27, 1542, a three-vessel armada under the command of Juan Rodriquez Cabrillo departed from Navidad on the west coast of Mexico. The flotilla, made up of the ships *San Salvador*, *Victoria*, and *San Miguel*, set out to explore the unknown (to Europeans) ocean to the north in search of the legendary cities of gold, a passage to Asia, and new areas for settlement. This area was *terra incognita* – the unknown territory. The expedition sailed north, exploring the Baja Peninsula until the end of September when the fleet made landfall at San Diego Bay.

At islands and prominent points that the searchers visited, a landing party would claim possession of the land for the King of Spain. In what must have seemed like a strange ritual to the natives, Cabrillo would place his hand on his sword and announce that he took possession of the land and was prepared to defend the claim from anyone who might contradict him. He would cut a nearby tree with the sword, move rocks from one place to another, and take water from the sea and pour it on the land. The party placed markers to attest their claim of possession and named the location. This ceremony to claim possession was the custom of the time.

Sailing north of Point Conception toward Monterey and beyond, Cabrillo encountered a rugged, stormy coastline whose mountains were covered with snow and ice. Strong winds, high surf and lack of places to anchor often kept the sailors from going ashore to explore. During one storm near Cape San Martin, the deck cargo from *Victoria* was lost overboard. After about a month, the fleet turned south to spend the winter in the sheltered anchorages in the Channel Islands.

The vessel *San Miguel* was leaking very badly and was in danger of sinking. The boat was hauled ashore so the crew could make repairs and reseal the seams between the hull planks. The site of this repair was probably present-day Cuyler Harbor on the island of San Miguel off Santa Barbara.

While wintering in the islands, relations with the natives were sometimes contentious. One sailor reported, "all the time the armada was in the Isla Capitana (San Miguel Island) the Indians there never stopped fighting us." Just before Christmas, a landing party sent ashore to get water was attacked by the island's residents. The sailors called out to the ship for help.

Cabrillo led the rescue party. As he came ashore, he lost his footing and broke some bones in the fall. Still, he refused to leave the island until all the men in the shore party were rescued. He was then taken back to the ship, but there was little anyone could do to treat his injuries. Realizing he was dying, Cabrillo turned over command of the expedition to his ship's pilot, Bartolome Ferrer. He then worked to bring the record of the voyage up to date, but was only able to complete part of the job before he died on January 3, 1543.

The armada remained in the islands until January 19, when they weighed anchor and resumed the difficult exploration of the coast. They sailed northward as far as Pt. Arena on the Mendocino Coast before turning south. Short on supplies, with the vessels in need of repair, the expedition sailed into Navidad, Mexico on April 14, 1543, nine months after embarking from that port and three and a half months after Capitan Cabrillo's death.

To this day, no one has found Cabrillo's gravesite. In fact, no one is certain on which of the offshore islands he is buried, but local legend holds that he is buried on San Miguel Island, off Santa Barbara. A memorial marker was placed there in 1937 overlooking Cuyler Harbor. Some think that he was buried on neighboring Santa Rosa Island. Still others assert Cabrillo's final resting place is on Santa Cruz Island, either in a cave or at Prisoners' Harbor. No one has claimed that he is buried on Anacapa, but one scholar credibly argues that Cabrillo was not laid to rest on any of the northern Channel Islands, but favors Catalina Island well to the south.

San Miguel Island remains one of the most remote and difficult to reach islands in the United States. From Santa Barbara, a boater encounters steep seas and often almost impenetrable fog. Two "formulas" work fairly well for reaching the island. One is to sail to Becher's Bay on eastern end of Santa Rosa Island that is south of San Miguel Island, anchor for the night, and then make the run to Cuyler Harbor on San Miguel Island early in the morning before the wind and waves build up. The other is to power up the coast from Santa Barbara and spend the night at Cojo Anchorage below Point Conception and again make an early crossing with the wind and waves on the quarter (sideways to the wind).

But once you have paid your "dues" and arrived at Cuyler Harbor on San Miguel Island, you will find outstanding diving and hiking where few others have visited. Giant elephant seals abound, and it is rewarding to arrange for an excursion with a park ranger. San Miguel Island is the westernmost of California's eight Channel Islands and the sixth-largest at 9,325 acres. Its highest peak is 831 foot San Miguel Hill. San Miguel is part of Channel Islands National Park and lies within Santa Barbara County. Almost all of the island (8,960 acres) has been designated as an archeological district on the National Register of Historic Places. The northwesterly winds and severe open ocean weather create cold and nutrient-rich water that is home to a diverse array of sea life not found on the southern islands.

MANILA GALLEONS

The Manila galleons were Spanish trading ships that sailed one or two times a year across the Pacific Ocean between Manila in the Philippine Islands and Acapulco in New Spain – present day Mexico.

The Manila-Acapulco galleon trade began in 1565 when Andrés de Urdaneta discovered a return route from Cebu City in the Philippines to Mexico. Urdaneta reasoned that the trade winds of the Pacific might move in a circular gyre as did the Atlantic winds. He reasoned that by sailing far to the north before heading east, he would pick up trade-winds that would bring him back to the west coast of North America. His prolonged course took him to 38 degrees North before turning east, but his hunch paid off, and he made a landfall near Cape Mendocino, California. Urdaneta then followed the coast south to San Blas and then to Acapulco. But his success was ill-fated, as many of his crew died on the long and insufficiently provisioned voyage.

By the eighteenth century, experience showed that a less northerly track was sufficient, but galleon navigators cautiously steered well clear of the forbidding and rugged, fogbound Alta California coast. It took four months to sail across the Pacific Ocean from Manila to Acapulco. The ships generally made their landfall well down the coast, somewhere between Point Conception and Cabo San Lucas. These were preeminently merchant ships, and the business of exploration lay outside their field, although chance discoveries were sometimes made.

The earliest exploration of Alta California was to look for possible way station locations for the sea-worn Manila galleons to prepare for the last leg of their journey. Early attempts were not successful, but several Manila galleons put in at Monterey in the later eighteenth century.

Trade served as the primary income-generating business for Spanish colonists living in the Philippine Islands between the fourteenth and seventeenth centuries. Over one hundred Manila galleons participated in the Manila-Acapulco trade between 1565 and 1815. Until 1593, three or more ships would set sail annually from each port, but the Manila trade became so lucrative that merchants located in Spain complained to King Philip II of lost revenues. This resulted in a law in 1593 that set a limit of just two ships being allowed to sail each year from either port.

To counter this limitation, ship owners constructed the largest class of ships known to have been built anywhere up to that time. Ranging from 1,700 to 2,000 tons, these giant galleons were reported to be able to carry up to a thousand passengers. The *Concepción*, wrecked in 1638, was approximately 160 feet long and displaced some 2,000 tons.

The galleons collected a variety of goods from the Spice Islands and Asia-Pacific for sale in the European markets - spices, porcelain, ivory, lacquerware, processed silk cloth, and more. The cargoes were transported by land across Mexico to Veracruz on the Gulf of Mexico, and then loaded onto galleons bound for Spain. The galleons sailed west across the Indian Ocean, around the Cape of Good Hope, and on to Spain, thus avoiding ports controlled by the competing powers of Portugal and the Netherlands. From the early days of exploration, the Spanish knew that the American continent was much narrower across the Panamanian isthmus than across Mexico. They attempted to establish a regular land crossing there, but the thick jungle and deadly malaria made it impractical at that time.

For over 200 years, hundreds of Manila galleons traveled from present-day Mexico to the Philippines on a route taking them around thirteen hundred miles south of the Hawaiian Islands. No historical records show any contact, but there are questions as to whether explorers accidentally arrived in the Hawaiian Islands two centuries before Captain James Cook's first visit in 1778. Ruy López de Villalobos commanded a fleet of six ships that left Acapulco in 1542 with a Spanish sailor named Juan Gaetano aboard as pilot. Depending on the interpretation, Gaetano's reports seemed to describe the discovery of Hawaii or the

Marshall Islands in 1555. If it was Hawaii, Gaetano would have been the first European to find the islands, but most scholars have dismissed this claim as lacking credibility.

Spain's routes were cloaked in secrecy to protect their ships from English pirates and the Dutch. For this reason, if the Spanish had found Hawaii during their voyages, they would not have published their findings, and the discovery would have remained unknown.

The Manila-Acapulco galleon trade ended when Mexico gained independence from Spain in 1821, after which the Spanish crown took direct control of the Philippines. By the mid-1800s, with the invention of steam powered ships and the opening of the Suez Canal, travel time from Spain to the Philippines was reduced to around 40 days. The era of the Spanish galleons had come to an end.

The wrecks of the Manila galleons are legends second only to the wrecks of the treasure ships in the Caribbean. Aside from the goods carried in the galleons, their trade allowed modern, liberal ideas to enter the Philippines, which eventually inspired the movement for independence from Spain.

The Philippine Declaration of Independence occurred on June 12, 1898. With the public reading of the *Act of the Declaration of Independence*, Filipino revolutionary forces under General Emilio Aguinaldo proclaimed the sovereignty and independence of the Philippine Islands from the colonial rule of Spain, which had been recently defeated at the Battle of Manila Bay during the Spanish-American War.

The declaration, however, was not recognized by the United States or Spain, and the Spanish government later ceded the Philippines to the United States in the 1898 Treaty of Paris that ended the Spanish-American War. It was almost fifty years later when the United States recognized Philippine independence on July 4, 1946 with the Treaty of Manila.

FROM WARFARE TO SPORT

Rowing is one of the oldest human activities in the world. What began as a method of transport and warfare eventually became a sport with a wide following. Today, it has it became a part of the cultural identity of the English speaking world.

Ever since the earliest recorded references to rowing, the sporting element has been present. A 1430 BC Egyptian inscription reports that the warrior Amenophis II was renowned for his feats of oarsmanship. In the *Aeneid*, written between 29-19 BC, Virgil mentions rowing forming part of the funeral games arranged by Aeneas in honor of his father. In the 13th century, Venetian festivals called "regata" included boat races among others.

The first known "modern" rowing races began as competition among the professional watermen who provided ferry and taxi service on the River Thames in London. Prizes for wager races were often offered by the London guilds and livery companies as well as by wealthy owners of riverside houses. The oldest race that is still held today is "Doggett's Coat and Badge," which was first contested in 1715. The race course is from London Bridge to Chelsea. During the nineteenth century these races were numerous and popular, attracting large crowds. Prize matches among professionals also became popular on other rivers throughout Great Britain, most notably on the River Tyne. In America, the earliest known rowing race dates back to 1756 in New York, when a pettiauger defeated a Cape Cod whaleboat.

Amateur rowing competition in England began towards the end of the eighteenth century. Documentary evidence from this period is sparse, but it is known that the Monarch Boat Club of Eton College and the Isis Club of Westminster School were both in existence in the 1790s. The Star Club and Arrow Club in London for gentlemen amateurs were also in existence before 1800. At the University of Oxford bumping races were first organized in 1815 when Brasenose College and Jesus College boat clubs had the first annual race while at Cambridge the first recorded races were in 1827. A bumps race is a form of rowing race in which a number of boats chase each other in single file as each boat attempts to catch ("bump") the boat in front without being caught by the boat behind. Brasenose won Oxford University's first Head of the River Race, and claims to be the oldest established boat club in the world. The 1829 boat race between Oxford and Cambridge Universities was the second known intercollegiate sporting event, following the first varsity cricket match by two years.

In America, a sizable rowing community also developed. Many rowing boats were built for the day to day activities in ports such as Boston, New York, and Philadelphia, and competition was inevitable. The first American race took place on the Schuylkill River in 1762 between six-oared barges, predecessors of today's lightweight rowing sculls. As the sport gained popularity, clubs were formed and scullers began racing for prizes. Races were often round trips to a stake and back, so that the start and finish could be watched. The public flocked to such events, and rowing became as popular in America during the 1800s as other professional sports are today. In 1824, ferrymen from the Whitehall Landing at Manhattan's Battery raced a crew from the British frigate HMS *Hussar* for $1,000. Thousands bet on the event, and the Americans won. In 1843, the first American college rowing club was formed at Yale University. The Harvard-Yale Regatta is the oldest intercollegiate sporting event in the United States, having been contested every year since 1852 except for occasional breaks due to major wars. The oldest continuous rowing club in America is the Detroit Boat Club in Michigan.

Today, the strongest rowing nations include Great Britain, the United States, Italy, France, Canada, Germany, New Zealand, Australia, and Romania.

Santa Barbara became heavily involved in rowing and paddling competition when the United States sponsored the 1984 Olympics rowing and paddling competitions at Lake Casitas. The athletes were housed at UCSB, and I and many other Santa Barbarans spent several years preparing for and conducting these events.

The Olympic rowing competition at Lake Casitas was held in racing shells of various sizes in races for one, two, four, and eight men and women rowers. Competitors came from throughout the world, but not the Soviet Union which boycotted the 1984 Olympics for political reasons.

The single person racing shell that won the men's Olympic gold medal is currently on display at the Santa Barbara Maritime Museum. The gold medal was won by Finland, and the silver and bronze medals were won by the German Democratic Republic and Canada respectively. The women's singles event was won by Romania, followed by the United States and Belgium.

To develop maximum speed, competitive rowing boats are designed to be strong but extremely lightweight. The single shell on display at Santa Barbara Maritime museum is twenty-eight feet long, but weighs just thirty-one pounds, excluding its oars.

International rowing competition is under the auspices of FISA, the "Fédération Internationale des Sociétés d'Aviron" (in French). The English equivalent is "International Federation of Rowing Associations." The federation was founded by representatives from France, Switzerland, Belgium, Adriatica (now a part of Italy) and Italy in Turin in 1892. It is the oldest international sports federation in the Olympic movement.

FISA first organized a European rowing championship in 1893. An annual world rowing championship was organized in 1962. Rowing has been conducted at the Olympic Games since 1900. It was not held at the first modern Games in 1896 due to bad weather.

Well-known rowers of recent years include Sir Steve Redgrave (UK), who won Olympic golds in five successive Olympics; Sir Matthew Pinsent (UK), who won golds in four successive Olympics; James Tomkins (Australia), three-time Olympic gold medalist; Rob Waddell (New Zealand) and Xeno Müller (Switzerland), opponents in the single sculls; Ekaterina Karsten (Belarus) in women's single sculls; Kathrin Boron (Germany) in women's double sculls and quadruples.

TREASURES?

Americans are collectors. Witness the countless thriving garage sales each Saturday across the nation. What may be a treasure to you may seem as trash to others and vice versa.

My treasures are nautical antiques, which to some may seem to be "nautical junk." Nevertheless, they mean much to me for a variety of reasons, and I enjoy handling them while reflecting on their origin and where they may have traveled across the oceans and years.

Part of the allure of nautical antiques is that most were once working gear from ships of the past that had traveled the oceans and seas of the world, encountering conditions ranging from nautical paradise to watery hell.

One of my nautical "treasures" is an old store-bought knife fitted in a handmade sheath. The sheath is made from two flat pieces of wood, each with a section cut away to match the length and width of the knife blade. With the two pieces joined together with twine, the cutouts form a hollow interior that fits the dimensions and shape of the blade. The workmanship is crude, but I can easily envision an old sailor on a square-rigged sailing ship passing his slow off-watch hours carving this necessary and useful tool that would soon assist him in his often dangerous work at sea.

Another "treasure" is a pair of oarlocks from a lifeboat of one of the last great ocean liners, the *Queen Mary*. Since the *Queen Mary* survives as a visitor attraction at Long Beach, I don't know how the oar locks found their way to a marine surplus shop. Nor do I have proof that the oar locks are authentic, but I believe they are.

With many antiques, it is not possible to obtain absolute proof of their age or origin. Frequently, a collector has to rely on the seller's integrity plus the overall visual and physical "feel" of an item based on prior experience and knowledge. Other items may be found with precise written documentation of origin that leaves no doubt.

The latter is true with an octant that I acquired some years ago. An octant is an earlier version of the sextant. Both came before the invention of today's Global Positioning Systems, and were used to determine a ship's location by measuring the angle between the Earth's horizon and the sun or stars. My octant is in its original wood case labeled with the builder's seal of "Spencer-Browning & Company Ltd." I checked the internet and found that Spencer-Browning made navigational tools in England between 1840 and 1870, which confirmed that my instrument was built during that period.

I am drawn to and moved by items built by the sailors themselves. They did so to preserve scarce funds, to pass long hours at sea, or to fill a need that could not be purchased. Two from my collection meet these criteria – a sewing kit and a shaving mirror. The 3 ½ inch by 6 inch mirror was manufactured, but a sailor had later carved out a piece of wood so the glass could be recessed to protect it from breaking. The top of the wood is curved with a hole drilled at the top so

the mirror could be hung on a bulkhead while the sailor shaved and otherwise spruced up. The sewing kit consists of an eight inch length of bamboo, hollowed out at one end, and with a cork-like plug made of carved wood and covered in sailor's knot work.

A grizzly item in the collection is a sailor's cosh. About twelve inches long, the cosh is constructed of numerous thin strips of whale baleen with a lead ball installed at each end, all covered with sailors knot-work. The result is a flexible, effective, and deadly weapon. Coshes were typically carried by a sailing ship's boatswain's mate as a tool to assist in maintaining order on-board. Ashore, members of press gangs used coshes for a quick knock on an unsuspecting head to add members to a ship's crew. Many sailors considered their cosh to be more effective than a knife as a means of protection.

Perhaps even more grizzly is a pair of iron leg irons that I purchased at an obscure and shady waterfront shop several years ago in England.

The irons are probably from the sixteenth or seventeenth centuries. I sometimes wonder what stories these ominous restraints could tell.

Ships in bottles are a part of any serious historic nautical collection. There are two major categories – professional and sailor-made. I searched for a good example of each. Fine professional ship models are made one at a time by craftsmen and not by manufacturers. My professional model is mounted in a Haig & Haig scotch whiskey bottle. (Robert Haig was censured by his church elders in 1655 for operating a still upon the Sabbath.) The model is a three-masted bark riding under full sail over deep blue water scattered with surging white-capped waves.

Also rigged as a three-masted bark, my sailor-made model is more crudely constructed and mounted in a much less pretentious bottle than the Haig & Haig. But I enjoy this crude model more than that of the skilled craftsman. I can envision a sailor passing long days on-deck a thousand miles off-shore, doing his best to recreate the proud ship beneath him, but with only a feeble result. But, this crude model is also an authentic creation from the era of "iron men and wooden ships."

Similar craftsman-verses-sailor workmanship is evident in two scrimshaw whale's teeth. Both are authentic, but the craftsman selected a tooth of very good quality, while the sailor had to settle for one that seemed to have needed urgent care by a whale-dentist. The craftsman copied a picture from the London Illustrated News of the ill-fated ship *Ann Alexander* being sunk by a whale in 1851. The sailor carved a crude ship from his imagination. The sailor gets my vote as creating a more authentic contribution to the history of the sea.

There are many other "treasures" in my collection, each with its own story that adds to the long and varied history of man and the sea. Some may see them as "nautical junk," but they are prizes to me.

ILLUSTRIOUS QUEEN

One of Santa Barbara's oldest and most illustrious institutions is the Santa Barbara Yacht Club. Historically, it has been far more than a place for boat owners to congregate.

One of the most significant and visible contributions of the Yacht Club can be observed any day of the week – the harbor's breakwater. Santa Barbara is endowed with towering mountains, a mild Mediterranean climate, panoramic views of the Pacific, terrain that discourages urban sprawl... but not a natural harbor. In 1836, Richard Henry Dana noted in Two Years Before The Mast, "This wind (the south-easter) is the bane of the coast of California. Between the months of November and April (including a part of each) which is the rainy season in this latitude, you are never safe from it, and accordingly, in the ports which are open to it, vessels are obliged, during these months, to lie at anchor at a distance of three miles from shore, with slip ropes on their cables ready to slip and go to sea at a moment's warning. The only ports which are safe from this wind are San Francisco and Monterey in the north and San Diego in the south."

Beginning in 1868, the City began petitioning the US Government for funds to build a breakwater at Santa Barbara. But the military and others argued that a more advantageous location would be forty-five miles north at Point Sal. Joseph Stearns finished building his wharf in front of the town, but the debate regarding the location of a harbor wore on and on through the years. When a severe storm in 1878 resulted in the loss of the Chapala Street Pier along with 1400 feet of Stearns Wharf, the need for a breakwater became more urgent.

Meanwhile, local yachting was becoming more prevalent by both local boat owners as well as wealthy yachtsmen who came to Santa Barbara each winter from their east coast estates. This increased activity in yachting ultimately resulted in the formation of the Santa Barbara Yacht Club in 1872. But through the ensuing years, bureaucracy, World War I, finance, and other issues continued to postpone the construction of a harbor at Santa Barbara. The Yacht Club continued its persistent campaign for the construction of a harbor breakwater. Santa Barbara Yacht Club member Major Max C. Fleischmann wrote of a check for $200,000, a substantial sum at that time, toward construction of a breakwater with a condition that the City of Santa Barbara match his donation with a similar amount.

The Yacht Club made many other contributions to the community to through the years, including attracting visitors to Santa Barbara by conducting a variety of regattas and sailing events, support and fundraising for local charities, acting as marine ambassador for visiting naval ships and military personnel, implementing and promoting positive programs for youth, and providing material enhancement to the City's waterfront.

All of these contributions to the community continue to this day. Santa Barbara Yacht Club has clearly played a major role in Santa Barbara's heritage. Now, one hundred and thirty two years after its official formation, the Yacht Club has compiled and published a comprehensive narrative that describes its long and fascinating history. Initially designed for its members, the Yacht Club has decided make it available to all Santa Barbarans. The over 300 page volume includes many rare and fascinating photographs, and is of "coffee table" quality. It will become a collectors item worthy of being handed down to future generations. Interested parties may purchase the book at Santa Barbara Yacht Club at the harbor by major credit card for $90.00 plus sales tax.

SANTA BARBARA'S MARITIME TREASURE

Ten years ago, a handful of volunteers decided that Santa Barbara deserved a maritime museum. The story of this area's unique and extensive maritime history needed to be preserved and presented for generations to come. Our area's story began thousands of years ago when coastal Chumash plied their Tomol canoes between the central coast and channel islands. Since then, it has been claimed by Spanish explorer Juan Rodriguez Cabrillo in 1542, written about by Richard Henry Dana in Two Years Before The Mast, and the site of many other historic events.

The founding volunteers were concerned that historic information and valuable artifacts may be lost, and it was therefore urgent that they be preserved and protected for future generations. Our vision was to locate a facility at Santa Barbara Harbor that could accommodate a small museum, but then . . . enter fate. The City of Santa Barbara had just reacquired the large Naval Reserve Building from the US Navy. The building had originally been built with funds provided by both the City and the Federal Government. Upon the outbreak of World War ll, the City sold its share of the building to the Navy for one dollar. During the war, the Navy used the building for port security and as a training facility.

At war's end, the City's problem became, what to do with the building? Our small group met with City personnel to see if some space could be allocated for a small museum. I recall that the City's initial plan had been to install a number of shops in the building's large drill hall area. But as our dream and community support for a maritime museum continued to grow, the final result was that the entire drill hall and its surrounding mezzanine would become the home of the Santa Barbara Maritime Museum.

Dozens of committed volunteers then began planning for the new museum. Maritime history had to be collected and compiled, artifacts located, the floor plan designed, construction drawings prepared, money raised, and much more. As word spread throughout the community, growing support allowed the dream to expand. The original plan of occupying one-half of the drill hall was expanded to encompass the entire hall as well as some surrounding office areas. The final design of the building included a extensive maritime museum, a museum store, ample restaurants upstairs and down (Endless Summer Bar-Cafe and the Waterfront Grill), and a community meeting room.

The result was a facility worthy of our community and its long and varied history. At the museum's entry, the walls are covered with Honduran paneling salvaged from the passenger steamer Hermosa which stopped at Santa Barbara in 1880 on its way to begin carrying passengers between San Pedro and Catalina Island. Rare historic photographs line a hallway o the entry's left.

Stepping through the museum's entry, you are first met by JIM, a large diving suit constructed of tough magnesium that allowed oil industry divers to work undersea at depths down to 2000 feet.

Moving into the main exhibition hall, visitors encounter a historic path that traces Santa Barbara's maritime history from the early Chumash to the present day. First in line is a Chumash Tomol canoe that was recently constructed by members of the local Chumash community. Further on are displays about early explorers, seal hunters, shore whaling, the supply ships that plied our early coast, Richard Henry Dana, and Santa Barbara's overall waterfront history.

Just past the Historic Path is a children's area that is both entertaining and educational. The adjacent area presents historical information about Santa Barbara's diving industry and includes historic diving helmets and equipment.

The museum incorporates many interactive exhibits that permit visitors to operate and observe various features. For example, a replica of a ship's pilot house includes contemporary navigational equipment and bridge controls. The visitor "steers" the ship and operates various controls while viewing the results on a large screen.

A prime exhibit displays two of the five cannons that were discovered at a shipwreck site off the coast of Goleta. Pushing a button results in the sound of the cannon firing. The cannons are on loan from the Goleta Historical Society.

The very popular and entertaining sports fishing exhibit includes a fighting chair, a fishing rod reel and line, and a projection screen. The museum visitor first selects which type of game fish he wishes to try to catch. Then, the screen shows the fighting fish and the fishing line begins tugging in coordination with the actions of the fish. If the visitor is successful, the screen will display accolades; if not, the fish breaks loose and swims away.

Additional museum exhibits include marine navigation and charting, Santa Barbara's yacht club, the tragic multiple shipwreck disaster at Point Honda, the sinking of the ship Cuba, and descriptions of the island ranches. Other displays include such subjects as model ships, the ocean environment, ocean trash, maritime safety, and weather. The huge power of the off-shore oceans is dramatically displayed in the storm at sea exhibit.

The list of intriguing exhibits continues. A twenty-eight foot rowing shell that won its division at the 1984 Olympics at Lake Casitas is on display. A large model of the Lockheed F-1 Flying Boat is suspended from the ceiling, and a museum visitor may operate controls that power-up the propellers. An exceptional experience is to operate the authentic submarine periscope that extends from the mezzanine through the roof of the museum. But, instead of sighting enemy warships, the actual view is of various areas of surrounding Santa Barbara.

Of course, a Santa Barbara maritime museum would not be compete without including surfing. The exhibit begins with surfing's origins in the 1800's and progresses through the key role of Santa Barbara's famous surfers including the Currens and George Greenough. The innovative camera that George designed to allow him to be the first to photograph from inside the tube of a wave is on display, along with the knee board he designed that revolutionized the sport of surfing. In my late teens, I skippered the Greenough's 59-foot sailing yawl "Sabrina" and sailed George and his brother Bill to various off-shore islands for surfing and fishing.

Santa Barbara's commercial fishing industry is well depicted in the museum, as is its renowned yachting history. Included in the yachting display is an eight-foot Sea Shell sailboat. First introduced to Santa Barbara in 1948 when my father purchased a Sea Shell assembly kit for my brother and me, the Sea Shell fleet rapidly grew and continues to prosper today. On Sundays during Santa Barbara's sailing season, you can see dozens of Sea Shells competing off of East Beach.

There are many other exhibits and programs at the museum, including lectures and productions in the unique Munger Theater. The exterior of the theater is configured as a historic sailing ship that dramatically projects outward from the second floor mezzanine.

This year is the tenth anniversary of the Santa Barbara Maritime Museum. Come down to see this Santa Barbara treasure between 10 AM to 6 PM during the summer months (closed Wednesdays). Or better yet, become involved as a volunteer of one of the many committees or activities of the museum. Donations of items of local maritime history for display not only benefits the visiting public, but also preserves them for future generations. Of course, as with all non-profit institutions donations are welcome and valued. The museum's web site is www.sbmm.org.

Happy Birthday, Santa Barbara Maritime Museum!

TRAVELS OF "TRAVELER"

Over the years, I have listened to many sailors expressing their dreams to "sail around the world," but only a handful have actually fulfilled their aspirations. One of the more bizarre followed a grand "bon voyage" party at Santa Barbara Harbor, after which well-wishers cheered as the forty-foot yawl slipped past the breakwater and was soon lost from sight over the horizon. Many of those watching yearned to trade places with the adventurers but with a sigh, slowly headed back to their seemingly monotonous lives. As I sailed into Ensenada Harbor three weeks later at the end of a race from Los Angeles, I spotted the yawl anchored near the breakwater. After we dropped our anchor, I rowed over to say hi to the crew, but found only the owner on-board. Dissention among the crew had resulted in their abandoning the yawl and its owner – a pretty short around the world voyage.

However, Barbara Burdick and Michael Lawler are an exception. A little over four years ago, I helped them purchase and outfit a 40-foot sloop for their planned circumnavigation. Just a few weeks ago, they successfully completed their over 30,000 mile around the world voyage. The following are some entries from Michael's blog as their trip neared completion.

- On our last night in San Diego, we went out with friends on their Catalina 32 [sailboat] to watch a couple of hundred boats hoist their spinnakers as they rounded the weather mark in the Wednesday night beer can race. We then went out to dinner at the Bali Hai – what a spectacular view of San Diego Harbor! We had a great time, but I got a little emotional when I realized this was the last time on this voyage that we would be going out to a restaurant for dinner (our last two nights in Catalina will be a barbecue on the beach.) The End Is Near!

- Over the past month or so, as the end of this incredible circumnavigation was drawing near, I would do certain tasks and realize, Wow, this is the last time I'll do that on this voyage. For example, for the last time:

- I raised a foreign country's courtesy flag (between Guatemala and Huatulco, Mexico)

- I changed the engine oil (Mazatlan)

- I got a haircut in a foreign country (La Paz, Mexico, $4)

- We did the laundry (or had it done for us, in La Paz, $4/load)

- I varnished the teak (La Paz)

- I caught a fish (mahi mahi, on passage between Magdalena Bay and Turtle Bay)

- I took the crew (Barbara and Brian) out to dinner in a foreign country (Ensenada)

- Cleared Customs and Immigration (San Diego)

- Just a few hours ago, we cast of the dock lines at our guest slip at the Southwestern Yacht Club in San Diego — for the last time (we will be at anchor in Catalina for the last two nights.)

- We are now on a night passage, and I am taking the graveyard watch from 0300 to 0600–for the last time.

- Brian went off watch an hour ago and I read in the Log Book: "Last log entry by b-law! Best experience of my life! Thanks dad!"

- I just picked up Catalina on radar! (It goes out 24 miles.)

- Barbara and Brian are off watch, asleep. I am so pleased and thankful that Barbara was able to rejoin me for the final leg up from Cabo San Lucas, and to have Brian with me since last August. Brian said it well in his toast at our dinner in Ensenada: "Finish strong!" And we are - finishing strong together.

- We are motoring in calm seas, doing 8.0 knots, and the engine is running well. In fact, all is well on board Traveler. And The End Is Near, indeed.

Team Traveler - Living The Dream!

JIMMY'S HABASOD

Upon reaching Boston on a business trip from Santa Barbara, I was determined to settle once and for all the argument regarding from which ocean springs the world's best seafood – the Atlantic or the Pacific. I was weary of New Englanders bragging that Pacific coast lobster was really crayfish and that for years Westerners have been consuming large quantities of imitation clam chowder.

After checking in, I approached a knowledgeable looking hotel employee and asked where I might find the best seafood restaurant in Boston. Without hesitation, he replied "Jimmy's Habasod." "Jimmy's Habasod?' I repeated to make sure I had this obviously historic New England name correct. "Yes", he verified, and I moved out in search of a cab. Settling into the seat, I conveyed my desired destination to the driver, "Jimmy's Habasod." "Right", the driver replied, and we sped off into the night.

After we drove for some time through the twisting streets of Boston, I was becoming a bit concerned as to where and what Jimmy's Habasod might be. But we soon reached the wharf area, and I was relieved that we were near a most logical location for a seafood restaurant - even if it did have a strange name of undecipherable meaning.

I felt even better when a bright sign appeared ahead. Unknowingly, I had been speaking like a native New Englander, and that "Jimmy's Habasod" was what we Westerners would improperly pronounce as Jimmy's <u>Harborside</u> Restaurant".

HOLE IN THE WALL

Wives of sailors often carry a heavy burden. When I was actively sailing trailer ed one-design boats, our driveway and garage were frequently reserved for boats rather than cars. When I began sailing a twenty-two foot Olympic Star Boat, the garage was a few feet too short for its door to be closed. My clever solution was to cut a hole in the garage wall so the boat 's bow could extend into a kitchen cabinet. It was fun to open the cabinet to show friends my boat's bow, but I don't think Joan was as amused.

SAILING AROUND THE AMERICAS

Last week, a past Santa Barbaran sailed into our harbor on a sixty-four foot sloop nearing the end of a unique challenge – sailing around North and South America by first starting at Seattle and crossing over the top of the North American continent "the wrong way". "Ocean Passage's" daring voyage through the Northwest Passage was a goal that few ships have achieved, but which is now more possible due to rapid warming of the Arctic. Bucking fierce tides and winds from west to east, Captain Mark Schrader and his crew were under severe pressure to reach the Atlantic before impassible winter set in. They made it, but just as the beginnings of impassible winter ice had begun to form. Well suited and familiar with such challenges, Schrader had previously sailed two adventurous but also lonely solo trips around the world, having surved fierce hurricane force winds in the process.

The voyage of "Ocean Watch" is unique - to sail over twenty-six thousand miles, circumnavigating both American continents with a mission "to build awareness throughout the Americas of the increasing threats to our fragile ocean environment and to mobilize North and South Americans to take action to improve the health of our oceans". The goal is to connect and engage the public in the following ways:

- On-shore activities in more than 51 port visits
- Maintaining an engaging website that provides information about the expedition and ocean health issues, daily crew logs and photos from Ocean Watch, and free educational curriculum in both English and Spanish – www. aroundtheamericas.org.

- Local, national and international media coverage

The project seeks to raise awareness of ocean-health issues including:

- Polar ice melt
- Coral reef health
- Ocean acidification
- Collapsing fisheries
- Ocean debris and pollution
- Changing sea levels and coastal erosion

There are two phases of the program – first, the actual voyage around North and South America. Then a second phase of analysis and dissemination of the information collected. Phase One has just over 950 miles remaining – about four percent of the total trip distance.

In the second phase all information, photographs, film and observations will be processed, followed by dissemination of the information to the public with particular emphasis on providing prepared curriculum and lesson plans for use by schools in both North and South America. Two books of the voyage and its findings will be published – one for adults and one for children. A documentary film will be prepared, and speaking arrangements will be available for a corporate tour. The film is expected to be shown on PBS and other educational outlets. It is hoped that "Ocean Watch" will be housed at the Pacific Science Center near the Seattle Space Needle for viewing by the public.

Fourteen countries have been visited by "Ocean Watch" on her voyage. When I was on-board, the electronic log showed she had covered 26,087 nautical miles, which converts to 29,347 miles traveled so far.

The voyage has had many challenges, including racing to reach calm waters in the face of the offset of arctic winter and growing ice, fierce following winds and seas that pushed the boat south in the Labrador Seas at seventeen knots (19 mph) with only one tiny jib flying, waiting out a 105 knot gale at Cape Horn, thousands of frustrating miles of contrary wind, and more.

David Rockefeller, Jr. and Captain Mark Schrader have been engaged in joint sailing expeditions for over two decades. On one occasion, they were sitting dockside in Naples, Italy during a 2006 voyage around the Tyrrhenian Sea, when Mark proposed the concept of an Americas circumnavigation that could bring visibility to the Sailors for the Sea Foundation and its mission to recruit ocean stewards. Thus, the "Around the Americas" expedition was conceived.

The founders felt it was important to link current ocean science research and education to the project. Pacific Science Center, a highly respected educational institution in Seattle that uses engaging hands-on activities to educate and inspire visitors of all ages, was recruited as the science and education partner for "Around the Americas". Because of the Center's expertise in curriculum development and informal education and their history developing bilingual educational materials, Pacific Science Center was a natural partner with Sailors for the Sea Foundation to develop and operate the educational component of the" Around the Americas" project. In addition, Pacific Science Center attracted strong science partners to the project that are active in oceanographic and atmospheric research, including the UW Applied Physics Laboratory, the Joint Institute for the Study of the Atmosphere and Ocean, and the MIT Sea Grant Program. Sailors for the Sea Foundation was founded by David Rockefeller, Jr. after his three years of service on the Pew Oceans Commission. Seeking to follow the successful model of other organizations, the organizers of the "Around the America's" project recruited volunteers who use and enjoy a natural resource and who are therefore highly motivated to become the protectors of it. Rockefeller therefore concentrated on recruiting other lifelong sailors to join the board of this new non-profit organization that would focus attention on and raise awareness of ocean conservation.

The remaining stops of "Ocean Passage's" voyage are Monterey Bay May 22-26, San Francisco May 26-June 5, Portland, Oregon June 10-12, Port Townsend, Washington June 16-17, and the completion of the voyage around the Americas at Seattle, Washington on June 17.

The "Around the Americas" voyage was initially made possible by generous lead grants from The Tiffany & Co. Foundation, Unilever, the Rockefeller Family Foundation along with major support from James Bishop, Osberg Construction Co, and the Osberg Family Trust. Additional financial support is needed to conduct Phase Two of the project in order to put the valuable tools and information into the hands of teachers, students and other institutions throughout North and South America. To learn more, go to www.aroundtheamericas.org.

HARD DAY'S NIGHT

Last week's column described the "Around Then Americas" voyage of the ketch *Ocean Watch* as she nears the end of her epic voyage at Seattle. As the crew readied to sail up California's coast, I was tempted to warn them of the rigors of passing the "Graveyard of the Pacific" between Points Conception and Arguello north of Santa Barbara. But who was I to give advice to such an experienced crew whose skipper had sailed alone twice around the world? The following internet report from one of the crewmembers indicates that perhaps I should have.

"May 24th, 2010 - Regular readers of these crew logs know that I enjoy invoking popular culture and/or golden oldies in this space from time to time, and last night, in one of the bleaker moments of a truly dreary evening, the old Beatles tune "Hard Day's Night" drifted into mind – it seemed like an apt description of the present situation and the previous 24-hours. After all, it had been a hard night, a hard day and then another hard night. But a more relevant metaphor might've been the title of a regular segment on the David Letterman show called "Stupid Human Tricks." If David could've uploaded a signal, he would've seen four downtrodden humans in the midst of something extremely stupid.

How ridiculous was it, pounding headfirst into seas cresting and breaking over *Ocean Watch*'s bow, while getting punched in the kisser by brisk winds well over 30-knots? On a scale of one to ten, it felt like a twelve. We saw one other boat all night, and their crew had the good sense to be heading south, away from the brunt of the blow. "What are those idiots doing out here on a night like this?" I asked my watch mate, before realizing the question was rhetorical. He shook his head. "Some people…" he replied, as his words, or maybe his very thoughts, were carried away on the wind.

There was a reason, of sorts, for the catastrophe; we were late for an appointment, namely a series of scheduled appearances at the Monterey Bay Aquarium. Because of this, much of the crew who'd signed on for the Santa Barbara-Monterey leg – including oceanographer Michael Reynolds, shore manager Bryan Reeves and teacher Zeta Strickland – had already been dispatched north via rental car to wend their way up the Pacific Coast Highway to stand in for the boat and the rest of us until we arrived.

For the core crew of four, that meant the first time we sailed as just a quartet on the entire expedition Around the Americas. We sure picked a divine trip to get to know one another a little better.

It began in Santa Barbara in the wee hours of Sunday morning; twelve hours later, we might as well have been in a Cuisinart. Speaking of the Beatles, the so-called Fab Four, of the four of us on *Ocean Watch*, I was certainly feeling the least fabulous. After writing yesterday's edition of the crew log – typing in gales is a hazard in this occupation – I started to experience those tell-tale, queasy signals: sweaty brow, dry mouth, emerging headache. It was all trending in the wrong direction. The last time I used seasickness medication was a good 25-years ago, but this was no time to extend the streak. Lots of guests over the course of our travels have had good luck with the remedy called Stugeron, so I caught Logan's eye and elaborately described what I had in mind.

"Pills," I said. In a jiffy, he came back with a pair. "One now, another in eight hours," he said. "Eat something with it." I choked down a wedge of bread slathered with peanut butter. "Good boy," he concluded. Thankfully, they did the trick.

And actually, I wasn't the only one feeling iffy. Continuing our record-breaking ways, last night was also the first time on the entire escapade that nobody stepped forth to make at least the rudiments of a hot meal. Logan did manage to pull a rotisserie chicken out of the fridge and set it on the counter. Now, Captain Schrader loves whole chickens more than fleas love dogs, and such a temptation is generally laid to waste in no time flat. The mound of bones left in the aftermath resembled something out of *CSI*. But not last night. Everyone picked at the thing over the course of the long evening, but there were still plenty for sandwiches left over.

To add insult to injury, the massive high-pressure system stalled to the west, coupled with the stationary low parked over the western states – the source of those compressed and funneled northerly winds raking coastal California – was sending frigid air our way (we understand that the forty-seven degree temperatures in San Francisco were a record low). So, yes, it may have been miserable, but at least it was freezing.

At sunset, a wispy string of high clouds signaled the start of the windiest stretch of the day with sustained winds over 30-knots and gusting as high as forty. I'm struggling to come up with a good adjective for the wave trains, but let's try "stupendous". Dusk brought little visual relief; I'd been longing for nightfall so I wouldn't have to look at the mess anymore, but there was a big, bright three-quarter-moon overhead that illuminated the seaway like a floodlight. It resembled Opening Night in Hell.

Through all of this, amazingly, we had cell-phone coverage. And David, downloading weather from his iPhone, kept promising that if we could just hold on a little longer, things would calm down and smooth out. Sometime after midnight, finally, wonderfully, that's what happened.

Logan and I came on watch at 0600 this morning, and there was a decided change to the weather. The breeze had indeed moderated and fallen into the 10-knot range. While the leftover waves were sloppy, the whitecaps had disappeared and everything was in the midst of flattening out. The beaming blue sky of the last several days was now laced with clouds ("Those are your friends," said Logan). And over there to starboard? Why, that was California.

I've driven up and down Route 1 a bunch of times and this is my second time taking it in from sea, but it never fails to amaze me in crazed, frenetic, freeway-happy California how stark, open and beautiful stands the coastline from Santa Barbara to Monterey Bay. On top of that, a pair of Laysan albatrosses – the only type seen in the far North Pacific – swooped and hovered atop the water. Before long, we were visited by scores of leaping brown porpoises, and then watched a series of stately orca whales nonchalantly swimming by.

Soon enough, now making 7-8 easy knots instead of 3-5 plodding ones, we were abeam of the noble lighthouse marking Point Sur, one of the prettiest places in one of our prettiest states. Monterey was just a few hours away. Who would have thought it? The Hard Day's Night had a sequel after all. The Gorgeous Day's Morning had begun."

ISLA CALIFIA

During the early sixteenth century settlers thought California was an island. Just as the fabled blind men who touched different parts of an elephant reached various and different conclusions as to what it looked like, colonists having only partial information made wrong assumptions about California. A chart entitled "Cette Californie et du Nouveau Mexique" published in 1705 and now on display at the Santa Barbara Maritime Museum incorrectly portrays the "island" of California. Although very distorted in shape and scale, the chart includes the familiar names of San Diego, Santa Barbara Channel, Monterey, and Mendocino.

Three hundred years later, a geologist actually discovered a lost and sunken island off the coast of Santa Barbara. Isla Calafia is presently 300 feet underwater, but it had been above sea level during the Ice Age around 20,000 years ago, according to Ed Keller, professor of geological sciences and environmental studies at UCSB. "We had been trying to understand the earthquake hazard in the Santa Barbara area," Keller related, "and were surprised to find what used to be an island out there."

The now submerged island is part of an underwater ridge that extends outward from the Ventura shoreline and continues westward through the Santa Barbara Channel The undersea ridge extends down the coast from Point Conception and then emerges to become part of South Mountain near Ventura. It is about 31 miles in length, three miles wide, and rises about 660 feet from the floor of the Santa Barbara Channel. During ancient times when the ridge jutted above the waves,

348

today's Santa Cruz, Anacapa, Santa Rosa and San Miguel Islands were all part of one single land mass.

It is possible that Isla Calafia may once again rise above the waves as the Santa Barbara region continues to be squeezed by the Pacific and North American tectonic plates. But don't hold your breath. It will not occur, if at all, for at least another 50,000 years.

"The island shows signs of coastal erosion, had sea cliffs that were 30 feet high, and was flat," Dr. Keller reported. He speculated that Columbian mammoths may have swum out to the island at the peak of the Ice Age around 20,000 years ago.

The underwater island is bordered by two major earthquake faults, one of which is capable of producing an earthquake with a 7.5 magnitude and possibly a resultant tsunami wave. Not far from the underwater island are pockets of natural gas. A dozen craters in the area suggest that gas blowouts may have occurred in the past.

Both the sunken island and our state may have been named for a mythical warrior queen who ruled a utopian island empire. Most Spanish names of locations in California were derived from religious terms, Native American names, geographic peculiarities and the like. But the word "California" itself does not appear to have been derived from any of these common sources. Who first applied the name to the present day State of California and when is not known. Scholars who researched the subject developed several theories, but none are conclusive. The first recorded use of the word "California" was found in a 1541 document regarding a breach of contract suit brought by Juan Castellon against explorer Hernan Cortez. In a letter by Franciscan Father Antonio de Meno that was introduced as evidence in the trial, Father Meno referred to the "Isla de California". Father Meno had accompanied Francisco de Ulloa on an expeditions in the Sea of Cortez in 1539, so it is possible that the name may have been in use at that earlier date.

Spanish explorer Hernan Cortez was the driving force behind the Ulloa expedition. After Vasco Nunez de Balboa had discovered the Pacific Ocean in 1513, Cortez was commissioned to explore the Pacific Ocean. Myths circulating at the time spoke of lands of great wealth in distant oceans. These myths depicted wondrous islands of gold that were inhabited by beautiful amazons and strange beasts which were guarded by rocky shores. Both the King of Spain and Cortez appear to have believed that there was at least some substance to these myths. As a reward for his services, Cortez was to be given the governorship for life of any island that he discovered.

But Cortez had lost his position in New Spain and needed an island of riches to renew his financial fortunes. In 1533 he commissioned Diego Bezerra de Mendoza to search the Pacific for islands. Bezerra's pilot, Ortuna Ximenes, murdered his captain and took over the expedition. Ximenes discovered the southern tip of what is today known as Baja California and thought that it was an island. Ximenes went ashore with a landing party and was killed by a party of natives. The survivors aboard the ship returned to the mainland of now Mexico with word of their discovery. On May 3, 1535 Cortes landed on his "island," claimed it for Spain, and named it Santa Cruz. It is not known if Cortes actually referred to his "island" informally as California, but it is easy to speculate that wishful thinking might have encouraged him to do so.

It is ironic that the word California can trace it's origin back to dreams of great wealth, beautiful women, strange beasts, difficult obstacles, and even murder. Certainly all have played a part in the history of our state. The conflicting accounts are such that full and complete information may never be known.

Note: There are many conflicting accounts of the early history of California and the derivation of its name. The above seems to be in the mainstream, but firm information may never be known.

THE LOG OF THE SAGINAW

Ship's logs are legal documents that specify the transport, activities and locations of ships. Historic logs are fascinating glimpses into the past. The following entries are from the log of the USS Saginaw. The USS Saginaw was a transitional vessel, a paddle wheel steam sailing sloop. Launched in 1859 for anti-piracy patrols in China, she was later deployed to the Pacific Squadron during the Civil War. The Saginaw's last duty was to serve as the supply ship for a team of divers working to blast a channel through the reef at Midway Atoll. She was wrecked at Kure Atoll fifty-five miles west of Midway Atoll in the Northwestern Hawaiian Islands on a return voyage. All of her crew and passengers were able to safely reach nearby Green Island the following day. They rigged a small boat to attempt a hazardous month-long voyage back to the main Hawaiian Islands. Tragically, four died in the rough surf upon landing on the island of Kauai. The remaining castaways were finally rescued after spending sixty-seven days on Green Island.

The following are log entries of the USS Saginaw's last days. (Clarifications have been added in parenthesis.)

October 29, 1870 – Making passage from Midway Island to San Francisco. Commences and until 4 a.m. Weather cloudy but pleasant, moderate breeze from Nd. and Ed (north and east). At 1 a.m. clewed up topgallant sails and furled them at 2. At 2:25 stopped the engine. At 3 took in main trysail. About 3:15 made (sighted) breakers ahead, backed engine and took in jib and clewed up topsail. At about 3:22 ship struck on the rocks. At about 3:35 the launch carried away. At about 3:40 the smokestack went over the side to leeward. Started to get 2d cutter inboard for launching to leeward. Commenced getting up provisions. From 4 to 8 a.m. During the first part of the watch the ship was thrown high upon the reef, and was fast breaking up. The sea broke over the ship fore and aft. Hoisted the 2d cutter inboard preparatory to launching it to leeward. All hands engaged in getting up provisions. Both fore and main holds were full of water and the sea pouring in through the side of the ship. At daylight part of the crew got ashore on the reef and the boats were launched to leeward. About 6:25 the forward half of the ship was carried away and washed up on the reef. At 6:30 cut away the mainmast. At 7 Wysman, marine, was washed overboard but got on shore. From 8 to 5:15 p.m. the crew engaged in saving everything possible from the wreck.

October 30 – Part of the crew at work on the wreck saving provisions, rigging, sails, etc. Party on shore engaged drying provisions and receiving stores from the wreck Weather pleasant. Wind from Nd. and Ed. Dug a well on the island, (Ocean Island), water brackish.

October 31 – Ocean Island. Party engaged on wreck, saving rigging, sails, etc. Second cutter (large rowboat) employed gathering drift wood. Party on shore engaged drying provisions and digging wells, no fresh water was found on the island.

Got condensers out of the ship's wheel houses with the contractors (and) boilers. Set up distiller on the island, no fresh water having been found.

November 1 – January 2, 1871 – On Ocean Island

January 3 – First part pleasant, middle and later part of the day squally with passing showers. Carpenter at work on new boat, fitted beams, planking, etc. Usual parties at work picking oakum (for caulking) and ripping off planking, etc. At 3:45 Hawaiian steamer Kilauea was sighted bearing N. by W. At 4:30 Kilauea passed northern end of island and dipped her colors, sent 1st cutter to communicate, but falling dark. 1st cutter returned and was hauled up. Served out extra quantity of flour, coffee, sugar, pickles etc.

January 4 – Weather clear and pleasant, moderate breeze from Nd. & Ed. At daylight sent 1st cutter out to steamer Kilauea and commenced preparations for leaving the island. At 10 a.m. Kilauea anchored off the passage. At 1 p.m. Captain Long representing the Hawaiian government came ashore and informed Captain Sicard that he had come to rescue his crew and notified him of the loss of the gig with Lieutenant John G. Talbot and three of his crew while attempting to land at Kilahi Kai about 5 miles form Hanalei Bay, Island of Kauai, 31 days after leaving Ocean Island. Sent provisions (pay dept.) chronometer and log books (navigator's dept.) and men's baggage on-board.

January 5 – At daylight commenced sending off all stores with all boats, also commenced securing stores to be left on the island.

At 5 p.m. got underway for Midway Island.

January 14 – At 9 a.m. sighted the Island of Oahu. At 4:55 p.m. entered the harbor and made fast to wharf. Transferred the crew, baggage and stores to the USS. Nyack.

The 133-year old wreck of the American warship *USS Saginaw* was recently discovered at Kure Atoll by a research group of NOAA. Among the most interesting discoveries in exploring the wreck was the ship's sounding lead in perfect condition. The lead with line attached should have been swung over the side to determine the depth when approaching shallow waters. It appears as if there was little warning preceded the *Saginaw's* impact. The artifacts' debris trails graphically record the initial strike, the ship's bow subsequently being swung to seaward by the breakers, and the eventual breakup of the entire vessel. The sunken artifacts of the *Saginaw* remain property of the U.S. Government, and are protected by federal and state preservation laws. Locations of historic shipwreck sites within Reserve boundaries are protected as sensitive data.

IT'S GETTING CROWDED OUT THERE

There has been a waterfall of articles in the media about sixteen-year-old Marina del Rey sailor Abby Sunderland's unsuccessful attempt to be the youngest to sail single-handed around the world and her subsequent rescue in the southern Indian Ocean. But most people are unaware that there have been many sailing voyages around the world over the years. There were sixty-six known successful circumnavigations between 1898 and 2007, and several more are underway today. We man never know who the first circumnavigator was. It may have happened thousands of years ago by a civilization that is not known today.

Sixteen year-old Australian Jessica Watson presently holds the record that Abby Sunderland was attempting to break. Jessica set out in an attempt to become the youngest person to sail solo around the world, non-stop and unassisted - a young woman alone, facing all that the sea and weather could throw at her for seven lonely months and over 22,000 nautical miles. She departed from Sydney on October 18, 2009, headed eastbound across the Pacific Ocean, Atlantic Ocean, the Indian Ocean, and returned to Sydney on May 15, 2010, just three days before her 17th birthday.

The first known single-handed circumnavigation of the world by sail was made by New Englander Joshua Slocum. After a long and varied career, he decided to attempt a sailing fete that no known person had accomplished before. In 1890 at Fairhaven, Massachusetts, he rebuilt "Spray, a 36' 9" sloop-rigged fishing boat that was destined to become one of the most famous sailboats of all time. Slocum wrote, "I had resolved on a voyage around the world, and as the wind on the morning of April 24, 1895 was fair, I weighed anchor at noon, set sail, and filled away from Boston, where the "Spray" had been moored snugly all winter". On June 27, 1898, after more than three years and more than 46,000 miles, Slocum sighted Newport, Rhode Island, and became the first known mariner to have circumnavigated the world. Unfortunately, Slocum's return went almost unnoticed. The Spanish-American War had begun two months earlier and was dominating the headlines. Later, after the end of the major hostilities, many American newspapers published articles describing Slocum's amazing epic voyage.

There are many records that have been set and broken in recent years.

- The first nonstop solo unassisted circumnavigation was completed by Bernard Moitessier of France in 1969 on his 39-ft ketch "Joshua" sailing via the five great capes.
- The first nonstop solo unassisted circumnavigation by a woman was by Australian Kay Cottee on her Cavalier 37 Sloop *Blackmores First Lady* commencing November 29, 1987 and finishing June 5, 1988 at an average speed of 116.93 miles per day. Her route departed Sydney, Australia, via St Paul's Rocks in the North Atlantic, and south past the five southernmost capes. Her total sailing time was 189 days 0 hours 32 minutes, logging 22,100 miles. The voyage was completed without touching land, and without any form of outside aid apart from radio contact. In the course of her voyage she set seven world records.
- The oldest nonstop circumnavigator was Minoru Saito of Japan at age 71
- The oldest circumnavigator making stops was Harry Heckel of Jacksonville Florida at age 89 over the period 1995 to 2005.)
- The first woman circumnavigator making stops was Krystyna Chojnowska-Liskiewicz of the Canary Islands 1976 to 1978 in the 32 foot "Mazurek".
- During his triple circumnavigation (one voyage circling the earth three times), Jon Sanders set the following records:

- First single-handed to complete five circumnavigations (two having been completed by Sanders in Perie Banou in 1981-82)
- First single-handed to complete three non-stop circumnavigations consecutively.
- First single-handed to complete a total of four non-stop circumnavigations (the first in 1981-82)
- First single-handed to complete more than one non-stop circumnavigation.
- First single-handed to complete five Cape Horn rounding's (one east-west, four west-east).
- First single-handed to complete four Cape Horn rounding's during non-stop circumnavigations.
- First single-handed to round the five southernmost capes four times.
- First single-handed to complete a circumnavigation using the east-west route (i.e. Cape Horn plus two other capes - Leeuwin and Good Hope).
- First single-handed to complete four circumnavigations using the west-east route (i.e. Cape Horn plus four other capes - Good Hope, Leeuwin, South East, Tasmanian and Southwest, New Zealand).
- First small yacht (less than 15.5m) skipper to complete five circumnavigations, crewed or single-handed
- Longest distance ever sailed continuously by any vessel - 71,023 nautical miles.
- Longest period ever spent alone at sea (657 days 21 hours 18 minutes).
- Believed first yachtsman to complete five circumnavigations via Cape Horn (as crewed or single-handed).
- First yachtsman to circumnavigate non-stop via the Horn west about and east about.
- First yachtsman to complete three consecutive non-stop circumnavigations.

I have identified six serious circumnavigation voyages presently underway, but there could easily be more. There is no formal registration procedure, and many sailors just take to sea without fanfare. French sailor

Francis Joyon recently set a stunning world record, having made his solo voyage in 57 days, 13 hours, 34 minutes, 6 seconds in a trimaran. Abby Sunderland's sixteen year old brother Zac Sunderland departed June 14, 2008 from Marina del Rey and arrived home July 16, 2009 after a successful voyage and became the youngest person to circumnavigate the world alone by sail. Mike Perham of England completed his around the world voyage on August 27, 2009 at age seventeen. Marta Sziłajtis-Obiegło of Poland finished on April 20, 2009. Natasza Caban, also of Poland, finished her voyage December 2, 2009. Commodore Dilip Donde, a clearance diver with India's Navy, became the first from India to complete a solo circumnavigation expedition. A clearance diver uses explosives and other underwater techniques to remove obstructions to make harbors and shipping channels safe to navigate. Perhaps that made a mere solo trip around the world seem somewhat tame.

The longest I have sailed alone is four days. The problem with sailing alone is knowing that if you fall overboard, are injured, or become ill, there will be no rapid assistance, if any at all. Whenever on deck, I attached a tether from my life vest to the boat, and I was far more careful than I ever had been on a crewed vessel.

MANILA GALLEONS

Two decades after Juan Rodriguez Cabrillo first explored the coast of California, other Spanish ships began appearing off of the California coast. For two hundred and fifty years, from 1565 until 1815, Spanish galleons set sail each year from Manila in the Philippines bound for Acapulco on the west coast of Mexico laden with silks, porcelain, and spices and other riches of the Orient.

Following carefully guarded sailing instructions, the captains steered their ships on a long and lonely passage across the Pacific Ocean to about 30 degrees north latitude in order to pick up favorable winds (a line approximately 160 miles south of San Diego). Upon sighting the first indications of land, the ships were quickly turned south in order to avoid the uncharted hazards of California's rugged coast. If all went well, the first land actually sighted by the sailors would be near the lower tip of the Baja Peninsula. Their course then was across the bay of Baja California and southward to Acapulco. From that port city, much of the cargo was sent overland on pack animals across Mexico to be loaded onto ships at Vera Cruz. Then, on to Cuba, where the richly laden ships would become part of the legendary treasure fleet that sailed each year bound for Spain.

But, the voyages seldom went well. Galleons often had to sail far north of 30 degree latitude in search of favorable winds. (a line about 160 miles south of today's San Diego) Very poor living conditions literally plagued the vessels and crew. Upon completing the crossing, food, water, and other essentials were either spoiled or expended. Many sailors had become sick from scurvy and other diseases during the crossings. Leaking and worn out from the long but still unfinished voyage, the ships were frequently in danger of sinking. The galleon captains sought ports of refuge along the California coast where they could restock vital supplies, make repairs, and revitalize their crew after the long trans-Pacific journey.

In 1594, the treasure laden galleon *San Augustin* sailed from Manila on a course to Acapulco. But she also had a secondary mission to scout for good ports of refuge along the California coast. The *San Augustin* made her first landfall near Trinidad Head, just south of the California-Oregon border. The ship then worked her way down the coast to Drakes Bay, just north of San Francisco. As she lay at anchor in the bay, a major storm developed and suddenly her anchor failed. The *San Augustin* washed ashore and became the first known shipwreck in California. Her surviving crew was able to salvage one of the galleon's launches, and soon began a long and arduous voyage back to civilization. Today, National Park Service archeologists continue their search for the remains of *San Augustin*.

Spanish mariners and explorers continued their exploration of western North America. Eight years after the loss of *San Augustin*, Sebastian Vizcaino sailed from Acapulco to explore upper California with three ships: *San Diego*, *Santo Tomas*, and *Tres Reyes*. The three ship flotilla traveled far to the north and then, one at a time, each turned back to Mexico. The *Santo Tomas* was first. After exploring as far north as Monterey, California, the ship returned to Spain carrying sailors who were too sick to continue the journey. *San Diego*, commanded by Vizcaino reached 43 degrees north latitude before turning back because of sickness among the crew. *Tres Reyes* returned last. During the voyage up the coast to 43 degrees north latitude (a line about as far north as Milwaukee, Wisconsin), her skipper and pilot died. With her leaders gone, the ship reversed course and headed south for home.

The Vizcaino expedition marked the end of official Spanish explorations of the California coast for almost two centuries. Often talked about expeditions to fortify and settle California did not happen. Yet, vessels continued to visit the coast. Spanish galleons continued to sail down the coast on their annual voyages. Some never made it to the safe harbor at Acapulco. In 1600, the galleon *Capitana* disappeared without a trace. *Nuestro de Senora Aguda* reportedly ran aground on a rock west of Catalina in 1641. Another galleon, *Francisco Xavier*, may have wrecked just south of the Columbia river in Oregon in 1707.

Other dangers lurked for the galleons off the California coast. The riches of the Pacific attracted raiders intent plundering the Spanish ships. English sea captain, Sir Francis Drake, explored the California coast in 1579 after attacking Spanish settlements in South America. He landed somewhere in California to repair his ship, the *Golden Hind*. The exact location of this landfall is not known. Most historians believe it was near San Francisco. Yet, some believe the ship stopped along the Santa Barbara Channel coast for repairs. Other English sea captains hunted the galleons. Thomas Cavendish looted and burned the Manila galleon *Santa Ana* off the tip of the Baja peninsula in 1587. George Compton pursued the galleon *San Sebastian* in 1754. The galleon's crew purposely ran the ship aground on Catalina Island to escape the raider. Compton captured and killed the surviving crew. Spain finally colonized California because of incidents like these and threats to her claims over the territory. Soldiers established a series of forts or presidios along the coast. With the presidios came the California missions. Soon, the Spanish required all ships sailing along the California coast, including the Manila galleons, to stop and be inspected.

Historian Hubert Bancroft wrote "that an old sailor of Santa Barbara told (me) that in 1872 he opened a grave on Santa Cruz Island, which had a wooden headboard on which could be deciphered the date of about 1660." Was this the final resting place of an unfortunate who died on a ship while passing the islands or is it the grave of a castaway from a long forgotten shipwreck? We will probably never know.

LESSONS FROM DEEPWATER HORIZON

My cousin, Curtis Ebbesmeyer, is an oceanographer in Seattle. The following is derived from his recent and timely article in the Wall Street Journal.

In the early 1990s, thousands of desperate Cuban balseros cast themselves adrift on rafts, tires

and any other makeshift craft that could float. They shoved off even from the island's far shore, adjusting their lives to the powerful Loop Current that pushes north from the Yucatan, rounds Cuba, rushes through the Florida Straits, and spills into the Atlantic, seeding the Gulf Stream. Many drowned or perished from thirst, but others survived to wash up on Florida's east coast.

Now, the Loop Current is in the news once again. Oil from the Deepwater Horizon gusher (please don't call it a "spill") has begun trickling into the current, prompting anxious speculation as to how much will be swept up and where it will be borne. Only a small quantity of surface oil has been seen entering the current, but much more oil swirls below. Given the complex nature of both petroleum and these marine waters, the underwater plumes will be extremely difficult to measure and track.

Oil is far from a homogenous substance, even before it becomes emulsified by waves, currents and the sun. It's a complex mixture of liquids, gases and waxy solids that vary widely in weight and solubility. Ocean waters are likewise not uniform; they are made up of distinct horizontal slabs, differentiated by temperature and salinity and propelled by wind and currents. Recent use of improved monitoring equipment indicates that in years to come some of the oil will wash up on European shores, some will reach the Arctic Ocean, and some will join other global conveyor belts of currents. Whales, dolphins and other animals will dive through the petro-infused slabs, suffering possible toxic exposures. The unprecedented deepwater injection of chemical dispersants to break up the petroleum before it reaches the surface may only worsen its impact. They may cause more oil to remain suspended longer in the submerged stratified slabs with no way to remove it.

The Atlantic Ocean is not the only route the oil will take. Each year, the Loop Current becomes "pregnant," bulging out toward Louisiana and Deepwater Horizon. At times, the current loops back tightly enough to squeeze this bulge like a tied-off balloon, releasing a constellation of spinning eddies. The unlucky Cuban balseros, who launched into the Loop Current in summer 1994, wound up swirling helplessly in these eddies and never neared Florida.

According to mapping by Mitchell Roffer's highly regarded ocean forecasting service, some of the current eddies have already veered west, and tentacles of oil have extended west past the Loop Current. One eddy already appears to have broken off and has begun crawling toward Texas. It may carry escaping oil deep underwater for several months, relieving the Florida, Alabama and Mississippi coasts and the upper water column where most marine life lies. But by August, it will have moved too far from the wellhead to continue capturing the oil, and more crude may leach out from Louisiana's spongy coastal wetlands, where it's now being absorbed. We will be seeing Deepwater Horizon's effects for many years to come.

Westward-bound oil from Deepwater Horizon will weather, clumping into tar balls. Most will wash up along "the graveyard of the Gulf," Texas's Great Bend coast, just as debris from Hurricane Katrina did. Ten years later, the Ixtoc One blowout that occurred further south in the Gulf of Mexico was a closer precedent for Deepwater Horizon. It lasted ten months and spewed more oil than any previous accident. Because it involved a Mexican company and happened outside U.S. waters, it did not register as forcefully in this country. But in 1989, the smaller but far more visible Exxon Valdez spill in Alaska delivered a wake-up call that still registers today. It demonstrated how vulnerable single-hulled tankers are, and it continues to show that spilled oil can persist in ecosystems for more than two decades.

Every 20 years or so, another oceanic oil spill or blowout reshapes our attitudes toward petroleum and to the environment as a whole. In 1969, twenty years after the advent of offshore drilling, the Union Oil spill off Santa Barbara forced us to confront the inherent risks and the cost of our hunger for fossil fuels. The source was the January 28, 1969, blow-out on Union Oil's Platform A, six miles offshore. Over a ten-day period, an estimated 80,000 to 100,000 barrels of crude oil spilled into the channel and onto the beaches of Santa Barbara County, fouling the coastline from Goleta to the Rincon and all four of the northern Channel Islands. Upwards of 10,000 birds were killed in the ecological disaster. The Santa Barbara spill prompted the great wave of environmental regulation of the early 1970s. It may also have motivated the oil companies to build for much higher waves and stronger currents. The oil spill prompted a Congressional moratorium in 1981 on new offshore oil leasing, with exceptions in the Gulf of Mexico and parts of offshore Alaska that remained in effect until 2008 when Congress did not renew it.

We will also learn much more from Deepwater Horizon, but at a substantial price.

Mr. Ebbesmeyer is co-author, with Eric Scigliano, of "Flotsametrics and the Floating World" (Smithsonian Books, 2009). He worked for three decades as a consulting oceanographer for environmental agencies and oil companies in Alaska, on Puget Sound, the Gulf of Mexico, the North Sea and the South China Sea. Ebbesmeyer founded the nonprofit Beachcombers' and Oceanographers' International Association in 1996 for which he writes and publishes the magazine *Beachcombers' Alert*. His website is www.beachcombersalert.com.

TALES FROM BOTTLES

One of the oldest and perhaps most reliable means of communication through history has been messages inserted into bottles and then dropped into the sea. The first known messages in waterproof containers were released around 310 BC by the Ancient Greek philosopher Theophrastus as part of an experiment to show that the Mediterranean Sea was formed by the inflowing Atlantic Ocean.

On his return to Spain following his first voyage to the New World, Christopher Columbus's ship encountered a severe storm. Columbus placed a report of his discovery in a sealed cask along with a note asking that it to be passed on to the Queen of Spain. He hoped the news would make it back even if he did not survive. Columbus survived, but the sealed report was never reported as being found.

In the 16th century, English navy ships at sea used bottled messages to send information ashore about enemy positions. Queen Elizabeth I created the official position of "Uncorker of Ocean Bottles," and anyone else opening the bottles could face the death penalty.

In 1784, Japanese seaman Chunosuke Matsuyama along with forty-three companions set out in search of a treasure thought to be buried on a Pacific island. A fierce storm blew their battered craft onto a coral reef. When the storm passed, Matsuyama and his friends realized that except for a few coconuts from uprooted palm trees there was nothing to eat. They survived for some time on small crabs, but there was no fresh water to drink. Matsuyama watched his friends slowly die one by one and realized that none of them, including himself, would ever see their families or homes again. Locating a bottle from the wreckage of his ship and using thin pieces of wood from a fallen coconut tree, he carefully carved a message, sealed it in the bottle, and then threw it into the sea. A century and a half later, the bottle washed ashore and was found by a Japanese seaweed collector. The bottle had come ashore at the village of Hiraturemura, the birthplace of Chunosuke Matsuyama.

One hundred years later, the crew of the Canadian bark "Lennie" mutinied and murdered its officers. The ship's steward was spared because he knew how to navigate. While actually steering the ship to the French coast, he told the mutineers he was heading for Spain. Secretly, he dropped several bottles over the side with messages that revealed the whole story. French authorities found one of the bottles, located and boarded the ship, and arrested the stunned mutineers.

During World War I, British soldier Thomas Hughes tossed a green ginger beer bottle into the English Channel containing a letter to his wife. He was killed two days later while fighting in France. The bottle was recovered from the River Thames eighty-five years later. Although the intended recipient had died in 1979, the letter was finally delivered two years later to Private Hughes eighty-six year old daughter who was then living in New Zealand.

In February 1916, the doomed crew of Zeppelin Airship L-19 dropped their last messages to superiors and loved ones into the North Sea. Six months later, the message container washed up on the Kattegat coast near Gothenburg, Sweden.

Paolina and Ake Viking were married in Sicily in the autumn of 1958, thanks to a far-traveling bottle. Two years earlier Ake, a bored young Swedish sailor on a ship far out at sea, had dropped a bottle overboard with a message asking any pretty girl who found it to write. Paolina's father, a Sicilian fisherman, picked it up and passed it to his daughter as a joke. Continuing the joke, Paolina sent off a note to the young sailor. Their correspondence quickly grew warmer. Ake visited Sicily, and their marriage soon followed that first meeting.

Eighty-eight shipwrecked migrants were rescued off the coast of Costa Rica in May 2005 after their SOS message in a bottle was recovered.

The oldest known message in a bottle spent 92 years 229 days at sea. It was released at 60° 50'N / 00° 38'W on April 25, 1914. It was recovered by fisherman Mark Anderson of Bixter, Shetland, UK, at 60° 50'N / 00° 37'W on December 10, 2006.

It is frequently impossible to predict the direction a bottle will take. Of two bottles dropped together off the Brazilian coast, one drifted east for 130 days and was found on a beach in Africa; the other bottle floated northwest for 190 days, finally reaching Nicaragua. Speed is also bound to vary according to wind and current. A bottle might be completely becalmed or, if caught up by the Gulf Stream at its swiftest, may travel as many as 100 miles a day.

The longest bottle voyage of all is thought to have been made by a bottle known as the Flying Dutchman. It was launched by a German scientific expedition in 1929 in the southern Indian Ocean. Inside was a message which could be read without breaking the bottle that asked the finder to report where he found it and then to throw it back into the sea. The bottle apparently caught an east going current which carried it to the southern tip of South America. There it was found, reported, and thrown back again several times. Eventually, the well-traveled bottle moved out into the Atlantic, then again into the Indian Ocean, passing roughly the spot where it had been originally dropped. Finally, in 1935, it was cast ashore on the west coast of Australia. The bottle had covered 16,000 miles in 2,447 days (a little over 6 1/2 years) at an average speed of more than six nautical miles a day.

Fragile as it is, a well-sealed bottle is one of the world's most seaworthy objects. It will b bob safely through hurricanes capable of sinking great ships. For most practical purposes, glass lasts forever. In 1954, eighteen bottles were salvaged from a ship that sank 250 years before off the coast of England. The liquor in them was unrecognizable, but the bottles were as good as new.

I have researched many of the countless reports of messages in bottles found after they had traveled thousands of miles from their origin. The number of bottles at sea at any given time is enormous.

From an ecological perspective, Americans use 2,500,000 plastic bottles every hour and throw away over 25,000,000,000 Styrofoam coffee cups every year. A modern glass bottle will take over 4000 years to decompose.

ILLUSTRIOUS QUEEN

One of Santa Barbara's oldest and most illustrious institutions is the Santa Barbara Yacht Club. Historically, it has been far more than a place for boat owners to congregate.

One of the most significant and visible contributions of the Yacht Club can be observed any day of the week – the harbor's breakwater. Santa Barbara is endowed with towering mountains, a mild Mediterranean climate, panoramic views of the Pacific, terrain that discourages urban sprawl... but not a natural harbor. In 1836, Richard Henry Dana noted in Two Years Before The Mast, "This wind (the south-easter) is the bane of the coast of California. Between the months of November and April (including a part of each) which is the rainy season in this latitude, you are never safe from it, and accordingly, in the ports which are open to it, vessels are obliged, during these months, to lie at anchor at a distance of three miles from shore, with slip ropes on their cables ready to slip and go to sea at a moment's warning. The only ports which are safe from this wind are San Francisco and Monterey in the north and San Diego in the south."

Beginning in 1868, the City began petitioning the US Government for funds to build a breakwater at Santa Barbara. But the military and others argued that a more advantageous location would be forty-five miles north at Point Sal. Joseph Stearns finished building his wharf in front of the town, but the debate regarding the location of a harbor wore on and on through the years. When a severe storm in 1878 resulted in the loss of the Chapala Street Pier along with 1400 feet of Stearns Wharf, the need for a breakwater became more urgent.

Meanwhile, local yachting was becoming more prevalent by both local boat owners as well as wealthy yachtsmen who came to Santa Barbara each winter from their east coast estates. This increased activity in yachting ultimately resulted in the formation of the Santa Barbara Yacht Club in 1872. But through the ensuing years, bureaucracy, World War I, finance, and other issues continued to postpone the construction of a harbor at Santa Barbara. The Yacht Club continued its persistent campaign for the construction of a harbor breakwater. Santa Barbara Yacht Club member Major Max C. Fleischmann wrote of a check for $200,000, a substantial sum at that time, toward construction of a breakwater with a condition that the City of Santa Barbara match his donation with a similar amount.

The Yacht Club made many other contributions to the community to through the years, including attracting visitors to Santa Barbara by conducting a variety of regattas and sailing events, support and fundraising for local charities, acting as marine ambassador for visiting navalships and military personnel, implementing and promoting positive programs for youth, and providing material enhancement to the City's waterfront.

All of these contributions to the community continue to this day. Santa Barbara Yacht Club has clearly played a major role in Santa Barbara's heritage. Now, one hundred and thirty two years after its official formation, the Yacht Club has compiled and published a comprehensive narrative that describes its long and fascinating history. Initially designed for its members, the Yacht Club has decided make it available to all Santa Barbarans. The over 300 page volume includes many rare and fascinating photographs, and is of "coffee table" quality. It will become a collectors item worthy of being handed down to future generations. Interested parties may purchase the book at Santa Barbara Yacht Club at the harbor by major credit card for $90.00 plus sales tax.

How happy is a clam?

Near that stage in their lives, only the most masochistic of molluscs could be expected to experience anything but a sense of imminent dread. Even the most comfortable of clams, however, can hardly be called the life and soul of the party. All they can expect is a watery existence, likely at any moment to be rudely interrupted by a man with a spade, followed by conveyance to a very hot place.

The saying that one is as happy as a clam is very definitely American and hardly known elsewhere. The fact is, we've lost its second half, which makes everything more clear. The full expression is "happy as a clam at high tide or happy as a clam at high water". Clam digging has to be done at low tide when there is a chance of finding them and extracting them. At high tide, clams are comfortably covered in water and able to feed, comparatively at ease and free of the risk that some hunter will rip them untimely from their sandy berths. That seems a good enough definition of "happy".

The adage in its shortened form was first recorded in the 1830s, although it is almost certainly a lot older. By 1848, the Southern Literary Messenger of Richmond, Virginia reported that the expression in its short form "is familiar to everyone".

Clamming is another relatively rare opportunity on California beaches. Pismo State Beach has historically been known as the "Clam Capital of the World." Clamming is best at minus tides (tide schedules are available at www.ClassicCalifornia.com). A California fishing license is required; limit is 10, each at least 4.5" in diameter. Unfortunately, the resident otters appreciate the shellfish also, so legal clams are now rare. But the decrease in clams has not decreased their popularity. Now held annually in November (Veteran's weekend), under warm Indian summer skies, the three-day Pismo Clam Festival includes live entertainment, a parade, a marching band review, a clam chowder cook-off, wine tasting, clam digging for the kids, and a celebration to honor the nation's veterans.

SANTA BARBARA'S MARITIME TREASURE

Ten years ago, a handful of volunteers decided that Santa Barbara deserved a maritime museum. The story of this area's unique and extensive maritime history needed to be preserved and presented for generations to come. Our area's story began thousands of years ago when coastal Chumash plied their Tomol canoes between the central coast and channel islands. Since then, it has been claimed by Spanish explorer Juan Rodriguez Cabrillo in 1542, written about by Richard Henry Dana in Two Years Before The Mast, and the site of many other historic events.

The founding volunteers were concerned that historic information and valuable artifacts may be lost, and it was therefore urgent that they be preserved and protected for future generations. Our vision was to locate a facility at Santa Barbara Harbor that could accommodate a small museum, but then . . . enter fate. The City of Santa Barbara had just reacquired the large Naval Reserve Building from the US Navy. The building had originally been built with funds provided by both the City and the Federal Government. Upon the outbreak of World War ll, the City sold its share of the building to the Navy for one dollar. During the war, the Navy used the building for port security and as a training facility.

At war's end, the City's problem became, what to do with the building? Our small group met with City personnel to see if some space could be allocated for a small museum. I recall that the City's initial plan had been to install a number of shops in the building's large drill hall area. But as our dream and community support for a maritime museum continued to grow, the final result was that the entire drill hall and its surrounding mezzanine would become the home of the Santa Barbara Maritime Museum.

Dozens of committed volunteers then began planning for the new museum. Maritime history had to be collected and compiled, artifacts located, the floor plan designed, construction drawings prepared, money raised, and much more. As word spread throughout the community, growing support allowed the dream to expand. The original plan of occupying one-half of the drill hall was expanded to encompass the entire hall as well as some surrounding office areas. The final design of the building included a extensive maritime museum, a museum store, ample restaurants upstairs and down (Endless Summer Bar-Cafe and the Waterfront Grill), and a community meeting room.

The result was a facility worthy of our community and its long and varied history. At the museum's entry, the walls are covered with Honduran paneling salvaged from the passenger steamer Hermosa which stopped at Santa Barbara in 1880 on its way to begin carrying passengers between San Pedro and Catalina Island. Rare historic photographs line a hallway on the entry's left.

Stepping through the museum's entry, you are first met by JIM, a large diving suit constructed of tough magnesium that allowed oil industry divers to work undersea at depths down to 2000 feet.

Moving into the main exhibition hall, visitors encounter a historic path that traces Santa Barbara's maritime history from the early Chumash to the present day. First in line is a Chumash Tomol canoe that was recently constructed by members of the local Chumash community. Further on are displays about early explorers, seal hunters, shore whaling, the supply ships that plied our early coast, Richard Henry Dana, and Santa Barbara's overall waterfront history.

Just past the Historic Path is a children's area that is both entertaining and educational. The adjacent area presents historical information about Santa Barbara's diving industry and includes historic diving helmets and equipment.

The museum incorporates many interactive exhibits that permit visitors to operate and observe various features. For example, a replica of a ship's pilot house includes contemporary navigational equipment and bridge controls. The visitor "steers" the ship and operates various controls while viewing the results on a large screen.

A prime exhibit displays two of the five cannons that were discovered at a shipwreck site off the coast of Goleta. Pushing a button results in the sound of the cannon firing. The cannons are on loan from the Goleta Historical Society.

The very popular and entertaining sports fishing exhibit includes a fighting chair, a fishing rod reel and line, and a projection screen. The museum visitor first selects which type of game fish he wishes to try to catch. Then, the screen shows the fighting fish and the fishing line begins tugging in coordination with the actions of the fish. If the visitor is successful, the screen will display accolades; if not, the fish breaks loose and swims away.

Additional museum exhibits include marine navigation and charting, Santa Barbara's yacht club, the tragic multiple shipwreck disaster at Point Honda, the sinking of the ship Cuba, and descriptions of the island ranches. Other displays include such subjects as model ships, the ocean environment, ocean trash, maritime safety, and weather. The huge power of the off-shore oceans is dramatically displayed in the storm at sea exhibit.

The list of intriguing exhibits continues. A twenty-eight foot rowing shell that won its division at the 1984 Olympics at Lake Casitas is on display. A large model of the Lockheed F-1 Flying Boat is suspended from the ceiling, and a museum visitor may operate controls that power-up the propellers. An exceptional experience is to operate the authentic submarine periscope that extends from the mezzanine through the roof of the museum. But, instead of sighting enemy warships, the actual view is of various areas of surrounding Santa Barbara.

Of course, a Santa Barbara maritime museum would not be compete without including surfing. The exhibit begins with surfing's origins in the 1800's and progresses through the key role of Santa Barbara's famous surfers including the Currens and George Greenough. The innovative camera that George designed to allow him to be the first to photograph from inside the tube of a wave is on display, along with the knee board he designed that revolutionized the sport of surfing. In my late teens, I skippered the Greenough's 59-foot sailing yawl "Sabrina" and sailed George and his brother Bill to various off-shore islands for surfing and fishing.

Santa Barbara's commercial fishing industry is well depicted in the museum, as is its renowned yachting history. Included in the yachting display is an eight-foot Sea Shell sailboat. First introduced to Santa Barbara in 1948 when my father purchased a Sea Shell assembly kit for my brother and me, the Sea Shell fleet rapidly grew and continues to prosper today. On Sundays during Santa Barbara's sailing season, you can see dozens of Sea Shells competing off of East Beach.

There are many other exhibits and programs at the museum, including lectures and productions in the unique Munger Theater. The exterior of the theater is configured as a historic sailing ship that dramatically projects outward from the second floor mezzanine.

This year is the tenth anniversary of the Santa Barbara Maritime Museum. Come down to see this Santa Barbara treasure between 10 AM to 6 PM during the summer months (closed Wednesdays). Or better yet, become involved as a volunteer of one of the many committees or activities of the museum. Donations of items of local maritime history for display not only benefits the visiting public, but also preserves them for future generations. Of course, as with all non-profit institutions donations are welcome and valued. The museum's web site is www. sbmm.org.

Happy Birthday, Santa Barbara Maritime Museum!

Guarding The Graveyard

Lying forty-five miles up the coast from Santa Barbara, Point Conception has been justly branded "a graveyard of the Pacific." In October 1542, as explorer Juan Rodríguez Cabrillo attempted to round the treacherous point, he encountered heavy winds and high seas that forced him to turn back to San Miguel Island where he later died from complications of a broken leg incurred from a fall. Cabrillo's second-in-command Bartolomé Ferrelo took charge and again attempted to round the point, but he too was unsuccessful. Such fierce conditions continue today, and modern craft frequently must anchor in the lee of the point to await better circumstances - sometimes for days. Several times, I have spent a miserable night off the point as our radar confirmed that the high winds and rough seas were preventing us from making any forward progress at all. Then, back to anchor in the lee of the point to wait and try again the next night.

Most of the California coast runs in a general north-south direction, but along the Santa Barbara channel, it changes to more of an east-west direction. At the western end of the channel, the coast makes an abrupt 90-degree turn northward. This treacherous transition point, where mariners following the coast have to make a severe course correction, was the site selected to build the Point Conception Lighthouse.

The following description by a Coast Guardsman who had been sent to Point Conception to do repairs provides a vivid description of the ominous and dangerous area. "The eerie sound of the fog horn and crashing waves against the cliff and the often foggy days gave the place a ghostly feeling. Of course no lighthouse worth its salt would be without a ghost story or two, and Point Conception had its stories too. I chose to heed the stories, given the overall feeling that the area gave out. On one occasion we had to replace the chimes on the light. On this given day, everyone was in a happy mood and the jokes were flying. Soon the crew started to joke about the Ghost at Conception. This, I guess, didn't sit well, because our tools started to go missing. We would put a wrench down then go to pick it up again only to not be able to find it. After searching high and low, it would later turn up at the bottom of the stairs. This happened several times during the day, making a half-day replacement job last all day. Needless to say, the jokes stopped. After that, whenever I would enter the lighthouse, I would knock on the door first and announce that we were there to service the light."

The first lighthouse on the point, a one-story Cape Cod style dwelling with a tower rising from its center, was built high on the sandstone cliffs of the point in 1856. The lens and steel tower had been fabricated in France and then transported around Cape Horn for installation at Point Conception. Supplies to construct the lighthouse were sea freighted down the coast from San Francisco and then off-loaded through the surf at Cojo Landing, just west of the point. The construction materials were then hauled by wagon through deep sand that at times reached the hubs of the wheels. Originally designed to house the old-fashioned Argand lamp and reflector system, the tower portion of the lighthouse was later torn down and reconstructed to accommodate the Lighthouse Board's decision to use a larger first-order Fresnel lens in the lantern room.

George Parkinson, picked to be the first keeper of the lighthouse, arrived on scene in 1855 and spent several months at the lighthouse without any duties or pay. Work on the new tower began in August, the lens showed up in September, and Parkinson was finally able to activate the light on February 1, 1856. Point Conception Lighthouse had become the sixth lighthouse in operation on the West Coast of the United States.

Parkinson, who ended up serving at the active light for only six months before being dismissed, wrote a letter of complaint to the Lighthouse Service that included the following passage. "Point Conception lies some sixty-five miles by land from the little village of Santa Barbara, the nearest point at which supplies can be obtained, the road to which place is only passable at very low water... the freight on goods amounts to more than my pay, and price rates at Santa Barbara are one-hundred percent over San Francisco rates. How to convey wood and water here I know not, the former being five or six miles off, the latter about 600 yards. That my situation here is truly distressing admits not of any doubt, cut off as I am from all communications and without means to live on. My pay has not been forthcoming in over four months."

Over the years, numerous changes were made to the station. In 1872, a first class, steam fog signal to replace an earlier fog bell was installed on a large flat area, 100 feet down the bluff from the lighthouse. In 1875, the Lighthouse Board reported, "The old dwelling at the station is in bad condition, and the best plan is to pull it down, leaving the tower by itself, and to build for the accommodation of the keepers two more cottages similar to the one built last year." In 1880, after no appropriation had been made to fulfill its 1875 request, the Lighthouse Board reported to Congress that because the aging original tower now required wooden supports to hold it up, it should be scrapped in favor of a new light to be constructed lower on the bluff where fog would be less likely to obscure the light. The $38,000 request was approved, and a new lighthouse was constructed in 1881. A large first-order lens was installed in the new tower and operated for the first time on June 20, 1882.

With its tower removed, the original lighthouse continued to serve as a lighthouse keeper dwelling for several more years. In 1906, a large duplex with six rooms and a bath for each of the occupying keepers was built, and in 1912, another dwelling was constructed to replace the original lighthouse, which had been removed. In 1967, an automated system was installed by the United States Coast Guard, and a lighthouse keeper and family were no longer required.

The 1882 first-order Fresnel lens was still in use in the tower in 1999. Originally, a 150-pound weight had to be cranked up every four hours to provide the energy to rotate the lens. When electricity reached the station, the system of gears and pulleys was replaced by an electric motor. With sixteen bull's-eye panels and making a revolution every eight minutes, the lens produced a two-second flash every thirty seconds. Sadly to traditionalists, and due to the expense of repairs necessary to keep the Fresnel lens revolving, a modern beacon is now in use.

The railroad was eventually extended to the area, and a depot and telegraph office were established about a mile from the lighthouse. In recent years Vandenberg Air Force Base restricts access from the northwest, and a private ranch restricts access from the adjoining land. It is sometimes possible to make arrangements for access well in advance by contacting the Coast Guard. But good news! Discussions are underway between the US Coast Guard and the Santa Barbara Maritime Museum that may see the giant lighthouse lens on display at the musuem within a few months.

Beware Of The Cosh

The cosh was an honored part of shipboard lore. Coshes were carried on sailing ships by the boatswain and his mates. Ashore, the cosh was a weapon of choice of press-gangs to "recruit" crew, and it was usually but not always a defensive weapon of sailors. Resembling the on-shore blackjack, coshes were the preferred method of defense to the knife, but they were no less deadly in skilled hands. But coshes were also useful in quieting a boisterous shipmate or maintaining order without unnecessarily causing death.

I am fortunate to have acquired a rare cosh several years ago. It is one of the favorite items in my collection, along with a pair of leg irons that compliment the task of handling an unruly sailor. It is a very rare and unusual cosh, with two lead-filled knobs needle-stitched at each end and then the entire weapon tarred. The shaft was made flexible using thin strips of whale baleen to make the force against a resting crewman's head even more powerful. The weapon is very nicely made, probably ashore by a craftsman rather than by a sailor aboard ship. It may have been carried by a Boatswain, Master-At-Arms, or Ship's Mate. Being very decorative, it would have been quite costly at the time, as opposed to cruder rope-made coshes, of which few have survived over time.

Coshes are on display at several maritime museums around the world, but they are relatively rare. One crudely constructed but less costly cosh consists of a wood shaft with two lead filled balls mounted at each end and then the whole needle-stitched in flax and varnished. Another is a Malacca (rattan) shafted cosh with the remains of the original leather wrist-loop still attached in a clove-hitch. It has tarred needle-hitched knobs and is varnished overall. It had rolled around on-board a sailing ship quite a lot, which caused lighter colored bands on the knobs at each end.

The English Royal Navy referred to coshes as "life preservers." One cosh that I observed was a particularly beautiful example for a deadly weapon. The entire surface was composed of six-strand coach-whipping in two colors which produced a unique "checkerboard" pattern. Unusual brass buttons were mounted at each end. Lead weighted, with one end slightly larger than the other, it would have been a most formidable weapon. The larger end had some flattened spots and a bit of damage to the coachwhipping, possibly due to contact with an errant crewmember's head. The cosh was fourteen inches long and estimated to have been constructed between 1840 and 1860. In trained hands, it would have been a quite deadly and serviceable weapon.

My cosh is now on display at the Santa Barbara Maritime Museum. Due to the aging and stiffening of the needle stitching, it is no longer possible to demonstrate how the cosh whips and accelerate its lead end for efficient contact with a victim's head.

Another time, I will describe and display my grim leg irons. But there are also some very pleasant items in my collection.

Native American Fisheries

Ethnological and anthropological evidence indicates that an abalone fishery flourished for many years among the Native Americans of the coastal regions and the Channel Islands. Whenever abalones were in sufficient quantities, they were the main shellfish item in the Indian's diet and among the Channel Island dwellers they were the principal food. This is attested to by the enormous quantities of abalone shells in the middens and shell mounds found along the coast from Monterey Bay south and among the Channel Islands.

Recently, radiocarbon dating techniques have been used to obtain fairly precise ages for these ancient fisheries. Red abalone shells from several sites on Santa Rosa Island were 5,370 to 7,400 years old. All shells were from middens with the exception of a sample which the Native Americans had placed in a cemetery containing over 100 skeletons. These skeletons had been buried in sitting positions with knees drawn up under their chins. Each skull had been painted a brilliant red which gradually faded on exposure to the air. Three of the skeletons were from strong people over 7 feet tall.

The Santa Rosa Island archaeological sites appear to be the oldest which have been radiocarbon dated on the Pacific coast, but one researcher stated, "We feel confident that there are many middens much older than these on both the Channel Islands and the Mainland, which are as yet undated."

Why is the Ocean Salty?

If you explore folk stories and mythology you will find that almost every culture has a story explaining how the oceans of the world became salty. The answer is really very simple. Salt in the ocean comes from rocks on land. Here's how it works -

Falling rain captures dissolved carbon dioxide from the surrounding air. This causes the rainwater to be slightly acidic due to carbonic acid which forms from the carbon dioxide and water. The rain erodes and the carbonic acid breaks down the rocks and the runoff carries it along in a dissolved state as ions. The ions in the runoff are carried to the streams and rivers and on to the ocean. Many of the dissolved ions are used by organisms in the ocean which removes them from the water. Others are not used up and are left for long periods of time where their concentrations increase over time.

The two ions that are present most often in seawater are chloride and sodium. These two make up over 90% of all dissolved ions in seawater. The concentration of salt in seawater (salinity) is about 35 parts per thousand. In other words, about 35 of 1,000 (3.5%) of the weight of seawater comes from the dissolved salts. In a cubic mile of seawater the weight of the salt (sodium chloride) would be about 120 million tons. And, just so you don't think seawater is worthless, a cubic mile of it also can contain up to 25 tons of gold and up to 45 tons of silver! But before you go out and try alchemy on seawater to become rich, just think about how big a cubic mile is.

By some estimates, if all the salt in the ocean could be removed and spread evenly over the Earth's entire land surface, it would form a layer more than 500 feet thick, about the height of a 40-story office building.

"Please pass the salt."

The British Royal Navy

England was once the greatest military power in the western world, and its foundation was the Royal Navy. The history of the Royal Navy can be traced to before the ninth century AD; however, it was formally created as the national naval force of England in 1660 following the restoration of King Charles II to the throne. It became the naval force of the United Kingdom of Great Britain after the unification of England and Scotland in 1707 when the English Navy merged with the much smaller Royal Scots Navy. England's navy had no defined moment of formation. It started out as a motley assortment of "King's ships" during the Middle Ages, assembling only when needed and then dispersing. It began taking shape as a standing navy during the 16th century, and finally became a regular establishment during the wars of the 17th century. The navy grew considerably during the global struggle with France which began in the late 1600's and culminated in the Napoleonic Wars, a time when the practice of fighting under sail was developed to its highest point.

Around the year 450 in Anglo-Saxon times, there was a "ship fyrd" (ship fund) for raising money and men for warships. Sandwich in the south of England was the main naval base, and was a strategic location where Vikings passing through the Straits of Dover could be spotted and the fleet alerted to intercept them before they could attack the Wessex coast. The first written record of an English victory was in the Anglo Saxon Chronicle in 871 by Athelstan, Alfred the Great's eldest brother. Alfred the Great has traditionally been recognized as the "founder of the navy".

Recent research reveals that in the year 825 seven Viking ships were fought by the English; in 882 two ships were fought; in 884 sixteen ships were fought; and in 895 a fleet of Danish ships were destroyed. Despite these English victories, Danish Viking raids continued to plunder the south coast of England. In 897, England's King Alfred the Great had a number ships built, each with over 60 oars. The new fleet went on to win a significant victory in the Battle of Poole Harbor, a large natural bay located in the south of England. King Alfred's ships also intercepted a number of Danish ships that had been ravaging Devon and the Isle of Wight. One of the fleeing Danish vessels was wrecked in Sussex, and its crew was hanged at Winchester.

The ensuing century of general peace saw considerable technological development, with sail yielding to steam, cannon supplanted by large shell-firing guns, and ended with a race to construct bigger and better battleships. But that race was ultimately a dead end, as aircraft carriers and submarines came to the fore. After its successes in World War II, the British Royal Navy yielded its preeminent place to the expanding United States Navy. The Royal Navy still remains one of the world's most capable navies and currently operates a large fleet of modern ships.

During the centuries of sail, naval life at sea was demanding and dangerous. Sailors generally went to sea as boys, and by the time they were 16 they could achieve the rating of seamen. They normally served at sea for another ten years before finally settling down and taking a shore or local sailing job. The idea of being single, free of responsibilities and well paid would have made a career at sea obviously alluring, but the attractions could also wear off. Only a small percentage of men stayed on at sea, rising to be naval petty officers or merchant shipmasters. In times of war or when recruiting was down, tough and press-gangs would be used to "recruit" men into the navy.

Patronage (sponsorship) was an essential ingredient in the success of the 18th-century Royal Navy. It allowed the best officers, those who held the prime commands and won key battles, to pick their followers. As professional men, they chose juniors who would reflect credit on them and help them to secure victories, prize money and profit. Similarly, ambitious young officers sought the patronage of the best Admirals - those who could help them. Captain Hugh Palliser, himself an officer of humble origins, brought James Cook into the officer corps as an act of patronage to command the first of several world expeditions. James Cook had escaped his humble background, while Palliser basked in explorer Captain Cook's reflected glory.

For many years, it was thought that women were rarely, if ever, allowed on board warships. This, like much else about life in the 18th-century Navy, was a Victorian invention that said more about the values of that time than it did about the realities. In fact, large numbers of women went to sea. Usually they were the wives of the petty officers - mature women who played important roles, including those of providing medical treatment and handling ammunition.

Not a few children were born on the warships, and some women signed on under assumed male identities. The fact that they were often not discovered is very revealing of the low incidence of bathing among the seafarers. The 18th-century mind preferred homely dirt and the occasional clean shirt to the terrors of cold water or the deep ocean. Those women who were officially on board soon made their presence felt. In 1797, crusty Admiral the Earl St. Vincent, issued an order demanding that the women reduce their consumption of water. If not, he proposed sending them all home on the next transport. It is unlikely he gave them the separate bathing rights enjoyed by the female members of our modern day navy.

Today, after over 1100 years of operations the British Royal Navy remains a blue water navy, and in terms of the combined displacement is the second-largest navy of the NATO alliance after that of the United States. As of 2010, there were 87 commissioned ships in the Royal Navy, including aircraft carriers, a helicopter carrier, landing platform docks, ballistic missile submarines, nuclear fleet submarines, guided missile destroyers, frigates, mine counter-measures and patrol vessels. Sixteen vessels of the Royal Fleet Auxiliary also contribute to the Royal Navy's order-of-battle. The Royal Navy's ability to project power globally is considered second only to the U.S. Navy.

Coast Survey

On February 10, 1807 President Thomas Jefferson signed a bill creating the United States Coast Survey, a new agency that would be responsible for conducting detailed surveys of the young nation's coastal areas and producing charts based on this work. The agency's creation followed the realization of an urgent need to ensure the safety of mariners, ships, and cargoes by supplying information about the shoals, reefs, and navigational hazards among which they moved while carrying the nation's commerce. The Survey was established under the supervision of Albert Gallatin, Secretary of Commerce, who in turn selected a young Swiss engineer, Ferdinand Hassler, then employed as a mathematics teacher at West Point, to head the new agency. But the U.S. Coast survey project was delayed by the War of 1812 and by difficulties in obtaining adequate surveying instruments, so the actual surveying of the coasts did not get underway until 1816.

Ferdinand Hassler was a perfectionist who envisioned the organization of the Survey's work to be divided into three branches – geodetic (measurement and representation of the <u>Earth</u>), hydrographic (the Earth's waters), and topographic (the Earth's elevations). Hassler believed the geodetic branch to be the most important.

The original idea for the Survey did not include geodetic work, but Hassler rightly saw that the Survey's work would prove truly useful and would stand the test of time only if its measurements were tied to known geodetically determined points on the Earth. His insistence caused lengthy delays in the work of the Survey and endless political problems with a Congress bent on more immediate, less precise results.

But ultimately it became the basis for the extremely accurate maps and charts that the Survey produced.

By the time of Hassler's death in 1843, the foundation for the survey of the coast had been laid and the detailed surveys of the ports and harbors were begun. Hassler was succeeded by Alexander Dallas Bache, a great grandson of Benjamin Franklin. Bache's academic and intellectual credentials were impeccable, and he followed Hassler's plan faithfully, adapting it to fit the needs of an expanding United States. The addition of Texas, California, Oregon, and Washington to the nation at the close of the Mexican War nearly doubled the length of coastline under the Survey's charge, but Bache was up to the expanded task.

The work of the Coast Survey resulted in the most accurate charts possible of the coastal waters of the nation, ensuring the safety and the reliability of maritime traffic. It also pioneered the techniques and equipment soon to be utilized by surveys in the country's interior. The work of the U.S. Geological Survey, the various state surveys, and the surveys of the Army's Topographical Corps were to some all extent grounded in the work of the Coast Survey. More importantly, the early creation of the Coast Survey lead to the federal government assuming responsibility for the development and distribution of maps and charts to promote the safety and welfare of the people. Thus, in more ways than one, our country became known from the coastline inward.

Several original Coast Survey charts are on display at the Santa Barbara Maritime Museum – a rare 1853 hand colored chart of the California coastline from San Francisco to San Diego and a 1852 chart of Cuyler Harbor on San Miguel Island. Also on display is and a copy of a painting "Reconnaissance of Island Harbors" that shows the two US Coast Survey vessels *Active* and *Ewing* at anchor at San Miguel Island when they were charting of the west coast.

Other historic charts on display include a 1705 chart depicting California when it was thought to be a large island and not part of the United States, a 1700's chart from the exploration of the west coast of North America by explorer George Vancouver, and a late 1700's chart of the world. An 1854 chart of Anacapa Island that was drawn by celebrated artist James McNeal Whistler is unique. Famous for paintings such as "Whistler's Mother," his chart unconventionally includes a flight of birds in its background.

The collection also includes modern charts of Santa Barbara's coastline and Channel Islands produced by the successor of the Coast Survey, the National Oceanographic and Atmospheric Administration. It's Office of Coast Survey is under the umbrella organization of the US Department of Commerce. These modern charts include three dimensional views of the coastline, islands, and ocean floor.

Sea Shells

Rain was falling on a dark afternoon in 1947 as my father drove my brother and me to Santa Barbara Harbor. He parked in front of Bill Smart's small ship's chandlery with its very limited stock. Most of his sales were by ordering items selected by customers from one of his catalogs. Our order had arrived in an eight-foot flat box. We quickly strapped it to our car's roof and headed home with high expectations and excitement.

The box was from the Haggerty Company in Rhode Island, and it contained what would become a boating phenomenon in Santa Barbara for years to come – Santa Barbara's first Sea Shell sailboat. The boat was a kit of precut pieces of plywood, long sections of spruce for mast and boom, fasteners, and instructions. Several days later, the small boat was assembled and had a bright coat of blue paint. Then to the harbor and its first sail. What a thrill it was to be sailing alone among the moored boats that composed the harbor's tenants in those days.

Being an organizer, my father soon persuaded others to order Sea Shells, and a racing program soon began. Unlike today, the first Santa Barbara Sea Shellers were mostly adults, but that soon changed, and the fleet today is primarily a large and very successful junior program. The secret of that success depended on enticing parents to take their sons and daughters to the harbor many weekends throughout the summer. The successful enticement was to have the last race of the day just for the parents, and that inducement continues to work sixty-two years later.

Today, the Sea Shell Association continues its tradition of introducing, nurturing and graduating youngsters from 8 to 15 into the exciting and challenging sport of sailing. The group teaches new skippers with little to no experience to become comfortable with their boats. As each skipper becomes more skilled, he or she graduates to higher competition levels. Many of Sea Shell alumni have continued their sailing as part of local high school, college, and even international sailing events.

The Sea Shell sailing season runs from April through October, with a long break in August. The first three Sundays of the season are allocated to orientation and instruction. A typical day at the beach begins at noon and ends by 5 pm. First, the boats are rigged at the harbor launching ramp, then sailed around to West Beach where the participants congregate for a "mast meeting" at 1 pm. Then, four races are conducted – three for the kids and the last one for the adults.

The foundation of Sea Shell program is centered on teaching youngsters to sail in a program with strong family participation. The club offers a low cost, family oriented sailing experience. There are still a few sailing Sundays remaining this year, which creates a good opportunity for interested parties to see the program in action and to make plans to join it next spring.

To keep the program affordable, the Sea Shell organization holds a wine tasting event each fall to raise funds for the coming year. This year's event will take place at Santa Barbara Harbor on Saturday October 2 from 4 pm until dusk. Its unique format is a progressive wine tasting event on a number of yachts in Marina One (the marina closest to Santa Barbara Yacht Club). Admission is thirty-five dollars, which entitles a participant to visit several yachts in the marina for wine tasting and munchies. For tickets, contact Angela Beardon at 964-6495 or angelabeardon@cox.net. You can also visit the Sea Shell web site at http://www.sbssa.org.

America's Cup Update

In 1851, a yacht named America won the 100 Guinea Cup, the prize for the winner of a race around England's Isle of Wight. When America finished, none of the English yachts were in sight and Queen Victoria asked who was second. The reply was, ""Ah, there is no second, Your Majesty." The winning crew donated the cup to the New York Yacht Club for future racing as a challenge trophy. Thus was born the America's Cup, named after the boat, not the country.

The most recent America's Cup competition was held last February in 90-foot multihull yachts at Valencia, Spain. The United States challenger, software billionaire Larry Ellison's "BMW Oracle Racing", beat the Spanish defender "Alinghi" 2-0, winning the Cup for San Francisco's Golden Gate Yacht Club, which now gets to decide the location, timing and type of boats for the next competition to be held in 2013. Since the America's Cup is a challenge-based competition where the winning Yacht Club makes the rules and hosts the subsequent event, the defenders generally make it difficult for the challengers to take the Cup home.

The defenders have announced that the next America's Cup competition will be feature newly designed 72-foot catamarans, the fastest boats ever used in the competition. "These are going to be brand-new, specially designed catamarans that are going to be up on the side with people hanging off." according to Russel Coutts, CEO of BMW Oracle Racing.

The format is to be a shorter race course at a venue with strong reliable winds. These factors favor San Francisco's candidacy, but final word on the host city won't come until later this year. Other lead locations under consideration are Valencia and an undisclosed Italian port, but the high probability is San Francisco Bay. Team officials announced that they wish to have the final competition in 2013, with a series of challenger races beginning in 2011 at various locations around the globe.

The BMW Oracle Racing team is keen to expand the sport's popularity and plans to make the America's Cup competition more television friendly, including having camera operators on-board the racing yachts. Reliable winds to minimize delays and made-for-TV backdrops like the Golden Gate Bridge and Alcatraz all work in San Francisco's favor.

Bygone Cup

A number of years ago, a good friend and collector of antiques from Boston bequeathed me two yachting half-models made of pewter and mounted on dark wooden plaques. Each had a metal plate in the lower right hand corner showing the name of the yacht – Reliance and Shamrock III. I was familiar with Englishman Sir Thomas Lipton's endless but unsuccessful quest to win the America's Cup, and that he had named all his entries Shamrock. With a bit of research, I found that Reliance and Shamrock III competed in the 1903 America's Cup and that the American yacht Reliance was the winner. That makes my commemorative models one hundred and seven years old!

The third of Lipton's Shamrock challengers was launched on Saint Patrick's Day, March 17, 1903, and was christened by the English Countess of Shaftesbury. Shamrock III underwent its first practice trials on March 31 on the River Clyde, sailing against earlier contender Shamrock I. One month later, Shamrock III snapped her mast, injuring several of her crew and killing one man through drowning.

On May 28, 1903, Lipton decided that the first and third Shamrock-named yachts would leave for the United States. It was the first time in Cup history that a challenger arrived before the Cup to train on the race course area with a trial horse. They could not be transported on a ship because the sly Americans made a rule that the yachts must reach the race course "on their own bottoms."

Lipton would be racing under burgee of the Royal Ulster Yacht Club of Ireland.

The contest was to be from August 22 to September 3, 1903 with the Cup to go to the yacht with the best record in a five race series. There were three race course options for the contest. The first was a 15 nautical mile course leeward to the Sandy Hook Lightship and then return. The second race course was a 30-nautical mile equilateral triangle, and the third was to be a 40-nautical miles leg to leeward to Sandy Hook Lightship and return. Since the two yachts were not identical in design, a corrected time handicap system was used to make the contest equal.

The results were an American runaway. In the first race, Reliance beat Shamrock III by seven minutes and three seconds on corrected time. The second race over the 30 mile triangular course was won by Reliance by one minute and 19 seconds on corrected time. During the third race, the fog was so thick that Shamrock III lost its way and Captain Robert Wringe decided to withdraw and sail directly to his mooring. Shamrock III had been beaten even more convincingly than Shamrock II in 1901. With three consecutive wins, the American yacht had to sail only three races of the five race contest.

A dejected Sir Thomas Lipton put Shamrock I and Shamrock III up for sale in the United States, but there were no takers. Both yachts sailed back to Great Britain.

A look at the following specifications of the 1903 British yacht and those for the next competition in 2013 contest show a great contrast. (2013 specifications are shown in parenthesis.)

Hull construction: All steel (Composite fiberglass); Mast: Steel (Composite fiberglass); Length overall: 134.5 ft. (72 ft.); Beam: 24.6 ft. (46 ft.) ; Displacement: 333,200 pounds (15,500 pounds), Sail area: 13,713 sq. ft. (3229 sq. ft.); Crew 56 (11). The 2013 yachts are expected to have speeds in excess of 30 knots (mph).

The beginning of the longest running sporting contest in history began in 1851 when Commodore John Cox Stevens, a charter member of the fledgling New York Yacht Club formed a six-person syndicate to build a yacht with the intention of taking her to England and making some money competing in yachting regattas and match races. The syndicate contracted with pilot-boat designer George Steers for a 101 foot schooner which was christened America and launched on May 3, 1851.

The following are the results of all America's Cup contests to date:

Year	Defender	Challenger	Record
1851	Aurora, England	America, USA	1-0
1870	Magic, USA	Cambria, England	1-0
1871	Columbia, USA	Livonia, England	4-1
1876	Madeline, USA	Countess of Dufferin, Canada	2-0
1881	Mischief, USA	Atalanta, Canada	4-1
1885	Puritan, USA	Genesta, GBR	2-0
1886	Mayflower, USA	Genesta, GBR	2-0
1887	Volunteer, USA	Thistle, Scotland	2-0
1893	Vigilant, USA	Valkyrie II, GBR	3-0
1895	Defender, USA	Valkyrie III, GBR	3-0
1899	Columbia, USA	Shamrock, Ireland	3-0
1901	Columbia, USA	Shamrock II, Ireland	3-0
1903	Reliance, USA	Shamrock III, Ireland	3-0
1920	Resolute, USA	Shamrock IV, Ireland	3-2
1930	Enterprise, USA	Shamrock V, Ireland	4-0
1934	Rainbow, USA	Endeavour, GBR	4-2
1937	Ranger, USA	Endeavour II, GBR	4-0
1958	Columbia, USA	Sceptre, GBR	3-1
1962	Weatherly, USA	Gretel, Australia	4-1
1964	Constellation, USA	Sovereign, GBR	4-0
1967	Intrepid, USA	Dame Pattie, Australia	4-0
1970	Intrepid, USA	Gretel II, Australia	4-1
1974	Courageous, USA	Southern Cross, Australia	4-0
1977	Courageous, USA	Australia, Australia	4-0
1980	Freedom, USA	Australia, Australia	4-1
1983	Liberty, USA	Australia II, Australia	4-3
1987	Kookaburra III, Australia	Stars & Stripes, USA	4-0
1988	Stars & Stripes, USA	New Zealand, NZ	2-0
1992	America 3, USA	Il Moro di Venezia, Italy	4-1
1995	Young America, USA	Team NZ, New Zealand	5-0

2000	Team NZ, New Zealand	Luna Rossa, Italy	5-0
2003	Team NZ, New Zealand	Alinghi, Switzerland	5-0
2007	Alinghi, Switzerland	Team NZ, New Zealand	5-2
2010	Alinghi, Switzerland	BMW Oracle Racing, USA	0-2
2013	Next America's Cup Contest		

SIR FRANCIS DRAKE

Francis Drake was born in England in early 1544, and went on to become one of the most famous explorers and sea warriors of all time.

His sea career began at age thirteen as an apprentice crewmember on a barque that traded in the waters of the English Channel. He became owner-master of the ship at age twenty after the death of its previous captain, who bequeathed it to him. Three years later, Drake made his first voyage to the New World as part of the fleet of his cousin, John Hawkins, an English shipbuilder, naval administrator and commander, merchant, navigator, and slave trader. In 1568, Drake was again with the Hawkins fleet when it was trapped by the Spaniards in the Mexican port of San Juan de Ulua. He escaped along with Hawkins, but the experience led him to a lifelong vengeance against the Spanish.

Seeking both revenge and wealth, Drake embarked on his first major independent enterprise in 1572, an attack on the Panama isthmus known as the Spanish Main. It was there that the silver and gold treasures of Peru were landed and sent overland to the Caribbean Sea and then reloaded onto galleons that sailed on to Spain. Drake left Plymouth in May with a crew of seventy-three men in two small vessels, the Pascha (70 tons) and the Swan (25 tons), with the intention to capture Nombre de Dios on the eastern shore of the isthmus.

His first raid came in late July, when Drake and his men captured both the town and its treasure. But upon discovering that Drake was bleeding profusely from a wound, his men insisted on withdrawing immediately to save his life and left the heavy treasure behind. Drake remained in the vicinity of the isthmus for almost a year, raiding Spanish shipping and attempting to capture a treasure shipment.

In 1573, Drake joined up with French buccaneer Guillaume Le Testu in an attack on a richly laden mule train. The raid succeeded beyond their wildest dreams netting over twenty tons of silver and gold. The treasure was too much for the few men to carry off, so they buried much of it, which may have given rise to subsequent stories of pirates and buried treasure.

The small band of adventurers dragged as much gold and silver as they could across eighteen miles of jungle-covered mountains to where they had left their small raiding boats. But upon arrival they discovered their boats had vanished! Downhearted, exhausted and hungry, the raiders had nowhere to go, and the Spanish were not far behind.

Drake rallied his men, buried the treasure on the beach and built a raft to sail himself and two volunteers ten miles along the fearsome surf-lashed coast to where he had left his flagship. The raft was continually awash, and the salt water and burning sun caused them much suffering. But they pushed onwards and finally reached the ship. When Drake finally stood on her deck, the crewmen he had left on-board were alarmed at his bedraggled appearance. Fearing the worst, they asked him how the raid had gone. Drake, in spite of everything, could not resist a joke and teased them by looking beaten and downhearted. He then looked up, laughed, pulled a necklace of Spanish gold from around his neck and said, "Our voyage is made, lads!" He was back in Plymouth August 9, 1573.

After the success of the Panama isthmus raid, Queen Elizabeth sent Drake on an expedition against the Spanish along the west coast of the Americas. Drake's fleet suffered great attrition. He was forced to scuttle both the Christopher and the Swan due to loss of men on the Atlantic crossing. He finally made landfall at the dismal Bay of San Julian in what is now Argentina. Explorer Ferdinand Magellan had called there half a century earlier and had put to death some mutineers. Drake's men cringed upon seeing the weathered and bleached skeletons on the grim Spanish gibbets. Following Magellan's example, Drake tried and executed Thomas Doughty, who was convicted of mutiny and treason. He then decided to remain the winter in San Julian before attempting to round the Strait of Magellan.

The three remaining ships of Drake's convoy then departed for the southern tip of South America. Drake made it to the Pacific a few weeks later, but violent storms destroyed one of the three ships in the strait and caused another to have to return to England, leaving only the Pelican (renamed Golden Hind) to carry on. The Golden Hind sailed north along the Pacific coast of South America, attacking Spanish ports and rifling towns as it went. Drake made good use of the more accurate charts found on the captured Spanish ships. Before reaching the coast of Peru, they stopped at Mocha Island where Drake was seriously injured by hostile Mapuches. Further north, they sacked the port of Valparaíso in Chile.

Nearing Lima, the Golden Hind captured a Spanish ship laden with 25,000 pesos of Peruvian gold - about six million of today's dollars. Drake then learned another Spanish ship, Nuestra Señora de la Concepción, was sailing west towards Manila. Giving chase, the privateers eventually captured the treasure ship which proved to be their most profitable trophy. The ship was carrying 80 pounds of gold, a golden crucifix, jewels, 13 chests full of royals of plate and 26 tons of silver!

On 17 June 1579, Drake landed somewhere north of Spain's northern-most claim at Point Loma (today's San Diego). He found a good port, landed, repaired and restocked his vessels. Staying on for a time, he maintained friendly relations with the natives. He claimed the land in the name of the Holy Trinity for the English Crown and named it Nova Albion - Latin for "New Britain." The exact location of the port was carefully guarded to keep it secret from the Spaniards, and several of Drake's maps may even have been altered for this purpose. Unfortunately, all first-hand records from the voyage, including logs, paintings and charts were lost when Whitehall Palace in London burned in 1698. A bronze plaque inscribed with Drake's claim to the new lands, Drake's Plate of Brass, fitting the description in Drake's own account, was discovered in Marin County, California. It was later declared a hoax. Another location often claimed to be Nova Albion is Whale Cove in Oregon, although there is no evidence to suggest this other than a general resemblance to a single map penned a decade after Drake's landing.

From Nova Albion, Drake and his men sailed north in search of a western opening to the Northwest Passage, a potentially valuable asset to the English at the time. During this venture, the sailors accurately mapped the westward trend of the northwestern corner of the North American continent, present-day British Columbia and Alaska. They had a rough voyage among the islands of the Alaskan panhandle, and were finally forced to turn back due to freezing weather.

Bawlf argues that Drake's ship reached 56°N, much farther north than was recorded. The reason for this false record, Bawlf writes, was for political reasons - competition with the Spanish in the Americas. Queen Elizabeth wanted to keep any information about the Northwest Passage secret, with the result that the location of Nova Albion and the highest latitude the expedition reached are still a source of controversy today. Drake's brother endured a long period of torture in South America at the hands of Spaniards, who sought intelligence from him about Francis Drake's voyage.

More about Sir Francis Drake's voyage around the world in a future column

COMPASS ROSE

The "compass rose" has appeared on charts and maps since the 1300's when portolan (our present day format) charts first made their appearance. The term "rose" came from the figure's compass points resembling the petals of the well-known flower. Originally, this device was used to indicate the directions of the winds (it was then known as a wind rose). The 32 points of the compass rose came from the directions of the eight major winds, the eight half-winds and the sixteen quarter-winds.

In the Middle Ages, the names of the winds were commonly known throughout the Medeterranean countries as tramontana (north), grecogreco (north east), levante (east), siroco (south east), ostro (south), lebeccio (southl west), ponente (west), and maestro (north west). On portolan charts you can see the initials of these winds labeled around the edge as T, G, L, S, O, L, P, and M. The 32 points are therefore simple bisections of the directions of the four winds. One of the first things western apprentice seamen had to know were the names of the points. Naming them all off perfectly was known as "boxing the compass".

There is no absolute standard for drafting a compass rose, and each school of cartographers seems to have developed their own. In the earliest charts, north was indicated by a spearhead above the letter T (for tramontana). This symbol evolved into a fleur-de-lys around the time of Columbus, and was first seen on Portuguese maps. Also in the 14th century, the L (for levante) on the east side of the rose was replaced with a cross, indicating the direction to Paradise (long thought to be in the east), or at least to where Christ was born (in the Levant).

The colors on the compass rose are supposedly the result of the need for graphic clarity rather than a mere cartographical whim. On a rolling ship at night with the compass illuminated by a flickering light, the helmsman needed to see figures that were as visible as possible. Therefore, the eight principle points of the compass are usually shown on the compass rose in black, which clearly stands out. Against this background, the points representing the half-winds are typically colored in blue or green, and since the quarter-wind points are the smallest, they are usually colored red.

Today, all nautical charts have a circle printed on them that resembles a compass divided into increments of 360 degrees. Superimposed is a second circle that is rotated several degrees compared with the first circle. The pair of circles constitute a modern compass rose. The first circle shows the direction of true north, the direction to the physical location of the north pole of Earth. The second circle shows the direction of north that a magnetic compass points to. This is the direction of magnetic north as opposed to true north. The magnetic field of Earth is not located at the same point on Earth as the geographic north pole, but is a few degrees off. The amount the magnetic field varies from the location of true north depends on where you are standing on Earth. At Santa Barbara, true north is actually about 13 degrees to the west of the direction of magnetic north shown on a compass. Mariners must adjust for this difference in order to be able to use their compass to steer to a desired destination. If they are plotting their course on a paper chart, they will use the magnetic north compass illustrated on their chart rather than the illustration of the true north compass. Modern electronic navigation devices such as global positioning systems can be programmed to show either magnetic or true course readings. Most mariners select the magnetic programs that match up with their compass.

MESSING AROUND IN BOATS

Many people often quote one small portion of a lovely, almost poetic ode to boats. Here, with the distractions of the action removed and substituted with either dots or dashes, is the entire ode to boats from *Wind in the Willows* by Kenneth Grahame.

"Is it so nice as all that?" asked the mole, shyly...

"Nice? It's the *only* thing," said the Water Rat Solemnly, as he leaned forward for his stroke. "*Believe me, my young friend, there is nothing -- absolutely nothing -- half so much worth doing as simply messing about in boats.*"

"Simply messing...about in boats -- or with boats... In or out of 'em it doesn't matter. Nothing seems to matter, that's the charm of it. Whether you get away, or whether you don't; whether you arrive at your destination or whether you reach somewhere else, or whether you never get anywhere at all, you're always busy, and you never do anything in particular; and when you've done it there's always something else to do, and you can do it if you like, but you'd much better not."

"Look here! If you've really nothing else on hand this morning, supposing we drop down the river together and have a long day of it.?"

Good advice!

1870 HARBOR PLAN

I have a rare Santa Barbara artifact in my office. It is a 1870 drawing titled "Sketch of Plan and Section of a Breakwater – Santa Barbara California". It shows our very small town, Stearns Wharf before its railroad connection had been built, and a planned 1320 yard long breakwater to be located in about fifty feet of water 1200 yards to seaward of Stearns Wharf. The breakwater was not planned to be connected to the shore. But why was it located three quarters of a mile out to sea? In 1870, there were very few engine powered boats. During southeast storms, sailing ships needed plenty of room to raise anchor and tack away from the dangers of Santa Barbara's storm tossed shores.

That breakwater was never built, but Santa Barbara finally got its breakwater in 1930, much closer to shore, but still detached from the land. But an unforeseen problem soon became apparent. Currents constantly carry sand down our coast, settling to the bottom in quieter waters such as those behind the protection of Santa Barbara's new breakwater. The west end of he breakwater was connected to the shore, but this didn't stop sand from passing through the spaces in the large rocks of the breakwater or building a sandbar at the breakwater's outer end. Leadbetter beach was allowed to form, and dredging was initiated to remove the sandbar every three or four years. As the harbor grew with more boats to be moored and greater protection was needed against southeast storms, it was decided to turn the sandbar into a breakwater extension by piling large rocks on it, and it remains so today.

SHIP'S BELL

The "Ship's Bell" system of chimes evolved from a crude sand clock dates back to the time of Columbus. This primitive clock was called a "sand" or "sandglass clock" and was an essential device for marking time at sea.

Records of epic voyages tell how sand clocks were used to measure time in half-hour increments. Watches or work shifts were organized into periods of four hours, a custom that is still widely used today. With a sandglass at his side, the helmsman would signal the passing of half-hour increments of time to all aboard by the number of strikes on the ships bell – a strike of one bell at the end of the first half hour, two at second and so on until reaching eight bells, which signaled the end of the watch. The tradition of the sand clock continued for hundreds of years and was replaced only upon the development of the mechanical clock that could withstand the rigors at sea.

The ship's name is traditionally engraved on its ship's bell, often with the year the ship was launched. Occasionally (especially on more modern ships) the bell will also carry the name of the shipyard that built the ship. If a ship's name is changed, maritime tradition requires that the original bell carrying the original name remains with the vessel. A ship's bell is a prized possession when a ship is broken up, and it often provides the only positive means of identification in the case of a shipwreck.

Bells have a centuries-long tradition of varied use in the navies and merchant fleets of the world. They have been used for signaling, keeping time, and providing alarm. Their functional and ceremonial uses have made them a symbol of considerable significance to the United States Navy.

Historically, bells cast from metal were first developed during the Bronze Age, achieving a particularly high level of sophistication in China. During the European Middle Ages, bells were used by Christians to signal divine services and to make special announcements. Christian and Buddhist monasteries historically used them to regulate daily activity, conceptually similar to later timekeeping in the U.S. Navy.

One of the earliest recorded references of the use of a shipboard bell was on the British sailing ship Grace Dieu around 1485. Ten years later an inventory of the English ship Regent indicated that it carried two "wache bells".

The sounding of a ship's bell found a natural application as a warning signal to other vessels during poor visibility and in dense fog. In 1676, one Henry Teonage serving as a chaplain with the British Mediterranean Fleet recorded, "so great a fog that we were fain to ring our bells, beat drums, and fire muskets often to keep us from falling foul one upon another". Ringing a ship's bell in fog soon became customary, and in 1858 British Naval Regulations made their use mandatory.

American ships of the Revolutionary War period and our early national years adopted many of the practices and traditions of the British Royal Navy, including the use of bells. In 1798, Paul Revere cast a bell weighing 242 pounds for the frigate Constitution, also known as "Old Ironsides". Today, maritime law requires all ships to carry an efficient bell.

It is interesting to note that a ship's bell contributed to the richest single prize captured by the American Navy during the War of Independence. While a Continental Navy Squadron under the command of Commodore Whipple lay to, wrapped in Newfoundland fog on a July morning in 1779, the sound of ships' bells and an occasional signal gun could be heard a short distance off. As the fog lifted, the Americans discovered that they had fallen in with the richly laden enemy Jamaican Fleet. Ten ships were captured as prizes which, together with their cargo, were valued at more than a million dollars.

The age-old practice of sounding the bell on the hour and half hour still has its place in our nuclear and missile oriented United States Navy, regulating daily routine, just as it did on our historic sailing vessels under in the late Eighteenth Century.

The ship's bell is also an essential link in a ship's fire alarm system. In the event of a fire, the bell is rung rapidly for at least five seconds, followed by one, two or three rings to indicate the location of a fire - forward, amidships, or aft. The bells are used in religious ceremonies, continuing their connection to religious origins. A custom that originated in the British Royal Navy was to baptize a child under the ship's bell, and sometimes the bell was filled with water and used as a christening bowl. Once the baptism is completed, the child's name was often inscribed inside the bell.

Traditionally, the bell is maintained by the ship's cook, while the ship's whistle is maintained by the ship's bugler. In actual practice, the bell is maintained by a person of the ship's division charged with the upkeep of that part of the ship where the bell is located. For this reason a deck seaman, quartermaster striker, or signalman striker may have the bell-shining duty.

In addition to continuing its role as a timepiece and alarm, the bell serves a ceremonial and memorial function. U.S. Navy bells, part of the many artifacts removed from decommissioned vessels, are preserved by the Naval Historical Center. They may be provided on loan to new namesake ships; naval commands with an historical mission or functional connection, and to museums and other institutions that are interpreting specific historical themes or creating displays of naval history.

United States Navy bells remain the permanent property of the US Government and the Department of the Navy. They serve to inspire and to remind our naval forces and personnel of their honor, courage, and commitment to the defense of our nation. Bells remain a powerful and tangible reminder of the history, heritage, and accomplishments of the naval service.

Early Sea Explorers

With water covering 70 percent of our planet, mankind has had to cross, explore, and adjust to the world's lakes, oceans and seaways since its beginning. We will never know the very earliest stories of these adventures, but much is known through archeological discoveries as well as early writings.

Hannu was an ancient Egyptian explorer who made the first recorded expedition of exploration. He is said to have sailed down the Red Sea to the southeastern areas of the Arabian peninsula (called Punt) around 2750 B.C. during Egypt's second dynasty. His voyage took him to what is now part of eastern Ethiopia and Somalia. He returned to Egypt with treasures that included spices and precious metals. Descriptions of his explorations have been found written in stone.

Scylax of Caryanda (Greece) explored the Middle East, including portions of the almost 2000 mile long Indus River. His small expedition sailed from the city of Caspatyrus in Pactyica (eastern Afghanistan), and traveled for a period of about three years. He was dispatched by the Emperor Darius of Persia (Iran), who wanted information in order to expand his empire with the intention of conquering India.

Zhang Qian (also called Chang Ch'ien) was a Chinese explorer who traveled to the steppes of Central Asia during the reign of Han dynasty Emperor Han Wudi, who reigned from 140 to 87 BC. He was the first person to bring information of the area to China. The Emperor sent

Zhang Qian to visit the Indo-European Yüeh-chih tribe of central Asia in order to establish trade relations. On his way northwest with about 100 men in 138 B.C., Zhang Qian was imprisoned by the nomadic Hsiung-nu people (the Huns) for 10 years. He finally escaped, made his way over 2,000 miles to the Yueh-chih tribe, and returned to China three years later. Years later, the Emperor sent him to visit the Wu-sun people to the northwest of China, another Indo-European tribe living in what is now Russia. His travels helped to opened up Chinese trade and the beginning the important "Silk Road" trading route.

Saint Brendan (486-578 AD) was an Irish abbot, monastery founder, and legendary sea voyager. He sailed in the Atlantic Ocean, traveling to the Hebrides Islands, Scotland, and perhaps to Wales and Brittany. He is also believed to have sailed to the Canary Islands off the northwest coast of Africa, the Azores Islands far off the coast of Portugal, and to Iceland. The Irish epic poem "Voyage of Brendan" recounts his voyages.

Eric the Red was born in Norway, but his family settled in western Iceland after his father was banished for murdering a man. Eric later killed two men in Iceland and was banished for three years. Hearing of the discovery by Gunnbjorn Olfsson of some islands that lay west of Iceland, Eric decided to sail there during his banishment. Departing in 982, he reached the harsh coast of eastern Greenland and then sailed south to the southern tip, which he explored over the next two years. Feuding with many people on Iceland, Eric wanted to start a new settlement without his enemies. He and 400 to 500 settlers in 14 ships arrived to settle Greenland in 986. After doing well for a while, the settlements experienced unusually cold weather, and some of the settlers returned to Iceland. The remaining settlers disappeared. It is thought that either the Inuit people attacked the settlers or they died from epidemics and starvation.

One of history's most famous explorers, Viking Leif Ericsson, Eric the Red's son, was probably the first European to voyage to Vinland (North America). Around 1000 AD, Ericsson and a crew of 35 sailed north from the lower tip of Greenland, along the coast of Baffin Island to Labrador, and then landed in what is now called Newfoundland where remains of an ancient Norse settlement have been found. Ericsson may have been preceded to Vinland by the Icelandic explorer Bjarni Herjulfsson who may have spotted the coast of North America in 985 or 986 when blown off his course from Iceland to Greenland.

Marco Polo was an Italian voyager and merchant who was one of the first Europeans to travel across Asia through China, visiting the Kublai Khan in Beijing. In the company of his father and uncle, Polo sailed south from Venice, Italy in the Mediterranean Sea to the Middle East, then overland to Persia (now Iran), then through the Pamir Mountains and the Gobi Desert, and then to China, exploring the area south of Beijing, including Yunan and Szechuan. Returning to Beijing, he turned east to Tankchow at the mouth of the Yangtse River, then south to Hangchow, China and along the coast to today's Vietnam and Sumatra. They then sailed west to Sri Lanka and India, back to Ormuz on the Persian Gulf, northwest overland to the Black Sea and Mediterranean Sea, and finally back to Venice. Polo told of his travels to a writer from Pisa named Rustichello who wrote "Book of Ser Marco Polo" around 1298. Marco Polo's accounts of his travels included the first Western record of porcelain, coal, gunpowder, printing, paper money, and silk.

Abu Abdullah Muhammad Ibn Battuta was a Moroccan explorer who traveled through Africa, the Middle East, and parts of the Far East. A Muslim, he set off on a Hajj (a pilgrimage to the holy town of Mecca) from Tangier Africa in 1325. He traveled for almost three decades, covering over 75,000 miles by boat and over land. He also traveled to China, Sri Lanka, Sumatra, and much of Africa.

The early travels of many other intrepid sailors were never recorded and have been lost to history.

Circumnavigation By Sail

I am not a candidate to sail around he world. My longest time at sea without touching land on a sailing vessel was three weeks. Initially, time seemed to pass very slowly, but I soon adjusted and the daily routine became normal – watches six hours on and six hours off twenty-four hours a day; weather changes ranging from dead calm to fierce storms; alone on-deck lashed to the mizzen mast steering through rough conditions; extreme boredom followed by urgent tasks; observing a few personnel clashes between inexperienced crewmembers; close calls; and always a concern of falling overboard with no one noticing as the ketch sailed onward and over the horizon. Finally arriving back on the mainland, it always seemed as if everything and everyone were moving at panic speeds, but soon I would fall back into the rhythm of "civilized" on-land living.

Through history, many crossing records that have been set by sailors around the world. Of the 240 crewmembers on five ships that set out with Magellan, only eighteen men and one ship survived to complete the circumnavigation. Magellan himself was not among them, having been killed not at sea, but by natives in the Philippines. The survivors were led by Spaniard Juan Sebastián Elcano, who assumed command of the expedition after Magellan's death.

The first person to sail single-handed around the world was New Englander Joshua Slocum aboard his sloop Spray. Between April 24, 1895 and June 27, 1898, Slocum crossed the Atlantic Ocean twice (to Gibraltar and back to South America), negotiated the Strait of Magellan at the tip of South America, crossed the Pacific Ocean, visited Australia and South Africa, crossed the Atlantic Ocean a third time, and finally reached home after a journey of 46,000 miles. His book, "Sailing Around The World" was a triumph when first published in 1899 and remains so today.

Dodge Morgan was the first American to sail alone around the globe without stopping in 1986. Sailing 60-foot American Promise, he set a world record passage time of 150 days 1 hour and 6 minutes, beating British sailor Chay Blyth who took 292 days to accomplish the same feat in 1971.

Here is the status of some voyages presently underway or recently completed.

French sailor Francis Joyon had no heat, no companions and little sleep for nearly two months as he sailed around the globe to completion in February 2004. But now he has a stunning world record, having made his solo voyage in 57 days, 13 hours, 34 minutes, 6 seconds in a trimaran (a sailboat with three hulls side by side), shattering the record held by Ellen MacArthur by two weeks. Joyon skirted the southern reaches of the globe in 95-foot speedster "Idec", which he built with parts gathered from other boats.

Another Polish sailor, Tomasz Lewandowski, had sailed around the world without stopping at any ports in 392 days in 2007-2008, but there is a dispute as to whether this circumnavigation could be classified as "non-stop" due to a to stop at East London as evidenced from receipts showing mooring for three nights at the marina and purchasing fuel.

Joanna Pajkowska of Poland completed solo and non-stop trip around the world January 8, 2009. Until then, no Polish yachtswoman achieved such a task. Her trip was the record fastest Polish single handed circumnavigation. The previous Polish record was set in 1980 by Henryk Jaskuła on S/Y Dar Przemyśla and stood at 344 days.

Marta Sziłajtis-Obiegło of Poland finished on April 20, 2009 Her voyage followed the Passat Route via Panama, the Galapagos Islands, the Island of Polynesia, Australia, Indian Ocean, South Africa, across the Atlantic Ocean to Brazil (to attend the carnival) and back to Venezuela. She called at fourteen harbors on her way.

Sailor Abby Sunderland's sixteen year old brother Zac departed June 14, 2008 from Marina del Rey and arrived home July 16, 2009, becoming the youngest person to circumnavigate the world alone by sail.

Mike Perham of England completed his around the world voyage on August 27, 2009 at age seventeen. He began sailing at the age of seven and never looked back. At fourteen, Mike became the youngest person to sail across the Atlantic single-handed. He still holds that world record today.

Natasza Caban of Poland finished her voyage December 2, 2009. Before departing she related, "I am not attempting to become famous. I'm going to sail solo around the world on a little boat to show to people that it is worth while having a dream. I want to make them believe in themselves by proving that persistence will lead them to their goals."

Commodore Dilip Donde, a clearance diver with India's Navy, became the first from India to complete a solo circumnavigation expedition. He departed in August of 2009, made four stops - Fremantle (Australia), Christ Church (New Zealand), Port Stanley (Falkland Islands) and Cape Town (South Africa), completing his voyage May 19, 2010. A clearance diver uses explosives and other underwater techniques to remove obstructions to make harbors and shipping channels safe to navigate. Perhaps that made a mere solo trip around the world seem somewhat tame.

Sixteen year old Australian Jessica Watson spent seven months at sea on her pink yacht sailed across the finish line of her round-the-world journey on May 15, 2010 and became the youngest sailor to circle the globe solo, nonstop and unassisted.

ABOUT THE AUTHOR

For several years, "Scuttlebutt" has appeared each week Santa Barbara's primary newspaper, the Sqnta Barbara News-Press. The column covers a wide range of marine -related topics of general interest for boaters and non-boaters alike. This book is a collection of selected articles from the column.

Author Bob Kieding has been a lifelong sailor. He began sailing an 8-foot, single-sailed pram at age eight, and went on to compete in one-design and off-shore yachts throughout the US and beyond. As a teenager, he worked as a paid hand on various yachts out of Santa Barbara Harbor. By 18, he had earned his first professional command as a paid yacht skipper, operating with a professional crew on Southern California waters on weekends and summers. Upon completing college at the University of California, he held several conventional on-land white-collar jobs, but kept returning to his first love, the sea.

In 1977, he purchased Santa Barbara's primary ship's chandlery, and then went on to open several other retail businesses at Santa Barbara's waterfront. Currently, he works with his son Ken operating Chandlery Yacht Sales, which specializes in sales of both new and used boats and yachts, plus marine systems design, equipment and electronics sales, installation services, and yacht delivery.

Bob's boating career involved sailing with a number of celebrities, including movie giants Humphrey Bogart, David Niven, and Dana Andrews He also sailed with celebrities form other walks of life such as the chairman of the board of Mercedes Benz, California Governor and Supreme Court Chief Justice Earl Warren, and movie maker John Ford.

Bob has held many community positions through the years, including president of the Santa Barbara Youth Foundation, chairman of the Junior Rowing Program for the1984 Olympics, trustee of the Santa Barbara Museum of Natural History, president of the Santa Barbara Semana Nautica Summer Sports Festival, and more. He was the primary founder of Santa Barbara's popular Maritime Museum.

The Kieding family has been active in boating for several generations. Bob's father, Ray Kieding, began sailing in the 1920's on Lake Michigan, and then brought his enthusiasm to California in 1946. Shortly after arriving, he bought a kit and with his two sons built an 8-foot pram Seashell sailboat. His enthusiasm resulted in what is now the oldest and largest sailboat racing fleet in Santa Barbara which is still going strong after more than 60 years. Over sixty families and eighty young skippers participate in the sailing program each year. Ray chaired the Santa Barbara Harbor Commission for many years, was a member of Santa Barbara Yacht Club, spearheaded the building of the first marina at Santa Barbara Harbor, and was active in many other nautical and community programs.

Boating is deeply etched in the Kieding family. Other family members who are active in boating and the boating business are son Ken Kieding, who is president of Chandlery Yacht Sales, and son-in-law Jamie Deardorff, who operates Chandlery Yacht Services. Bob Kieding has been a life-long writer, and was recognized with a writing award from Eleanor Roosevelt. He continues to write a weekly marine column for the Santa Barbara News-Press in addition to working at Chandlery Yacht Sales.

BIBLIOGRAPHY

The Untold Story of Chinese Fishermen in Santa Barbara and the Channel Islands. Linda Bentz

Channel Islands - Charles Hillinger 1998

Umbrella Guide To California Lighthouses - Sharlene and Ted Nelson 1993

Channel Islands National Park - Lighthouse Friends

Lone Woman Of Ghalas-Hat - Rice D. Oliver

Lecture by Vail descendants Nita Vail and Will Woolley

Credit is given to -

Robert Schwemmer

Santa Barbara Maritime Museum Curator Abbey Chamberlain

Author/researcher Justin Ruhge.

The Minerals Management Service of the U.S. Department of the Interior.

Linda Kieding